American Contexts

Multicultural Readings for Composition

Audrey B. Joyce

Pasco-Hernando Community College

New York • San Francisco • Boston
London • Toronto • Sydney • Tokyo • Singapore • Madrid
Mexico City • Munich • Paris • Cape Town • Hong Kong • Montreal

Senior Vice President/Publisher: Joseph Opiela
Executive Marketing Manager: Ann Stypuloski
Production Manager: Denise Phillip
Project Coordination, Text Design, and Electronic Page Makeup: UG / GGS Information
    Services, Inc.
Cover Designer/Manager: Nancy Danahy
Cover Illustration: Lisa Henderling/Stock Illustration Source, Inc.
Manufacturing Buyer: Lucy Hebard
Printer and Binder: Courier Corporation
Cover Printer: Coral Graphics

For permission to use copyrighted material, grateful acknowledgment is made to the
copyright holders on pp. 427–430, which are hereby made part of this copyright page.

Library of Congress Cataloging-in-Publication Data

American contexts: multicultural readings for composition/ [compiled by] Audrey B. Joyce.
    p. cm.
    Includes bibliographical references and index.
    ISBN 0-205-32462-2 (alk. paper)
    1. Readers--Social sciences. 2. Pluralism (Social sciences)--Problems, exercises, etc. 3.
Ethnic relations--Problems, exercises, etc. 4. Ethnic groups--Problems, exercises, etc. 5.
English language--Rhetoric. 6. College readers. I. Joyce, Audrey B.

PE1127.S6 A48 2003
808'.0427--dc21   2002067901

Please visit our website at *http://www.ablongman.com*

ISBN 0-205-32462-2

2   3   4   5   6   7   8   9   10—CRW—05   04   03

Contents

Contents

> "No matter whether the slave girl be as black as ebony or
> as fair as her mistress. In either case, there is no shadow
> of law to protect her from insult, from violence, or even
> from death. . . ."

> "During this time, I succeeded in learning to read and
> write. In accomplishing this I was compelled to resort to
> various stratagems."

> "Materially, psychologically, and culturally, part of the
> nation's heritage is Negro American, and whatever it
> becomes will be shaped in part by the Negro's presence."

> "There was no chance to warn Bailey that he was
> dangerously late, that everybody had been worried and
> that he should create a good lie or, better, a great one."

never blamed me, for this was the way she knew it would be with my wonderful new education."

PART 4: NATIVE AMERICAN WRITERS   323

Thematic Contents

COMMUNITIES

CONFLICT AND VIOLENCE

Thematic Contents

COMMUNITIES

CONFLICT AND VIOLENCE

EARLY MEMORIES

FRIENDS AND MENTORS

HERITAGE AND TRADITIONS

FRIENDS AND MENTORS

HERITAGE AND TRADITIONS

HUMOR, IRONY, AND SATIRE

IDENTITY AND SELF-ESTEEM

JUSTICE AND EQUALITY

NATURE AND PLACE

POPULAR CULTURE

SOCIAL PROBLEMS

SPORTS

WORK AND INCOME

Rhetorical Contents

EXPOSITORY

Note: These essays may have some autobiographical sections.

Preface

American Contexts contains forty nonfiction readings that shed light on the meaning of terms such as identity, family, heritage, assimilation, justice, and equality, which are the core of the study of multiculturalism in the United States. Following the categories used by the U.S. Census Bureau, these readings are divided into four ethnic/racial groups of writers: African American, Hispanic American, Asian American, and Native American.

What makes American Contexts unique is that all authors and selections (including expository and argumentative essays, memoirs, and autobiography) meet three criteria. First, all forty authors are highly regarded American writers from one of the four ethnic/racial groups recognized by the Census. Every writer selected is an award-winning, respected writer, such as Henry Louis Gates, Jr., Gary Soto, Bharati Mukherjee, and N. Scott Momaday. Second, these authors are recognized as spokespersons for their groups. They have written books and essays on current, often controversial, socioeconomic issues. Some of the writers, such as Nikki Giovanni, Elizabeth Cook-Lynn, Vine Deloria, and Jesus Colon, also have engaged in political activism. Thus, knowledgeable, affected members of a group address the issues of importance to members of that group. It is the voice of the "insider" that the reader will hear. Finally, the authors write about a wide variety of topics (such as bilingual education, dropouts, gang warfare, and single mothers) that are debated in today's media. The readings should help readers better understand how writers from different ethnic groups address these current issues. These topics should appeal both to students from a minority racial/ethnic group and to those from the dominant culture.

The ethnic/racial classification is that designation used by the writer or listed in biographical references. For example, Frederick Douglass, whose father was white, considered himself African American. Many of the Native American writers, such as Joseph Bruchac and Inez Petersen, are of mixed heritage; their essays often focus on their efforts to understand and honor their heritage. The broad term "Asian American" includes immigrants from countries such as China and Japan that were former enemies. The essay "Beyond Our Shadows" by Helen Zia shows how being viewed as "Asian American" has affected her. As seen in the battle over the last census, the division of human populations into racial/ethnic groups is itself an interesting and controversial topic, suitable for a class discussion.

The introduction to each of the four parts consists of a brief overview of that group's history in the United States and a list of important milestones (dates, laws, and events). Even for those students familiar with U.S. history, this introduction will call attention to events that may not have been fully discussed in a conventional textbook. Reviewing this history will help students better understand the context of essays that follow. For example, the essays by Pablo Medina and Gustavo Perez Firmat both refer to events following the Cuban immigration of 1960. Students can better understand the reading by Maya Angelou once they are aware of the "separate but equal" laws of the time.

Following the historical introduction, the ten essays in each part are arranged by the author's date of birth. Before each selection, students will find biographical and critical notes that will be of assistance in understanding the essay. The biographical notes present basic information on the writer, including education and current work. For instance, the biographical notes on Luis Rodriguez discuss his former involvement with gangs; this information will help the reader understand why Rodriguez is so active in fighting gang membership.

The critical notes provide information on some of the major concerns of that writer, in particular those themes that appear in the selection that follows. For example, students learn of Cornel West's interest in both economic and moral issues, two concerns that recur in his essay "Beyond Affirmative Action." In some cases, the notes discuss briefly a major book by the writer, such as Ralph Ellison's *Invisible Man* or Amy Tan's *The Joy Luck Club*. These critical notes should aid students in analyzing the essay that follows.

Along with each selection, readers will find questions for discussion, research, and writing. All these questions should elicit critical thinking; repeatedly the questions ask "why." They require students to extend an answer, to explain the reasons "why" for their response. Although each question/suggestion can be used as a "writing prompt," instructors should select those most suitable for their students' abilities and probable interests. Some instructors will want to focus solely on questions dealing with identity formation and/or multicultural issues; others may prefer to use one of the "springboards for writing" assignments that broaden out from other topics discussed in the reading. In all cases, the writing topics, sometimes controversial, should lend themselves readily to student discussion and writing. For instance, Louis Owens in "Water Witch" discusses the importance of guns and hunting in his life, affording students an opportunity to write on the much debated issue of gun control laws.

Placed before the selection, the "Preparing to Read" questions can be used for group work, class discussion, or journal writing. These introductory questions, which help to give students a "set" before reading, make this a usable book for those students who still need assistance in improving reading skills. These are open-ended, sometimes provocative questions, which allow students to consider an issue and express their opinions. The questions lead students into the reading.

The first set of questions following the selection, "Writing About the Reading," asks the students to respond to specific questions about the text. Questions require students to interpret, analyze, compare, predict, infer, and argue. Students sometimes are required to explain the meaning of one of the author's statements. They are asked why an author begins or ends an essay in a certain way, why the writer has included certain types of support, what are the causes and consequences of certain events, and whether or not a writer is justified in making an assertion. These questions are suitable for a close reading, a class discussion, or an interpretative paper.

The second set of questions after the selection, "Writing from Your Own Experience," asks the students to recall, consider, and write an essay about events in their own lives similar to those discussed in, or suggested by, the reading. These questions, best viewed as writing prompts, are well suited to personal essays that require students to reflect thoughtfully on their own experiences. For example, if the writer has discussed how he has turned his life around, the students may be asked to write about some way in which they have made a positive change in their lives and the reasons for this change. Or, if a writer has discussed someone who has served as a mentor, students may be asked to recall someone who assumed the role of mentor in their lives and the reason that they chose this person. Those students who hesitate to write about themselves are encouraged to write about the experiences of other people, either real or fictional.

The last group of questions, "Writing from Research," lists a variety of research projects that require the students to go beyond the text to expand their knowledge of this ethnic/racial group. For instance, after reading the selection "Un Poquito de Tu Amor" by Sandra Cisneros, students are asked to research a traditional holiday, such as Cinco de Mayo, celebrated by an ethnic/racial group. David Mura's "Where the Body Meets Memory" discusses his parents' experience in a relocation camp during World War II. One of the following questions asks students to write a paper about the reasons for these camps. Many of the research questions ask students to investigate the contribution of members of this ethnic/racial group to a field, such as politics, business, sports, or the arts. The instructor also may wish to use the historical introduction or Milestones list for research projects. To assist the students with research, a selected bibliography and a list of selected Internet resources appear at the end of each of the four parts.

Questions asking for comparisons are found both at the end of each part and at the end of this book. Following each of the four parts, students will find suggestions for comparing essays by writers from within the same ethnic/racial group. To compare writers from different ethnic/racial categories, students can use the suggested topics in "Connecting Writers Across Ethnic/Racial Groups" at the end of the book. Additionally, the Thematic Table of Contents allows comparison of topics (such as assimilation, early memories, families, violence, and justice) discussed by writers from separate groups.

Finally, students will find the Glossary at the end of the book to be of assistance in understanding many of the terms, often from sociology, used in this text. These terms also may lend themselves to class discussion and/or research projects.

In a typical semester course, an instructor would not expect students to read and write on all the selections. One instructor could decide to use a few selected shorter readings from each of the four parts. Another instructor, with a different student population or instructional goal, might choose to use a few of the longer, more complex readings from just one or two parts of *American Contexts*.

By using readings in *American Contexts* as the basis for discussion, research, and writing, students will come to a better understanding of themselves and others. As students review the cultural adaptations made by others, they will have an opportunity to reflect on their own experiences in establishing identity. Observing the broad range of issues of concern to a group, students will come to understand that although writers view the world from the perspective of their cultural heritage, all writers from the same group do not necessarily think alike, that group labels and stereotypes are often misleading. Through their reading and writing, students will become better acquainted with the diversity and interrelationship of groups that comprise America today.

I appreciate the support of Marion D. Bullock and Stanley M. Giannet, Pasco-Hernando Community College, and Maura Snyder, Professor Emerita, Saint Leo University, in developing this book. Thanks also to Joseph Opiela at Longman Publishers for his encouragement and valuable suggestions.

To the many reviewers who provided detailed and full critiques, I give a special acknowledgment: Cathryn Amdahl, Harrisburg Area Community College; Anne Bliss, University of Colorado at Boulder; Lenore Dowling, Rio Hondo Community College; Jeff Henderson, Kalamazoo Valley Community College; Dolores Johnson, Marshall University; Elizabeth Leyson, Fullerton College; Richard Marback, Wayne State University; Ollie Oviedo, Eastern New Mexico University; Merry G. Perry, University of South Florida; Mary Trachsel, University of Iowa; Randy Woodland, University of Michigan.

Finally, I would like to express my appreciation to my husband for his understanding and assistance.

Audrey B. Joyce

Part 1

African American Writers

INTRODUCTION

The ten essays in Part 1, selected from the large body of writing by African Americans, show an individual's perspective on some aspect of racism, the discriminatory treatment of a minority group because of a trait such as skin color, which continues to be an important issue in American society. Arranged in order of the author's birthdate, the readings include topics of interest to the contemporary reader and lend themselves readily to subjects for class discussion and student writing.

The perspective of these African American writers will be of interest to readers of all ethnic/racial backgrounds. These writings will help readers to examine how much of a person's self-image comes from identification with a particular ethnic/racial group. Additionally, students will come to a better understanding of an individual African American writer's perspective on political, economic, and social issues. Students will better understand how the journey toward freedom, justice, and social equality has affected African Americans.

Recent media accounts of Thomas Jefferson's African American descendants have interested Americans in the tangled relationships between masters and slaves in the pre–Civil War period. Works such as Toni Morrison's *Beloved* have made all Americans more aware of the enduring impact of slavery, which remains an intellectual challenge to those who would realize the ideals of the American Dream. **Harriet Ann Jacobs** and **Frederick Douglass,** the first two writers in this part, are enduring voices from the era of slavery. The excerpts from their inspiring autobiographies demonstrate how both were determined to find freedom despite the oppression they faced. Douglass, separated from his mother from early childhood, confirms that slavery disrupted the normal human bonds of family and community. His autobiography, a triumph of the human spirit, narrates the self-education of Douglass as he teaches himself to read and write in

1

defiance of the laws of the time. In Jacobs's autobiography, the reader sees how African American women faced sexual oppression by their masters. Both writers eventually escaped to the North, where they wrote their memoirs and worked in the abolitionist cause. Their works help to put a human face on the topic of slavery.

Maya Angelou makes vivid the Jim Crow era, a period (1880s through 1960s) when laws and social customs discriminated against African Americans and kept them segregated as "outsiders." As shown in the selection from Angelou's autobiography, intimidation and violence were ever-present threats to African Americans. Her narrative, with its presentation of the segregated seating in the local movie theater, further shows the reader how the days of "separate but equal" laws affected daily life.

During the Jim Crow years, many African Americans, seeking better economic and educational opportunities, moved from the agricultural South to the cities of the North and West. One outcome of this migration was the Harlem Renaissance, in which African American writers, musicians, and artists flourished. **Ralph Ellison,** who moved to New York in the 1930s, represents this cultural movement. In his essay, Ellison argues that African American contributions are an integral part of the "mainstream" society. Ellison's 1952 novel *Invisible Man* is a vivid portrayal of African American life during this Jim Crow period.

The third period of African American history includes the years of the 1960s to the present.

The 1960s were a time of ongoing struggle for social, economic, and political equality as African Americans began to defy the Jim Crow segregation statutes. While Dr. Martin Luther King, Jr., advocated policies of nonviolence and assimilation, more militant leaders, such as Malcolm X, favored cultural pluralism. In her essay, civil rights activist **Nikki Giovanni** reflects on her participation in this historic struggle and its legacy. Her essay leads naturally into student discussion of this important turning point as legal segregation ended with the Civil Rights Law of 1964.

At present, most African Americans and members of the dominant group have widely differing perceptions of the gains made since the 1960s. Although the majority of whites emphasize the progress made, the majority of African Americans see a society that, despite their long presence in the United States and their many contributions, continues to discriminate against them. Five writers discuss some of the topics on which there is disagreement, even in the African American community. These issues, often the subject of current media coverage, allow students to take a stand on these still controversial topics.

The first essay in this group, by **Claude M. Steele,** raises the issue of educational achievement of African Americans. Using examples from his research, Steele discusses the debilitating effects of racial stereotypes on student achievement. College students should find his essay provocative, especially as raising educational standards is an ongoing important political issue that affects them personally.

In the 1970s, the federal government developed a number of affirmative action programs designed to help victims of past discrimination attain equality with the dominant group. However, many conservatives oppose affirmative action, calling it "reverse discrimination." The essay by **Cornel West** on "the necessity and limits of affirmative action" allows students to explore whether and how to redress past wrongs.

Henry Louis Gates, Jr., concerns himself with the issue of identity for middle-class African Americans, what it means to be "authentically black." Raising the issue of class differences within the African American population, Gates considers how much an educated and successful African American is obligated to the one-third of the black population remaining in the impoverished, urban underclass. For many students, whatever their ethnic/racial group, the topic of upward mobility will become a personal issue as they become the first in their families to attend college.

The treatment of African Americans at the hands of law enforcement officers has led to racial tensions and even racial riots. In her challenging essay, **Barbara Reynolds** argues that the criminal justice system, especially "racial profiling," discriminates against African Americans.

Although African Americans have excelled in college and professional sports, **Marcus Mabry** feels that many of these athletes are exploited. His essay should enable students to explore the role of sports in college and in society. Because sports are of interest to most readers, students should find his discussion thought provoking.

Students may find a discussion of the following terms and "milestones" helpful in better understanding the essays and in developing topics for further research.

IMPORTANT MILESTONES

1863	The Emancipation Proclamation declared that slaves held in Confederate states were free.
1865	The Thirteenth Amendment freed all African Americans in the United States.
1896	*Plessy v. Ferguson:* Separate facilities were permitted for African Americans, but these facilities were to be equal to those of whites. This Supreme Court decision resulted in segregated schools, buses, trains, hospitals, and prisons. Many states passed laws forbidding marriage between blacks and whites.

1950	**Integration of Armed Forces:** President Truman's executive order integrated the Armed Forces for the first time.
1954	***Brown* v. *Topeka Board of Education:*** The Supreme Court said that the "separate but equal" school system denied African American children equal protection under the law. No longer could there be two separate public school systems, nor did the law protect the concept of separation of Americans by race.
1955	In Montgomery, Alabama, Rosa Parks refused to move to the back of the bus.
1957	Governor Orval Faubus called out the National Guard to prevent African American students from attending an all-white high school in Little Rock, Arkansas.
1963	In June, civil rights disruptions occurred after Medgar Evers, director of the Mississippi NAACP, was assassinated. In August, Dr. Martin Luther King, Jr., gave his "I Have a Dream" speech to 250,000 supporters gathered at the Lincoln Memorial. Assassination of President John Kennedy in November.
1964	**Civil Rights Law:** The law provided for equal rights in voting, education, and public accommodation.
1965	Assassination of Malcolm X.
1968	Assassinations of Martin Luther King, Jr., and Robert Kennedy.
1968	**Civil Rights Act:** This law eliminated many forms of housing discrimination.
1970	The Equal Employment Opportunity Commission ordered businesses, universities, and agencies to have "hiring, promotion, and admission" policies favoring African Americans. This "affirmative action" policy was to be in effect until the organization reflected the racial composition of society.
1978	***University of California* v. *Bakke:*** The Supreme Court outlawed admissions programs based on rigid affirmative action standards.
1991	In hearings of the Senate Judiciary Committee, Clarence Thomas, nominated to the Supreme Court, defended himself from charges of sexual harassment by Anita Hill.

Selection 1

Incidents in the Life of a Slave Girl, Written by Herself

HARRIET ANN JACOBS

Harriet Ann Jacobs (1813–1897) *recounted the events of her life under the pseudonym of "Linda Brent." Born into slavery, Jacobs, at the age of twelve, became the property of a master (the one she calls "Dr. Flint") who threatened her with unwanted sexual advances and prevented her from marrying the African American man she loved. As a means of fending off Dr. Flint, Jacobs then became the mistress of another white man by whom she had two children. Jacobs managed to escape from slavery after hiding for seven years in a tiny storeroom. In 1842, "passing" as a white woman, Jacobs traveled to New York where she worked as a domestic and began writing her autobiography. During the Civil War, Jacobs worked as a nurse and a teacher with newly freed African Americans. She spent her later years in Washington, D.C.*

In 1855, an abolitionist newspaper in New York published sections of Incidents; *the complete book was published in 1861. Jacobs's autobiography is notable for its treatment of slavery from the perspective of a woman. Jacobs shows how, even under the separations and hardships caused by slavery, she maintained a close and loving relationship with family members, including her grandmother, her parents, and her two children.*

In the following excerpt, Jacobs emphasizes the dilemma of enslaved African American women who had to endure both the sexual advances of the master and the jealous hostility of his wife. With its frank revelation of sexual exploitation, Jacobs's autobiography defies the conventional morality of the time. Incidents, *the first important book written by an African American woman, is considered by critics to be a seminal work that influenced many later African American women writers.*

PREPARING TO READ

1. Why do you think that people today are more aware of and less tolerant of sexual harassment than in the past?

2. Explain whether you think that the lyrics of some popular songs (such as "rap") are degrading to women.

3. Why do you agree (or disagree) that today men and women receive equal treatment in U.S. society?

4. What do you think are some of the important qualities of a good husband or wife and why do you think these characteristics are important?

INCIDENTS IN THE LIFE OF A SLAVE GIRL

Childhood

I was born a slave; but I never knew it till six years of happy childhood had passed away. My father was a carpenter, and considered so intelligent and skilful in his trade, that, when buildings out of the common line were to be erected, he was sent for from long distances, to be head workman. On condition of paying his mistress two hundred dollars a year, and supporting himself, he was allowed to work at his trade and manage his own affairs. His strongest wish was to purchase his children; but, though he several times offered his hard earnings for that purpose, he never succeeded. In complexion my parents were a light shade of brownish yellow, and were termed mulattoes. They lived together in a comfortable home; and, though we were all slaves, I was so fondly shielded that I never dreamed I was a piece of merchandise, trusted to them for safe keeping, and liable to be demanded of them at any moment. I had one brother, William, who was two years younger than myself—a bright, affectionate child. I had also a great treasure in my maternal grandmother, who was a remarkable woman in many respects. She was the daughter of a planter in South Carolina, who, at his death, left her mother and his three children free, with money to go to St. Augustine, where they had relatives. It was during the Revolutionary War; and they were captured on their passage, carried back, and sold to different purchasers. Such was the story my grandmother used to tell me; but I do not remember all the particulars. She was a little girl when she was captured and sold to the keeper of a large hotel. I have often heard her tell how hard she fared during childhood. But as she grew older she evinced so much intelligence, and was so faithful, that her master and mistress could not help seeing it was for their interest to take care of such a valuable piece of property. She became an indispensable personage in the household, officiating in all capacities, from cook and wet nurse to seamstress.

• • •

To this good grandmother I was indebted for many comforts. My brother Willie and I often received portions of the crackers, cakes, and preserves she made to sell; and after we ceased to be children we were indebted to her for many more important services.

Such were the unusually fortunate circumstances of my early childhood. When I was six years old, my mother died; and then, for the first time, I learned, by the talk around me, that I was a slave. My mother's mistress was the daughter of my grandmother's mistress. She was the foster sister of my mother; they were both nourished at my grandmother's breast. In fact, my mother had been weaned at three months old, that the babe of the mistress might obtain sufficient food. They played together as children; and, when they became women, my mother was a most faithful servant to her whiter foster sister. On her death-bed her mistress promised that her children should never suffer for any thing; and during her lifetime she kept her word. They all spoke kindly of my dead mother, who had been a slave merely in name, but in nature was noble and womanly. I grieved for her, and my young mind was troubled with the thought who would now take care of me and my little brother. I was told that my home was now to be with her mistress; and I found it a happy one. No toilsome or disagreeable duties were imposed upon me. My mistress was so kind to me that I was always glad to do her bidding and proud to labor for her as much as my young years would permit. I would sit by her side for hours, sewing diligently, with a heart as free from care as that of any free-born white child. When she thought I was tired, she would send me out to run and jump; and away I bounded, to gather berries or flowers to decorate her room. Those were happy days—too happy to last. The slave child had no thought for the morrow; but there came that blight, which too surely waits on every human being born to be a chattel.

When I was nearly twelve years old, my kind mistress sickened and died. As I saw the cheek grow paler, and the eye more glassy, how earnestly I prayed in my heart that she might live! I loved her; for she had been almost like a mother to me. My prayers were not answered. She died, and they buried her in the little churchyard, where, day after day, my tears fell upon her grave.

I was sent to spend a week with my grandmother. I was now old enough to begin to think of the future; and again and again I asked myself what they would do with me. I felt sure I should never find another mistress so kind as the one who was gone. She had promised my dying mother that her children should never suffer for any thing; and when I remembered that, and recalled her many proofs of attachment to me, I could not help having some hopes that she had left me free. My friends were almost certain it would be so. They thought she would be sure to do it, on account of my mother's love and faithful service. But, alas! we all know that the memory of a faithful slave does not avail much to save her children from the auction block.

After a brief period of suspense, the will of my mistress was read, and we learned that she had bequeathed me to her sister's daughter, a child of five years old. So vanished our hopes. My mistress had taught me the precepts of God's Word: "Thou shalt love thy neighbor as thyself." "Whatsoever ye would that men should do unto you, do ye even so unto them." But I was her slave, and I suppose she did not recognize me as her neighbor. I would give much to blot out from my memory that one great wrong. As a child, I loved my mistress; and, looking back on the happy days I spent with her, I try to think with less bitterness of this act of injustice. While I was with her, she taught me to read and spell; and for this privilege, which so rarely falls to the lot of a slave, I bless her memory.

She possessed but few slaves; and at her death those were all distributed among her relatives. Five of them were my grandmother's children, and had shared the same milk that nourished her mother's children. Notwithstanding my grandmother's long and faithful service to her owners, not one of her children escaped the auction block. These God-breathing machines are no more, in the sight of their masters, than the cotton they plant, or the horses they tend.

The Trials of Girlhood

During the first years of my service in Dr. Flint's family, I was accustomed to share some indulgences with the children of my mistress. Though this seemed to me no more than right, I was grateful for it and tried to merit the kindness by the faithful discharge of my duties. But I now entered on my fifteenth year—a sad epoch in the life of a slave girl. My master began to whisper foul words in my ear. Young as I was, I could not remain ignorant of their import. I tried to treat them with indifference or contempt. The master's age, my extreme youth, and the fear that his conduct would be reported to my grandmother, made him bear this treatment for many months. He was a crafty man and resorted to many means to accomplish his purposes. Sometimes he had stormy, terrific ways that made his victims tremble; sometimes he assumed a gentleness that he thought must surely subdue. Of the two, I preferred his stormy moods, although they left me trembling. He tried his utmost to corrupt the pure principles my grandmother had instilled. He peopled my young mind with unclean images, such as only a vile monster could think of. I turned from him with disgust and hatred. But he was my master. I was compelled to live under the same roof with him—where I saw a man forty years my senior daily violating the most sacred commandments of nature. He told me I was his property; that I must be subject to his will in all things. My soul revolted against the mean tyranny. But where could I turn for protection? No matter whether the slave girl be as black as ebony or as fair as her mistress. In either case, there is no shadow of law to protect her from insult, from violence, or even from death; all these are inflicted by fiends who bear the shape of men. The mistress, who ought to protect the helpless victim, has no other feelings towards her but those of jealousy and rage. The degradation, the wrongs, the vices, that grow out of slavery, are more than I can describe. They are greater than you would willingly believe. Surely, if you credited one half the truths that are told you concerning the helpless millions suffering in this cruel bondage, you at the North would not help to tighten the yoke. You surely would refuse to do for the master, on your own soil, the mean and cruel work which trained bloodhounds and the lowest class of whites do for him at the South.

Everywhere the years bring to all enough of sin and sorrow; but in slavery the very dawn of life is darkened by these shadows. Even the little child, who is accustomed to wait on her mistress and her children, will learn, before she is twelve years old, why it is that her mistress hates such and such a one among the slaves. Perhaps the child's own mother is among those hated ones. She listens to violent outbreaks of jealous passion and cannot help understanding what is the cause. She will become prematurely knowing in evil things. Soon she will learn to tremble when she hears her master's footfall. She will be compelled to realize that she is no longer a child. If God has bestowed beauty upon her, it will prove her greatest curse. That which commands admiration in the white woman only hastens the degradation of the female slave. I know that some are too much brutalized by slavery to feel the humiliation of their position; but many slaves feel it most acutely and shrink from the memory of it. I cannot tell how much I suffered in the presence of these wrongs nor how I am still pained by the retrospect. My master met me at every turn, reminding me that I belonged to him and swearing by heaven and earth that he would compel me to submit to him. If I went out for a breath of fresh air, after a day of unwearied toil, his footsteps dogged me. If I knelt by my mother's grave, his dark shadow fell on me even there. The light heart which nature had given me became heavy with sad forebodings. The other slaves in my master's house noticed the change. Many of them pitied me; but none dared to ask the cause. They had no need to inquire. They knew too well the guilty practices under that roof; and they were aware that to speak of them was an offense that never went unpunished.

I longed for some one to confide in. I would have given the world to have laid my head on my grandmother's faithful bosom, and told her all my troubles. But Dr. Flint swore he would kill me, if I was not as silent as the grave. Then, although my grandmother was all in all to me, I feared her as well as loved her. I had been accustomed to look up to her with a respect bordering upon awe. I was very young, and felt shamefaced about telling her such impure things, especially as I knew her to be very strict on such subjects. Moreover, she was a woman of a high spirit. She was usually very quiet in her demeanor; but if her indignation was once roused, it was not very easily quelled. I had been told that she once chased a white gentleman with a loaded pistol because he insulted one of her daughters. I dreaded the consequences of a violent outbreak; and both pride and fear kept me silent. But though I did not confide in my grandmother, and even evaded her vigilant watchfulness and inquiry, her presence in the neighborhood was some protection to me. Though she had been a slave, Dr. Flint was afraid of her. He dreaded her scorching rebukes. Moreover, she was known and patronized by many people; and he did not wish to have his villainy made public. It was lucky for me that I did not live on a distant plantation but in a town not so large that the inhabitants were ignorant of each other's affairs. Bad as are the laws and customs in a slaveholding community, the doctor, as a professional man, deemed it prudent to keep up some outward show of decency.

O, what days and nights of fear and sorrow that man caused me! Reader, it is not to awaken sympathy for myself that I am telling you truthfully what I suffered in slavery. I do it to kindle a flame of compassion in your hearts for my sisters who are still in bondage, suffering as I once suffered.

I once saw two beautiful children playing together. One was a fair white child; the other was her slave and also her sister. When I saw them embracing each other and heard their joyous laughter, I turned sadly away from the lovely sight. I foresaw the inevitable blight that would fall on the little slave's heart. I knew how soon her laughter would be changed to sighs. The fair child grew up to be a still fairer woman. From childhood to womanhood her pathway was blooming with flowers and overarched by a sunny sky. Scarcely one day of her life had been clouded when the sun rose on her happy bridal morning.

How had those years dealt with her slave sister, the little playmate of her childhood? She, also, was very beautiful; but the flowers and sunshine of love were not for her. She drank the cup of sin, and shame, and misery, whereof her persecuted race are compelled to drink.

In view of these things, why are ye silent, ye free men and women of the North? Why do your tongues falter in maintenance of the right? Would that I had more ability! But my heart is so full, and my pen is so weak! There are noble men and women who plead for us, striving to help those who cannot help themselves. God bless them! God give them strength and courage to go on! God bless those, everywhere, who are laboring to advance the cause of humanity!

The Jealous Mistress

I would ten thousand times rather that my children should be the half-starved paupers of Ireland than to be the most pampered among the slaves of America. I would rather drudge out my life on a cotton plantation, till the grave opened to give me rest, than to live with an unprincipled master and a jealous mistress. The felon's home in a penitentiary is preferable. He may repent, and turn from the error of his ways, and so find peace; but it is not so with a favorite slave. She is not allowed to have any pride of character. It is deemed a crime in her to wish to be virtuous.

Mrs. Flint possessed the key to her husband's character before I was born. She might have used this knowledge to counsel and to screen the young and the innocent among her slaves; but for them she had no sympathy. They were the objects of her constant suspicion and malevolence. She watched her husband with unceasing vigilance; but he was well practised in means to evade it. What he could not find opportunity to say in words he manifested in signs. He invented more than were ever thought of in a deaf and dumb asylum. I let them pass, as if I did not understand what he meant; and many were the curses and threats bestowed on me for my stupidity. One day he caught me teaching myself to write. He frowned, as if he was not well pleased; but I suppose he came to the conclusion that such an accomplishment might help to advance his favorite scheme. Before long, notes were often slipped into my hand. I would return them, saying "I can't read them, sir." "Can't you?" he replied; "then I must read them to you." He always finished the reading by asking, "Do you understand?" Sometimes he would complain of the heat of the tea room and order his supper to be placed on a small table in the piazza. He would seat himself there with a well-satisfied smile and tell me to stand by and brush away the flies. He would eat very slowly, pausing between the mouthfuls. These intervals were employed in describing the happiness I was so foolishly throwing away and in threatening me with the penalty that finally awaited my stubborn disobedience. He boasted much of the forbearance he had exercised towards me and reminded me that there was a limit to his patience. When I succeeded in avoiding opportunities for him to talk to me at home, I was ordered to come to his office, to do some errand. When there, I was obliged to stand and listen to such language as he saw fit to address to me. Sometimes I so openly expressed my contempt for him that he would become violently enraged, and I wondered why he did not strike me. Circumstanced as he was, he probably thought it was better policy to be forbearing. But the state of things grew worse and worse daily. In desperation I told him that I must and would apply to my grandmother for protection. He threatened me with death, and worse than death, if I made any complaint to her. Strange to say, I did not despair. I was naturally of a buoyant disposition, and always I had a hope of somehow getting out of his clutches. Like many a poor, simple slave before me, I trusted that some threads of joy would yet be woven into my dark destiny.

I had entered my sixteenth year, and every day it became more apparent that my presence was intolerable to Mrs. Flint. Angry words frequently passed between her and her husband. He had never punished me himself, and he would not allow anybody else to punish me. In that, respect, she was never satisfied; but, in her angry moods, no terms were too vile for her to bestow upon me. Yet I, whom she detested so bitterly, had far more pity for her than he had, whose duty it was to make her life happy. I never wronged her or wished to wrong her; and one word of kindness from her would have brought me to her feet.

After repeated quarrels between the doctor and his wife, he announced his intention to take his youngest daughter, then four years old, to sleep in his apartment. It was necessary that a servant should sleep in the same room, to be on hand if the child stirred. I was selected for that office and informed for what purpose that arrangement had been made. By managing to keep within sight of people, as much as possible, during the day time, I had hitherto succeeded in eluding my master, though a razor was often held to my throat to force me to change this line of policy. At night I slept by the side of my great aunt, where I felt safe. He was too prudent to come into her room. She was an old woman and had been in the family many years. Moreover, as a married man, and a professional man, he deemed it necessary to save appearances in some degree. But he resolved to remove the obstacle in the way of his scheme; and he thought he had planned it so that he should evade suspicion. He was well aware how much I prized my refuge by the side of my old aunt, and he determined to dispossess me of it. The first night the doctor had the little child in his room alone.

The next morning, I was ordered to take my station as nurse the following night. A kind Providence interposed in my favor. During the day Mrs. Flint heard of this new arrangement, and a storm followed. I rejoiced to hear it rage.

After a while my mistress sent for me to come to her room. Her first question was, "Did you know you were to sleep in the doctor's room?"

"Yes, Ma'am."

"Who told you?"

"My master."

"Will you answer truly all the questions I ask?"

"Yes, ma'am."

"Tell me, then, as you hope to be forgiven, are you innocent of what I have accused you?"

"I am."

She handed me a Bible, and said, "Lay your hand on your heart, kiss this holy book, and swear before God that you tell me the truth."

I took the oath she required, and I did it with a clear conscience.

"You have taken God's holy word to testify your innocence," said she. "If you have deceived me, beware! Now take this stool, sit down, look me directly in the face, and tell me all that has passed between your master and you."

I did as she ordered. As I went on with my account her color changed frequently, she wept and sometimes groaned. She spoke in tones so sad that I was touched by her grief. The tears came to my eyes; but I was soon convinced that her emotions arose from anger and wounded pride. She felt that her marriage vows were desecrated, her dignity insulted; but she had no compassion for the poor victim of her husband's perfidy. She pitied herself as a martyr; but she was incapable of feeling for the condition of shame and misery in which her unfortunate, helpless slave was placed.

Yet perhaps she had some touch of feeling for me; for when the conference was ended, she spoke kindly and promised to protect me. I should have been much comforted by this assurance if I could have had confidence in it; but my experiences in slavery had filled me with distrust. She was not a very refined woman and had not much control over her passions. I was an object of her jealousy and, consequently, of her hatred; and I knew I could not expect kindness or confidence from her under the circumstances in which I was placed. I could not blame her. Slaveholders' wives feel as other women would under similar circumstances. The fire of her temper kindled from small sparks, and now the flame became so intense that the doctor was obliged to give up his intended arrangement.

I knew I had ignited the torch, and I expected to suffer for it afterwards; but I felt too thankful to my mistress for the timely aid she rendered me to care much about that. She now took me to sleep in a room adjoining her own. There I was an object of her especial care, though not of her especial comfort, for she spent many a sleepless night to watch over me. Sometimes I woke up, and found her bending over me. At other times she whispered in my ear, as though it was her husband who was speaking to me, and listened to hear what I would answer. If she startled me, on such occasions, she would glide stealthily away; and the next morning she would tell me I had been talking in my sleep and ask who I was talking to. At last, I began to be fearful for my life. It had been often threatened; and you can imagine, better than I can describe, what an unpleasant sensation it must produce to wake up in the dead of night and find a jealous woman bending over you. Terrible as this experience was, I had fears that it would give place to one more terrible.

My mistress grew weary of her vigils; they did not prove satisfactory. She changed her tactics. She now tried the trick of accusing my master of crime, in my presence, and gave my name as the author of the accusation. To my utter astonishment, he replied, "I don't believe it; but if she did acknowledge it, you tortured her into exposing me." Tortured into exposing him! Truly, Satan had no difficulty in distinguishing the color of his soul! I understood his object in making this false representation. It was to show me that I gained nothing by seeking the protection of my mistress, that the power was still all in his own hands. I pitied Mrs. Flint. She was a second wife, many years the junior of her husband, and the hoary-headed miscreant was enough to try the patience of a wiser and better woman. She was completely foiled and knew not how to proceed. She would gladly have had me flogged for my supposed false oath; but, as I have already stated, the doctor never allowed anyone to whip me. The old sinner was politic. The application of the lash might have led to remarks that would have exposed him in the eyes of his children and grandchildren. How often did I rejoice that I lived in a town where all the inhabitants knew each other! If I had been on a remote plantation, or lost among the multitude of a crowded city, I should not be a living woman at this day.

The secrets of slavery are concealed like those of the Inquisition. My master was, to my knowledge, the father of eleven slaves. But did the mothers dare to tell who was the father of their children? Did the other slaves dare to allude to it, except in whispers among themselves? No, indeed! They knew too well the terrible consequences.

My grandmother could not avoid seeing things which excited her suspicions. She was uneasy about me, and tried various ways to buy me; but the never changing answer was always repeated: "Linda does not belong to *me*. She is my daughter's property, and I have no legal right to sell her." The conscientious man! He was too scrupulous to *sell* me; but he had no scruples whatever about committing a much greater wrong against the helpless young girl placed under his guardianship, as his daughter's property. Sometimes my persecutor would ask me whether I would like to be sold. I told him I would rather be sold to anybody than to lead such a life as I did. On such occasions he would assume the air of a very injured individual and reproach me for my ingratitude. "Did I not take you into the house and make you the companion of my own children?" he would say. "Have I ever treated you like a negro? I have never allowed you to be punished, not even to please your mistress. And this is the recompense I get, you ungrateful girl!" I answered that he had reasons of his own for screening me from punishment and that the course he pursued made my mistress hate me and persecute me. If I wept, he would say, "Poor child! Don't cry! Don't cry! I will make peace for you with your mistress. Only let me arrange matters in my own way. Poor, foolish girl! you don't know what is for your own good. I would cherish you. I would make a lady of you. Now go, and think of all I have promised you."

I did think of it.

Reader, I draw no imaginary pictures of Southern homes. I am telling you the plain truth. Yet when victims make their escape from this wild beast of Slavery, Northerners consent to act the part of bloodhounds and hunt the poor fugitive back into his den, "full of dead men's bones, and of all uncleanness." Nay, more, they are not only willing, but proud, to give their daughters in marriage to slaveholders. The poor girls have romantic notions of a sunny clime and of the flowering vines that all the year round shade a happy home. To what disappointments are they destined! The young wife soon learns that the husband in whose hands she has placed her happiness pays no regard to his marriage vows. Children of every shade of complexion play with her own fair babies, and too well she knows that they are born unto him of his own household. Jealousy and hatred enter the flowery home, and it is ravaged of its loveliness.

Southern women often marry a man knowing that he is the father of many little slaves. They do not trouble themselves about it. They regard such children as property, as marketable as the pigs on the plantation; and it is seldom that they do not make them aware of this by passing them into the slave-trader's hands as soon as possible and thus getting them out of their sight. I am glad to say there are some honorable exceptions.

I have myself known two Southern wives who exhorted their husbands to free those slaves towards whom they stood in a "parental relation," and their request was granted. These husbands blushed before the superior nobleness of their wives' natures. Though they had only counselled them to do that which it was their duty to do, it commanded their respect and rendered their conduct more exemplary. Concealment was at an end, and confidence took the place of distrust.

Though this bad institution deadens the moral sense, even in white women, to a fearful extent, it is not altogether extinct. I have heard Southern ladies say of Mr. Such a one, "He not only thinks it no disgrace to be the father of those little niggers, but he is not ashamed to call himself their master. I declare, such things ought not to be tolerated in any decent society!"

WRITING ABOUT THE READING

5. Frequently, Jacobs interrupts the narrative to comment, from her present perspective, on her motives, thoughts, and emotions as she went through these experiences. What do Jacobs's comments reveal about the psychology of the writer?

6. Explain why it could be argued that the institution of slavery was harmful to both African American and white women.

7. Jacobs frequently addresses the reader directly. Using evidence from the text, describe the "ideal reader" that she seems to be addressing.

8. What does Jacobs mean when she writes that she prefers her "children should be the half-starved paupers of Ireland than to be the most pampered among the slaves of America" and why does she say this?

9. Readers often use the word "moving" when speaking of Jacobs's autobiography. Explain why you think that this is an appropriate (or inappropriate) word to describe her writing.

WRITING FROM YOUR OWN EXPERIENCE

Note: In these assignments, write about your own experience or use that of someone you know, read about, or saw in a film/TV show.

10. Mrs. Flint treated Jacobs harshly because she saw the girl as a rival for her husband's affection. Explain the reason why you participated in a competition with another person (or people) and the consequences of this rivalry.

11. As an enslaved person, Jacobs was subject to mistreatment and abuse. Have you ever seen anyone mistreated or been mistreated yourself? Why did this abuse occur and what were the results of this experience?

12. Jacobs regarded slavery as an intolerable situation from which she had to escape. Think of a time when you felt that you had to escape from an intolerable situation. Why did you feel this way and what was the outcome of your experience?

WRITING ABOUT RESEARCH

13. Jacobs's autobiography provides the reader with many details about life during the pre-Civil War period. Research some aspect of African American life during this period. Consider:

    (a) The journey from Africa to America, known as the "middle passage."

    (b) Folk beliefs, crafts, and traditions brought from Africa.

    (c) The contributions of African Americans to agriculture.

    (d) The lives of free African Americans in the North.

    (e) Living conditions (such as food and housing) and/or culture of enslaved African Americans.

    (f) The relationship between Eli Whitney's invention of the cotton gin in 1793 and the expansion of slavery.

    (g) The 1712 uprising of African Americans in New York.

14. One of the most famous events of the pre-Civil War period was the Nat Turner rebellion of 1831. Why did this rebellion occur and what were the consequences?

15. What was the contribution of Crispus Attucks, an African American, to the American War for Independence?

16. Research the accusations by the supporters of Anita Hill that Clarence Thomas sexually harassed her. Explain whether you think that these charges were justified or not.

Narrative of the Life of Frederick Douglass, an American Slave, Written by Himself

FREDERICK DOUGLASS

Frederick Douglass *(1818–1895) was born into slavery, the son of Harriet Bailey and an unknown white man (most likely the owner of the Maryland plantation where Douglass lived as a young child). From 1826–1833, Douglass was a house servant in Baltimore, where he managed to learn to read and write. In 1833, his owner sent him to work as a laborer on a plantation where conditions were harsh and brutal punishments common. In 1838, Douglass escaped to the North, where he quickly became a well-known speaker and writer against the evils of slavery.*

As a result of his speeches on behalf of the antislavery movement and the publication of his autobiography in 1845, Douglass became a well-known public figure. Although living in the North, Douglass, an escaped slave, still was not legally free. Always in danger of being captured and returned to his master, Douglass had to move to England for two years. Douglass only became legally free after some of his admirers raised the money to purchase his freedom. During the Civil War, Douglass helped recruit African American men for service with the Union army. In his later years, he continued to write and to speak out for the rights of African Americans.

In this excerpt from his autobiography, Douglass shows that slavery had harmful effects on all people, even on the wife of Master Hugh, a woman who initially wished to be kind and teach him to read. His simple and direct account of the hardships of slavery, including the separation of families and cruel beatings, has made his autobiography an enduring classic.

PREPARING TO READ

1. What do you think are the characteristics of an "educated" person and why do you choose these characteristics?
2. Why do most families today emphasize the need for young people to attain a good education?

3. Think of a current ethical dilemma (such as the arguments over abortion, stem cell research, or cloning human beings). What are some of the ethical issues involved and why is this a difficult decision for many people?

4. In the pre–Civil War period, some people defied the law and helped African Americans escape from slavery. Explain whether you agree that, if there is a conflict between conscience and the law, people have a right to break the law.

NARRATIVE OF THE LIFE OF FREDERICK DOUGLASS, AN AMERICAN SLAVE, WRITTEN BY HIMSELF

Chapter II

My master's family consisted of two sons, Andrew and Richard; one daughter, Lucretia, and her husband, Captain Thomas Auld. They lived in one house, upon the home plantation of Colonel Edward Lloyd. My master was Colonel Lloyd's clerk and superintendent. He was what might be called the overseer of the overseers. I spent two years of childhood on this plantation in my old master's family. It was here that I witnessed the bloody transaction recorded in the first chapter; and as I received my first impressions of slavery on this plantation, I will give some description of it, and of slavery as it there existed. The plantation is about twelve miles north of Easton, in Talbot county, and is situated on the border of Miles River. The principal products raised upon it were tobacco, corn, and wheat. These were raised in great abundance; so that, with the products of this and the other farms belonging to him, he was able to keep in almost constant employment a large sloop, in carrying them to market at Baltimore. This sloop was named Sally Lloyd, in honor of one of the colonel's daughters. My master's son-in-law, Captain Auld, was master of the vessel; she was otherwise manned by the colonel's own slaves. Their names were Peter, Isaac, Rich, and Jake. These were esteemed very highly by the other slaves, and looked upon as the privileged ones of the plantation; for it was no small affair, in the eyes of the slaves, to be allowed to see Baltimore.

Colonel Lloyd kept from three to four hundred slaves on his home plantation, and owned a large number more on the neighboring farms belonging to him.

• • •

The home plantation of Colonel Lloyd wore the appearance of a country village. All the mechanical operations for all the farms were performed here. The shoemaking and mending, the blacksmithing, cartwrighting, coopering, weaving, and grain-grinding, were all performed by the slaves on the home plantation. The whole place wore a business-like aspect very unlike the neighboring farms. The number of houses, too, conspired to give it advantage over the neighboring farms. It was called by the slaves the *Great House Farm*. Few privileges were esteemed higher, by the slaves of the out-farms, than that of being selected to do errands at the Great House Farm. It was associated in their minds with greatness. A representative could not be prouder of his election to a seat in the American Congress, than a slave on one of the out-farms would be of his election to do errands at the Great House Farm. They regarded it as evidence of great confidence reposed in them by their overseers; and it was on this account, as well as a constant desire to be out of the field from under the driver's lash, that they esteemed it a high privilege, one worth careful living for. He was called the smartest and most trusty fellow, who had this honor conferred upon him the most frequently. The competitors for this office sought as diligently to please their overseers, as the office-seekers in the political parties seek to please and deceive the people. The same traits of character might be seen in Colonel Lloyd's slaves, as are seen in the slaves of the political parties.

The slaves selected to go to the Great House Farm, for the monthly allowance for themselves and their fellow-slaves, were peculiarly enthusiastic. While on their way, they would make the dense old woods, for miles around, reverberate with their wild songs, revealing at once the highest joy and the deepest sadness. They would compose and sing as they went along, consulting neither time nor tune. The thought that came up, came out—if not in the word, in the sound;—and as frequently in the one as in the other. They would sometimes sing the most pathetic sentiment in the most rapturous tone, and the most rapturous sentiment in the most pathetic tone. Into all of their songs they would manage to weave something of the Great House Farm. Especially would they do this, when leaving home. They would then sing most exultingly the following words:—

"I am going away to the Great House Farm!
O, yea! O, yea! O!"

This they would sing, as a chorus, to words which to many would seem unmeaning jargon, but which, nevertheless, were full of meaning to themselves. I have sometimes thought that the mere hearing of those songs would do more to impress some minds with the horrible character of slavery, than the reading of whole volumes of philosophy on the subject could do.

I did not, when a slave, understand the deep meaning of those rude and apparently incoherent songs. I was myself within the circle; so that I neither saw nor heard as those without might see and hear. They told a tale of woe which was then altogether beyond my feeble comprehension; they were tones loud, long, and deep; they breathed the prayer and complaint of souls boiling over with the bitterest anguish. Every tone was a testimony against slavery, and a prayer to God for deliverance from chains. The hearing of those wild notes always depressed my spirit, and filled me with ineffable sadness. I have frequently found myself in tears while hearing them. The mere recurrence to those songs, even now, afflicts me; and while I am writing these lines, an expression of feeling has already found its way down my cheek. To those songs I trace my first glimmering conception of the dehumanizing character of slavery. I can never get rid of that conception. Those songs still follow me, to deepen my hatred of slavery, and quicken my sympathies for my brethren in bonds. If any one wishes to be impressed with the soul-killing effects of slavery, let him go to Colonel Lloyd's plantation, and, on allowance-day, place himself in the deep pine woods, and there let him, in silence, analyze the sounds that shall pass through the chambers of his soul,—and if he is not thus impressed, it will only be because "there is no flesh in his obdurate heart."

I have often been utterly astonished, since I came to the north, to find persons who could speak of the singing, among slaves, as evidence of their contentment and happiness. It is impossible to conceive of a greater mistake. Slaves sing most when they are most unhappy. The songs of the slave represent the sorrows of his heart; and he is relieved by them, only as an aching heart is relived by its tears. At least, such is my experience. I have often sung to drown my sorrow, but seldom to express my happiness. Crying for joy, and singing for joy, were alike uncommon to me while in the jaws of slavery. The singing of a man cast away upon a desolate island might be as appropriately considered as evidence of contentment and happiness, as the singing of a slave; the songs of the one and of the other are prompted by the same emotion.

• • •

Chapter IV

Mr. Hopkins remained but a short time in the office of overseer. Why his career was so short, I do not know, but suppose he lacked the necessary severity to suit Colonel Lloyd. Mr. Hopkins was succeeded by Mr. Austin Gore, a man possessing, in an eminent degree, all those traits of character indispensable to what is called a first-rate overseer.

Mr. Gore had served Colonel Lloyd, in the capacity of overseer, upon one of the out-farms, and had shown himself worthy of the high station of overseer upon the home or Great House Farm.

Mr. Gore was proud, ambitious, and persevering. He was artful, cruel, and obdurate. He was just the man for such a place, and it was just the place for such a man. It afforded scope for the full exercise of all his powers, and he seemed to be perfectly at home in it. He was one of those who could torture the slightest look, word, or gesture, on the part of the slave, into impudence, and would treat it accordingly. There must be no answering back to him; no explanation was allowed a slave, showing himself to have been wrongfully accused. Mr. Gore acted fully up to the maxim laid down by slaveholders,—"It is better that a dozen slaves suffer under the lash, than that the overseer should be convicted, in the presence of the slaves, of having been at fault." No matter how innocent a slave might be—it availed him nothing, when accused by Mr. Gore of any misdemeanor. To be accused was to be convicted, and to be convicted was to be punished; the one always following the other with immutable certainty. To escape punishment was to escape accusation; and few slaves had the fortune to do either, under the overseership of Mr. Gore. He was just proud enough to demand the most debasing homage of the slave, and quite servile enough to crouch, himself, at the feet of the master. He was ambitious enough to be contented with nothing short of the highest rank of overseers, and persevering enough to reach the height of his ambition. He was cruel enough to inflict the severest punishment, artful enough to descend to the lowest trickery, and obdurate enough to be insensible to the voice of a reproving conscience. He was, of all the overseers, the most dreaded by the slaves. His presence was painful; his eye flashed confusion; and seldom was his sharp, shrill voice heard, without producing horror and trembling in their ranks.

Mr. Gore was a grave man, and, though a young man, he indulged in no jokes, said no funny words, seldom smiled. His words were in perfect keeping with his looks, and his looks were in perfect keeping with his words. Overseers will sometimes indulge in a witty word, even with the slaves; not so with Mr. Gore. He spoke but to command, and commanded but to be obeyed; he dealt sparingly with his words, and bountifully with his whip, never using the former where the latter would answer as well. When he whipped, he seemed to do so from a sense of duty, and feared no consequences. He did nothing reluctantly, no matter how disagreeable; always at his post, never inconsistent. He never promised but to fulfil. He was, in a word, a man of the most inflexible firmness and stone-like coolness.

His savage barbarity was equalled only by the consummate cool-ness with which he committed the grossest and most savage deeds upon the slaves under his charge. Mr. Gore once undertook to whip one of Colonel Lloyd's slaves, by the name of Demby. He had given Demby but few stripes, when, to get rid of the scourging, he ran and plunged himself into a creek, and stood there at the depth of his shoul-ders, refusing to come out. Mr. Gore told him that he would give him three calls, and that, if he did not come out at the third call, he would shoot him. The first call was given. Demby made no response, but stood his ground. The second and third calls were given with the same result. Mr. Gore then, without consultation or deliberation with any one, not even giving Demby an additional call, raised his musket to his face, taking deadly aim at his standing victim, and in an instant poor Demby was no more. His mangled body sank out of sight, and blood and brains marked the water where he had stood.

A thrill of horror flashed through every soul upon the plantation, excepting Mr. Gore. He alone seemed cool and collected. He was asked by Colonel Lloyd and my old master, why he resorted to this ex-traordinary expedient. His reply was, (as well as I can remember,) that Demby had become unmanageable. He was setting a dangerous exam-ple to the other slaves,—one which, if suffered to pass without some such demonstration on his part, would finally lead to the total subver-sion of all rule and order upon the plantation. He argued that if one slave refused to be corrected, and escaped with his life, the other slaves would soon copy the example; the result of which would be, the freedom of the slaves, and the enslavement of the whites. Mr. Gore's defence was satisfactory. He was continued in his station as overseer upon the home plantation. His fame as an overseer went abroad. His horrid crime was not even submitted to judicial investigation. It was committed in the presence of slaves, and they of course could neither institute a suit, nor testify against him; and thus the guilty perpetrator of one of the bloodiest and most foul murders goes unwhipped of jus-tice, and uncensured by the community in which he lives.

• • •

Chapter VII

I lived in Master Hugh's family about seven years. During this time, I succeeded in learning to read and write. In accomplishing this, I was compelled to resort to various stratagems. I had no regular teacher. My mistress, who had kindly commenced to instruct me, had, in compliance with the advice and direction of her husband, not only ceased to instruct, but had set her face against my being instructed by any one else. It is due, however, to my mistress to say of her, that she did not adopt this course of treatment immediately. She at first lacked the depravity indispensable to shutting me up in mental darkness. It was at least necessary for her to have some training in the exercise of irresponsible power, to make her equal to the task of treating me as though I were a brute.

My mistress was, as I have said, a kind and tender-hearted woman; and in the simplicity of her soul she commenced, when I first went to live with her, to treat me as she supposed one human being ought to treat another. In entering upon the duties of a slaveholder, she did not seem to perceive that I sustained to her the relation of a mere chattel, and that for her to treat me as a human being was not only wrong, but dangerously so. Slavery proved as injurious to her as it did to me. When I went there, she was a pious, warm, and tender-hearted woman. There was no sorrow or suffering for which she had not a tear. She had bread for the hungry, clothes for the naked, and comfort for every mourner that came within her reach. Slavery soon proved its ability to divest her of these heavenly qualities. Under its influence, the tender heart became stone, and the lamblike disposition gave way to one of tiger-like fierceness. The first step in her downward course was in her ceasing to instruct me. She now commenced to practise her husband's precepts. She finally became even more violent in her opposition than her husband himself. She was not satisfied with simply doing as well as he had commanded; she seemed anxious to do better. Nothing seemed to make her more angry than to see me with a newspaper. She seemed to think that here lay the danger. I have had her rush at me with a face made all up of fury, and snatch from me a newspaper, in a manner that fully revealed her apprehension. She was an apt woman; and a little experience soon demonstrated, to her satisfaction, that education and slavery were incompatible with each other.

From this time I was most narrowly watched. If I was in a separate room any considerable length of time, I was sure to be suspected of having a book, and was at once called to give an account of myself. All this, however, was too late. The first step had been taken. Mistress, in teaching me the alphabet, had given me the *inch,* and no precaution could prevent me from taking the *ell.*

The plan which I adopted, and the one by which I was most successful, was that of making friends of all the little white boys whom I met in the street. As many of these as I could, I converted into teachers. With their kindly aid, obtained at different times and in different places, I finally succeeded in learning to read. When I was sent on errands, I always took my book with me, and by going one part of my errand quickly, I found time to get a lesson before my return. I used to carry bread with me, enough of which was always in the house, and to which I was always welcome; for I was much better off in this regard than many of the poor white children in our neighborhood. This bread I used to bestow upon the hungry little urchins, who, in return, would give me that more valuable bread of knowledge. I am strongly tempted to give the names of two or three of those little boys, as a testimonial of the gratitude and affection I bear them; but prudence forbids;—not that it would injure me, but it might embarrass them; for it is almost an unpardonable offence to teach slaves to read in this Christian country. It is enough to say of the dear little fellows, that they lived on Philpot Street, very near Durgin and Bailey's shipyard. I used to talk this matter of slavery over with them. I would sometimes say to them, I wished I could be as free as they would be when they got to be men. "You will be free as soon as you are twenty-one, *but I am a slave for life!* Have not I as good a right to be free as you have?" These words used to trouble them; they would express for me the liveliest sympathy, and console me with the hope that something would occur by which I might be free.

I was now about twelve years old, and the thought of being *a slave for life* began to bear heavily upon my heart. Just about this time, I got hold of a book entitled "The Columbian Orator." Every opportunity I got, I used to read this book. Among much of other interesting matter, I found in it a dialogue between a master and his slave. The slave was represented as having run away from his master three times. The dialogue represented the conversation which took place between them, when the slave was retaken the third time. In this dialogue, the whole argument in behalf of slavery was brought forward by the master, all of which was disposed of by the slave. The slave was made to say some very smart as well as impressive things in reply to his master—things which had the desired though unexpected effect; for the conversation resulted in the voluntary emancipation of the slave on the part of the master.

In the same book, I met with one of Sheridan's mighty speeches on and in behalf of Catholic emancipation. These were choice documents to me. I read them over and over again with unabated interest. They gave tongue to interesting thoughts of my own soul, which had frequently flashed through my mind, and died away for want of utterance. The moral which I gained from the dialogue was the power of truth over the conscience of even a slaveholder. What I got from Sheridan was a bold denunciation of slavery, and a powerful vindication of human rights. The reading of these documents enabled me to utter my thoughts, and to meet the arguments brought forward to sustain slavery; but while they relieved me of one difficulty, they brought on another even more painful than the one of which I was relieved. The more I read, the more I was led to abhor and detest my enslavers. I could regard them in no other light than a band of successful robbers, who had left their homes, and gone to Africa, and stolen us from our homes, and in a strange land reduced us to slavery. I loathed them as being the meanest as well as the most wicked of men. As I read and contemplated the subject, behold! that very discontentment which Master Hugh had predicted would follow my learning to read had already come, to torment and sting my soul to unutterable anguish. As I writhed under it, I would at times feel that learning to read had been a curse rather than a blessing. It had given me a view of my wretched condition, without the remedy. It opened my eyes to the horrible pit, but to no ladder upon which to get out. In moments of agony, I envied my fellow-slaves for their stupidity. I have often wished myself a beast. I preferred the condition of the meanest reptile to my own. Any thing, no matter what, to get rid of thinking! It was this everlasting thinking of my condition that tormented me. There was no getting rid of it. It was pressed upon me by every object within sight or hearing, animate or inanimate. The silver trump of freedom had roused my soul to eternal wakefulness. Freedom now appeared, to disappear no more forever. It was heard in every sound, and seen in every thing. It was ever present to torment me with a sense of my wretched condition. I saw nothing without seeing it, I heard nothing without hearing it, and felt nothing without feeling it. It looked from every star, it smiled in every calm, breathed in every wind, and moved in every storm.

I often found myself regretting my own existence, and wishing myself dead; and but for the hope of being free, I have no doubt but that I should have killed myself, or done something for which I should have been killed. While in this state of mind, I was eager to hear any one speak of slavery. I was a ready listener. Every little while, I could hear something about the abolitionists. It was some time before I found what the word meant. It was always used in such connections as to make it an interesting word to me. If a slave ran away and succeeded in getting clear, or if a slave killed his master, set fire to a barn, or did any thing very wrong in the mind of a slaveholder, it was spoken of as the fruit of *abolition*. Hearing the word in this connection very often, I set about learning what it meant. The dictionary afforded me little or no help. I found it was "the act of abolishing;" but then I did not know what was to be abolished. Here I was perplexed. I did not dare to ask any one about its meaning, for I was satisfied that it was something they wanted me to know very little about. After a patient waiting, I got one of our city papers, containing an account of the number of petitions from the north, praying for the abolition of slavery in the District of Columbia, and of the slave trade between the States. From this time I understood the words *abolition* and *abolitionist*, and always drew near when that word was spoken, expecting to hear something of importance to myself and fellow-slaves. The light broke in upon me by degrees. I went one day down on the wharf of Mr. Waters; and seeing two Irishmen unloading a scow of stone, I went, unasked, and helped them. When we had finished, one of them came to me and asked me if I were a slave. I told him I was. He asked, "Are ye a slave for life?" I told him that I was. The good Irishman seemed to be deeply affected by the statement. He said to the other that it was a pity so fine a little fellow as myself should be a slave for life. He said it was a shame to hold me. They both advised me to run away to the north; that I should find friends there, and that I should be free. I pretended not to be interested in what they said, and treated them as if I did not understand them; for I feared they might be treacherous. White men have been known to encourage slaves to escape, and then, to get the reward, catch them and return them to their masters. I was afraid that these seemingly good men might use me so; but I nevertheless remembered their advice, and from that time I resolved to run away. I looked forward to a time at which it would be safe for me to escape. I was too young to think of doing so immediately; besides, I wished to learn how to write, as I might have occasion to write my own pass. I consoled myself with the hope that I should one day find a good chance. Meanwhile, I would learn to write.

The idea as to how I might learn to write was suggested to me by being in Durgin and Bailey's ship-yard, and frequently seeing the ship carpenters, after hewing, and getting a piece of timber ready for use, write on the timber the name of that part of the ship for which it was intended. When a piece of timber was intended for the larboard side, it would be marked thus—"L." When a piece was for the starboard side, it would be marked thus—"S." A piece for the larboard side forward, would be marked thus—"L. F." When a piece was for starboard side forward, it would be marked thus—"S. F." For larboard aft, it would be marked thus—"L. A." For starboard aft, it would be marked thus— "S. A." I soon learned the names of these letters, and for what they were intended when placed upon a piece of timber in the ship-yard. I immediately commenced copying them, and in a short time was able to make the four letters named. After that, when I met with any boy who I knew could write, I would tell him I could write as well as he. The next word would be, "I don't believe you. Let me see you try it." I would then make the letters which I had been so fortunate as to learn, and ask him to beat that. In this way I got a good many lessons in writing, which it is quite possible I should never have gotten in any other way.

During this time, my copy-book was the board fence, brick wall, and pavement; my pen and ink was a lump of chalk. With these, I learned mainly how to write. I then commenced and continued copying the Italics in Webster's Spelling Book, until I could make them all without looking on the book. By this time, my little Master Thomas had gone to school, and learned how to write, and had written over a number of copy-books. These had been brought home, and shown to some of our near neighbors, and then laid aside. My mistress used to go to class meeting at the Wilk Street meetinghouse every Monday afternoon, and leave me to take care of the house. When left thus, I used to spend the time in writing in the spaces left in Master Thomas's copy-book, copying what he had written. I continued to do this until I could write a hand very similar to that of Master Thomas. Thus, after a long, tedious effort for years, I finally succeeded in learning how to write.

WRITING ABOUT THE READING

5. What were the steps by which Douglass managed to learn to read and why was he motivated to undertake his education?
6. What ethical dilemma did the wife of Master Hugh face when she wanted to teach Douglass to read?
7. Based on Douglass's autobiography, why do you think that slave owners passed laws against teaching enslaved African Americans to read?
8. Douglass describes many interesting people with whom he came in contact. How and why do the details Douglass uses make a person "come alive" for the reader?
9. The enslaved African Americans always lived under the threat of the master's anger and consequent harsh treatment. How and why did their singing reflect the harsh conditions of their existence?
10. Why did Douglass sometimes feel that being educated was a burden to him?

WRITING FROM YOUR OWN EXPERIENCE

Note: In these assignments, write about your own experience or use that of someone you know, read about, or saw in a film/TV show.

11. Douglass describes many people who had an influence (positive or negative) on his development as a young man. Consider a

teacher, coach, or mentor who has influenced your life. How and why did this person influence you?

12. Faced with a difficult choice, the wife of Master Hugh decided to abandon Douglass's education. Choose a time when you faced a difficult choice. Explain why you made this choice and the consequences of this decision.

13. Douglass shows how the enslaved African Americans found it necessary to employ subterfuge and role-playing skills to survive when dealing with those who had power over their lives. Recall a time when you had to use similar strategies when dealing with a person in power. What strategy did you use and what were the outcomes of this experience?

WRITING ABOUT RESEARCH

14. What role did African American abolitionists play in turning the nation's attention to the issue of slavery? Consider one of the following:
    (a) Harriet Jacobs
    (b) David Ruggles
    (c) Charles Remond
    (d) Harriet Tubman
    (e) Sojourner Truth

15. How and why did African Americans participate in the Civil War?

16. Choose a more recent war (such as World Wars I and II, the Korean War, or the Vietnam War) and explain the participation of African Americans in that war.

17. What was the role of the mutual aid societies and churches (such as the African Union Society, the Free African Society, or the African Methodist Episcopal Church) in the lives of the approximately 250,000 free African Americans who lived in the North by 1860?

Selection 3

What Would America Be Like Without Blacks

RALPH ELLISON

Ralph Ellison *(1914–1994) has had enormous influence both as a writer and as a cultural historian. Born in Oklahoma City, Ellison first planned to become a musician, entering Tuskegee Institute in 1936 to study classical composition. During his early years, Ellison also was influenced by the work of many jazz musicians. In 1937, Ellison moved to New York, where he began to write essays and fiction for several periodicals. After serving in the Merchant Marine during World War II, Ellison held a number of jobs while he worked on* Invisible Man, *which was published to great acclaim in 1952. Ellison then had a long and distinguished career as a visiting lecturer at major universities. He also was presented with honorary doctorates by many universities, including Brown University (1980). He received the Presidential Medal of Freedom (1969) and was appointed a charter member of the National Council on the Arts and Humanities. In 1975, Oklahoma City, Ellison's birthplace, named a public library in his honor.*

Ellison's distinguished book, Invisible Man, *quickly earned him praise from critics. His novel received several major awards, including the National Book Award (1952), and was recognized as one of the most important postwar novels. In* Invisible Man, *Ellison explores the distinctive experience of African Americans and their struggle against the dominant white society that treated them in the 1950s as if they were invisible, not fully human. He employs references to jazz as a symbol of the protagonist's conflict between freedom and order, of the risks inherent in improvisation and self-determination. Rather than scorning the traditional African American culture, Ellison was one of the earliest writers to emphasize its richness and value.*

In the following essay, Ellison answers the question posed by the provocative title by insisting that African American culture is an inseparable part of American culture, that the American identity cannot be envisioned without the African American contribution. "What Would America Be Like Without Blacks," originally published in Time *magazine (1970), was reprinted in 1986 as part of a collection of essays by Ellison,* Going to the Territory. *The essay is one of the strongest affirmations of the valuable contributions made to American life by African Americans.*

PREPARING TO READ

1. Explain what is meant by the terms "outsider" and "scapegoat" and explain why you would define these terms in this way.
2. Why do you think that the dominant society today is more accepting of the contributions of African Americans than it was in the 1950s?
3. Why has African American music, such as jazz, become an accepted part of the "cultural mainstream"?

WHAT WOULD AMERICA BE LIKE WITHOUT BLACKS

The fantasy of an America free of blacks is at least as old as the dream of creating a truly democratic society. While we are aware that there is something inescapably tragic about the cost of achieving our democratic ideals, we keep such tragic awareness segregated to the rear of our minds. We allow it to come to the fore only during moments of great national crisis.

On the other hand, there is something so embarrassingly absurd about the notion of purging the nation of blacks that it seems hardly a product of thought at all. It is more like a primitive reflex, a throwback to the dim past of tribal experience, which we rationalize and try to make respectable by dressing it up in the gaudy and highly questionable trappings of what we call the "concept of race." Yet, despite its absurdity, the fantasy of a blackless America continues to turn up. It is a fantasy born not merely of racism but of petulance, of exasperation, of moral fatigue. It is like a boil bursting forth from impurities in the bloodstream of democracy.

In its benign manifestations, it can be outrageously comic—as in the picaresque adventures of Percival Brownlee who appears in William Faulkner's story "The Bear." Exasperating to his white masters because his aspirations and talents are for preaching and conducting choirs rather than for farming, Brownlee is "freed" after much resistance and ends up as the prosperous proprietor of a New Orleans brothel. In Faulkner's hands, the uncomprehending drive of Brownlee's owners to "get shut" of him is comically instructive. Indeed, the story resonates certain abiding, tragic themes of American history with which it is interwoven, and which are causing great turbulence in the social atmosphere today. I refer to the exasperation and bemusement of the white American with the black, the black American's ceaseless (and swiftly accelerating) struggle to escape the misconceptions of whites, and the continual confusing of the black American's racial background with his individual culture. Most of all, I refer to the recurring fantasy of solving one basic problem of American democracy by "getting shut" of the blacks through various wishful schemes that would banish them from the nation's bloodstream, from its social structure, and from its conscience and historical consciousness.

This fantastic vision of a lily-white America appeared as early as 1713, with the suggestion of a white "native American," thought to be from New Jersey, that all the Negroes be given their freedom and returned to Africa. In 1777, Thomas Jefferson, while serving in the Virginia legislature, began drafting a plan for the gradual emancipation and exportation of the slaves. Nor were Negroes themselves immune to the fantasy. In 1815, Paul Cuffe, a wealthy merchant, shipbuilder, and landowner from the New Bedford area, shipped and settled at his own expense thirty-eight of his fellow Negroes in Africa. It was perhaps his example that led in the following year to the creation of the American Colonization Society, which was to establish in 1821 the colony of Liberia. Great amounts of cash and a perplexing mixture of motives went into the venture. The slaveowners and many Border-state politicians wanted to use it as a scheme to rid the country not of slaves but of the militant free Negroes who were agitating against the "peculiar institution." The abolitionists, until they took a lead from free Negro leaders and began attacking the scheme, also participated as a means of righting a great historical injustice. Many blacks went along with it simply because they were sick of the black and white American mess and hoped to prosper in the quiet peace of the old ancestral home.

Such conflicting motives doomed the Colonization Society to failure, but what amazes one even more than the notion that anyone could have believed in its success is the fact that it was attempted during a period when the blacks, slave and free, made up eighteen percent of the total population. When we consider how long blacks had been in the New World and had been transforming it and being Americanized by it, the scheme appears not only fantastic, but the product of a free-floating irrationality. Indeed, a national pathology.

Nevertheless, some of the noblest of Americans were bemused. Not only Jefferson but later Abraham Lincoln was to give the scheme credence. According to historian John Hope Franklin, Negro colonization seemed as important to Lincoln as emancipation. In 1862, Franklin notes, Lincoln called a group of prominent free Negroes to the White House and urged them to support colonization, telling them, "Your race suffers greatly, many of them by living among us, while ours suffers from your presence. If this is admitted, it affords a reason why we should be separated."

In spite of his unquestioned greatness, Abraham Lincoln was a man of his times and limited by some of the less worthy thinking of his times. This is demonstrated both by his reliance upon the concept of race in his analysis of the American dilemma and by his involvement in a plan of purging the nation of blacks as a means of healing the badly shattered ideals of democratic federalism. Although benign, his motive was no less a product of fantasy. It envisaged an attempt to relieve an inevitable suffering that marked the growing pains of the youthful body politic by an operation which would have amounted to the severing of a healthy and indispensable member.

Yet, like its twin, the illusion of secession, the fantasy of a benign amputation that would rid the country of black men to the benefit of a nation's health not only persists; today, in the form of neo-Garveyism, it fascinates black men no less than it once hypnotized whites. Both fantasies become operative whenever the nation grows weary of the struggle toward the ideal of American democratic equality. Both would use the black man as a scapegoat to achieve a national catharsis, and both would, by way of curing the patient, destroy him.

What is ultimately intriguing about the fantasy of "getting shut" of the Negro American is the fact that no one who entertains it seems ever to have considered what the nation would have become had Africans *not* been brought to the New World, and had their descendants not played such a complex and confounding role in the creation of American history and culture. Nor do they appear to have considered with any seriousness the effect upon the nation of having any of the schemes of exporting blacks succeed beyond settling some fifteen thousand or so in Liberia.

We are reminded that Daniel Patrick Moynihan, who has recently aggravated our social confusion over the racial issue while allegedly attempting to clarify it, is co-author of a work which insists that the American melting pot didn't melt because our white ethnic groups have resisted all assimilative forces that appear to threaten their identities. The problem here is that few Americans know who and what they really are. That is why few of these groups—or at least few of the children of these groups—have been able to resist the movies, television, baseball, jazz, football, drum-majoretting, rock, comic strips, radio commercials, soap operas, book clubs, slang, or any of a thousand other expressions and carriers of our pluralistic and easily available popular culture. And it is here precisely that ethnic resistance is least effective. On this level the melting pot did indeed melt, creating such deceptive metamorphoses and blending of identities, values, and life-styles that most American whites are culturally part Negro American without even realizing it.

If we can resist for a moment the temptation to view everything having to do with Negro Americans in terms of their racially imposed status, we become aware of the fact that for all the harsh reality of the social and economic injustices visited upon them, these injustices have failed to keep Negroes clear of the cultural mainstream; Negro Americans are in fact one of its major tributaries. If we can cease approaching American social reality in terms of such false concepts as white and nonwhite, black culture and white culture, and think of these apparently unthinkable matters in the realistic manner of Western pioneers confronting the unknown prairie, perhaps we can begin to imagine what the United States would have been, or not been, had there been no blacks to give it—if I may be so bold as to say—color.

For one thing, the American nation is in a sense the product of the American language, a colloquial speech that began emerging long before the British colonials and Africans were transformed into Americans. It is a language that evolved from the king's English but, basing itself upon the realities of the American land and colonial institutions—or lack of institutions, began quite early as a vernacular revolt against the signs, symbols, manners, and authority of the mother country. It is a language that began by merging the sounds of many tongues, brought together in the struggle of diverse regions. And whether it is admitted or not, much of the sound of that language is derived from the timbre of the African voice and the listening habits of the African ear. So there is a *de'z* and *do'z* of slave speech sounding beneath our most polished Harvard accents, and if there is such a thing as a Yale accent, there is a Negro wail in it—doubtlessly introduced there by Old Yalie John C. Calhoun, who probably got it from his mammy.

Whitman viewed the spoken idiom of Negro Americans as a source for a native grand opera. Its flexibility, its musicality, its rhythms, freewheeling diction, and metaphors, as projected in Negro American folklore, were absorbed by the creators of our great nineteenth-century literature even when the majority of blacks were still enslaved. Mark Twain celebrated it in the prose of *Huckleberry Finn*; without the presence of blacks, the book could not have been written. No Huck and Jim, no American novel as we know it. For not only is the black man a co-creator of the language that Mark Twain raised to the level of literary eloquence, but Jim's condition as American and Huck's commitment to freedom are at the moral center of the novel.

In other words, had there been no blacks, certain creative tensions arising from the cross-purposes of whites and blacks would also not have existed. Not only would there have been no Faulkner; there would have been no Stephen Crane, who found certain basic themes of his writing in the Civil War. Thus, also, there would have been no Hemingway, who took Crane as a source and guide. Without the presence of Negro American style, our jokes, our tall tales, even our sports would be lacking in the sudden turns, the shocks, the swift changes of pace (all jazz-shaped) that serve to remind us that the world is ever unexplored, and that while a complete mastery of life is mere illusion, the real secret of the game is to make life swing. It is its ability to articulate this tragic-comic attitude toward life that explains much of the mysterious power and attractiveness of that quality of Negro American style known as "soul." An expression of American diversity within unity, of blackness with whiteness, soul announces the presence of a creative struggle against the realities of existence.

Without the presence of blacks, our political history would have been otherwise. No slave economy, no Civil War; no violent destruction of the Reconstruction; no K.K.K. and no Jim Crow system. And without the disenfranchisement of black Americans and the manipulation of racial fears and prejudices, the disproportionate impact of white Southern politicians upon our domestic and foreign policies would have been impossible. Indeed, it is almost impossible to conceive of what our political system would have become without the snarl of forces—cultural, racial, religious—that make our nation what it is today.

Absent, too, would be the need for that tragic knowledge which we try ceaselessly to evade: that the true subject of democracy is not simply material well-being but the extension of the democratic process in the direction of perfecting itself. And that the most obvious test and clue to that perfection is the inclusion—*not* assimilation—of the black man.

• • •

Since the beginning of the nation, white Americans have suffered from a deep inner uncertainty as to who they really are. One of the ways that has been used to simplify the answer has been to seize upon the presence of black Americans and use them as a marker, a symbol of limits, a metaphor for the "outsider." Many whites could look at the social position of blacks and feel that color formed an easy and reliable gauge for determining to what extent one was or was not American. Perhaps that is why one of the first epithets that many European immigrants learned when they got off the boat was the term "nigger"—it made them feel instantly American. But this is tricky magic. Despite his racial difference and social status, something indisputably American about Negroes not only raised doubts about the white man's value system but aroused the troubling suspicion that whatever else the true American is, he is also somehow black.

Materially, psychologically, and culturally, part of the nation's heritage is Negro American, and whatever it becomes will be shaped in part by the Negro's presence. Which is fortunate, for today it is the black American who puts pressure upon the nation to live up to its ideals. It is he who gives creative tension to our struggle for justice and for the elimination of those factors, social and psychological, which make for slums and shaky suburban communities. It is he who insists that we purify the American language by demanding that there be a closer correlation between the meaning of words and reality, between ideal and conduct, our assertions and our actions. Without the black American, something irrepressibly hopeful and creative would go out of the American spirit, and the nation might well succumb to the moral slobbism that has ever threatened its existence from within.

When we look objectively at how the dry bones of the nation were hung together, it seems obvious that some one of the many groups that compose the United States had to suffer the fate of being allowed no easy escape from experiencing the harsh realities of the human condition as they were to exist under even so fortunate a democracy as ours. It would seem that some one group had to be stripped of the possibility of escaping such tragic knowledge by taking sanctuary in moral equivocation, racial chauvinism, or the advantage of superior social status. There is no point in complaining over the past or apologizing for one's fate. But for blacks, there are no hiding places down here, not in suburbia or in penthouse, neither in country nor in city. They are an American people who are geared to what *is* and who yet are driven by a sense of what it is possible for human life to be in this society. The nation could not survive being deprived of their presence because, by the irony implicit in the dynamics of American democracy, they symbolize both its most stringent testing and the possibility of its greatest human freedom.

WRITING ABOUT THE READING

4. Why does the historical survey of the movement to rid the United States of African Americans prepare the reader for the next section of the essay?
5. Using evidence from the essay, what would Ellison's response probably be to those who favor cultural pluralism?

6. What is the tone of this essay and why do you think that the tone is appropriate (or inappropriate)?
7. Explain what you think Ellison means when he speaks of "soul" as announcing "the presence of a creative struggle against the realities of existence."
8. Ellison compares the language spoken by Americans and the British. What are some of the differences he lists and what does he say are the reasons for these differences?

WRITING FROM YOUR OWN EXPERIENCE

Note: In these assignments, write about your own experience or use that of someone you know, read about, or saw in a film/TV show.

9. Recall a time when you were treated as an "outsider" or "scapegoat." Why did this situation occur and what were some of the consequences of this treatment?
10. Ellison argues that African Americans have contributed to the "cultural mainstream." Think of a prominent contemporary African American who has made such a contribution. Why would you choose this person to support Ellison's statement?
11. Ellison argues that "perfection of the self" is the true goal of democracy. Many Americans, such as Benjamin Franklin, have undertaken self-improvement programs. Have you ever undertaken a program to improve yourself? How and why did you engage in this effort to "perfect" yourself?
12. Ellison speaks of the tragicomic view of life. Recall a time when you were involved in an event that could be described as "tragicomic." Why would you use this word to describe this situation and what was the effect of this experience on you?

WRITING ABOUT RESEARCH

13. Ellison discusses some of the contributions of African Americans to the language. In recent years, there has been a controversy about the teaching of Ebonics, a dialect of American English spoken by some African Americans. Take a position supporting one side or the other on this issue and explain the reasons for your position.
14. Ellison explains that the movement to send African Americans to Liberia was popular in the nineteenth century. How and why has Liberia become one of the more prosperous African countries?

15. Why was the Harlem Renaissance an important development in African American culture?

16. Why do most leading anthropologists agree that modern humans have their origin in Africa?

17. In recent years, numerous African Americans have received recognition for their writing. Explore the life and work of an African American writer who is not included in this anthology. What has been this writer's contribution to American literature?

    Consider:

    (a) James Baldwin

    (b) Toni Cade Bambara

    (c) Amiri Baraka (LeRoi Jones)

    (d) Gwendolyn Brooks

    (e) Lorraine Hansberry

    (f) Langston Hughes

    (g) Zora Neale Hurston

    (h) Charles Johnson

    (i) Toni Morrison

    (j) Alice Walker

    (k) August Wilson

    (l) Richard Wright

Selection 4

My Brother Bailey
and Kay Francis

MAYA ANGELOU

Maya Angelou *(1928–) has had a successful and varied career as a writer, editor, dancer, singer, actress, lecturer, director, and screen producer. Angelou's* I Know Why the Caged Bird Sings *(1970), the first of her five autobiographies, was nominated for a National Book Award. Angelou has received many other awards for both her writing and acting, including honorary degrees from several universities and recognition by the* Ladies Home Journal *as one of the 100 most influential women of the time. At President Clinton's 1993 inauguration, Angelou was chosen for the honor of reading aloud one of her poems.*

I Know Why the Caged Bird Sings *tells the story of an African American girl growing up during the 1930s. The young Angelou learns to cope with and to transcend the rigid rules that govern her life. The following selection from the popular autobiography is set in the South, where she and her brother, Bailey, were sent to live with their grandmother and uncle, who ran a general store. The young girl has to learn how to endure and survive, living under the "Jim Crow" racial segregation she finds in this small, Southern town.*

PREPARING TO READ

1. Support or refute the following statement: Children who live with only one parent (or with relatives other than parents) are adversely affected by this living arrangement.
2. Why do you think parents today are often more reluctant to use corporal punishment than in past years?
3. Sometimes light-skinned persons of partial African American ancestry "pass" or identify themselves as "white." Explain why you think they do this and whether you think it is "right" for them to "pass"?
4. Explain whether you think that today many African American students choose to segregate themselves from whites (such as by sitting at an all "African American" table in the cafeteria)?

MY BROTHER BAILEY AND KAY FRANCIS

Weekdays revolved on a sameness wheel. They turned into themselves so steadily and inevitably that each seemed to be the original of yesterday's rough draft. Saturdays, however, always broke the mold and dared to be different.

Farmers trekked into town with their children and wives streaming around them. Their board-stiff khaki pants and shirts revealed the painstaking care of a dutiful daughter or wife. They often stopped at the Store to get change for bills so they could give out jangling coins to their children, who shook with their eagerness to get to town. The young kids openly resented their parents' dawdling in the Store and Uncle Willie would call them in and spread among them bits of sweet peanut patties that had been broken in shipping. They gobbled down the candies and were out again, kicking up the powdery dust in the road and worrying if there was going to be time to get to town after all.

Bailey played mumbledypeg with the older boys around the chinaberry tree, and Momma and Uncle Willie listened to the farmers' latest news of the country. I thought of myself as hanging in the Store, a mote imprisoned on a shaft of sunlight. Pushed and pulled by the slightest shift of air, but never falling free into the tempting darkness.

In the warm months, morning began with a quick wash in unheated well water. The suds were dashed on a plot of ground beside the kitchen door. It was called the bait garden (Bailey raised worms). After prayers, breakfast in summer was usually dry cereal and fresh milk. Then to our chores (which on Saturday included weekday jobs)—scrubbing the floors, raking the yards, polishing our shoes for Sunday (Uncle Willie's had to be shined with a biscuit) and attending to the customers who came breathlessly, also in their Saturday hurry.

Looking through the years, I marvel that Saturday was my favorite day in the week. What pleasures could have been squeezed between the fan folds of unending tasks? Children's talent to endure stems from their ignorance of alternatives.

After our retreat from St. Louis, Momma gave us a weekly allowance. Since she seldom dealt with money, other than to take it in and to tithe to the church, I supposed that the weekly ten cents was to tell us that even she realized that a change had come over us, and that our new unfamiliarity caused her to treat us with a strangeness.

I usually gave my money to Bailey, who went to the movies nearly every Saturday. He brought back Street and Smith cowboy books for me.

One Saturday Bailey was late coming back from the Rye-al-toh. Momma had begun heating water for the Saturday-night baths, and all the evening chores were done. Uncle Willie sat in the twilight on the front porch mumbling or maybe singing, and smoking a ready-made. It was quite late. Mothers had called in their children from the group games, and fading sounds of "Yah . . . Yah . . . you didn't catch me" still hung and floated into the Store.

Uncle Willie said, "Sister, better light the light." On Saturdays we used the electric lights so that last-minute Sunday shoppers could look down the hill and see if the Store was open. Momma hadn't told me to turn them on because she didn't want to believe that night had fallen hard and Bailey was still out in the ungodly dark.

Her apprehension was evident in the hurried movements around the kitchen and in her lonely fearing eyes. The Black woman in the South who raises sons, grandsons and nephews had her heartstrings tied to a hanging noose. Any break from routine may herald for them unbearable news. For this reason, Southern Blacks until the present generation could be counted among America's arch conservatives.

Like most self-pitying people, I had very little pity for my relatives' anxiety. If something indeed had happened to Bailey, Uncle Willie would always have Momma, and Momma had the Store. Then, after all, we weren't their children. But I would be the major loser if Bailey turned up dead. For he was all I claimed, if not all I had.

The bath water was steaming on the cooking stove, but Momma was scrubbing the kitchen table for the umpteenth time.

"Momma," Uncle Willie called and she jumped. "Momma." I waited in the bright lights of the Store, jealous that someone had come along and told these strangers something about my brother and I would be the last to know.

"Momma, why don't you and Sister walk down to meet him?"

To my knowledge Bailey's name hadn't been mentioned for hours, but we all knew whom he meant.

Of course. Why didn't that occur to me? I wanted to be gone. Momma said, "Wait a minute, little lady. Go get your sweater, and bring me my shawl."

It was darker in the road then I'd thought it would be. Momma swung the flashlight's arc over the path and weeds and scary tree trunks. The night suddenly became enemy territory, and I knew that if my brother was lost in this land he was forever lost. He was eleven and very smart, that I granted, but after all he was so small. The Bluebeards and tigers and Rippers could eat him up before he could scream for help.

Momma told me to take the light and she reached for my hand. Her voice came from a high hill above me and in the dark my hand was enclosed in hers. I loved her with a rush. She said nothing—no "Don't worry" or "Don't get tender-hearted." Just the gentle pressure of her rough hand conveyed her own concern and assurance to me.

We passed houses which I knew well by daylight but couldn't recollect in the swarthy gloom.

"Evening, Miz Jenkins." Walking and pulling me along.

"Sister Henderson? Anything wrong?" That was from an outline blacker than the night.

"No ma'am. Not a thing. Bless the Lord." By the time she finished speaking we had left the worried neighbors far behind.

Mr. Willie Williams' Do Drop Inn was bright with furry red lights in the distance and the pond's fishy smell enveloped us. Momma's hand tightened and let go, and I saw the small figure plodding along, tired and old-mannish. Hands in his pockets and head bent, he walked like a man trudging up the hill behind a coffin.

"Bailey." It jumped out as Momma said, "Ju," and I started to run, but her hand caught mine again and became a vise. I pulled, but she yanked me back to her side. "We'll walk, just like we been walking, young lady." There was no chance to warn Bailey that he was dangerously late, that everybody had been worried and that he should create a good lie or, better, a great one.

Momma said, "Bailey, Junior," and he looked up without surprise. "You know it's night and you just now getting home?"

"Yes, ma'am." He was empty. Where was his alibi?

"What you been doing?"

"Nothing."

"That's all you got to say?"

"Yes, ma'am."

"All right, young man. We'll see when you get home."

She had turned me loose, so I made a grab for Bailey's hand, but he snatched it away. I said, "Hey, Bail," hoping to remind him that I was his sister and his only friend, but he grumbled something like "Leave me alone."

Momma didn't turn on the flashlight on the way back, nor did she answer the questioning Good evenings that floated around us as we passed the darkened houses.

I was confused and frightened. He was going to get a whipping and maybe he had done something terrible. If he couldn't talk to me it must have been serious. But there was no air of spent revelry about him. He just seemed sad. I didn't know what to think.

Uncle Willie said, "Getting too big for your britches, huh? You can't come home. You want to worry your grandmother to death?" Bailey was so far away he was beyond fear. Uncle Willie had a leather belt in his good hand but Bailey didn't notice or didn't care. "I'm going to whip you this time." Our uncle had only whipped us once before and then only with a peach-tree switch, so maybe now he was going to kill my brother. I screamed and grabbed for the belt, but Momma caught me. "Now, don't get uppity, miss, 'less you want some of the same thing. He got a lesson coming to him. You come on and get your bath."

From the kitchen I heard the belt fall down, dry and raspy on naked skin. Uncle Willie was gasping for breath, but Bailey made no sound. I was too afraid to splash water or even to cry and take a chance of drowning out Bailey's pleas for help, but the pleas never came and the whipping was finally over.

I lay awake an eternity, waiting for a sign, a whimper or a whisper, from the next room that he was still alive. Just before I fell exhausted into sleep, I heard Bailey: "Now I lay me down to sleep, I pray the Lord my soul to keep, if I should die before I wake, I pray the Lord my soul to take."

My last memory of that night was the question, Why is he saying the baby prayer? We had been saying the "Our Father, which art in heaven" for years.

For days the Store was a strange country, and we were all newly arrived immigrants. Bailey didn't talk, smile or apologize. His eyes were so vacant, it seemed his soul had flown away, and at meals I tried to give him the best pieces of meat and the largest portion of dessert, but he turned them down.

Then one evening at the pig pen he said without warning, "I saw Mother Dear."

If he said it, it was bound to be the truth. He wouldn't lie to me. I don't think I asked him where or when.

"In the movies." He laid his head on the wooden railing. "It wasn't really her. It was a woman named Kay Francis. She's a white movie star who looks just like Mother Dear."

There was no difficulty believing that a white movie star looked like our mother and that Bailey had seen her. He told me that the movies were changed each week, but when another picture came to Stamps starring Kay Francis he would tell me and we'd go together. He even promised to sit with me.

He had stayed late on the previous Saturday to see the film over again. I understood, and understood too why he couldn't tell Momma or Uncle Willie. She was our mother and belonged to us. She was never mentioned to anyone because we simply didn't have enough of her to share.

We had to wait nearly two months before Kay Francis returned to Stamps. Bailey's mood had lightened considerably, but he lived in a state of expectation and it made him more nervous than he was usually. When he told me that the movie would be shown, we went into our best behavior and were the exemplary children that Grandmother deserved and wished to think us.

It was a gay light comedy, and Kay Francis wore long-sleeved white silk shirts with big cuff links. Her bedroom was all satin and flowers in vases, and her maid, who was Black, went around saying "Lawsy, missy" all the time. There was a Negro chauffeur too, who rolled his eyes and scratched his head, and I wondered how on earth an idiot like that could be trusted with her beautiful cars.

The whitefolks downstairs laughed every few minutes, throwing the discarded snicker up to the Negroes in the buzzards' roost. The sound would jag around in our air for an indecisive second before the balcony's occupants accepted it and sent their own guffaws to riot with it against the walls of the theater.

I laughed, too, but not at the hateful jokes made on my people. I laughed because, except that she was white, the big movie star looked just like my mother. Except that she lived in a big mansion with a thousand servants, she lived just like my mother. And it was funny to think of the whitefolks' not knowing that the woman they were adoring could be my mother's twin, except that she was white and my mother was prettier. Much prettier.

The movie star made me happy. It was extraordinary good fortune to be able to save up one's money and go see one's mother whenever one wanted to. I bounced out of the theater as if I'd been given an unexpected present. But Bailey was cast down again. (I had to beg him not to stay for the next show.) On the way home he stopped at the railroad track and waited for the night freight train. Just before it reached the crossing, he tore out and ran across the tracks.

I was left on the other side in hysteria. Maybe the giant wheels were grinding his bones into a bloody mush. Maybe he tried to catch a boxcar and got flung into the pond and drowned. Or even worse, maybe he caught the train and was forever gone.

When the train passed he pushed himself away from the pole where he had been leaning, berated me for making all that noise and said, "Let's go home."

One year later he did catch a freight, but because of his youth and the inscrutable way of fate, he didn't find California and his Mother Dear—he got stranded in Baton Rouge, Louisiana, for two weeks.

WRITING ABOUT THE READING

5. Why does Angelou's family punish Bailey harshly for coming home late?

6. Why is it ironic that the white audience adores the actress, Kay Francis?

7. How and why does Angelou learn about the harsh realities of racism in the South?

8. How and why does Angelou's way of dealing with racism differ from that of her grandmother?

9. Why does the first section of this narrative prepare the reader for the second part?

10. Why is the experience of Angelou, newly arrived in the South, similar to that of immigrants who are new to the United States?

WRITING FROM YOUR OWN EXPERIENCE

Note: In these assignments, write about your own experience or use that of someone you know, read about, or saw in a film/TV show.

11. Angelou writes as an adult recalling the important events of her childhood. Remember a childhood event that made a strong impression on you. Why did the incident move you and what influence did it have on your later life?

12. Angelou writes about some of the "unending tasks" that were required of her as a child. Why were you required (or not required) to carry out tasks when you were a child and what are your feelings about these duties?

13. Uncle Willie severely punishes Bailey for coming home late. Think about a time when someone punished you in some way. How were you disciplined and why was the punishment effective (or ineffective)?

WRITING ABOUT RESEARCH

14. Why did the Supreme Court ruling in the case of *Plessy* v. *Ferguson* (*1896*) result in the growth of "Jim Crow" laws?

15. Why did the arguments used in *Brown* v. *Board of Education, Topeka* (*1954*) convince the courts that school segregation was unjust?

16. What role did the NAACP (National Association for the Advancement of Colored People) play in challenging "Jim Crow" laws?

17. What was the participation of African Americans (such as the "Brotherhood of Sleeping Car Porters and Maids") in the union movement of this era?

18. Choose one prominent African American from the pre-1960s era and explain how this person provided leadership or inspiration to African Americans. Consider:

(a) Nat King Cole
(b) W.E.B. DuBois
(c) Dorothy Dandridge
(d) Marcus Garvey
(e) Billie Holliday
(f) Lena Horne
(g) Jack Johnson
(h) Joe Louis
(i) Hattie McDaniel
(j) Philip Randolph
(k) Booker T. Washington

Selection 5

Our Sons Under Siege

BARBARA REYNOLDS

Barbara Reynolds *(1942–), journalist, editor, and ordained minister, received a B.A. degree from Ohio State University in 1966. Following many years as a reporter in Cleveland and Chicago, Reynolds was chosen to be a Nieman fellow in journalism at Harvard University (1976–1977). In 1977, she won a National Headliner Award for outstanding contribution to journalism. From 1983 to 1996, she was an editor and columnist for* USA Today *newspaper. In the 1990s, Reynolds studied divinity at Howard University and the United Theological Seminary in Dayton. She then became minister of a church in the Washington, D.C. area. She is currently working on biographies of Andrew Young and Coretta Scott King.*

Reynolds often describes herself as a representative African American woman and writes from this viewpoint. "Our Sons Under Siege" was first printed in Essence *magazine (1999), one of the leading publications for African American women. In this article, Reynolds expresses the fears of many African American women about the safety of their sons.*

PREPARING TO READ

1. Why are some African Americans skeptical about the belief that law enforcement officers are there to protect them?
2. Why do factors (such as gender, social class, and/or racial/ethnic group) usually affect a person's attitude toward law enforcement officers?
3. Why do you think that "racial profiling" is a controversial issue today?
4. Choose one law or rule at your college (or in your city) that you would like to eliminate or change. Why would you change this law or rule and what do you think would be the probable effects of this change?

OUR SONS UNDER SIEGE

With law-enforcement officers widely endorsing the controversial practice of racial profiling, all Black folks are at risk of being stopped by cops. But young Black men face the worst danger, as they're most likely to become victims of police violence, even when they have committed no crimes. This is the story of young men slain by police, and the families left to mourn them—and seek justice in a system where cops have all the power to manipulate the facts to protect their own.

• • •

My heart catches in my throat as I stand at the window of my suburban Maryland home and watch my 18-year-old son drive away to meet friends for the evening. Often before I hand him the car keys, I anoint him with oil, lay my hands on him and remind him of God's love and protection. And with all that, sometimes I still can't sleep until I hear him unlock the door. My son insists I fuss over him too much, but in the three short years he has been a driver, he has already been stopped by cops more times than I have been in the 30 years I've had my license. Once I asked him if he thought the police were there to serve and protect him. He laughed, confessing that the idea had never crossed his mind.

The fact is, my son is a young Black man in a nation where White cops can stop him on any pretext, and things can get out of hand. That's what happened to Amadou Diallo, a 22-year-old immigrant from Guinea, West Africa, gunned down last February 4 in The Bronx, New York, by a circle of White cops who say they mistook him for a rape suspect. As the young man reached for his wallet so he could identify himself, gunfire rained down. The cops fired 41 shots; 19 bullets pierced Diallo's body, killing him.

When I think of Diallo, I think also of countless Black men and boys who, like my son, are vulnerable to police aggression for no reason other than the color of their skin. The growing number of cases like Diallo's has the mothers of even very young Black boys trying to protect them from the people who should be ensuring their safety. "My son is only 7 years old," said one New York City mother in the aftermath of the Diallo killing, "and he kept saying, 'But Mommy, why didn't he just tell them he didn't do it?' I used the incident to teach him that, although he must always live by the law, he should avoid attracting the attention of the police at all costs. I told him that cops are unpredictable and some of them are violent, that they tend to see

Blacks as criminals even when we have done nothing wrong. I told him if he is ever in trouble on the street, he should look for a grand-mother type and ask her to help him. He should not go to a cop. I hated saying all this, but I really felt that as my son grows up he needs to understand that some cops, especially some White cops, are not his friends."

Black mothers across the country are teaching their sons the same lesson, aware that their boys do not have the luxury of childish innocence. "Police departments are engaged in an us-against-them campaign utilizing paramilitary models and racial profiling," explains Ron Daniels, executive director of the New York-based Center for Constitutional Rights, a nonprofit organization that seeks social justice through litigation. The Center's lawyers have filed suit against the City of New York, demanding that the NYPD's elite Street Crimes Unit, which was responsible for Diallo's death, be disbanded or that its policies of racial profiling be stopped. They allege that the unit's use of racial profiling has resulted in officers' illegally stopping and searching thousands of people of color. Too often, those detained end up dead.

Three Mothers' Sons

The popular notion perpetuated in the media is that those who die at the hands of police are part of a destructive element that con-tributes to that other urban nightmare, Black-on-Black crime. But that is far from the truth. Take a close look at the sons of Donna Dymally, Narves Gammage and Emma Jones, all felled by police violence. These three young Black men left the house one day, encountered the cops and never came home.

Like many mothers who've lost children to police brutality, Donna Dymally, a Los Angeles schoolteacher, spends much of her time protesting police violence. Even though the protests rekindle her own pain, Dymally says, "The only way we can hope to make change is to keep speaking out." Her only son, Marc Fitzsimmons, 28, was killed by police on July 2, 1998, when he volunteered to go to the bank for his sister. The family never saw him again, not even his body.

"The police claimed they got a 911 call that someone had at-tacked a 74-year-old woman with a butcher knife," Dymally says. "They confronted my son on the street. They said he attacked them with a knife or some kind of meat cleaver, and so they shot him in the chest." But a coroner's report shows Marc was shot in the back. And a *Los Angeles Sentinel* writer, Robin Lloyd-Starkes, who happened upon the scene, recalled seeing Marc sitting on the curb handcuffed, bleed-ing, disoriented, rocking back and forth. "He was there for quite a while, and I wondered why he wasn't being taken to the hospital," Lloyd-Starkes said. "He was a real small guy. I didn't see a weapon. When I found out he had died, I was stunned."

When Marc didn't return home, his family called the Missing Persons Bureau. They didn't know then that he was lying in the morgue, booked under the name of John Doe. When police finally notified the family of Marc's death five days after the shooting, a heartsick Dymally went to the coroner's office to identify him. "I was told I could not see his body, because he'd already been identified by his fingerprints," she says. Her voice sounds numb, as if the horror of that day is still too much to admit.

"We had a memorial, but we never had a funeral because I never saw my son." During the next three months, Dymally repeatedly petitioned to be allowed to view Marc's body, but she never received an answer. Then, in October, the coroner's office contacted her to say that Marc had been cremated. Devastated, Dymally refused the ashes they offered her. "I wasn't sure what was being offered belonged to my son," she says.

Dymally is sure that police cremated the body to cover up evidence of their crime. Though the family has filed to obtain police records, the LAPD has refused to turn over the official report, making a civil suit difficult. In a letter to the family's lawyer, the department stated that it was under no obligation to release the report because Marc Fitzsimmons "was the suspect in this incident and not the victim," and only victims or their representatives are entitled to a full report.

"My son had no criminal record and no history of drugs," Dymally says. "His step-grandfather is Mervyn Dymally, a former congressman and lieutenant governor of California, and I was on the board of directors of the Jefferson Park Improvement Project, which tries to improve community relations. My son was an honor student, accepted at UCLA at age 15. If this could happen to him, it could happen to anyone."

It also happened to Syracuse, New York, businessman Jonny Gammage, the 31-year-old son of Narves Gammage. Jonny's only crime was that on October 12, 1995, he was driving through the streets of Pittsburgh in a Jaguar belonging to his cousin, Pittsburgh Steelers player Ray Seals. Cops stopped him for "driving erratically" and "tapping his brakes." He emerged from the car carrying a cellular phone that police said they thought was a gun. A fight broke out, and police subdued Jonny by standing or sitting on his back. The coroner ruled he "died as a result of compression of the neck and upper chest." In 1997 a predominantly White jury deadlocked in the trial of two White cops who were charged in his death. No one went to jail.

"My son's death slammed me into another world," says Gammage, now 58. "Johnny had a bachelor's degree in psychology from the University of Buffalo. He worked with troubled teens, coaching them in baseball and job skills, and he marched against drugs. He wanted to improve people's lives. He had never been arrested, never been in trouble in his life, he wasn't a criminal. He was just trying to come home."

Grief has taken its toll: "I can't sleep at night," Gammage says, adding, "I sometimes break down. I am so angry. I hurt as badly as the mothers of those kids shot in Colorado, but people in power say nothing to us." But through prayer she is getting stronger. "I used to not speak up and speak out, but now I do. I am bolder and more confident," she says.

Emma Jones, a legal clerk in New Haven, Connecticut, probate court, knows just what Gammage is facing as she tries to heal. On April 14, 1997, Jones's youngest son, Malik, 21, was shot to death by a White cop in East Haven, a town with 26,000 people, less than 300 of them Black, but with no Blacks on the police force. Police say they pursued Malik after an unidentified motorist told a cop he was driving recklessly. The officer, Robert Flodquist, radioed for help and was joined by another officer. In the course of the chase, Flodquist blocked Malik's path with his van. When the car stopped, the officer exited his van and approached the car, which started rolling backward. Flodquist said he believed the driver was trying to run him over and so, fearing for his life, he shot him.

But Samuel Cruz, a passenger in Malik's car, tells another story, one of sheer terror. In statements to an investigator, Cruz said that when Malik stopped, Officer Flodquist ran up to the car and pounded on the driver's window, breaking it with his gun. He fired once at Malik in the driver's seat, then pumped several more bullets into the car. Cruz added that he himself escaped death only because Malik shielded his body, blocking the hail of bullets.

Flodquist, admitting he broke the driver's window with his gun, told investigators: "The first shot hit him in the left chest area. The shot appeared to have no effect on the operator, and he gave me a defiant, go-to-hell look. He did not stop the car; it continued to turn in to me . . . I then fired several more times . . . I do not recall how many . . . ." The medical examiner's report later revealed that Malik had been shot four times.

In an open letter, portions of which were published in the Black monthly *Umoja News*, Emma Jones wrote, "Every single day . . . I have passed or sat at the scene where the murder took place." Describing how she raced to her son after someone called to tell her of the shooting, she continued: "I see the crystal-clear picture of Malik being dragged from the passenger side of the vehicle, savagely brutalized and left for a long time, face down, bleeding uncontrollably, with his feet still inside the car ... It so reminded me of the KKK lynchings that many of us know too well, where there were picnics and family celebrations upon the execution and murder of a Black man."

Five months later, the state's attorney ruled that Officer Flodquist's actions were "reasonable and justified," despite testimony that Malik's car was rolling backward much too slowly to endanger Flodquist's life. Since the ruling, Jones has gathered more than 30,000 petitions and letters, from virtually every town and city in Connecticut, calling for the arrest of Flodquist. Her protest—and the tent she has set up at the scene of the shooting to gather signatures—has created a backlash among local Whites, who let her know in brutal terms that they believe Malik got what he deserved.

"We've received hate mail from the KKK and threatening telephone calls," she says. "Terrorists have come at night, knocking on my door and breaking windows, and every shrine we put up to honor Malik has been torn down." Still the family persists in the quest for justice. Backed by the mayor of New Haven and the town's police chief, Jones has written the U.S. Justice Department requesting a federal Grand Jury investigation into her son's death. She has also filed a civil lawsuit against the East Haven Police Department and the officers present at the shooting. Convinced that racial profiling accounts for why her son was stopped in the first place, Jones vows not to quit.

The Truth About Racial Profiling

Racial profiling has become such a hot issue in Black and Brown communities that Vice-President Al Gore has made it a campaign issue. And in June, President Bill Clinton ordered federal law-enforcement agencies to begin collecting data on the race and gender of those whom they stop to question or arrest. Study after study shows that drivers are being pulled over, searched and harassed by police for no other reason than the fact that they are Black. For example, between 1988 and 1991, along a section of the New Jersey Turnpike, African-Americans made up only 13.5 percent of the motorists and 15 percent of the speeders, but were 46 percent of those stopped. And in 1992, after viewing videotapes obtained from a Florida county sheriffs office, *The Orlando Sentinel* found that although Blacks made up less than 10 percent of the motorists along a stretch of I-95, they were 70 percent of those stopped. In Maryland, where my son drives, just 17.5 percent of the traffic violators on a particular stretch of the interstate in 1995 and 1996 were Black, but state records show that Blacks represented 73 percent of those searched.

Yet Morton Feldman, spokesman for the American Federation of Police and Concerned Citizens, insists the practice of racial profiling has been misrepresented. "When it is a dark night, and the driver has tinted windows, we have no foreknowledge of who's in the car," he says. "If it is an all-Black area, the majority of stops will be Blacks." But Feldman's analysis ignores the fact that cops disproportionately stop Blacks in White areas too. "If 20 people get off the train and 19 are White guys in suits and one is a Black female, guess who gets followed?" Gary McLhinney, president of the Baltimore Fraternal Order of Police, was quoted as saying in a *New York Times Magazine* article. As justification for the use of racial profiling, one top-ranking New Jersey law-enforcement officer, Colonel Carl A. Williams, asserted that most traffickers of cocaine and marijuana were people of color. In the charged atmosphere that saw two young Black men and a Hispanic man shot by state troopers after a traffic stop last year, Williams's remarks quickly got him fired.

Organizations such as the October 22 Coalition Against Police Brutality, the National Lawyers Guild and the Anthony Baez Foundation have documented more than 1,000 men, women and young people killed by law-enforcement agents since 1990. The victims came from 42 states and Washington, D.C., and the majority were people of color. The actual number of police slayings may be much higher, but accurate figures are hard to come by because the Justice Department does not keep national data on police use of deadly force. And while the news media may record shots fired in the war in Kosovo, somehow they fail to give the same attention to police shootings in Black and Brown communities right here at home.

What is driving all the hostility, the fear and suspicion cops seem to harbor toward people of color, and young Black men in particular? Former NAACP board member and Washington, D.C.-based radio talkshow host Joe Madison offers this bit of insight: "Virtually all Americans are conditioned to believe that Blacks are inferior," he says. "The police bring that conditioning to their jobs. They believe it is their job to control Blacks, to dominate and oppress them."

Many cops don't even bother to deny that they practice racial profiling, and some give statistics to show they have reason to fear Blacks. One frequently cited figure: Black males between the ages of 14 and 24 make up 1 percent of the nation's population, yet they commit more than 28 percent of homicides. Such statistics obscure the fact that hundreds of White offenders go uncaught and unpunished simply because cops are busy "profiling" Blacks. Even highly visible Black men, including actor Wesley Snipes, former pro football star Marcus Allen and Christopher Darden, prosecutor in the O.J. Simpson murder trial, have experienced the inconvenience of being stopped by cops for driving while Black. In fact, in a 1997 interview with Bryant Gumbel, actor Will Smith said that he got pulled over twice a month. Once, when he asked why, he was told, "You're a nigger with a nice car."

No Justice for a Judge's Son

Concern for my own son, and for all the mothers and fathers who have lost, or are at risk of losing, their loved ones to police violence brought me out of my home last April to attend a national day of protest against police brutality organized by the Center for Constitutional Rights. I sat on the steps of the U.S. Capitol for an entire day and listened as scores of mothers and fathers spoke through strained voices and fresh tears about how they had experienced a parent's worst nightmare—that knock at the door, that phone call breaking the silence of midnight to inform them their loved one is now a body in the morgue.

Cops invariably describe a police slaying as a good shoot, meaning the killing was justified by cops' fear for their own lives or other extenuating circumstances. The courts overwhelmingly support the police, most often ruling that the fatalities were "reasonable and justified." But that day on the steps of the Capitol, more than a hundred Black, Asian, Native American and Hispanic parents saw it differently. As they attempted to make sense of the hate pouring from smoking guns that made grotesque holes in the flesh of their children, they told of how police attempted to cover up some shootings by withholding police records, putting off notification of families, delaying medical care and even going so far as to try to cover up their crime by cremating victims without permission and refusing to issue an official explanation.

One mother who gave voice to the pain of losing a son was my neighbor, Dorothy Copp Elliott, whose ex-husband, Archie Elliott, Jr., is a general district judge in Portsmouth, Virginia. In 1974, Elliott moved with her then-5-year-old son, Archie "Artie" Elliott, III, to Prince George's County, Maryland, one of the most affluent suburbs in the nation. Later Artie would attend Virginia State University, majoring in business administration. Artie, who had never been convicted of any crime, helped support himself through college by doing construction work. His goal was to own his own company and build a home for his mother and younger brother but that was not to be.

There is little argument that on June 18, 1993, Artie stopped for drinks with friends after work, then headed home. At about 4:00 P.M., less than three minutes from his home, he was pulled over by a White cop who said he was "driving erratically." When Artie failed sobriety tests, the officer decided to arrest him. It was 91 Fahrenheit, and Artie was shirtless, wearing nothing but jeans shorts and tennis shoes without socks. The officer cuffed Artie's hands behind his back and searched him for weapons—and found none.

Then police backup arrived, and an incredible tale unfolded. Police reported that after they put him, still handcuffed, in the front passenger seat of the squad car and fastened the seat belt across his chest, Artie, restrained as he was, got hold of a gun and aimed it at them. After yelling for him to drop the gun and fearing for their lives, they fired at him 22 times; 14 bullets penetrated his body, killing him.

Elliott said her son never owned a gun. And police never explained where the gun came from that Artie allegedly produced after he had been handcuffed and searched. The Elliotts brought a civil suit against the police department, but it was dismissed, and the Supreme Court has declined to hear the case. "Never a day goes by that I don't miss my son," Elliott says. "I think about the irony of my son's father, Archie, a judge in Virginia, dispensing justice in a system where we can't get justice ourselves." Like many mothers who have lost sons to police violence, Elliott's activism keeps her going. She has participated in more than one hundred protests, marches and forums on police brutality and has started a scholarship fund in her son's name for a deserving high-school student. But grief still overwhelms her at odd moments. "At one march where Martin Luther King, III, was present, I began screaming and sobbing uncontrollably," she recalls. "It dawned on me that there would never be an Archie IV." She remains determined not to rest until the police are prosecuted. "The cops used my son for target practice," she says bitterly. Inspired by the example set by thousands who protested in New York, resulting in the indictment of police in the Diallo case, protestors demonstrate weekly at the Prince George's County courthouse, demanding the indictment of the cops who killed Archie Elliott, III. Activists such as Dick Gregory, the Reverend Walter Fauntroy and Joe Madison have all been jailed in the protests. And for the first time in her life, this soft-spoken mother has been arrested and gone to jail herself.

A National Movement

For each of us gathered, that day at the Capitol was an overwhelming parade of pain. At dusk I walked to my car wringing wet from tears and frustration, praying for the mothers and fathers and praying for my own son. Only one thing is sure: The mothers and fathers of the slain children no longer have to bear this cross alone. Their grief is fueling a national movement spearheaded by such groups as the Congressional Black Caucus, the Nation of Islam, associations of Black cops, lawyers, preachers, schoolteachers, beauticians, leftists, White liberals, Black nationalists and progressives of all stripes. Leaders such as the Reverend Al Sharpton, activists such as Joe Madison and Ron Daniels, and opinion-shapers such as *Essence* publisher and CEO Edward T. Lewis are proposing numerous solutions, including the curbing of the street-crimes units that are running rampant in Black communities. One approach, says Sharpton, is to set up civilian-complaint review boards that have the authority to subpoena cops charged with misconduct and to recommend termination or suspension of those found guilty. In addition, Sharpton and others propose that federal funds be withheld from police departments with citizen complaints about the use of excessive force. They are also pushing for residency laws requiring cops who patrol a particular area to live in that jurisdiction. Cops who know a neighborhood, they reason, are less likely to mistake law-abiding citizens for lawbreakers. [See box at end of story for how you can join the national fight against police brutality—and protect yourself in an encounter with cops.]

While the search for remedies continues, many families are left with the question of how to soothe the anguish of a broken heart. If sheer sadness could be chiseled in stone, Evadine Bailey is the model for that sculpture. Her deep hurt has etched grooves in her face; her smile tries in vain to break through. In a Manhattan hotel, with daughter Angela at her side, she described how, on Halloween night, 1997, her 22-year-old son Patrick, a Wall Street clerk with dreams of becoming a stockbroker, was shot to death by police inside the apartment building that his parents owned and that he managed in Brooklyn. According to a report issued by Brooklyn district attorney Charles Hynes, four uniformed cops were hailed by a man who told them that Patrick Bailey had pointed a shotgun at him during a dispute. Cops say they followed the man to the building where the alleged dispute took place and found Patrick with a shotgun. According to the report, the cops chased Patrick into the first-floor hallway of the apartment building, where they say he pointed the shotgun at them. As he tried to flee to the basement, they opened fire, killing him. Hynes concluded that the facts of the case did not support charges against the officers, who believed they were in imminent danger.

Witnesses presented a different case. One bystander, Chucky McDaniels, said in a TV news interview that the cops did not identify themselves before firing on Patrick. "They just kicked the door in and started shooting," he said. McDaniels insisted that Patrick was not holding a gun, but police later retrieved an unloaded, inoperable shotgun that they identified as the weapon brandished by Patrick during the encounter. Another witness, Deborah Chuck, who was in the first-floor hallway at the time of the shooting, recalled that as Patrick lay bleeding and gasping for breath, one officer ground a knee into his chest, handcuffed him, and vowed to kill him. Chuck, too, does not recall Patrick holding a gun during the confrontation with police.

In October 1998, Patrick's parents filed a $155 million civil lawsuit in U.S. District Court in Brooklyn, claiming that the cops responsible for their son's death were guilty of "overly aggressive policing." The complaint also alleges that the cops left Patrick to die, citing an independent autopsy showing that he could have survived his wounds had he been taken to the hospital sooner.

Since losing her son, Bailey has developed a litany of things she no longer does: eat pizza, go to baseball games, see movies. "These are things we did together; I can't do them without him," she sighs. "I often can't sleep at night. I lie awake staring at the ceiling. I don't believe this pain will ever go away. I want the cops punished."

Bailey has always said that unless the cops who killed Patrick were removed from active duty, they would kill again. Diallo's killing, the spark that ignited thousands of marchers in New York City to lay their anger and their anguish before the nation, might never have happened if officials had heeded her prophetic words. But Bailey's plea for the cops to be taken off the streets fell on deaf ears. Less than two years later, Kenneth Boss, one of the White cops acquitted in the killing of Patrick Bailey, was one of the four accused of murdering Amadou Diallo.

What to Do in Police Presence

Black cops, in and out of uniform, are not immune to racial profiling and police violence. Chief Deputy U.S. Marshal Matthew Fogg, a Black agent in Washington, D.C., who recently won $4 million in a discrimination suit against the head of the U.S. Department of Justice, described federal marshals and other law-enforcement agents in Tennessee passing out "nigger-hunting licenses" and using enlarged photographs of Dr. Martin Luther King, Jr., for target practice.

But while under attack themselves, many Black law-enforcement agents are launching programs and holding seminars to teach people of color how to survive encounters on city streets and highways with police who act illegally. Lawyer Van Jones, for example, has founded the Ella Baker Center for Human Rights. Based in San Francisco and named after one of

King's top aides, the center exists to teach people the necessary survival skills. Van Jones, along with the Bay Area Police Watch and the New York City Police Watch, offers this advice to those who may be confronted by police:

- When pulled over, keep hands in plain view.
- Always be polite. Never bad-mouth police.
- Make no sudden movements.
- If cops ask to search you or your possessions, you have the right to say "I don't consent" and ask "Am I free to go?" Assert your rights calmly, in a way that does not escalate the situation. The truth is, if the cops want to search you, they will, but later whatever they find may be excluded from court evidence if you can prove it came during an unlawful and unwarranted search.
- Don't try to talk your way out of trouble. Anything you say can be used against you.
- Don't complain or warn them you are going to file a complaint.
- Try to remember the officers' badge numbers and write them down as soon as possible after the encounter, as well as a detailed account of the incident. Record names and phone numbers of potential witnesses. Photograph any injuries to yourself or damage to your property as possible evidence should the case go to trial.

WRITING ABOUT THE READING

5. Who is Reynolds addressing in this article and why do you think that this is her intended audience?
6. Suppose the author were to discuss this issue with a more hostile audience, such as a group of law enforcement officers. How and why would Reynolds probably need to make changes in the essay?
7. Reynolds tells about a New York City mother who advises her seven-year-old son how to behave with the police. What do you predict will be the probable effect of this advice on the child?
8. Choose one of the anecdotes (such as the death of Archie Elliott, III) that Reynolds uses to illustrate police brutality. Why do you

think that this anecdote is effective (or ineffective) in supporting Reynolds's beliefs.

9. What do you think Reynolds means when she writes that young African American boys do not have the "luxury of childish innocence"?

10. Explain whether you think that Reynolds's use of emotional appeal strengthens or weakens this essay.

WRITING FROM YOUR OWN EXPERIENCE

Note: In these assignments, write about your own experience or use that of someone you know, read about, or saw in a film/TV show.

11. Think of a time when you had an encounter with a law enforcement officer. How did the officer treat you and what were the consequences of this encounter?

12. When young people move away from home to live on their own, as at college, many parents become concerned about the safety of their children. What are some of their concerns and why do you think these concerns are justified (or unjustified)?

13. Near the end of the essay, Reynolds provides a list of practical suggestions for behavior when stopped by the police. Think of a time when you heeded (or ignored) some advice given to you by your mother or father. Why did you heed or ignore this advice and what were the consequences of your choice?

WRITING ABOUT RESEARCH

14. In discussing police violence, Reynolds mentions the case of Amadou Diallo, who she states was "gunned down" by the New York City Police. Another notorious case is that of Rodney King in Los Angeles. Choose one of these cases to research and explain whether you think that the charges of police brutality were justified or not.

15. Why have recent initiatives, such as the program of community policing, been effective (or ineffective) in improving relations of law enforcement officers with the communities they serve?

16. Reynolds blames the practice of racial profiling for the death of many innocent African American men. Explain whether you agree (or disagree) that racial profiling is justified.

Black Is the Noun

NIKKI GIOVANNI

Nikki Giovanni *(1943–) is a poet, writer, and educator who was an active participant in the civil rights movement of the 1960s and early 1970s. After receiving a B.A. from Fisk University (1967), she organized the first Black Arts Festival in Cincinnati, Ohio, and founded an African American drama group, The New Theatre. She taught at Rutgers Livingston College (1968–1972) and became a professor of English at Virginia Polytechnic Institute in 1990. Her numerous awards include a National Book Award nomination for* Gemini *(1971). She also has received honorary doctorates from many universities, including Fisk University (1988). In 1998, Giovanni was inducted into the Literary Hall of Fame for Writers of African Descent at Chicago State University.*

Although Giovanni took a militant, revolutionary stance in her early writing, by the 1970s, she began to focus more on introspection and personal relationships. Besides taking pride in her African American heritage, Giovanni stresses writing as a means to seeking the truth and making the world a better place.

In the essay "Black Is the Noun" from the book, Racism 101 *(1994), Giovanni begins with a current personal experience, an encounter with a law enforcement officer, as a starting point to consider her life and racial issues past and present.*

PREPARING TO READ

1. Consider the goals, challenges, interests, and opportunities of today's students. What are some of the characteristics of college students today and the reasons why you would choose these characteristics?
2. A common comparison in literature is that of life to a journey. Explain whether you think that this is a good comparison.

3. In this essay, Giovanni says that map reading is a minor but necessary skill in modern life. What are some of the "minor skills" necessary for survival in college and why are they necessary?
4. Why is the word "experiment" often used to describe America?

BLACK IS THE NOUN

It is late. The poet has just opened her second pack of cigarettes. The poet smokes like a chimney. She fears the day when the possession of cigarettes, not just their use, will be illegal. The light is on in her den though her window blinds are closed. She did not wear her seat belt today. They know. She knows they know. Contemplating her fingernails she notices, to her horror, a speck of grease. She has, once again, eaten fried chicken. It won't be long before they come for her. What should she do? Finding no answer, she ambles to the refrigerator, opens the freezer, and takes out peach sorbet. If she must go, she will go her way.

I've had my fun . . . if I don't get well any more.

—J. McShann

I knew I was old when, one evening last spring, I was driving from Blacksburg to Princeton to attend a party. I had finished early but a friend was driving with me and she couldn't get off from work. We left about five-thirty in the evening, driving my car, a candy-apple-red MR2. We had on the requisite jeans and T-shirts. I am always cold so I had on a sweatshirt. We were short-coiffured, medium-nailed, no-makeup, modern sort of women on a fun drive to a fun place. We stopped for coffee, smoked, munched the sandwiches we had made— were, in other words, going about our business. Ginney has two talents that I not only do not possess but do not aspire to: she can spell and she can read a map. My idea of getting around is to go to the furthest point and make the appropriate ninety-degree turn. For example, in order to reach Princeton from Blacksburg, I would go to Washington, D.C., and turn left. But Ginney can read a map so she angled us onto the Pennsylvania turnpike, around Philadelphia, and onto the New Jersey turnpike. I don't like to be picky about things because I lack certain skills myself, but I do think it is not asking too much for employees to know where things are located. You know, you go into Kroger's looking for, say, tomato purée. You would expect to find this in the canned-vegetable section, only it isn't. It's located with sauces. You ask someone wearing a Kroger shirt and you should get that answer. You expect the turnpike officials who take your money at the toll booths to know which exit to take for something as well known as Princeton.

I have an aunt, well, actually I have two aunts, but I only want to talk about one of them. My aunt, and I will not designate which, has trouble with her night vision. She is not quite as blind as a bat but she . . . well . . . has trouble. And there are, possibly, these genetic transfers. I don't think I've reached that stage yet but sometimes it is difficult to see what exactly the signs are saying. It had gotten quite dark, we had stopped for coffee several times, and I, as driver, was happy to be on a turnpike with large green signs. When we were handed off from the Pennsylvania to the New Jersey I asked the woman in the booth which exit I should take for Princeton. Had she just said, "Honey, I ain't got no idea where no Princeton is. It's been a long day and nothing has gone right. My left foot is hurting 'cause I cut that corn but it's not healing right and maybe I have diabetes. You know when a corn won't heal that's a sign of diabetes. My mother had sugar and she lost her whole leg right up to the knee . . . " or something like that, I would have been understanding. "Yes," I would have said, "I've heard that corns that won't heal are a sign of sugar. My mother's best friend, Ann Taylor, from over in Knoxville was just telling me about it when I was passing through last June." And she and I could have visited a bit while Ginney looked at the map and plotted our course. But no, she says, with authority, "Take Exit 19," and we set out with the confidence of the innocently assured.

We were lost immediately; there was nothing that made sense on that exit, it was three-thirty in the morning, and, worst of all, I began to despair. We turned the light on in the car so that Ginney could see the map but, golly, those lines are very, very small and the car was in motion and bingo! The blue lights were shining in back of me. I pulled over, popped the Dells tape out of the cassette, ground out my cigarette, grabbed my seat belt, and waited for the highway patrolman. "Your registration and license, please." I had the registration with my gas card in the front but my driver's license was in my purse in the trunk. I looked up to explain my problem when he turned his flashlight into the car. He saw two McDonald's coffees, an ashtray full of cigarettes, and us—two lost, tired old ladies. "Where are you coming from?" he asked. "Roanoke, Virginia." I always answer Roanoke because nobody knows where Blacksburg is. "How long have you been on the road?" "Since about five-thirty. We're lost. We're trying to get to Princeton." "Well," he explained, "you're way out of your way. You've got another fifty miles to go." He gave us directions and said, "Drive carefully." "I'll get my driver's license now," I offered. "Oh, no, ma'am. You-all just get where you're going. Have a safe evening."

Something in me clicked. A few years ago he would have given me a ticket. A few years ago whether I was lost or not I would have been written up. But we were just two little ole ladies in what he probably thought was my son's car in the middle of the night trying to get to Princeton. I turned to Ginney: "We are old. He saw old woman. You drive."

Going to Chicago . . . sorry but I can't take you.

—W. Basie

In *Star Trek II: The Wrath of Khan*, Khan, a criminal Kirk was responsible for putting on some planet way the hell out of nowhere, finally makes his escape. He is living for only one reason: he wants to kill Kirk. Khan and Kirk fool around for a couple of hours while Khan tortures and kills people and . . . finally . . . gets *The Enterprise* in his grip. Spock, of course, sees the problem and goes to the rescue. The awful weapon is turned on Khan and he is killed. But wait! Khan will have the last word even after death. Khan has trapped *The Enterprise* and it will implode because the crystals it needs cannot feed the engine. They all will die and Khan, the evil Ricardo Montalban, whom I actually liked in *Fantasy Island*, will prove that evil triumphs over good even when evil can't be there to gloat about it. Spock knows the answer but Kirk cannot bear to see his friend give his life. Spock understands that either he gives his life or they all give their lives. He sneaks away from Kirk only to encounter McCoy. He uses the Spock maneuver to knock McCoy out but at the last minute whispers: "Remember." And does his mind meld. Spock steps into the chamber, feeds the engine, and awaits his death. By now Kirk is on the deck, upset, quite naturally, about losing Spock. "The needs of the many," Spock says, "outweigh the needs of the few . . . or in this case, the one. I will always be your friend." He gives Kirk the Spock sign with the split fingers and dies. The next thing we see is Spock's funeral service and *The Enterprise* pushing his casket out into space. By this time I am embarrassing my son by actually heaving in the theater. I cannot believe Spock is dead. I will not accept it. But Tom points out to me that Spock's casket is headed for the Genesis planet. *Star Trek III* will bring him back. I cannot see it. If he's dead, how can he come back to life? In all our myths only one man was able to do that. But Spock did tell McCoy something: "Remember."

I love *Star Treks*. They are nothing more than Greek myths of heroic people doing extraordinary deeds with style and wit. No one on the good ship *Enterprise* will ever be short of courage. The television series, which was actually quite short-lived, marked a new era in television by obliging audiences to respect—and even to admire—differences among people. They talked to rocks in "The Huerta" and spirits in "The Companion"; they came back to defy death at the OK Corral by not recognizing the power of bullets; they stopped a war between two planets by making them confront the reality and pay the price of the killing; they gave us television's first interracial kiss. But Spock said: "Remember."

The Search for Spock opens with Kirk and McCoy meeting Spock's father with a flag. Spock's mom is Jane Wyatt, formerly married to Jim Anderson on *Father Knows Best*. No one ever mentions the divorce but when you see how the kids came out you could easily see why she might have wanted to make her way to another planet. Mrs. Spock, Jane, is not seen. Since she is human she's probably off crying her eyes out over losing her only child. Mr. Spock, the Vulcan, is not emotional so he stands to talk. "Where are his memories?" Mr. Spock asks. He knows his son is dead and he can accept that. But where are his memories? Kirk and McCoy have no idea what he is talking about. "My son was a great man," Mr. Spock all but bellows. "His memories are valuable to us. We can store them so that others will learn from what he knew. You must find his body and retract from his brain his memories."

Star Trek perfectly epitomizes the sixties vehicle. You had a courageous white boy; a logical Vulcan; an Asian scientific transportation officer; an Irish, emotional doctor; and, the ultimate genius of *Star Trek*, Uhurua, a black woman who was the voice of the entire federation. Toni Morrison once wrote: "The Black woman is both a ship and a safe harbor." Uhurua proved that. Of all the possible voices to send into space, the voice of the black woman was chosen. Why? Because no matter what the words, that voice gives comfort and welcome. The black woman's voice sings the best notes of which Earthlings are capable. Hers is the one voice that suggests the possibility of harmony on planet Earth. Scholars are now studying what made the slavers bring females on the slave ships. The slavers could not have been so stupid as to think they could get as much work from a woman as from a man. There is the theory that since the women ran the markets and worked the farms the white man understood that in order for his agriculture to prosper he would need the women. I think not. I think there was a cosmic plan; a higher reason. In order to have a *civilization*, the black woman was needed. In order for one day this whole mess to make sense, the black woman was needed. So that one day forgiveness would be possible, the black woman was needed. I need not, I'm sure, point out the fact that the first black child born in what would become the United States was a black female. The first poet. But more, I believe the first voice to be lifted in song was the voice of a black woman. It may have been the "faith of our fathers," but it was our mothers who taught it to us. And when that faith was transformed what do we have? A half Earthling, half other-world being, saying to the doctor: "Remember."

Like Alex Haley's ancestor, who preserved his past by passing along his name, the slaves told their story through song. Isn't that why we sing "Swing Low, Sweet Chariot"? Isn't that why we know "Pass Me Not, O Gentle Savior"? Isn't that the reason our legacy is "You Got to Walk This Lonesome Valley"? "Were You There When They Crucified My Lord?" To W. E. B. Du Bois, the spirituals were sorrow songs, perhaps because he saw himself as so different from the slaves who sang them. But the spirituals were not and are not today sorrow songs but records of our history. How else would a people tell its story if not through the means available? And as James Cone has said, the spirituals testified to the *somebodiness* of our people. We made a song to be a quilt to wrap us "in the bosom of Abraham." "Over my head, I see trouble in the air. . . . There must . . . be a God, somewhere." We knew "He didn't take us this far to leave us." We brought a faith to the barbarians among whom we found ourselves, and the very humbleness of our souls defeated the power of their whips, ropes, chains, and money. "Give yourself to Jesus." Not your money, not a new church that you will sit in with other white people like yourself, not a new organ, none of those things . . . yourself. And all we had was a song and a prayer. Who would have remembered us had we not raised our voices?

Had Spock been a black American, his father would have gone to church to ask the Lord for help. And his help would have come like the strength that came to Emmett Till's mother: "I know that's my boy," when the sheriff asked what she could contribute to the trial of Till's killers. "I know it's my boy," Mrs. Mobley, Till's mother, said when she opened the casket. "I want the world to see what they did to my boy." Didn't she roll the rock away? Two thousand years ago the angels said, *"He is not here."* Mrs. Mobley said: "Here is my boy. Look." And the world was ashamed. Spock told McCoy to remember. And McCoy didn't even know what he had.

They went in search of the body and, movies being movies, they found a young Vulcan boy on Genesis and brought him home. But McCoy had the memories all along. He just didn't know what he had.

Money won't change you, but time is taking you on.

—J. Brown

Much evidence to the contrary, I am a sixties person. It's true that I didn't do T-shirts or drugs and I never went to jail. I argued a lot in coffeehouses and tried at one point to be a social drinker. It didn't work. I can't hold liquor at all. But I was nonetheless a sixties person and continue to be today because I actually believe in the people. That was never just rhetoric to me, though it has often been my undoing.

Believing in the people is dangerous because the people will break your heart. Just when you know in your heart that white people are not worth a tinker's damn and the future depends on us, some black person will come along with some nihilistic crap that makes you rethink the whole thing.

I was never more than a foot soldier and not a very good one at that. I observed and I wrote. And the more I observed, the more amazed I was by our need to deny our own history—our need to forget, not to remember. The contradictions were especially evident to me, perhaps, because I attended Du Bois's school, Fisk University. How ironic that Fisk's Jubilee Singers kept the spirituals alive, yet the students at Fisk were anxious to deny that their ancestors were slaves; if people were to be believed, nobody but me ever had slaves in their family.

The fact of slavery is no more our fault than the fact of rape. People are raped. It is not their choice. How the victim becomes responsible for the behavior of the victimizer is well beyond my understanding. How the poor are responsible for their condition is equally baffling. No one chooses to live in the streets; no one chooses to go to sleep at night hungry; no one chooses to be cold, to watch their children have unmet needs. No one chooses misery, and our efforts to make this a choice will be the damnation of our souls. Yet such thinking is one of the several troubling legacies we have inherited from DuBois.

Du Bois needed to believe that he was different. That if only the "better" white people would distinguish between the "better" black folk, "the talented tenth," they could make a "better" person. I think not. The normal ninety have to be respected for the trials and tribulations they have endured. They've been "'buked and they've been scorned." They bore the lash while they cleared the fields, planted and created in this wilderness. Am I against books and learning? Hardly. But just because my tools are words, I do not have the right to make mine the only tools. It is disturbing that wordsmiths like Henry Louis Gates, Jr., can say to those of physical prowess, "the odds are against your" succeeding in professional athletics (in a recent article in *Sports*

Illustrated). The odds are more against any young man or woman of color being tenured at Harvard. Gates was not deterred in his determination to succeed in his chosen field and he does not have the right to discourage others. Those young men on city playgrounds know that, indeed, basketball is the way out. Without that skill no school would be interested in them . . . no high school . . . no college. The academically excellent can use their words to sneer but the young men know that's the only open door. Is it right? I think not. I would like to see choice come into everybody's life. But there are no good choices on the streets these days. The conservatives don't care and the black intellectuals are trying to justify the gross neglect of the needs of black America. The Thomas Sowells, the Shelby Steeles no more or less than the Clarence Thomases and the Louis Sullivans are trying mighty hard to say, "I am not like them." We know that, we who are "them." We also know that they have no character. We know they are in opportunistic service. The very least they owe is the honesty that says, "I got here distinguishing myself from you." Clarence is against affirmative action? Shelby is against affirmative action? Since when? Since the people fought so that neither of these men would have to die for their choice of wives? So that Yale would admit a poor boy from Pin Point, Georgia? When did affirmative action become an insult? Shortly after you were granted tenure at your university? You don't like being made to feel you can honestly do your job because affirmative action made someone hire you? There is a solution. Quit. You think life is hard for you because you're viewed as a group? Try living in Newark or D.C. or Harlem and knowing that you will never be allowed by what Margaret Walker calls "those unseen creatures who tower over us omnisciently and laugh" to realize your dreams and potential.

Am I blaming Du Bois for his children? You bet. The black conservatives belong to Du Bois. Booker T. Washington, born in slavery, reared in the coal-mining districts of West Virginia, walked his way to Hampton, worked his way through the Institute, labored in the red clay of Alabama among some of the most vicious white folks outside of Mississippi to build Tuskegee; he tried to empower black folks. Is there a quarrel with the Atlanta Exposition speech? Somebody, other than the black conservatives, show me where this nation is not still "as separate as the fingers of a hand" and how we would not all be better off if we would "come together as a fist" for economic development. Du Bois wanted to vote? So do we all. Didn't Martin Luther King, Jr., have something to say about "Southern Negroes not being allowed to vote while Northern Negroes have nothing to vote for"? Didn't Frederick Douglass ask, "What does your fourth of July mean to me?" Washington and Garvey wanted black people to come to the table with some fruits from their labor. Both Washington and Garvey knew we needed and need, in Margaret Walker's words, "something all our own." Why did Du Bois fight them? What an ironic twist of fate that Du Bois was the beneficiary of Garvey's dreams. That Du Bois was the Renaissance Man who spent his last days in Ghana, a black independent nation, under a black president. How ironic that Louis Sullivan and Clarence Thomas are beneficiaries of the struggles of the sixties.

You better think . . . think about what you're trying to do to me.

—A. Franklin

I am a black American. Period. The rest is of no particular interest to me. Afro-American, African American, whatever. I believe that if I remain a black American I force all others to become and claim their other Americanisms. They are white Americans, Irish-Americans, Jewish-Americans, or whatever hyphens they would like to use. The noun is "black"; American is the adjective.

I do not fool myself often. I laugh about definitions because laughter is, well, so much more pleasant. I am not a particularly well person. I have lived too long with sick people to think I have escaped their malady. Every now and then, for one reason or another, someone will ask to interview me or talk with me or I will skim back through what has been said of my work just to, well, more or less see how I am progressing. I have always laughed at the critics' saying I am bitter and full of hate. Nothing could be further from the truth. I am not envious or jealous either. I am just me. And I do have strong feelings about that. I do not and did not and most likely will not ever feel that I have to justify that. I do not have to be a role model, a good person, a credit to the race. When I look at Phillis Wheatly, Harriet Tubman, Monroe Trotter, Frederick Douglass, Sojourner Truth, Booker T. Washington, George Washington Carver, for that matter W. E. B. Du Bois, James Weldon Johnson, Langston Hughes, Nella Larsen, James Baldwin, and I cannot possibly exhaust the list but, hey, Malcolm X, Elijah Muhammed, Martin Luther King, Sr. and Jr., just to name a few, the race has built up a big enough account for me to charge whatever I'd like. Doesn't Toni Morrison have a character named Stamped Paid? Perfect. Black America is well in advance of the Sunday-school tithing of the folks with whom we live.

I had the great pleasure of meeting Anna Hedgeman when she visited Fisk University during, I think, my junior year. She was talking to honors history about Frederick Douglass: "Every time I see that statue of Lincoln sitting below the Emancipation Proclamation I want to have a statue of Frederick Douglass standing behind him guiding his hand." I could see that. Lincoln was an interesting white man who did the right thing, finally, by freeing the slaves in the states where he had no power to enforce his decree. But hey, why be so picky? He did it. True. But not for me. Not for Cornelia Watson so that she could birth John Brown Watson in freedom and he could marry Louvenia Terrell and they could conceive Yolande Watson and she could marry Gus Giovanni and they could conceive me. No. Not for me. Lincoln didn't care about Cornelia Watson. Nor conceptionalize me. Near the end of *Song of Solomon* Morrison has Milkman finally review his life: it is the women who wanted him to live. Or as the father in *Sounder* says to his son, "I beat the DEATH they had planned for me; I want you to beat the LIFE." Am I saying I'm glad we have Presidents' Day instead of Lincoln's Birthday and Washington's Birthday? No. I like my holidays to have real names. But I also know I don't owe those people any great affection or loyalty. They do not love me or mine. That, by the way, means I live in a narrow world. Well, maybe not so narrow. Maybe a more accurate way of looking at it is that I will not have my world or my worth determined by people who mean me ill.

It's been a long time coming . . . but my change is gonna come.

—S. Cooke

Like most people approaching their fiftieth birthdays (I was born in 1943), I have contemplated the meaning of my people. I have wondered why we were chosen for this great, cosmic experience. We were not the first slaves in human history nor were we even the first chattel. We were, however, the first slaves who chose to live among the enslavers. That is about the only thing that gives me hope. If God could part the Red Sea for Moses, surely the Atlantic Ocean posed no insoluble problem. I have contemplated what life must have been like around 1865 or so when freedom became a possibility. Why didn't we seek boats to take us to Haiti, which was already a free, black republic? Why didn't we start great treks, not just a few wagon trains here and there, to the uncharted lands of this nation? What made us determined to fight it out essentially where we were? Some books tell us we loved enslavement—we didn't have to worry about our care or our duties. Some books say we didn't know where to go. Some books tell us we believed the promises of Emancipation that we would be given forty acres and a mule. Mostly I think it was cosmic. The spirituals show us people willing to "wait on the Lord." Though "sometimes I feel like a motherless child . . . a long way from home," though we knew "the rock cried out No Hiding Place," though we had the "Good News" that "I got a crown up in the Heavens," we "were there when they crucified my Lord." We were chosen to be witnesses. Like Job in his patience, like Samson in his foolishness, "my soul is a witness . . . for my Lord." And without that faith there is no foundation for this nation. America may not be the best nation on earth, but it has conceived loftier ideals and dreamed higher dreams than any other nation. America is a heterogeneous nation of many different peoples of different races, religions, and creeds. Should this experiment go forth and prosper, we will have offered humans a new way to look at life; should it fail, we will simply go the way of all failed civilizations. The spirituals teach us that the problem of the twentieth century is not the problem of the color line. The problem of the twentieth century is the problem of civilizing white people.

When I was a little girl you could still buy things at the five-and-dime. You could buy those paddles with the ball attached that you would sit and whack for hours; you could buy jacks and pick up sticks. You could buy spin tops that you pulled a string around and the top would go spinning off. If your surface was rocky the top would falter and fall; if your tip had a nick it would jump and fall; if your release of the string was not smooth it would jerk and fall. If you wanted your top to spin the longest you did everything you could to get and keep things smooth.

You read my letter, baby . . . sure must have read my mind.

—B. Eckstine

The poet lights her fortieth cigarette. She will go over her limit as she opens a new pack. It is her favorite time of the day, when morning begins fusing itself into night, bringing that nether light to the sky. The poet recommends life. She likes the idea of the human experiment going forth. She knows her people are more than capable. The worst blows have been thrown and parried. This is only the cleanup. Perhaps, she thinks, she should treat herself to something wonderful. Fish. Fried fish. The poet remembers her grandmother's joy at fried fish and extra salt. Yes. And maybe a cold beer to salute her mother. Good job, mommy. I'm here; not necessarily crazy; looking forward to tomorrow. No mother could do more. Maybe, the poet thinks, I'll buy a lottery ticket. The forty-first cigarette is lit. First thing in the morning. Fish and a lottery ticket. Hey . . . we're going to make it.

WRITING ABOUT THE READING

5. Giovanni begins her essay with an encounter with a law officer. Why does this encounter reveal that there have been changes in herself and in society?

6. Why does Giovanni state that *Star Trek* "perfectly epitomizes the sixties"?

7. Why does she say that it is only appropriate that the voice of an African American woman was chosen to send into space?

8. Why is Giovanni critical of Du Bois and "his children"?

9. What does the author mean when she argues that "black" is a noun, not an adjective, and why does she say this?

10. How and why does the last paragraph relate to the first paragraph to "frame" the essay?

WRITING FROM YOUR OWN EXPERIENCE

Note: In these assignments, write about your own experience or use that of someone you know, read about, or saw in a film/TV show.

11. Heading toward Princeton, the writer becomes lost and takes a wrong exit. Recall a time when you became lost. Why did you become lost and what were some of the consequences of this experience?

12. Based on the concept of life as a journey, being "lost" can take on an additional meaning. Choose a time when someone could describe you as "losing your way in life." Why did you become lost and what were the consequences of this experience?

13. Giovanni writes of her love of the *Star Trek* TV series and movies. Provide an example of some TV show (or movie, book, or video game) that was influential on your earlier years. Why did it appeal to you and what were the consequences of your interest?

14. Giovanni writes about the influence of TV, a modern technology of the 1950s and 1960s, on her life. Choose one example of modern technology that has become common in recent years. How and why has this modern technology influenced your life? Consider products such as camcorders, cell phones, computers, microwaves, or video games.

WRITING ABOUT RESEARCH

15. Giovanni describes herself as a "foot soldier" in the Civil Rights Movement of the sixties. Research the life of a prominent African American leader of the sixties (such as Dr. Martin Luther King, Jr., or Malcolm X). What was this leader trying to accomplish and to what extent was this person successful?

16. During the Civil Rights Movement, there were many acts of resistance against those in favor of integration. Choose one of the following events (or a similar episode from this period) to research. What were the causes and the major consequences of this action?

    (a) Governor Orval Faubus's resistance to school integration in Little Rock in 1957.

    (b) Mississippi Governor Ross Barnett's refusal to admit African Americans to the state university in 1962.

    (c) Governor George Wallace's refusal to admit African Americans to the University of Alabama in 1963.

    (d) The murder of Medgar Evers of the NAACP in 1963.

    (e) The death of four African American children in the bombing of a Birmingham church in 1963.

    (f) The death of several civil rights workers in 1964–1965.

17. What efforts were necessary to pass a Voting Rights Act in 1965 and to conduct voter registration drives?

Race and the Schooling of Black Americans

CLAUDE M. STEELE

Claude M. Steele *(1946–), social psychologist and educator, earned a B.A. from Hiram College, Ohio (1967). He received both M.A. (1969) and Ph.D. (1971) degrees from Ohio State University. He received a Center for Advanced Study in the Behavior Sciences fellowship in 1994. Currently, Steele serves as a consulting editor to several professional journals, including* Psychological Review, *and is a professor in the Department of Psychology at Stanford University.*

Steele has conducted research and written many professional articles on the educational achievement of African Americans. He explains some of his findings in "Race and the Schooling of Black Americans," a much-discussed article, originally published in The Atlantic Monthly *(1992). Steele believes that racism causes all African American students, even brilliant scholars with no financial disadvantages, to have difficulty in college. Steele asserts that because African American students are burdened with a daunting, negative stereotype, they often reject (or "disidentify" with) education. In this article, Steele suggests some measures that colleges can undertake to help African American students overcome "stereotype vulnerability" and to succeed in college.*

PREPARING TO READ

1. What are some of the characteristics of a good teacher and what are the reasons for your choice?
2. Explain whether you think that modern technology (such as that used for TV courses, computer programs, the Internet, or distance learning) will change education for the better.
3. Explain whether you think a person's friends have a strong influence on whether or not that person is a good student.
4. Why do you think that colleges should (or should not) use tests, such as the ACT or SAT, to select students for admission?

RACE AND THE SCHOOLING
OF BLACK AMERICANS

My former university offered minority students a faculty mentor to help shepherd them into college life. As soon as I learned of the program, I volunteered to be a mentor, but by then the school year was nearly over. Undaunted, the program's eager staff matched me with a student on their waiting list—an appealing nineteen-year-old black woman from Detroit, the same age as my daughter. We met finally in a campus lunch spot just about two weeks before the close of her freshman year. I realized quickly that I was too late. I have heard that the best way to diagnose someone's depression is to note how depressed you feel when you leave the person. When our lunch was over, I felt as gray as the snowbanks that often lined the path back to my office. My lunchtime companion was a statistic brought to life, a living example of one of the most disturbing facts of racial life in America today: the failure of so many black Americans to thrive in school. Before I could lift a hand to help this student, she had decided to do what 70 percent of all black Americans at four-year colleges do at some point in their academic careers—drop out.

I sense a certain caving-in of hope in America that problems of race can be solved. Since the sixties, when race relations held promise for the dawning of a new era, the issue has become one whose persistence causes "problem fatigue"—resignation to an unwanted condition of life.

This fatigue, I suspect, deadens us to the deepening crisis in the education of black Americans. One can enter any desegregated school in America, from grammar school to high school to graduate or professional school, and meet a persistent reality: blacks and whites in largely separate worlds. And if one asks a few questions or looks at a few records, another reality emerges: these worlds are not equal, either in the education taking place there or in the achievement of the students who occupy them.

As a social scientist, I know that the crisis has enough possible causes to give anyone problem fatigue. But at a personal level, perhaps because of my experience as a black in American schools, or perhaps just as the hunch of a myopic psychologist, I have long suspected a particular culprit—a culprit that can undermine black achievement as effectively as a lock on a schoolhouse door. The culprit I see is stigma, the endemic devaluation many blacks face in our society and schools. This status is its own condition of life, different from class, money, culture. It is capable, in the words of the late sociologist Erving Goffman, of "breaking the claim" that one's human attributes have on people. I believe that its connection to school achievement among black Americans has been vastly underappreciated.

This is a troublesome argument, touching as it does on a still unhealed part of American race relations. But it leads us to a heartening principle: if blacks are made less racially vulnerable in school, they can overcome even substantial obstacles. Before the good news, though, I must at least sketch in the bad: the worsening crisis in the education of black Americans.

Despite their socioeconomic disadvantages as a group, blacks begin school with test scores that are fairly close to the test scores of whites their age. The longer they stay in school, however, the more they fall behind; for example, by the sixth grade blacks in many school districts are two full grade levels behind whites in achievement. This pattern holds true in the middle class nearly as much as in the lower class. The record does not improve in high school. In 1980, for example, 25,500 minority students, largely black and Hispanic, entered high school in Chicago. Four years later only 9,500 graduated, and of those only 2,000 could read at grade level. The situation in other cities is comparable.

Even for blacks who make it to college, the problem doesn't go away. As I noted, 70 percent of all black students who enroll in four-year colleges drop out at some point, as compared with 45 percent of whites. At any given time nearly as many black males are incarcerated as are in college in this country. And the grades of black college students average half a letter below those of their white classmates. At one prestigious university I recently studied, only 18 percent of the graduating black students had grade averages of B or above, as compared with 64 percent of the whites. This pattern is the rule, not the exception, in even the most elite American colleges. Tragically, low grades can render a degree essentially "terminal" in the sense that they preclude further schooling.

Blacks in graduate and professional schools face a similarly worsening or stagnating fate. For example, from 1977 to 1990, though the number of Ph.D.s awarded to other minorities increased and the number awarded to whites stayed roughly the same, the number awarded to American blacks dropped from 1,116 to 828. And blacks needed more time to get those degrees.

Standing ready is a familiar set of explanations. First is societal disadvantage. Black Americans have had, and continue to have, more than their share: a history of slavery, segregation, and job ceilings; continued lack of economic opportunity; poor schools; and the related problems of broken families, drug-infested communities, and social isolation. Any of these factors—alone, in combination, or through accumulated effects—

can undermine school achievement. Some analysts point also to black American culture, suggesting that, hampered by disadvantage, it doesn't sustain the values and expectations critical to education, or that it fosters learning orientations ill suited to school achievement, or that it even "opposes" mainstream achievement. These are the chestnuts, and I had always thought them adequate. Then several facts emerged that just didn't seem to fit.

For one thing, the achievement deficits occur even when black students suffer no major financial disadvantage—among middle-class students on wealthy college campuses and in graduate school among black students receiving substantial financial aid. For another thing, survey after survey shows that even poor black Americans value education highly, often more than whites. Also, as I will demonstrate, several programs have improved black school achievement without addressing culturally specific learning orientations or doing anything to remedy socioeconomic disadvantage.

Neither is the problem fully explained, as one might assume, by deficits in skill or preparation which blacks might suffer because of background disadvantages. I first doubted that such a connection existed when I saw flunk-out rates for black and white students at a large, prestigious university.

• • •

From elementary school to graduate school, something depresses black achievement at every level of preparation, even the highest. Generally, of course, the better prepared achieve better than the less prepared, and this is about as true for blacks as for whites. But given any level of school preparation (as measured by tests and earlier grades), blacks somehow achieve less in subsequent schooling than whites (that is, have poorer grades, have lower graduation rates, and take longer to graduate), no matter how strong that preparation is. Put differently, the same achievement level requires better preparation for blacks than for whites—far better: among students with a C+ average at the university I just described, the mean American College Testing Program (ACT) score for blacks was at the 98th percentile, while for whites it was at only the 34th percentile. This pattern has been documented so broadly across so many regions of the country, and by so many investigations (literally hundreds), that it is virtually a social law in society—as well as a racial tragedy.

Clearly, something is missing from our understanding of black underachievement. Disadvantage contributes, yet blacks underachieve even when they have ample resources, strongly value education, and are prepared better than adequately in terms of knowledge and skills. Something else has to be involved. That something else could be of just modest importance—a barrier that simply adds its effect to that of other disadvantages—or it could be pivotal, such that were it corrected, other disadvantages would lose their effect.

That something else, I believe, has to do with the process of identifying with school. I offer a personal example:

I remember conducting experiments with my research adviser early in graduate school and awaiting the results with only modest interest. I struggled to meet deadlines. The research enterprise—the core of what one does as a social psychologist—just wasn't ME yet. I was in school for other reasons—I wanted an advanced degree, I was vaguely ambitious for intellectual work, and being in graduate school made my parents proud of me. But as time passed, I began to like the work. I also began to grasp the value system that gave it meaning, and the faculty treated me as if they thought I might even be able to do it. Gradually I began to think of myself as a social psychologist. With this change in self-concept came a new accountability; my self-esteem was affected now by what I did as a social psychologist, something that hadn't been true before. This added a new motivation to my work; self-respect, not just parental respect, was on the line. I noticed changes in myself. I worked without deadlines. I bored friends with applications of arcane theory to their daily lives. I went to conventions. I lived and died over how experiments came out.

Before this transition one might have said that I was handicapped by my black working-class background and lack of motivation. After the transition the same observer might say that even though my background was working-class, I had special advantages: achievement-oriented parents, a small and attentive college. But these facts alone would miss the importance of the identification process I had experienced: the change in self-definition and in the activities on which I based my self-esteem. They would also miss a simple condition necessary for me to make this identification: treatment as a valued person with good prospects.

I believe that the "something else" at the root of black achievement problems is the failure of American schooling to meet this simple condition for many of its black students. Doing well in school requires a belief that school achievement can be a promising basis of self-esteem, and that belief needs constant reaffirmation even for advantaged students. Tragically, I believe, the lives of black Americans are still haunted by a specter that threatens this belief and the identification that derives from it at every level of schooling.

The Specter of Stigma and Racial Vulnerability

I have a good friend, the mother of three, who spends consider-able time in the public school classrooms of Seattle, where she lives. In her son's third-grade room, managed by a teacher of unimpeachable good will and competence, she noticed over many visits that the extra-ordinary art work of a small black boy named Jerome was ignored—or, more accurately perhaps, its significance was ignored. As genuine art talent has a way of doing—even in the third grade—his stood out. Yet the teacher seemed hardly to notice. Moreover, Jerome's reputa-tion, as it was passed along from one grade to the next, included only the slightest mention of his talent. Now, of course, being ignored like this could happen to anyone—such is the overload in our public schools. But my friend couldn't help wondering how the school would have responded to this talent had the artist been one of her own, middle-class white children.

Terms like "prejudice" and "racism" often miss the full scope of racial devaluation in our society, implying as they do that racial de-valuation comes primarily from the strongly prejudiced, not from "good people" like Jerome's teacher. But the prevalence of racists—deplorable though racism is—misses the full extent of Jerome's bur-den, perhaps even the most profound part.

He faces a devaluation that grows out of our images of society and the way those images catalogue people. The catalogue need never be taught. It is implied by all we see around us: the kinds of people revered in advertising (consider the unrelenting racial advocacy of Ralph Lauren ads) and movies (black women are rarely seen as ro-mantic partners, for example); media discussions of whether a black can be President; invitation lists to junior high school birthday parties; school curricula; literary and musical canons. These details create an image of society in which black Americans simply do not fare well. When I was a kid, we captured it with the saying "If you're white you're right, if you're yellow you're mellow, if you're brown stick around, but if you're black get back."

In ways that require no fueling from strong prejudice or stereo-types, these images expand the devaluation of black Americans. They act as mental standards against which information about blacks is evaluated: that which fits these images we accept; that which contra-dicts them we suspect. Had Jerome had a reading problem, which fits these images, it might have been accepted as characteristic more read-ily than his extraordinary art work, which contradicts them.

These images do something else as well, something especially pernicious in the classroom. They set up a jeopardy of double devalua-tion for blacks, a jeopardy that does not apply to whites. Like anyone, blacks risk devaluation for a particular incompetence, such as a failed test or a flubbed pronunciation. But they further risk that such performances will confirm the broader, racial inferiority they are suspected of. Thus, from the first grade through graduate school, blacks have the extra fear that in the eyes of those around them their full humanity could fall with a poor answer or a mistaken stroke of the pen.

Moreover, because these images are conditioned in all of us, collectively held, they can spawn racial devaluation in all of us, not just in the strongly prejudiced. They can do this even in blacks themselves: a majority of black children recently tested said they like and prefer to play with white rather than black dolls—almost fifty years after Kenneth and Mamie Clark, conducting similar experiments, documented identical findings and so paved the way for *Brown* v. *Topeka Board of Education*. Thus Jerome's devaluation can come from a circle of people in his world far greater than the expressly prejudiced—a circle that apparently includes his teacher.

In ways often too subtle to be conscious but sometimes overt, I believe, blacks remain devalued in American schools, where, for example, a recent national survey shows that through high school they are still more than twice as likely as white children to receive corporal punishment, be suspended from school, or be labeled mentally retarded.

Tragically, such devaluation can seem inescapable. Sooner or later it forces on its victims two painful realizations. The first is that society is preconditioned to see the worst in them. Black students quickly learn that acceptance, if it is to be won at all, will be hard-won. The second is that even if a black student achieves exoneration in one setting—with the teacher and fellow students in one classroom, or at one level of schooling, for example—this approval will have to be rewon in the next classroom, at the next level of schooling. Of course, individual characteristics that enhance one's value in society—skills, class status, appearance, and success—can diminish the racial devaluation one faces. And sometimes the effort to prove oneself fuels achievement. But few from any group could hope to sustain so daunting and everlasting a struggle. Thus, I am afraid, too many black students are left hopeless and deeply vulnerable in America's classrooms.

"Disidentifying" with School

I believe that in significant part the crisis in black Americans' education stems from the power of this vulnerability to undercut identification with schooling, either before it happens or after it has bloomed.

Jerome is an example of the first kind. At precisely the time when he would need to see school as a viable source of self-esteem, his teachers fail to appreciate his best work. The devalued status of his race devalues him and his work in the classroom. Unable to entrust his sense of himself to this place, he resists measuring himself against its values and goals. He languishes there, held by the law, perhaps even by his parents, but not allowing achievement to affect his view of himself. This psychic alienation—the act of not caring—makes him less vulnerable to the specter of devaluation that haunts him. Bruce Hare, an educational researcher, has documented this process among fifth-grade boys in several schools in Champaign, Illinois. He found that although the black boys had considerably lower achievement-test scores than their white classmates, their overall self-esteem was just as high. This stunning imperviousness to poor academic performance was accomplished, he found, by their de-emphasizing school achievement as a basis of self-esteem and giving preference to peer-group relations—a domain in which their esteem prospects were better. They went where they had to go to feel good about themselves.

But recall the young student whose mentor I was. She had already identified with school, and wanted to be a doctor. How can racial vulnerability break so developed an achievement identity? To see, let us follow her steps onto campus: Her recruitment and admission stress her minority status perhaps more strongly than it has been stressed at any other time in her life. She is offered academic and social support services, further implying that she is "at risk" (even though, contrary to common belief, the vast majority of black college students are admitted with qualifications well above the threshold for whites). Once on campus, she enters a socially circumscribed world in which blacks—still largely separate from whites—have lower status; this is reinforced by a sidelining of minority material and interests in the curriculum and in university life. And she can sense that everywhere in this new world her skin color places her under suspicion of intellectual inferiority. All of this gives her the double vulnerability I spoke of: she risks confirming a particular incompetence, at chemistry or a foreign language, for example; but she also risks confirming the racial inferiority she is suspected of—a judgment that can feel as close at hand as a mispronounced word or an ungrammatical sentence. In reaction, usually to some modest setbacks, she withdraws, hiding her troubles from instructors, counselors, even other students. Quickly, I believe, a psychic defense takes over. She disidentifies with achievement; she changes her self-conception, her outlook and values, so that achievement is no longer so important to her self-esteem. She may continue to feel pressure to stay in school—from her parents, even from the potential advantages of a college degree. But now she is psychologically insulated from her academic life, like a disinterested visitor. Cool, unperturbed. But, like a painkilling drug, disidentification undoes her future as it relieves her vulnerability.

• • •

To make matters worse, once disidentification occurs in a school, it can spread like the common cold. Blacks who identify and try to achieve embarrass the strategy by valuing the very thing the strategy denies the value of.

Thus pressure to make it a group norm can evolve quickly and become fierce. Defectors are called "oreos" or "incognegroes." One's identity as an authentic black is held hostage, made incompatible with school identification. For black students, then, pressure to disidentify with school can come from the already demoralized as well as from racial vulnerability in the setting.

Stigmatization of the sort suffered by black Americans is probably also a barrier to the school achievement of other groups in our society, such as lower-class whites, Hispanics, and women in male-dominated fields. For example, at a large midwestern university I studied, women match men's achievement in the liberal arts, where they suffer no marked stigma, but underachieve compared with men (get lower grades than men with the same ACT scores) in engineering and pre-medical programs, where they, like blacks across the board, are more vulnerable to suspicions of inferiority.

"Wise" Schooling

> When they approach me they see . . . everything and anything except me. . . .[this] invisibility. . . occurs because of a peculiar disposition of the eyes. . . .
>
> —Ralph Ellison, *Invisible Man*

Erving Goffman, borrowing from Gays of the 1950s, used the term "wise" to describe people who don't themselves bear the stigma of a given group but who are accepted by the group. These are people in whose eyes the full humanity of the stigmatized is visible, people in whose eyes they feel less vulnerable. If racial vulnerability undermines black school achievement, as I have argued, then this achievement should improve significantly if schooling is made "wise"—that is, made to see value and promise in black students and to act accordingly.

And yet, although racial vulnerability at school may undermine black achievement, so many other factors seem to contribute—from the debilitations of poverty to the alleged dysfunctions of black American culture—that one might expect "wiseness" in the classroom to be of little help. Fortunately, we have considerable evidence to the contrary. Wise schooling may indeed be the missing key to the school-house door.

• • •

And research involving hundreds of programs and schools points to the same conclusion: black achievement is consistently linked to conditions of schooling that reduce racial vulnerability. These include relatively harmonious race relations among students; a commitment by teachers and schools to seeing minority-group members achieve; the instructional goal that students at all levels of preparation achieve; desegregation at the classroom as well as the school level; and a de-emphasis on ability tracking.

That erasing stigma improves black achievement is perhaps the strongest evidence that stigma is what depresses it in the first place. This is no happy realization. But it lets in a ray of hope: whatever other factors also depress black achievement—poverty, social isolation, poor preparation—they may be substantially overcome in a schooling atmosphere that reduces racial and other vulnerabilities, not through unrelenting niceness or ferocious regimentation but by wiseness, by seeing value and acting on it.

What Makes Schooling Unwise

But if wise schooling is so attainable, why is racial vulnerability the rule, not the exception, in American schooling?

One factor is the basic assimilationist offer that schools make to blacks: You can be valued and rewarded in school (and society), the schools say to these students, but you must first master the culture and ways of the American mainstream, and since that mainstream (as it is represented) is essentially white, this means you must give up many particulars of being black—styles of speech and appearance, value priorities, preferences—at least in mainstream settings. This is asking a lot. But it has been the "color-blind" offer to every immigrant and minority group in our nation's history, the core of the melting-pot ideal, and so I think it strikes most of us as fair. Yet non-immigrant minorities like blacks and Native Americans have always been here, and thus are entitled, more than new immigrants, to participate in the defining images of the society projected in school. More important, their exclusion from these images denies their contributive history and presence in society. Thus, whereas immigrants can tilt toward assimilation in pursuit of the opportunities for which they came, American blacks may find it harder to assimilate. For them, the offer of acceptance in return for assimilation carries a primal insult: it asks them to join in something that has made them invisible.

• • •

The fact is that blacks are *not* outside the American mainstream but, in Ellison's words, have always been "one of its major tributaries." Yet if one relied on what is taught in America's schools, one would never know this. There blacks have fallen victim to a collective self-deception, a society's allowing itself to assimilate like mad from its constituent groups while representing itself to itself as if the assimilation had never happened, as if progress and good were almost exclusively Western and white. A prime influence of American society on world culture is the music of black Americans, shaping art forms from rock-and-roll to modern dance. Yet in American schools, from kindergarten through graduate school, these essentially black influences have barely peripheral status, are largely outside the canon. Thus it is not what is taught but what is not taught, what teachers and professors have never learned the value of, that reinforces a fundamental unwiseness in American schooling, and keeps black disidentification on full boil.

Deep in the psyche of American educators is a presumption that black students need academic remediation, or extra time with elemental curricula to overcome background deficits. This orientation guides many efforts to close the achievement gap—from grammar school tutoring to college academic-support programs—but I fear it can be unwise. Bruno Bettelheim and Karen Zelan's article "Why Children Don't Like to Read" comes to mind: apparently to satisfy the changing sensibilities of local school boards over this century, many books that children like were dropped from school reading lists; when children's reading scores also dropped, the approved texts were replaced by simpler books; and when reading scores dropped again, these were replaced by even simpler books, until eventually the children could hardly read at all, not because the material was too difficult but because they were bored stiff. So it goes, I suspect, with a great many of these remediation efforts. Moreover, because so many such programs target blacks primarily, they virtually equate black identity with substandard intellectual status, amplifying racial vulnerability. They can even undermine students' ability to gain confidence from their achievement, by sharing credit for their successes while implying that their failures stem from inadequacies beyond the reach of remediation.

• • •

The Elements of Wiseness

For too many black students school is simply the place where, more concertedly, persistently, and authoritatively than anywhere else in society, they learn how little valued they are.

Clearly, no simple recipe can fix this, but I believe we now understand the basics of a corrective approach. Schooling must focus more on reducing the vulnerabilities that block identification with achievement. I believe that four conditions, like the legs of a stool, are fundamental.

- If what is meaningful and important to a teacher is to become meaningful and important to a student, the student must feel valued by the teacher for his or her potential and as a person. Among the more fortunate in society, this relationship is often taken for granted. But it is precisely the relationship that race can still undermine in American society. As Comer, Escalante, and Treisman have shown, when one's students bear race and class vulnerabilities, building this relationship is the first order of business—at all levels of schooling. No tactic of instruction, no matter how ingenious, can succeed without it.

- The challenge and the promise of personal fulfillment, not remediation (under whatever guise), should guide the education of these students. Their present skills should be taken into account, and they should be moved along at a pace that is demanding but doesn't defeat them. Their ambitions should never be scaled down but should instead be guided to inspiring goals even when extraordinary dedication is called for. Frustration will be less crippling than alienation. Here psychology is everything: remediation defeats, challenge strengthens—affirming their potential, crediting them with their achievements, inspiring them.

But the first condition, I believe, cannot work without the second, and vice versa. A valuing teacher-student relationship goes nowhere without challenge, and challenge will always be resisted outside a valuing relationship. (Again, I must be careful about something: in criticizing remediation I am not opposing affirmative-action recruitment in the schools. The success of this policy, like that of school integration before it, depends, I believe, on the tactics of implementation. Where students are valued and challenged, they generally succeed.)

- Racial integration is a generally useful element in this design, if not a necessity. Segregation, whatever its purpose, draws out group differences and makes people feel more vulnerable when they inevitably cross group lines to compete in the larger society. This vulnerability, I fear, can override confidence gained in segregated schooling unless that confidence is based on strongly competitive skills and knowledge—something that segregated schooling, plagued by shortages of resources and access, has difficulty producing.

- The particulars of black life and culture—art, literature, political and social perspective, music—must be presented in the mainstream curriculum of American schooling, not consigned to special days, weeks, or even months of the year, or to special-topic courses and programs aimed essentially at blacks. Such channeling carries the disturbing message that the material is not of general value. And this does two terrible things: it wastes the power of this material to alter our images of the American mainstream—continuing to frustrate black identification with it—and it excuses in whites and others a huge ignorance of their own society. The true test of democracy, Ralph Ellison has said, "is . . . the inclusion—not assimilation—of the black man."

Finally, if I might be allowed a word specifically to black parents, one issue is even more immediate: our children may drop out of school before the first committee meets to accelerate the curriculum. Thus, although we, along with all Americans, must strive constantly for wise schooling, I believe we cannot wait for it. We cannot yet forget our essentially heroic challenge: to foster in our children a sense of hope and entitlement to mainstream American life and schooling, even when it devalues them.

WRITING ABOUT THE READING

5. According to the author, why do many African Americans become alienated from school?
6. Steele presents the reasons (the "familiar set of explanations") often given to explain the problems African Americans face in school. Why does Steele believe that these reasons are not sufficient to explain the problem?
7. Why does Steele write that African Americans who defy group norms are often criticized?
8. How and why does Steele's narrative of his own experience in graduate school support his position?

9. Why does the author believe that remediation programs are harmful?

10. After analyzing the problem, Steele presents his solution to the problem. Why does he believe that his solution will work?

WRITING FROM YOUR OWN EXPERIENCE

Note: In these assignments, write about your own experience or use that of someone you know, read about, or saw in a film/TV show.

11. Recall a time when you were able to overcome an obstacle (such as passing a difficult class) in obtaining an education. What were some of the reasons that the obstacle was successfully overcome?

12. Choose a teacher who was important in your education. Explain why this teacher was influential and the results of this person's influence.

13. Steele states that friends often pressure African American students to "disidentify" with school. Did your friends ever urge you to do (or not do) something that you felt was wrong? Why did they pressure you and what were the consequences of this pressure?

WRITING ABOUT RESEARCH

14. What are some of the programs offered at your college to help students succeed? Explain whether you think that these programs are successful or not.

15. Many states now use extensive testing programs to measure student and school achievement. Research this testing movement and explain why you think it has been effective (or ineffective) in improving education.

16. Many educators are studying "resiliency," the ability of some students to overcome socioeconomic conditions and succeed in school. Research this topic and explain why some students, even under adverse conditions, are successful.

17. Steele states: "A prime influence of American society on world culture is the music of black Americans, shaping art forms from rock-and-roll to modern dance." Choose an African American

who has been a prominent singer, musician, or dancer. Why is this person considered to be a major figure in his/her field? Consider:

(a) Alvin Ailey
(b) Marian Anderson
(c) Louis "Satchmo" Armstrong
(d) Sammy Davis
(e) Duke Ellington
(f) Ella Fitzgerald
(g) Judith Jamison
(h) Jessye Norman

The Two Nations
of Black America

HENRY LOUIS GATES, JR.

Henry Louis Gates, Jr. *(1950–), a noted writer, editor, scholar, and teacher, received a B.A. from Yale University and M.A. and Ph.D. degrees from Cambridge University. At Harvard University, he is the W.E.B. Du Bois Professor of the Humanities, chair of the Afro-American Studies Department, and director of the W.E.B. Du Bois Institute for Afro-American Research. Gates has received numerous awards, including a Woodrow Wilson Fellowship, a MacArthur Prize Fellowship, and an American Book Award.*

As a recognized scholar and literary critic, Gates has explored the relationship of African American writing to the traditional literary canon. Gates defines himself as a centrist who rejects extreme positions of all kinds, who acknowledges the fluid relationship between African American and white cultures in the United States. In a world fragmented by social class, racial, and cultural differences, he esteems education as a necessary means to understanding the diversity of human experience and achieving cultural tolerance. Gates believes, as he has stated in the introduction to his best-known book Loose Canons *(1992), "There is no tolerance without respect—and no respect without knowledge."*

Many successful African Americans, like Gates, have concerned themselves with the obligation, if any, of the educated middle-class African American to those who are less fortunate. In the following essay, Gates reviews his own undergraduate experience, as one of many middle-class African Americans newly attending Yale. He then considers the social transformations that resulted in a division in culture and aspirations between middle-class and impoverished African Americans. "The Two Nations of Black America" (1998) comes from The Brookings Review, *an academic journal of issues in the social sciences, sponsored by The Brookings Institution in Washington, D.C.*

PREPARING TO READ

1. Explain whether you agree that after graduating from college, you will have an obligation to "give back to" or actively support the community from which you came.

2. In this essay, Gates uses a number of terms, including "a brother," "colleague," "gangsta" lifestyle, "leader," "Milquetoast," "Uncle Tom," and "radical." How would you define one of these terms and why would you define it this way?
3. When you first entered college, why were you surprised about the things you discovered about your fellow students or college life?
4. Consider your group of college friends and associates as a small community. What are some of the characteristics of this community and the reasons for your listing these attributes?

THE TWO NATIONS OF BLACK AMERICA

Six black men, each intellectually superior in his own way, graduated from Yale College in the class of 1966. Each had managed, through some luck and a lot of pluck, to penetrate the ironclad barriers that had kept the blacks matriculating at Yale to a fixed number for several decades. When I entered Yale two years later, 95 black men and women entered with me.

We were, to a person, caught up in the magic of the moment. Our good fortune was to have been selected to be part of the first "large" group of blacks included in Yale's commitment to educate "1,000 male leaders" each year. But we wondered: what would becoming a true black leader entail—for ourselves and for our people outside those hallowed Ivy walls? What sort of sacrifices and obligations did this special ticket to success bring along with it? We worried about this—out loud, often, and noisily.

Mostly we did our worrying in our long languid dinners in the colleges or in bull sessions in our suites, but our ritualized worrying space was our weekly meetings of the Black Student Alliance at Yale, headed by our black and shining prince, Glenn de Chabert. Our first item of business was always "recruitment," how to get more black students to join us at New Haven. "This place is lily white," de Chabert would complain. "We are flies in the buttermilk." Brimming to overflow with maybe 200 students, the year's first meeting of the BSAY looked like Harlem to me! I basked in the warmth generated by the comfort of the range of brown colors in that room, but I also shuddered (as unnoticeably as I could) as I contemplated the awesome burden of leadership that we felt or were made to feel, fulfilling our obligations to "help the community." After all, "the revolution" was unfolding around the country and we, along with students like us at Harvard,

Columbia, Princeton, Amherst, and Wesleyan, were to be its vanguard. This burden was no mere abstraction. The trial of New Haven's Black Panthers, and of one of their leaders, Bobby Seale, was under way just a block or two away at New Haven's federal courthouse.

It astonishes me today how sharp my black colleagues were, how thoughtful beyond their years, how mature. For some reason, I long assumed that most of these guys were up from the ghetto, first generation college. After all, our uniforms of the day, dashikis and blue jeans, obliterated our variety of social distinctions. Names like Baskerville and Irving, Reed and Robinson, Schmoke and de Chabert, Barrington Parker the Third, meant nothing particular to me. Only later would I discover that my contemporaries were no strangers to the idea of college. Had it not been for affirmative action, we would have met at Howard or Morehouse. They were not so much a new black middle-class bourgeoisie recruited to scale the ladder of class as the scions of an old and colored middle class, recruited to integrate a white male elite. We clung to a soft black nationalist politics to keep ourselves to the straight and narrow.

For me one crucial scene of instruction on the path of a more or less nationalist politics came while I was watching a black program that had been produced by students at Howard. In the film, a student, happily dating a white co-ed, comes to see the error of his ways after a campus visit by Maulana Ron Karenga. What a figure Karenga was—brown bald head, African robes, dark sun glasses. This was one bad dude, bad enough to make this guy in the film turn his back on love and come on home! I'm not sure it had ever occurred to me before this that there was "a way to be 'black,'" that one could be in the program or outside of it.

Of course I knew what an Uncle Tom was, but even Uncle Tom was still part of the extended family. No one ever talked about banishing him from the tribe. Before this. But this was a new day. A new generation, a vanguard within the vanguard of civil rights leadership, was demanding Black Power, the right to take over, and declaring venerable elders like Martin Luther King, Jr., to be too old, too tired, too Milquetoast to be effective keepers of Black Power's incandescent flare. Dr. King was especially symptomatic, moving away as he had done from an exclusively race-based politics to a more broadly conceived analysis that would bring "poor people" together. Where did a movement based on poverty leave all of us who were discovering an Afro-coifed dashiki-clad "blackness" long forcibly hidden from our view? Even the Black Panthers, Marxists that they claimed to be, manipulated the trappings of nationalist garb and rhetoric to maximize their appeal in a program that would eventually lead out of the black community and straight into a coalition with the brown and red and white truly poor.

J. Edgar Hoover and his FBI, apparently, were not aware of, or especially concerned about, what Freud called "the narcissism of tiny differences" within the black movement. For Hoover, the Panthers were black, they were radical, they were Communist-inspired. And they could be dealt with.

Systematic repression has a curious way of hampering the evolution of a movement. And not only were the Black Panthers repressed, Dr. King was assassinated—in retrospect the most dramatic act of violent repression in the wing of the movement that was beginning to embrace a class-based organizing principle that sought to reorder American society. Dr. King was killed. People like Huey Newton were imprisoned. And people as unlike as Elijah Mohammed and Vernon Jordan, Jesse Jackson, and my new compatriots at Yale were being invited to integrate a newly expanded American upper middle class. The vanguard of black cultural nationalist political consciousness, in other words, became the vanguard in the race's broad movement across the great divide that had for so long prevented genuine economic mobility up the great American ladder of class.

Somehow, in the late sixties, in the aftermath of the King assassination, what was held to be "authentically" black began to change. Ghetto culture was valorized; the "bourgeois" lifestyle that the old guard leaders of the civil rights establishment embodied was held to be too great a price to pay for our freedom, or at least to admit to. We wanted to be "real," to "be down with the people," to be successful, yes, but to appear to be "black" at the same time. And to be black was to be committed to a revolution of values, or mores and manners, of economic relationships. We were "a people." The best way to dramatize this kinship was to dress, walk, talk like a "brother."

Above all, being black meant that we were at one with "the revolution," standing tall and firm in defense of "the people," and that revolutionary vanguard, the persecuted and harassed Black Panther Party for Self-Defense. We went on strike on April 15, 1970, two weeks before Nixon and Henry Kissinger invaded Cambodia. We struck because Bobby Seale, we felt deeply, was not being tried fairly just down the street, bound and gagged as he was at the worst moment of the trial. The strike rally was glorious. It seemed as if 100,000 people crowded onto the New Haven Green on May Day of 1970. Kingman Brewster, Yale's dynamic president, offered them food and shelter in the residential colleges. Each stained glass window of the sacred cathedral of learning that we called "Sterling" stood intact at week's end. De Chabert had never spoken more impressively, never been more daring or inspiring.

However, graduation inevitably came, calling us to the newly expanded opportunities in graduate and professional schools and then on to similarly expanded opportunities in the broader professional and academic world. I went off to Cambridge, England, and when I returned a few years later to teach at Yale, so very much had changed. Any pretense that black admissions would be anything but staunchly and firmly middle class had ended during my absence. The new black middle class was perpetuating itself. Affirmative action, under assault by the Supreme Court's 1978 Bakke decision and wounded, still was functioning to increase the size of the middle class exponentially by a factor of four. Meanwhile, the gradual disappearance of industrial jobs in the cities was cutting off that upwardly mobile class escalator that so many in the middle class had been able to scale.

Thenceforth, in one of the most curious social transformations in the class structure in recent American history, two tributaries began to flow, running steadily into two distinct rivers of aspiration and achievement. By 1990, the black middle class, imperiled though it might feel itself to be, had never been larger, more prosperous, or more relatively secure. Simultaneously, the pathological behavior that results from extended impoverishment engulfed a large part of a black underclass that seemed unable to benefit from a certain opening up of American society that the civil rights movement had long envisioned and had finally made possible, if only for some. And for the first time ever, that inability to benefit seemed permanent.

Gangsterism became the handmaiden of hopelessness. Even middle-class children, well-educated, often, and well-heeled, found value in publicity celebrating a "gangsta" lifestyle. Cultural forms such as Rap and Hip Hop, "the CNN of the black community," valorized violence, homophobia, misogyny, anti-Semitism, and a curious form of masochistic self-destruction. And then life began to imitate art—the gangsterism of the art of Hip Hop liberalized itself in the reciprocal murders of Tupac and Biggie Smalls—and the bizarre nightmare inversion of popular black values manifested itself in a most public way.

Which brings us to the present—for the African-American community, the best of times and the worst of times. We have the largest black middle class in our history and the largest black underclass. In 1990, 2,280,000 black men were in prison, or probation, or parole, while 23,000 earned a college degree. That's a ratio of 99 to 1, compared with a ratio of 6 to 1 for white men.

What do we do about this? What do we not do?

First of all, we have to stop feeling guilty about our success. Too many of us have what psychologists call "the guilt of the survivor," deep anxieties about leaving the rest of our fellow blacks in the inner city of despair. We need to feel the commitment to service, not to guilt. Our community and our families prepared us to be successful. "Get all the education you can," they told us over and over—and we did.

Second, we don't have to fail in order to be black. As odd and as crazy as this sounds. Far too many young black kids say that succeeding is "white." Had any of us said this sort of thing when we were growing up, our families and friends would have checked us into a mental institution. We need more success individually and collectively.

Third, we don't have to pretend any longer that 35 million people can ever possibly be members of the same economic class. The entire population of Canada is 27 million. Canadians are not all members of one economic class. Nor do they speak with one single voice, united behind one single leader. As each of us knows, we have never been members of one social or economic class and never will be. The best we can strive for is that the class differentials within the black community—the bell curve of class—cease their lopsided ratios because of the pernicious nature of racial inequality.

So how do we do this? How do we "fight the power" in a post-civil rights world in which Bull Connors and George Wallace are no longer the easy targets? A world in which the rhetoric of the civil rights era sounds hollow and empty? A world in which race differences and class differentials have been ground together in a crucible of misery and squalor, in such a way that few of us can tell where one stops and the other begins? I certainly have no magic cures.

But we do know that the causes of poverty within the black community are both structural and behavioral. Scholars as diverse as philosopher Cornel West and sociologist William Julius Wilson have pointed this out, and we are foolish to deny it. A household composed of a 16-year-old mother, a 32-year-old grandmother, and a 48-year-old great grandmother cannot possibly be a site for hope and optimism. Our task, it seems to me, is to lobby for those social programs that have been demonstrated to make a difference for those motivated to seize these expanded opportunities.

More important, we have to demand a structural change in this country, the equivalent of a Marshall Plan for the cities. We have to take people off welfare, train them for occupations relevant to a 21st-century, high-tech economy, and put them to work. Joblessness, as Wilson maintains, is our biggest crisis.

And while I favor such incentives as tax breaks to generate new investment in inner cities, youth apprenticeships with corporations, expanded tax credits for earned income, and tenant ownership of inner-city property, we have to face the reality that most of our inner cities are simply not going to become overnight oases of prosperity. We should think about moving black inner-city workers to the jobs rather than hold our breath and wait for new factories to resettle in the inner city.

It is only by confronting the twin realities of white racism, on the one hand, and our failures to take the initiative and break the cycle of poverty, on the other, that we, the remnants of W. E. B. Du Bois's Talented Tenth, will be able to assume a renewed leadership role for, and with, the black community. To continue to repeat the same old stale formulas; to blame "the man" for oppressing us all, in exactly the same ways; to scapegoat Koreans, Jews, or even Haitians for the failure of black Americans to seize local entrepreneurial opportunities is to fail to accept our role as leaders of our own community. Not to demand that each member of the black community accept individual responsibility for her or his behavior—whether that behavior assumes the form of black-on-black homicide, gang members violating the sanctity of the church, unprotected sexual activity, gangster rap lyrics, whatever—is for us to function merely as ethnic cheerleaders selling woof tickets from campus or suburbs, rather than saying the difficult things that may be unpopular with our fellows. Being a leader does not necessarily mean being loved; loving one's community means daring to risk estrangement and alienation from it in the short run in order to break the cycle of poverty and despair in which we find ourselves, over the long run. For what is at stake is nothing less than the survival of our country, and the African-American people themselves.

Those of us on campus can also reach out to those of us left behind on the streets. The historically black colleges and universities and Afro-American Studies departments in this country can institutionalize sophomore and junior year internships for community development through organizations such as the Children's Defense Fund. Together we can combat teenage pregnancies, black-on-black crime, and the spread of AIDS from drug abuse and unprotected sexual relations, and counter the spread of despair and hopelessness in our communities. Dr. King did not die so that half of us would make it, half of us perish, forever tarnishing two centuries of agitation for our equal rights. We, the members of the Talented Tenth, must accept our historical responsibility and live Dr. King's credo that none of us is free until all of us are free. And that all of us are brothers and sisters, as Dr. King said so long ago—white and black, Protestant and Catholic, Gentile and Jew and Muslim, rich and poor—even if we are not brothers-in-law.

WRITING ABOUT THE READING

5. Why did Gates and his friends at Yale feel a responsibility to be leaders?

6. What is Gates's attitude about being "authentically black" and why does he feel this way?

7. According to the writer, why has "gangsterism" had an adverse effect on the African American community?

8. What do you think Gates means when he states ". . . the causes of poverty within the black community are both structural and behavioral"?

9. Describe the intended audience for this essay and the reasons why you think that this is the audience.

WRITING FROM YOUR OWN EXPERIENCE

Note: In these assignments, write about your own experience or use that of someone you know, read about, or saw in a film/TV show.

10. Gates states that some middle-class African Americans feel guilty about their success. Think of a time when you were successful (as in winning an award) and felt guilty about your success and/or obligated to those less successful. Why did you feel this way and what were the results of your feeling this way?

11. Much of this essay deals with trying to live up to the expectations others have of us. What expectations do others have of you (or you have of yourself) and why do you think that these expectations are reasonable (or unreasonable)?

12. Gates writes of the necessity of taking the initiative to break the cycle of poverty. Think of a time when you took the initiative to make a change in your life. Why did you initiate this change and what were the results of this act?

13. The writer states that being a leader means sometimes taking the risk of becoming unpopular with one's fellows. Recall a time when you risked losing a friend or becoming unpopular with your group. Why did you take this risk and what were the consequences of your actions?

14. As a student at a predominantly white college, Gates, of necessity, had to interact with the white majority and members of minority groups other than African Americans. Consider an experience you have had with a friend or colleague from a racial/ethnic group

other than your own. Why was this experience successful or unsuccessful and what insight did you gain from it?

WRITING ABOUT RESEARCH

15. Gates writes that if he had not attended Yale, he probably would have attended one of the historically African American colleges. Choose one historically African American college (such as Bethune-Cookman, Fisk, Howard, Morehouse, or Tuskeegee). How and why was this college established and developed?

16. Explain whether you think there is a need today for African American studies departments in colleges.

17. Many African Americans write newspaper articles or columns on current socioeconomic issues. Choose one such writer and explain why you agree (or disagree) with this person's views. Consider a writer for the op-ed page of your local paper or a national figure, such as Colin Powell, Jesse Jackson, William Raspberry, Brent Staples, William Julius Wilson, or Cornel West.

Beyond Affirmative Action: Equality and Identity

CORNEL WEST

Cornel (Ronald) West *(1953–), social critic and philosopher, earned an A.B. degree in 1973 from Harvard University, and M.A. (1975) and Ph.D. (1980) degrees from Princeton. From 1989–1994, West served as Professor of Religion and Director of the Afro-American Studies Department at Princeton. He then was appointed Professor of Afro-American Studies and Professor of the Philosophy of Religion at Harvard University. He is widely known as a writer, social commentator, intellectual, and public figure.*

West has stated that the greatest challenge for all Americans is to create and sustain a multiracial democracy that incorporates empathy and compassion. To create such a democracy, one without racism and oppression, West advocates combining Marxism and Christianity. As an intellectual with a moral vision, West believes that it is his vocation to ask critical questions of those in power, to bring to their attention issues of social misery. West also challenges individuals to use the power of their minds to better themselves and their communities.

West's twofold concern with economic and moral issues can be discerned in "Beyond Affirmative Action: Equality and Identity," which was included in Race Matters *(1993). West blames both poverty and "self-loathing" for what he sees as a crisis among many African Americans. To address this crisis, West first calls for financial measures, a redistribution of wealth beyond the goals of affirmative action policies. He then addresses the necessity for African Americans to affirm the value of "black identity" and to form coalitions with other people working for social progress.*

PREPARING TO READ

1. Explain whether you think that it is the role of the government to take measures to assist the poor in our society.
2. Explain whether you think that popular culture (i.e., movies, music, and TV) contributes to a positive (or negative) self-concept for African Americans?

3. Sometimes people from other countries characterize Americans as acting as though "money is everything." Explain why they make this criticism and whether you think it is justified or not.

4. Why do you think that many college students today major in business rather than the liberal arts, education, or the social sciences?

BEYOND AFFIRMATIVE ACTION: EQUALITY AND IDENTITY

The fundamental crisis in black America is twofold: too much poverty and too little self-love. The urgent problem of black poverty is primarily due to the distribution of wealth, power, and income—a distribution influenced by the racial caste system that denied opportunities to most "qualified" black people until two decades ago.

The historic role of American progressives is to promote redistributive measures that enhance the standard of living and quality of life for the have-nots and have-too-littles. Affirmative action was one such redistributive measure that surfaced in the heat of battle in the 1960s among those fighting for racial equality. Like earlier *de facto* affirmative action measures in the American past—contracts, jobs, and loans to select immigrants granted by political machines; subsidies to certain farmers; FHA mortgage loans to specific home buyers; or GI Bill benefits to particular courageous Americans—recent efforts to broaden access to America's prosperity have been based upon preferential policies. Unfortunately, these policies always benefit middle-class Americans disproportionately. The political power of big business in big government circumscribes redistributive measures and thereby tilts these measures away from the have-nots and have-too-littles.

Every redistributive measure is a compromise with and concession from the caretakers of American prosperity—that is, big business and big government. Affirmative action was one such compromise and concession achieved after the protracted struggle of American progressives and liberals in the courts and in the streets. Visionary progressives always push for substantive redistributive measures that make opportunities available to the have-nots and have-too-littles, such as more federal support to small farmers, or more FHA mortgage loans to urban dwellers as well as suburban home buyers. Yet in the American political system, where the powers that be turn a skeptical eye toward any program aimed at economic redistribution, progressives must secure whatever redistributive measures they can, ensure their enforcement, then extend their benefits if possible.

If I had been old enough to join the fight for racial equality in the courts, the legislatures, and the board rooms in the 1960s (I *was* old enough to be in the streets), I would have favored—as I do now—a class-based affirmative action in principle. Yet in the heat of battle in American politics, a redistributive measure in principle with no power and pressure behind it means no redistributive measure at all. The prevailing discriminatory practices during the sixties, whose targets were working people, women, and people of color, were atrocious. Thus, an *enforceable* race-based—and later gender-based—affirmative action policy was the best possible compromise and concession.

Progressives should view affirmative action as neither a major solution to poverty nor a sufficient means to equality. We should see it as primarily playing a negative role—namely, to ensure that discriminatory practices against women and people of color are abated. Given the history of this country, it is a virtual certainty that without affirmative action racial and sexual discrimination would return with a vengeance. Even if affirmative action fails significantly to reduce black poverty or contributes to the persistence of racist perceptions in the workplace, without affirmative action black access to America's prosperity would be even more difficult to obtain and racism in the workplace would persist anyway.

This claim is not based on any cynicism toward my white fellow citizens; rather, it rests upon America's historically weak will toward racial justice and substantive redistributive measures. This is why an attack on affirmative action is an attack on redistributive efforts by progressives unless there is a real possibility of enacting and enforcing a more wide-reaching class-based affirmative action policy.

In American politics, progressives must not only cling to redistributive ideals, but must also fight for those policies that—out of compromise and concession—imperfectly conform to those ideals. Liberals who give only lip service to these ideals, trash the policies in the name of *realpolitik*, or reject the policies as they perceive a shift in the racial bellwether give up precious ground too easily. And they do so even as the sand is disappearing under our feet on such issues as regressive taxation, layoffs or takebacks from workers, and cutbacks in health and child care.

Affirmative action is not the most important issue for black progress in America, but it is part of a redistributive chain that must be strengthened if we are to confront and eliminate black poverty. If there were social democratic redistributive measures that wiped out black poverty, and if racial and sexual discrimination could be abated through the good will and meritorious judgments of those in power, affirmative action would be unnecessary. Although many of my liberal and progressive citizens view affirmative action as a redistributive measure whose time is over or whose life is no longer worth preserving,

I question their view because of the persistence of discriminatory practices that increase black social misery, and the warranted suspicion
that good will and fair judgment among the powerful does not loom
as large toward women and people of color.

• • •

If the elimination of black poverty is a necessary condition of
substantive black progress, then the affirmation of black humanity, especially among black people themselves, is a sufficient condition of
such progress. Such affirmation speaks to the existential issues of what
it means to be a degraded African (man, woman, gay, lesbian, child) in
a racist society. How does one affirm oneself without reenacting negative black stereotypes or overreacting to white supremacist ideals?

The difficult and delicate quest for black identity is integral to
any talk about racial equality. Yet it is not solely a political or economic matter. The quest for black identity involves self-respect and
self-regard, realms inseparable from, yet not identical to, political
power and economic status. The flagrant self-loathing among black
middle-class professionals bears witness to this painful process. Unfortunately, black conservatives focus on the issue of self-respect as if
it were the one key that would open all doors to black progress. They
illustrate the fallacy of trying to open all doors with one key: they
wind up closing their eyes to all doors except the one the key fits.

Progressives, for our part, must take seriously the quest for self-
respect, even as we train our eye on the institutional causes of black
social misery. The issues of black identity—both black self-love and
self-contempt—sit alongside black poverty as realities to confront and
transform. The uncritical acceptance of self-degrading ideals, that call
into question black intelligence, possibility, and beauty not only com-
pounds black social misery but also paralyzes black middle-class efforts to defend broad redistributive measures.

This paralysis takes two forms: black bourgeois preoccupation with
white peer approval and black nationalist obsession with white racism.

The first form of paralysis tends to yield a navel-gazing posture
that conflates the identity crisis of the black middle class with the state
of siege raging in black working-poor and very poor communities.
That unidimensional view obscures the need for redistributive measures that significantly affect the majority of blacks, who are working
people on the edge of poverty.

The second form of paralysis precludes any meaningful coalition
with white progressives because of an undeniable white racist legacy
of the modern Western world. The anger this truth engenders impedes
any effective way of responding to the crisis in black America. Broad

redistributive measures require principled coalitions, including multiracial alliances. Without such measures, black America's sufferings deepen. White racism indeed contributes to this suffering. Yet an obsession with white racism often comes at the expense of more broadly based alliances to affect social changes and borders on a tribal mentality. The more xenophobic versions of this viewpoint simply mirror the white supremacist ideals we are opposing and preclude any movement toward redistributive goals.

How one defines oneself influences what analytical weight one gives to black poverty. Any progressive discussion about the future of racial equality must speak to black poverty and black identity. My views on the necessity and limits of affirmative action in the present moment are informed by how substantive redistributive measures and human affirmative efforts can be best defended and expanded.

WRITING ABOUT THE READING

5. Why does West describe some government programs other than affirmative action as "redistributive measures"?
6. Why does West say that affirmative action programs play a negative role?
7. Why does the writer think that the "acceptance of self-degrading ideals" is harmful?
8. What does West mean by "the black nationalist obsession with white racism" and why is he critical of this movement?
9. Why do some statements show that West knows that some readers may not agree with his position?
10. Explain how and why the organization of this essay supports the writer's opening statement about the problem.

WRITING FROM YOUR OWN EXPERIENCE

Note: In these assignments, write about your own experience or use that of someone you know, read about, or saw in a film/TV show.

11. Have you ever had a sudden increase or decrease in money? How and why did the change in financial status affect your behavior and/or self-concept?
12. Think of a government economic program of which you have some knowledge (such as subsidized school lunches, student loans, FHA

mortgage loans, or Social Security). Why would you argue that this is a necessary (or unnecessary) government program?

13. Compare two people that you know, one with high self-esteem and one with low self-esteem. Which person would you prefer as a friend and why would you choose this person?

WRITING ABOUT RESEARCH

14. What are some of the reasons that people support (or oppose) affirmative action?

15. Why is affirmative action an issue in business (such as in hiring, promotion, or awarding of contracts to small businesses)?

16. What are some of the arguments for and against raising the minimum wage?

17. Why do some people believe that African Americans should receive reparations for their unpaid work during the years of slavery?

When the Game Is Over

MARCUS MABRY

Marcus Mabry *(1967–), journalist, was graduated from Stanford University with B.A. degrees in both English and French Literature. He then went on to study at the Sorbonne in France, and earn M.A.s in International Relations and English. Currently Mabry is a Senior Editor for* Newsweek International *magazine.*

In his 1995 memoir, White Bucks and Black-Eyed Peas, *Mabry writes about his path to success in the dominant society and the internal conflicts caused by this success. Raised in a family that often had to depend on welfare to survive, Mabry received a scholarship to an exclusive prep school. Mabry then was exposed to a white, upper-class life far different from the one he had known before. His writing often explores the meaning of success for educated African Americans who live in two worlds, who often feel like outsiders in both the white and African American communities.*

In "When the Game Is Over," Mabry deplores the exploitation of African American athletes by colleges. He believes that, too often, these athletes concentrate on sports and neglect their studies, leaving them with few options when their athletic career ends. The essay was originally printed in Black Collegiate Magazine *(1993).*

PREPARING TO READ

1. Explain whether you think that schools and colleges put too much emphasis on sports.
2. Choose the one sport that most interests you and explain why you like this sport.
3. Explain why you would (or would not) consider qualities in addition to physical skill to describe a person as a "great athlete."
4. Explain whether you agree that colleges today should emphasize physical fitness and individual sports more than team sports.

WHEN THE GAME IS OVER

Eric Ramsey had it all. He had been a star defensive back at football powerhouse Auburn University. He had been popular with classmates and a local hero. He made it to the National Football League. In short, Ramsey had everything that a poor African-American kid who liked to play football could dream of. Then it all came crashing down. In 1991, after spending five years at Auburn and signing with the Kansas City Chiefs, Ramsey told the truth about his experience as an African-American athlete at Auburn. Coaches taunted African-American players, racism ran rampant in the football program, and Auburn coach Pat Dye fixed a collateral-free loan for Ramsey, in direct violation of NCAA rules.

Sitting before a hearing at the Congressional Black Caucus this past November, Ramsey and his wife told of the exploitation that African-American athletes suffered and of the harassment that dogged them since they came forward. Tears welling up in her eyes, Twilitta Ramsey said, "We did it because for five years we saw Black athletes get abused mentally and physically by coaches. And after their football eligibility was over, or if they were injured, they were thrown away like dirty dishrags."

Ramsey's story is only one version of a tragedy that has struck many African-American collegiate athletes when the game is over. Ramsey was smart enough to go to classes and get his education despite coaches prodding him to do less thinking about books and more thinking about football. (Last year Robert Smith, star running back at Ohio State University, quit the team because he said he was told, "You're here to play football. You take school too seriously.") Many African-American athletes graduate as functional illiterates or don't graduate at all. "Graduation rates for Black athletes are abysmal," says Charles S. Farrell, president of Sports Perspectives International, an advocacy group for athletes, particularly African-American ones. "Only about 25 percent of Black scholarship athletes in Division I, the NCAA's top competitive division, receive college degrees after six years."

Anecdotes abound of African-American athletes who were intensely recruited by schools, then abandoned when they arrived, with no attention paid to their cultural or social, not to mention academic, well-being. With little or no support outside of their athletic training, some get into trouble almost as soon as they get into college. Recently two University of Maryland football players were charged with going on a spending spree with a stolen credit card. A University of Louisville football player was accused of raping a student in her campus apartment. In the past year and a half, 15 Arizona State University basketball and football players were charged with crimes ranging from sexual assault to illegal credit card use. Fourteen of the 15 are African Americans.

Some experts say that despite greater attention being paid to college athletes and collegiate sports scandals, the problem of the exploited African-American athlete is getting worse. "The decline of academic achievement among many of America's talented and gifted athletes has accelerated," says David L. Smith, president of SET Communications Inc. and a former college and pro athlete himself. The NCAA will get more than $1 billion in the next seven years from network TV to broadcast games, says Smith. Sales in sports marketing topped $8 billion last year—despite the recession. "The multibillion dollar sports industry has grown at the expense of the intellectual, emotional, social, and economic needs of its participants. The sports industry has merged into the entertainment industry on the backs of free athletic talent."

Often promising athletes, a large proportion of them African Americans, arrive on campus with one thing in mind: playing their sport and playing it well. They are often from disadvantaged backgrounds. Many, like Ramsey, are the first people in their families to go to college. The students and their parents are unfamiliar with college and often at the mercy of the coaches who direct them. "Only the athletes are amateurs," says Smith. The dreams of riches and a life in professional sports are far more glamorous than cracking the books. And many student-athletes are intoxicated by them. "Coaches tell them all along that if they go full speed every practice and win games, they will be rich when they leave," says Ramsey. "What really happens is that they leave with broken, patched, aching bones, and no college degree."

In many ways the problems of African-American college athletes are symptomatic of society's problems: from the American obsession with "living large," fast cars, and fat steaks, to the persistent view of African-American men as little more than sports commodities. In professional sports too, African-American athletes complain of prejudice and a lack of empowerment. Perhaps more importantly, African Americans are still grossly underrepresented in the front offices and head coaching and manager positions in every sport, at the college and the professional level. African-Americans are still seen by many whites as incapable of doing anything more than jumping, running, and tackling. But racism is an insufficient explanation for the exploitation of these athletes. For instance, while only four percent of coaches are African-American, about 25 percent of the approximately 100 coaches under NCAA sanctions for violating recruitment rules are African-American, according to NCAA statistics.

And many experts say that the African-American community and the young men who play college sports are also to blame. "Our athletes too often buy into the myth that their only chance of success is through sports, even though the odds are far better that they can become a doctor or lawyer than a professional athlete," says Farrell. The African-American community does not work to challenge its youth to put the same amount of energy into the classroom that they do on the field. He says, "Black youths aspire to become the next Michael Jordan while ignoring the classroom."

Meanwhile, college sports officials claim they have already improved the way they do business. "The reform movement to improve college sports started in the early '80s," says Charles M. Neinas, executive director of the College Football Association, an organization of 67 major football playing universities, independent of but linked to the NCAA. A group of concerned college and university presidents, athletic directors, and coaches got together to discuss the failings and corruption of college sports. Subsequently they met formally as the NCAA President's Commission to recommend changes to the NCAA: stricter rules and less intense recruiting and training schedules. Many coaches were upset that the administrative brass was interfering in their arena. Neinas points out that football coaches themselves reduced the off-campus recruiting season from 200 days to fewer than eight weeks and that coaches prompted legislation to prohibit alumni and boosters from becoming involved in the recruiting process, offering free cars and apartments.

And specific colleges have responded to critics as well. The University of Maryland has a support program for freshmen athletes that includes everything from study skills to social skills to stress management. Some colleges, like Stanford University, have academic support programs for athletes. At Stanford there is an optional study hall nightly for athlete-students. Students who fall below a C− average are required to attend.

Clearly, more can be done. More African-American coaches and athletic directors in more colleges and universities could serve as role models for these athletes and help them make the adjustments to college life. Many athlete advocacy groups argue that recruiting must be overhauled. The current cutthroat system allows, even encourages, schools to offer prospective recruits under-the-table deals and illegal perks that distort the student-athlete's goals even before he gets to school. Farrell suggests that scholarships be issued on a five-year basis rather than renewed year to year. "That would allow athletes to feel more secure in the pursuit of a degree, rather than permit coaches to have the power of life and death over an athlete," says Farrell.

Congress is threatening action of its own. Senator Bill Bradley of New Jersey, a former college and pro basketball player, and Representative Aldolphous Towns of New York have introduced the Coach and Athletes Bill of Rights, a college sports reform bill. It would supersede the NCAA's self-monitoring and would create federal penalties for colleges that abuse student-athletes or recruit illegally. Many experts attribute the progress in college sports so far to be the result of the threat of federal action.

Auburn University initially denied Eric Ramsey's charges, although Coach Dye, who was forced out as athletic director after Ramsey made the allegations in the fall of 1991, admitted that Auburn had broken some NCAA rules in dealing with Ramsey. The NCAA is still conducting an investigation into the charges. Meanwhile, Ramsey paid a high cost for coming forward with his allegations. He is sure he was released from the Kansas City Chiefs because of it. He is certain that he can't find a place on any NFL team because Coach Dye pulled strings to have him ostracized. He and his wife are now going to school in the Washington area and trying to make a new life for themselves, away from the threats and harassment they say they received from Auburn boosters after Eric broke his silence.

Ramsey's revelations may make a difference at Auburn, but no number of Congressional Black Caucus hearings alone will be able to end the exploitation of African-American college athletes. That will not happen until colleges get serious about policing themselves and until African-American student-athletes and their parents demand an education with their competition. But even that may not be enough to reverse a system of exploitation that has become so ingrained. It may take an act of Congress to get coaches and administrators to treat athletes like whole people—or at least like college students.

WRITING ABOUT THE READING

5. Why does Mabry begin his essay with a narrative about the experience of Eric Ramsey?

6. What does the writer mean when he compares African American athletes to "sports commodities" and why does he use this choice of words?

7. Why does Mabry state that the conflict between sports and academics is the reason that many student-athletes do not finish their degree?

8. Why does the author state that the "sports industry has merged into the entertainment industry"?

9. Why does the writer often use the term "student-athlete" rather than just "athlete"?

10. Why do you think Mabry singles out African American athletes in particular?

11. Mabry offers several suggestions to correct the problem he has identified. Choose one of these recommendations and explain why you think this is a workable (or impractical) solution to this problem.

WRITING FROM YOUR OWN EXPERIENCE

Note: In these assignments, write about your own experience or use that of someone you know, read about, or saw in a film/TV show.

12. Choose a time when you felt a conflict between academics and sports (or other responsibilities such as family or work). Why was there a conflict and what were some of the consequences of this conflict?

13. Mabry believes that colleges are exploiting athletes, using them for their own ends. Think of a time when you felt you were "being used" by someone. Why did you feel this way and what were some of the results of this situation?

14. Mabry advocates college support programs that include study skills, social skills, and stress management. Suppose you had to develop a "safety net" program to make education more successful for minority students. What would the program include and why would you include these activities?

WRITING ABOUT RESEARCH

15. Choose a prominent African American athlete, business leader, entertainer, government leader, musician, scientist, or singer to investigate. Why was this person able to achieve success in his/her field? Consider:

   (a) Alvin Ailey (dancer)
   (b) Mohammed Ali (athlete)

(c) Marian Anderson (singer)

(d) Arthur Ashe (athlete)

(e) Louis "Satchmo" Armstrong (musician)

(f) Sammy Davis (entertainer)

(g) Duke Ellington (musician)

(h) Ella Fitzgerald (singer)

(i) Judith Jamison (dancer)

(j) Joe Louis (athlete)

(k) Michael Jordan (athlete)

(l) Jessye Norman (singer)

(m) Jesse Owens (athlete)

(n) Colin Powell (Secretary of State)

(o) Condoleezza Rice (government official)

(p) Jackie Robinson (athlete)

(q) Serena Williams (athlete)

(r) Venus Williams (athlete)

(s) Tiger Woods (athlete)

16. Why was the Negro League (baseball) established and what were some of the major events in its history?

17. Why was Jesse Owens's victory in the Olympics so important a milestone for African Americans?

COMPARING SELECTIONS: AFRICAN AMERICAN WRITERS

1. Suppose that you have been asked to choose either the essay by **Barbara Reynolds** or that by **Cornel West** to publish in your local college/city newspaper. You would like to choose the one that would appeal most to the readers of this paper. Explain which one you would choose and the reasons for your choice.

2. Compare the insights you have gained into the experience of enslaved peoples from the memoirs of **Harriet Ann Jacobs** and **Frederick Douglass.**

3. Both **Maya Angelou** and **Frederick Douglass** had to learn, as children, how to deal with the potential threat of the white society. Compare their narratives and explain what similarities and differences there are in the way they deal with racism.

4. Consider what **Nikki Giovanni** has to say about **Frederick Douglass** and the institution of slavery. How does Nikki Giovanni view Douglass and why does she view him this way?

5. Compare the discussion of African American music in the essays by **Ralph Ellison** and **Nikki Giovanni.**

6. Compare and contrast the views on assimilation of **Ralph Ellison** and **Henry Louis Gates, Jr.**

7. Compare **Maya Angelou's** fears for her brother to the fears for African American men expressed by **Barbara Reynolds.**

8. Evaluate **Nikki Giovanni's** behavior and reaction when stopped by a law enforcement officer in view of **Barbara Reynolds's** discussion of this issue.

9. Compare the recommendations made by **Marcus Mabry** to improve academics in light of **Claude M. Steele's** explanation of what factors are needed for success in college. Why do you think Mabry agrees with/differs from Steele's position?

10. Compare the discussion of the importance of self-esteem in the essays by **Claude M. Steele** and **Cornel West.**

11. Consider **Henry Louis Gates's** discussion of the duty to those who are less fortunate in view of **Cornel West's** redistribution of wealth proposal. What would be West's probable response to Gates?

12. Compare the importance of education in the lives of **Frederick Douglass** and **Henry Louis Gates, Jr.**

13. How and why were the lives of **Nikki Giovanni** and **Henry Louis Gates, Jr.,** influenced by the events of the 1960s?

SELECTED BIBLIOGRAPHY—AFRICAN AMERICAN WRITERS

Abel, Elizabeth, Barbara Christian, and Helene Moglen, eds. *Female Subjects in Black and White: Race, Psychoanalysis, Feminism.* Berkeley: Univ. of California Press, 1997.

Angelou, Maya. *Even the Stars Look Lonesome.* New York: Random House, 1997.

———. *Wouldn't Take Nothing for My Journey Now.* New York: Random House, 1993.

Auerbach, Susan, ed. *Encyclopedia of Multiculturalism.* New York: Marshall Cavendish, 1994.

Baldwin, James. *Collected Essays.* New York: The Library of America, 1998.

———. "The Fight: Patterson vs. Liston." *The Twentieth Century Treasury of Sports.* eds. Al Silverman and Brian Silverman. New York: Viking, 1992. 27–38.

———. "Stranger in the Village." In *The Oxford Book of Essays.* Ed. John Gross. New York: Oxford Univ. Press, 1991. 621–633.

Baraka, Amiri. *The Autobiography of Leroy Jones/Amiri Baraka.* New York: Freundlich Books, 1984.

Bell-Scott, Patricia. *Life Notes: Personal Writings by Contemporary Black Women.* New York: W.W. Norton & Co., 1994.

Berry, Mary Frances, and John W. Blassingame. *Long Memory: The Black Experience in America.* New York: Oxford Univ. Press, 1982.

Bibliographic Guide to Black Studies. Boston: Hall, 1975–current.

Callahan, John F., ed. *The Collected Essays of Ralph Ellison.* New York: The Modern Library, 1995.

Chapman, Abraham, ed. *Black Voices: An Anthology of Afro-American Literature.* New York: Mentor, 1968.

Davis, Angela Y. *Women, Race and Class.* New York: Vintage, 1983.

Davis, Charles T., and Henry Louis Gates, Jr., eds. *The Slave's Narrative.* Oxford: Oxford Univ. Press, 1985.

Delgado, Richard, and Jean Stefancic, eds. *Critical White Studies: Looking Behind the Mirror.* Philadelphia: Temple Univ. Press, 1997.

Donalson, Melvin, ed. *Cornerstones: An Anthology of African American Literature.* New York: St. Martin's Press, 1996.

Duneier, Mitchell. *Slim's Table: Race, Respectability, and Masculinity.* Chicago: Univ. of Chicago Press, 1992.

Dyer, Richard. *White.* London: Routledge, 1997.

Dyson, Michael Eric. *Reflecting Black: African-American Cultural Criticism.* Minneapolis: Univ. of Minnesota Press, 1993.

———. *Race Rules: Navigating the Color Line.* New York: Vintage/Random, 1997.

Early, Gerald, ed. *Lure and Loathing: Essays on Race, Identity, and the Ambivalence of Assimilation.* New York: Penguin Press, 1993.

Ellison, Ralph. "The Battle Royal." *The Twentieth Century Treasury of Sports.* eds. Al Silverman and Brian Silverman. New York: Viking, 1992. 167–176.

Ferguson, Robert. *Representing Race: Ideology, Identity and the Media.* London: Arnold, 1998.

Gates, Henry Louis, Jr. *Loose Canons: Notes on the Culture Wars.* New York: Oxford Univ. Press, 1992.

———. *Thirteen Ways of Looking at a Black Man.* New York: Random House, 1997.

Gates, Henry Louis, Jr., and Nellie Y. McKay, eds. *The Norton Anthology of African American Literature.* New York: W.W. Norton & Co., 1997.

Giovanni, Nikki. *Racism 101.* New York: William Morrow and Co., Inc., 1994.

Golden, Marita, and Susan Richards Shreve, eds. *Skin Deep: Black Women and White Women Write About Race.* New York: Doubleday, 1995.

Haley, Alex. *The Autobiography of Malcolm X.* New York: Ballantine Books, 1965.

Hooks, Bell. *Ain't I a Woman: Black Women and Feminism.* Boston: South End, 1981.

———. *Talking Back: Thinking Feminist, Thinking Black.* Boston: South End, 1989.

Hutchinson, Earl Ofari. *The Assassination of the Black Male Image.* New York: Simon and Schuster, 1994.

Ignatiev, Noel, and John Garvey, eds. *Race Traitor.* New York: Routledge, 1996.

Index to Black Periodicals. Boston: Hall, 1950.

Johnson, Charles. *Being & Race: Black Writing Since 1970.* Bloomington: Indiana Univ. Press, 1988.

Jordan, Casper. *A Bibliographic Guide to African-American Women Writers.* Westport: Greenwood, 1993.

Kolko, Beth E., Lisa Nakamura, and Gilbert B. Rodman, eds. *Race in Cyberspace.* New York: Routledge, 2000.

Kornblum, William. *Sociology in a Changing World.* 4th ed. Fort Worth: Harcourt Brace, 1997.

Lipsitz, George. *The Possessive Investment in Whiteness: How White People Profit from Identity Politics.* Philadelphia: Temple Univ. Press, 1998.

Lubiano, Wahgneema, ed. *The House That Race Built: Black Americans, U.S. Terrain.* New York: Pantheon, 1997.

Mabry, Marcus. *White Bucks and Black-Eyed Peas: Coming of Age Black in White America.* New York: Scribner, 1995.

Magill, Frank. *Masterpieces of African-American Literature.* New York: HarperCollins, 1992.

Majors, Richard, and Janet Mancini Billson. *Cool Pose: The Dilemmas of Black Manhood in America.* New York: Simon and Schuster, 1992.

Marger, Martin N. *Race and Ethnic Relations: American and Global Perspectives.* Belmont, CA: Wadsworth Pub. Co., 1997.

Mosley, Walter, Manthia Diawara, Clyde Taylor, and Regina Austin. *Black Genius: African American Solutions to African American Problems.* New York: W.W. Norton & Co., 1999.

Olson, James S. *The Ethnic Dimension in American History.* 2nd ed. New York: St. Martin's Press, 1994.

Omi, Michael, and Howard Winant. *Racial Formation in the United States: From the 1960s to the 1990s.* 2nd ed. New York: Routledge, 1994.

Peavey, Charles. *Afro-American Literature and Culture Since World War II: A Guide to Information Sources.* Detroit: Gale, 1979.

Ploski, Harry. *Reference Library of Black America.* 5 Vols. Detroit: Gale, 1990.

Roediger, David R., ed. *Black on White: Black Writers on What It Means to Be White.* New York: Schocken, 1998.

Rothenberg, Paula S. *Race, Class, and Gender in the United States.* New York: St. Martin's Press, 1998.

Rywell, Martin. *Afro-American Encyclopedia.* 10 Vols. North Miami: Educational Book Pub., 1974.

Salem, Dorothy. *African American Women: A Biographical Dictionary.* New York: Garland, 1993.

Schneider, Bart, ed. *Race: An Anthology in the First Person.* New York: Crown, 1997.

The State of Black America 1999. The National Urban League.

Walker, Alice. *In Search of Our Mothers' Gardens.* San Diego: Harcourt Brace Jovanovich, 1983.

West, Cornel. *Keeping Faith: Philosophy and Race in America*. New York: Routledge, 1993.

———. *Race Matters*. Boston: Beacon Press, 1993.

Williams, Michael. *The African American Encyclopedia*. 6 Vols. New York: Marshall Cavendish, 1993.

SELECTED INTERNET RESOURCES—AFRICAN AMERICAN WRITERS

Note: Unless otherwise noted, all URL addresses listed begin with http://www.

African Americans in the Sciences.
<princeton.edu/~mcbrown/display/faces.html/>

African and African American Collections at University of California–Berkeley. <lib.berkeley.edu/ Collections/Africana/>

African American Census Data. <thuban.com/census/index.html>

African Studies Center: University of Pennsylvania. <sas.upenn.edu/ African_Studies/AS.html.>

American Studies: Black History and Literature. "Writing Black" <keele.ac.uk/ depts/as/ Literature/amlit.black.html>

Black Studies Library Website: Ohio State University. <lib.ohio-state.edu/ OSU_profile/ >bslweb/lib.html>

Center for African American Studies at UCLA. <sscnet.ucla.edu/caas/>

Ethnic Studies at the University of Southern California. <usc.edu/isd/archives/ ethnicstudies>

Everythingblack.com.

Internet Resources for Students of Afro-American History and Culture—Rutgers University. <libraries.rutgers.edu/rulib/socsci/hist/afrores.html>

University of Georgia Institute for African American Studies. <uga.edu/~iaas>

The University of Pittsburgh African American Collection. <library.pitt.edu/libraries/ african-american/>

U.S. Census Bureau. <census.gov>

Part 2

Hispanic American Writers

INTRODUCTION

Hispanic Americans, the fastest growing ethnic group in the United States, soon will surpass the number of African Americans to become the largest minority group. The term *Hispanics* (or "Latinos") includes both those of Hispanic descent born in the United States and those who were foreign-born but immigrated to this country. All Hispanic Americans share a heritage that is a mixture of Spanish, Native American, and African American cultures. Despite their common heritage, however, the various Hispanic American subgroups differ in the reasons they came to the United States, their length of time in this country, and their current socioeconomic status. Despite the collective label "Hispanics," there are wide differences between and within subgroups.

The ten authors in this part (from Mexican American, Puerto Rican American, and Cuban American subgroups) represent the wide diversity of Hispanic positions on social, economic, and political issues. Their controversial, often antagonistic, views will show the reader some of the many divisions within the group labeled "Hispanic." Because these writers are arranged in order of date of birth, the reader can compare the views of writers from the same generation but from different subgroups of the Hispanic population.

MEXICAN AMERICANS

During the early nineteenth century, thousands of citizens of the United States moved into the Southwest, then part of Mexico, where they came into conflict with the earlier settlers. In the 1840s, conflict broke out between the two countries. After Mexico was defeated in the War of 1848, its lands (present-day California, Arizona, New Mexico,

Nevada, Utah, Colorado, and Texas) became part of the United States. The small population of original Mexican Americans (often designated as "Spanish Americans" or "Latin Americans") now found themselves to be a conquered, often impoverished, minority in their former lands. **Joseph Torres**, a writer representative of this group, points out that the Spanish names of many towns, especially in the Southwest, are a reminder of this early Hispanic heritage.

Since the mid-nineteenth century, the vast majority of Mexican Americans have been voluntary immigrants, employed in the United States whenever there was a demand for cheap labor. From the 1940s through the mid-1960s, the "bracero" program allowed Mexicans to work as temporary, legal farmworkers. After the program ended, poor Mexican workers, with or without visas, continued to seek employment in the United States. Thus, as **Richard Rodriguez** explains, the current Mexican American population is a mixture of those who are both legally and illegally in the States. Today, the Mexican Americans (also called "Chicanos") comprise more than half of the Hispanic ethnic group. Five writers, **Sandra Cisneros, Richard Rodriguez, Luis Rodriguez, Gary Soto**, and **Christine Granados**, represent the Mexican American subgroup.

PUERTO RICAN AMERICANS

Puerto Rican Americans, who form the second largest Hispanic subgroup are not immigrants but citizens of the United States. Because they may travel freely to and from the mainland, many working-class Puerto Rican Americans have migrated to the Northeast to find employment. **Jesus Colon** represents this group as he writes about his experiences as a worker in New York. Another Puerto Rican American writer, **Judith Ortiz Cofer**, focuses on the common assumptions about Hispanic women.

CUBAN AMERICANS

Following the Spanish American War, small groups of Cubans, often political exiles, settled in Florida and New York. After 1959, a large group of the educated and affluent middle class fled to the United States because of Fidel Castro's takeover of the Cuban government. The United States enthusiastically welcomed these political refugees, who hoped to overthrow Castro and return to Cuba. The Cuban American population grew after a second wave of immigration took place in

1980, and Cuban Americans now comprise about 5 percent of the Hispanic group. **Pablo Medina** describes the culture shock faced by Cuban Americans upon their arrival, while **Gustavo Perez Firmat** contemplates the assimilation of his children into the dominant culture.

OTHER HISPANICS

The diversity of today's Hispanic population has been further increased by immigration from Central and South America and the Caribbean. These immigrants (including Dominicans, Nicaraguans, Colombians, and Guatemalans) continue to come to the United States because of poor economic conditions and/or political instability at home.

IMPORTANT MILESTONES

1848	After its defeat in the War of 1848, Mexico was forced to sell its land (present-day California, Arizona, New Mexico, Nevada, Utah, and Colorado) and to recognize Texas as a U.S. state.
1898	Following the Spanish American War, Puerto Rico became a territory of the United States.
1917	Puerto Ricans were granted the status of U.S. citizens.
1942	U.S. government established a "bracero" program to allow for legal, temporary farmworkers. Following the end of this program in the 1960s, undocumented Mexican immigrants continued to enter the United States illegally.
1959	Following Fidel Castro's takeover of the government of Cuba, thousands of Cubans fled to the United States.
1961	**The Bay of Pigs**: The U.S. government supported an attempt by exiles to invade Cuba. The attempt failed, and the United States placed a trade embargo on Cuba.
1960s	Cesar Chavez organized the United Farm Workers, which pressed for better wages and working conditions.
1965	*Immigration and Nationality Act*: This act ended ethnic quotas based on national origins and limited

immigration from the Western Hemisphere to 120,000 per year.

1974   The Equal Educational Opportunity Act made bilingual education available to Hispanic students.

1976   An amendment to the 1965 Immigration and Nationality Act limited immigrants from Mexico to 20,000 per year.

1980   **The Mariel Boatlift**: A second wave of migration came to the United States from Cuba.

1986   *Immigration Reform and Control Act*: This act imposed several penalties on businesses that employed undocumented workers. It also gave residency status to undocumented workers who had lived continuously in the United States since 1982.

Sketches from *A Puerto Rican in New York*

"Hiawatha into Spanish"; "Easy Job, Good Wages"; "I Heard a Man Crying"; "Kipling and I"; "A Hero in the Junk Truck"; and "Little Things Are Big."

JESUS COLON

Jesus Colon *(1901–1974), writer and political activist, came to the United States at the age of 16. In New York, he first supported himself as a laborer while learning English.* Colon *then became a writer for several New York newspapers, including* El Machete Criollo, El Nuevo Mundo, The Daily Worker, *and* Liberation. *Colon also founded and operated a small publishing house, Hispanic Publishers (Editorial Hispanica), and was active in the movement for Puerto Rican independence.*

As a Spanish-speaking immigrant of Afro-Puerto Rican heritage, Colon faced discrimination because of his language, his race, and his working-class status. His sketches of immigrant life, A Puerto Rican in New York, *were originally published in 1961. In these sketches, Colon often uses wit and humor to write about serious issues of discrimination. One of the first Puerto Rican immigrants to write in English, Colon became an inspiration to many later "Nuyorican" writers.*

PREPARING TO READ

1. Why is a person who has goals (or "dreams") often more successful than a person without such dreams or goals?
2. Compare the "dreams" of new immigrants to those individuals whose families have been in the United States for more than one generation. Why are there some similarities and differences in the "dreams" of the two groups?
3. Why is a person's work important in developing that person's self-concept or sense of identity?

4. Why is it that new immigrants (even those with some education and training) often work at "menial" jobs?

SKETCHES FROM A PUERTO RICAN IN NEW YORK

Hiawatha into Spanish

The old *New York World* was a great paper. I bought it mainly for the Heywood Broun column "It Seems To Me," and for the pages and pages of Help Wanted Ads. I got many a "good" porter job through these Help Wanted pages of the *New York World*. Once, I also got myself a job as a translator from these same pages.

Those were the days of the silent films. A film agency somewhere in the Times Square area was asking for a person who could translate the explanatory material like "One Year Later," into Spanish, so that the films could be used in Latin America. Half a penny a word was to be paid. The translator was to work in his own home and all transactions were to be done through the mail. The agency gave a post office box number to which you were supposed to write.

I wrote. The agency mailed me the material to be translated for one short film. I returned the completed translation. Then they sent me a small check, and more work. It seems that they were satisfied.

Time passed. My old Oliver typewriting machine continued to grind translations of inspirational thoughts such as: "The morning after," "One week after," "Five years after." Sometimes a description or historical paragraph such as an introduction to a striking panorama or a scene helped to break the monotony of the hackneyed phrase and the routine short dialogue.

During the early twenties, the episode or chapter of a serial was a standard feature accompanying the main picture in a movie house. At the end of the episode the hero or more often the heroine was left hanging by two fingers from the edge of a cliff or surrounded by half a dozen lions in the middle of an African jungle. The idea was to excite enough curiosity for you to return next week to see what surely appeared, from all logical deduction, like certain death for the hero or heroine. But—what do you know! She or he was miraculously saved from a horrible ending by one of the thousand props that the director always had ready to extract from his shirt sleeve and the serial went on and on for months. Today, you can only see these serials chapter by chapter every week in cheapest of the movie houses or on the most idiotic of the TV programs.

To me, these serials were a gold mine. I was the first to wish the hero eternal life—the longer the serials, the more money I could earn.

One morning I received a long poem that was supposed to be the life of a young American Indian. It was to be used in one of those nature pictures full of rushing rivers, whispering pine trees, bounding deer and flocks of birds suddenly rising out of the thick foliage frightened by the unexpected appearance of "man." The poem was long. The name of the poem was "Hiawatha" by Henry Wadsworth Longfellow. Well, at last I got something worth translating! For a few days I concentrated on making a comparative study of the English and Spanish meter, poetic accent, rhyme and rhythm, before I actually tackled the task of translating the poem itself. It was work. It was fun. Some additional explanation in prose helped in giving clarity and unity to the many natural scenes in the film. The poem itself was broken into sections and these were inserted among the panoramic sequences. When I finished the translation I felt I had done a good job of it.

Hiawatha was sent to the film agency. A few days later I received a complimentary letter with a check. The letter also invited me to come to the office on a certain date. I was being offered steady employment at the agency at a weekly salary.

I got up very early the day of the appointment. I took a great deal of time washing, dressing and combing my hair so that I would look my best. I wore my Sunday suit. The office took up about half an entire floor, way up in a tall building. I asked for the man who had signed the letter. Yes, he was in.

The minute I told him who I was and showed him the letter he himself had signed offering me steady work as a translator, he assumed a cold and impersonal attitude. He made it short and to the point. "Yes, I wrote that letter. I invited you to come to translate for us here at the office." And, pointing to the other side of the room he added "That was to be your desk and typewriter. But I thought you were white."

Then and there that day in the early twenties, I added one more episode to the maturing serial of my life.

Easy Job, Good Wages

This happened early in 1919. We were both out of work, my brother and I. He got up earlier to look for a job. When I woke up, he was already gone. So I dressed, went out and bought a copy of the *New York World* and turned its pages until I got to the "Help Wanted Unskilled" section of the paper. After much reading and re-reading the same columns, my attention was held by a small advertisement. It read: "Easy job. Good wages. No experience necessary." This was followed by a number and street on the west side of lower Manhattan. It sounded like the job I was looking for. Easy job. Good wages. Those four words revolved in my brain as I was travelling toward the address indicated in the advertisement. Easy job. Good wages. Easy job. Good wages. Easy . . .

The place consisted of a small front office and a large loft on the floor of which I noticed a series of large galvanized tubs half filled with water out of which I noticed protruding the necks of many bottles of various sizes and shapes. Around these tubs there were a number of workers, male and female, sitting on small wooden benches. All had their hands in the water of the tub, the left hand holding a bottle and with the thumb nail of the right hand scratching the labels.

The foreman found a vacant stool for me around one of the tubs of water. I asked why a penknife or a small safety razor could not be used instead of the thumb nail to take off the old labels from the bottles. I was expertly informed that knives or razors would scratch the glass thus depreciating the value of the bottles when they were to be sold.

I sat down and started to use my thumb nail on one bottle. The water had somewhat softened the transparent mucilage used to attach the label to the bottle. But the softening did not work out uniformly somehow. There were always pieces of label that for some obscure reason remained affixed to the bottles. It was on those pieces of labels tenaciously fastened to the bottles that my right hand thumb nail had to work overtime. As the minutes passed I noticed that the coldness of the water started to pass from my hand to my body giving me intermittent body shivers that I tried to conceal with the greatest of effort from those sitting beside me. My hands became deadly clean and tiny little wrinkles started to show especially at the tip of my fingers. Sometimes I stopped a few seconds from scratching the bottles, to open and close my fists in rapid movements in order to bring blood to my hands. But almost as soon as I placed them in the water they became deathly pale again.

But these were minor details compared with what was happening to the thumb of my right hand. From a delicate, boyish thumb, it was growing by the minute into a full blown tomato colored finger. It was the only part of my right hand remaining blood red. I started to look at the workers' thumbs. I noticed that these particular fingers on their right hands were unusually developed with a thick layer of corn-like surface at the top of their right thumb. The nails on their thumbs looked coarser and smaller than on the other fingers—thumb and nail having become one and the same thing—a primitive unnatural human instrument especially developed to detach hard pieces of labels from wet bottles immersed in galvanized tubs.

After a couple of hours I had a feeling that my thumb nail was going to leave my finger and jump into the cold water in the tub. A numb pain imperceptibly began to be felt coming from my right thumb. Then I began to feel such pain as if coming from a finger bigger than all of my body.

After three hours of this I decided to quit fast. I told the foreman so, showing him my swollen finger. He figured I had earned 69 cents at 23 cents an hour.

Early in the evening I met my brother in our furnished room. He started to exchange experiences of our job hunting for the day. "You know what?" my brother started, "early in the morning I went to work where they take labels off old bottles—with your right hand thumb nail . . . Somewhere on the west side of lower Manhattan. I only stayed a couple of hours. 'Easy job . . . Good wages' . . . they said. The person who wrote that ad must have had a great sense of humor." And we both had a hearty laugh that evening when I told my brother that I also went to work at the same place later in the day.

Now when I see ads reading, "Easy job. Good wages," I just smile an ancient, tired, knowing smile.

I Heard A Man Crying

Around 1918 I was living in a rooming house on Atlantic Avenue in Brooklyn. I was working then as a scaler. Long distances, long hours and the dirtiest kind of work you could imagine.

As the ships came in, a scaling crew moved in to clean the ship from top to bottom. Cleaning was done especially at the bottom, underneath the machine room, and inside and around the furnaces.

If the ship was an oil tanker, you had to go down to the bottom of that tank ship after the oil was pumped off and collect the oil that the pump was unable to swallow, with a small tin shovel and pail. The pail was placed on a hook at the end of a rope and hoisted up by those working on deck. Pay was better "down below" than on deck, so I always chose to work inside the tanker. As the job was about finished we were supposed to "paint" the inside of the oil tank with Portland cement by just throwing cement at the inside walls of the oil-moist tank. Imagine twenty or twenty-five men throwing cement at the oily walls of an enclosed tank!

When we came out, our faces, eyes, brows and hair looked old and gray. We looked like the grandfathers of our own selves. Some winters when the snow and ice covered the river solidly, the temperature down below at the bottom of the oil tank was below zero. Good thing that we were given rubber boots which fastened at the top of our thighs and rubber pants, jackets and hats that made us look like old seafarers.

Everywhere we went at the bottom of that tank, we were followed by a long electrical wire at the end of which there were three or four electric bulbs protected from breakage by a wire net. Sometimes when we gave the order to hoist the pail filled with oil and we kept looking up at that hole through which a ray of sun kept mocking at us down below, the edge of the pail might abruptly hit the edge of the hole way up there and a splash of ice cold oil would come spattering down and smear your face and neck. Sometimes the oil used to run down your back until it reached the very tip of your spine . . . and more. So, no matter how you scrubbed yourself, some of the oil always remained all over your body from your head to your toes. When I took the old crosstown trolley car with its spongy yellow straw seats and sat in one of them on my way home, I usually left a mark of black moist oil like a great heart parted right down the middle.

It was way into the evening when I came in from my scaling job. I was very tired. The room was very cold, I chose to get into bed with all my clothes on instead of going through the task of starting a fire in the dead coal stove in the middle of the room. (Why is it so difficult for tropical people to start a fire in a hard coal stove?)

As if coming from way out in space through the cracks in my window and from the crevices dividing the door and the floor I heard a very low moaning sound. It went up and down like a wave. Then there was silence for a minute or two and then it started all over again in a repressed way as if the person from whom the crying, moaning sound came did not want to be heard by anybody. Then as if the pain or emotion could not be held back anymore a piercing cry full of self-pity and desperation came distinctly to my ears. At last I could trace clearly from whence it came. It was from another room on the same floor. I knocked at the door of the room. After a short pause, the door was opened by a man who then turned and sat himself on a narrow bed which filled the room.

He covered his face with his hands and then let his crying run fully. I could see that the man was robust, built strong as a bull. He was possibly accustomed to heavy work out of doors. It was sad, yes, tragic, to listen to such a specimen of man crying. So clumsily and innocently strong was he.

In between the minutes that he could control his emotions and his natural shyness, he told me of missing a boat where he was working as a coal passer. The boat belonged to a Spanish shipping company. He himself was Spanish. A story of the ignorance of the language, of fear of the immigration laws, of shyness and of pride, not to beg, not to ask for anything, followed.

The man had not eaten since . . . he didn't remember how many days. He was actually starving, gradually dying of hunger.

Have you ever heard a man crying? A young strong man crying? Crying of hunger in the midst of what is supposed to be the greatest and richest city in the world? It is the saddest, most tragic sight you could ever imagine.

At that hour we left the rooming house and went to the nearest restaurant. He ate as if he had never eaten before in his life.

Next day I took him to an old iron junk yard in which they were asking for young strong men. The job was to break old iron parts of machinery with a sledge hammer. My new Spanish friend wielded the big sledge hammer with the gracefulness and ease of a young girl skipping a thin rope on the sidewalk.

For the first few days I managed to bring him to his place of work. Then he would wait for me in the evening at the wide door of the junk yard until he learned how to take the trolley car that would take him to and from the rooming house where we were living.

I moved. I don't remember the last time I saw that burly, strong young Spaniard.

But I will never forget as long as I live, his deep anguished crying of hunger that night—long, long ago.

Kipling and I

Sometimes I pass Debevoise Place at the corner of Willoughby Street . . . I look at the old wooden house, gray and ancient, the house where I used to live some forty years ago . . .

My room was on the second floor at the corner. On hot summer nights I would sit at the window reading by the electric light from the street lamp which was almost at a level with the window sill.

It was nice to come home late during the winter, look for some scrap of old newspaper, some bits of wood and a few chunks of coal and start a sparkling fire in the chunky fourlegged coal stove. I would be rewarded with an intimate warmth as little by little the pygmy stove became alive puffing out its sides, hot and red, like the crimson cheeks of a Santa Claus.

My few books were in a soap box nailed to the wall. But my most prized possession in those days was a poem I had bought in a five and ten cent store on Fulton Street. (I wonder what has become of these poems, maxims and sayings of wise men that they used to sell at the five and ten cent stores?) The poem was printed on gold paper and mounted in a gilded frame ready to be hung in a conspicuous place in the house. I bought one of those fancy silken picture cords finishing in a rosette to match the color of the frame.

I was seventeen. This poem to me then seemed to summarize the wisdom of all the sages that ever lived in one poetical nutshell. It was what I was looking for, something to guide myself by, a way of life, a compendium of the wise, the true and the beautiful. All I had to do was to live according to the counsel of the poem and follow its instructions and I would be a perfect man—the useful, the good, the true human being. I was very happy that day, forty years ago.

The poem had to have the most prominent place in the room. Where could I hang it? I decided that the best place for the poem was on the wall right by the entrance to the room. No one coming in and out would miss it. Perhaps someone would be interested enough to read it and drink the profound waters of its message . . .

Every morning as I prepared to leave, I stood in front of the poem and read it over and over again, sometimes half a dozen times. I let the sonorous music of the verse carry me away. I brought with me a handwritten copy as I stepped out every morning looking for work, repeating verses and stanzas from memory until the whole poem came to be part of me. Other days my lips kept repeating a single verse of the poem at intervals throughout the day.

In the subways I loved to compete with the shrill noises of the many wheels below by chanting the lines of the poem. People stared at me moving my lips as though I were in a trance. I looked back with pity. They were not so fortunate as I who had as a guide to direct my life a great poem to make me wise, useful and happy.

And I chanted:

If you can keep your head when all about you
Are losing theirs and blaming it on you . . .

If you can wait and not be tired by waiting
Or being hated don't give way to hating . . .

If you can make one heap of all your winnings
And risk it on a turn of pitch and toss . . .
And lose and start again at your beginnings . . .

"If," by Kipling, was the poem. At seventeen, my evening prayer and my first morning thought. I repeated it every day with the resolution to live up to the very last line of that poem.

I would visit the government employment office on Jay Street. The conversations among the Puerto Ricans on the large wooden benches in the employment office were always on the same subject. How to find a decent place to live. How they would not rent to Negroes or Puerto Ricans. How Negroes and Puerto Ricans were given the pink slips first at work.

From the employment office I would call door to door at the

piers, factories and storage houses in the streets under the Brooklyn and Manhattan Bridges. "Sorry, nothing today." It seemed to me that that "today" was a continuation and combination of all the yesterdays, todays and tomorrows.

From the factories I would go to the restaurants looking for a job as a porter or dishwasher. At least I would eat and be warm in a kitchen.

"Sorry". . . "Sorry". . .

Sometimes I was hired at ten dollars a week, ten hours a day including Sundays and holidays. One day off during the week. My work was that of three men: dishwasher, porter, busboy. And to clear the sidewalk of snow and slush "when you have nothing else to do." I was to be appropriately humble and grateful not only to the owner but to everybody else in the place.

If I rebelled at insults or at a pointed innuendo or just the inhuman amount of work, I was unceremoniously thrown out and told to come "next week for your pay." "Next Week" meant weeks of calling for the paltry dollars owed me. The owners relished this "next week."

I clung to my poem as to a faith. Like a potent amulet, my precious poem was clenched in the fist of my right hand inside my second hand overcoat. Again and again I declaimed aloud a few precious lines when discouragement and disillusionment threatened to overwhelm me.

If you can force your heart and nerve and sinew
To serve your turn long after you are gone . . .

The weeks of unemployment and hard knocks turned into months. I continued to find two or three days of work here and there. And I continued to be thrown out when I rebelled at the ill treatment, overwork and insults. I kept pounding the streets looking for a place where they would treat me half decently, where my devotion to work and faith in Kipling's poem would be appreciated. I remember the worn out shoes I bought in a secondhand store on Myrtle Avenue at the corner of Adams Street. The round holes in the soles that I tried to cover with pieces of carton were no match for the frigid knives of the unrelenting snow.

One night I returned late after a long day of looking for work. I was hungry. My room was dark and cold. I wanted to warm my numb body. I lit a match and began looking for some scraps of wood and a piece of paper to start a fire. I searched all over the floor. No wood, no paper. As I stood up, the glimmering flicker of the dying match was reflected in the glass surface of the framed poem. I unhooked the poem from the wall. I reflected for a minute, a minute that felt like an eternity. I took the frame apart, placing the square glass upon the small table. I tore the gold paper on which the poem was printed, threw its pieces inside the stove and placing the small bits of wood from the frame on top of the paper I lit it adding soft and hard coal as the fire began to gain strength and brightness.

I watched how the lines of the poem withered into ashes inside the small stove.

A Hero in the Junk Truck

How many times have we read boastful statements from high educational leaders in our big newspapers that while other countries ignore the history and culture of the United States, our educational system does instruct our children in the history and traditions of other countries.

As far as instruction in the most elementary knowledge of Latin America is concerned, we are forced to state that what our children receive is a hodgepodge of romantic generalities and chauvinistic declarations spread further and wider by Hollywood movies.

We do not have to emphasize that the people are not to blame.

Blame rests on those persons and reactionary forces that represent and defend the interests of finance capital in education.

Last summer my wife and I had an experience that could be presented as proof of our assertion.

We were passing by, on bus No. 37, my wife and I.

"Look, Jesus, look!" said my wife pointing excitedly to a junk truck in front of the building that was being torn down. A truck full of the accumulated debris of many years was parked with its rear to the sidewalk, littered with pieces of brick and powdered cement.

Atop the driver's cabin of the truck and protruding like a spangled banner, was a huge framed picture of a standing figure. Upon his breast was a double line of medals and decorations.

"Did you notice who the man was in that framed picture?" my wife asked insistently as the bus turned the corner of Adams and Fulton Street.

"Who," I answered absent mindedly.

"Bolivar," my wife shouted.

"Who did you say he was?" I inquired as if unduly awakened from a daze.

"Bolivar, Bolivar," my wife repeated excitedly and then she added, "and to think that he is being thrown out into a junk truck," she stammered in a breaking voice.

We got out of the bus in a hurry. Walked to where the truck was about to depart with the dead waste of fragments of a thousand things. The driver caught us staring at the picture.

"What do you want?" he shouted to us in a shrill voice above the noise of the acetylene torch and the electric hammers.

"You know who he is," I cried back pointing at the picture tied atop the cabin of the driver's truck like Joan of Arc tied to the flaming stake.

"I don't know and I don't care," the driver counter-blasted in a still higher pitch of voice. But I noticed that there was no enmity in the tone of his voice, though loud and ear-drum breaking.

"He is like George Washington to a score of Latin American countries. He is . . ."

"You want it?" he interrupted in a more softened voice.

"Of course!" my wife answered for both of us, just about jumping with glee.

As the man was unroping Bolivar from atop the truck cabin, the usual group of passersby started clustering around and encircling us—the truck driver, my wife, myself and Bolivar's painting standing erect and magnificent in the middle of us all.

"Who is he, who is he?" came the question of the inquiring voices from everywhere. The crowd was huddled on top of us, as football players ring themselves together bending from their trunks down when they are making a decision before the next play. "Who is he, I mean, the man in the picture?" they continued to ask.

Nobody knew. Nobody seemed to care really. The question was asked more out of curiosity than real interest. The ones over on the third line of the circle of people craned their necks over the ones on the second and the first lines upping themselves on their toes in order to be able to take a passing glance at the picture. "He is not American, is he?" someone inquired from the crowd.

My wife finally answered them with a tinge of pride in her voice. "He is Simon Bolivar, the liberator of Latin America."

Curiosity fulfilled, everybody was on his way again. Only my wife, myself and Bolivar remained.

Well, what to do next. It was obvious that the bus driver would not allow us in the bus with such a large framed painting going back home. Fortunately we have a very good American friend living in the Borough Hall neighborhood.

"Let us take him to John's place until we find a person with a car to take Bolivar to our home," I said. My wife agreed.

We opened the door of John's apartment.

"I see that you are coming with very distinguished company today: 'Bolivar,' " he said, simply and casually as if he had known it all his life.

John took some cleaning fluid and a soft rag and went over the whole frame in a loving and very tender manner.

We heard a knock at the door. In came a tall and very distinguished looking man dressed in black, a blend of Lincoln and Emerson in his personality. "He is a real representative of progressive America," John whispered to us. The Reverend spoke quietly and serenely. Looking at the picture he said just one word:

"Bolivar!"

And we all felt very happy.

Little Things Are Big

It was very late at night on the eve of Memorial Day. She came into the subway at the 34th Street Pennsylvania Station. I am still trying to remember how she managed to push herself in with a baby on her right arm, a valise in her left hand and two children, a boy and girl about three and five years old, trailing after her. She was a nice looking white lady in her early twenties.

At Nevins Street, Brooklyn, we saw her preparing to get off at the next station—Atlantic Avenue—which happened to be the place where I too had to get off. Just as it was a problem for her to get on, it was going to be a problem for her to get off the subway with two small children to be taken care of, a baby on her right arm and a medium sized valise in her left hand.

And there I was, also preparing to get off at Atlantic Avenue, with no bundles to take care of—not even the customary book under my arm without which I feel that I am not completely dressed.

As the train was entering the Atlantic Avenue station, some white man stood up from his seat and helped her out, placing the children on the long, deserted platform. There were only two adult persons on the long platform some time after midnight on the eve of last Memorial Day.

I could perceive the steep, long concrete stairs going down to the Long Island Railroad or into the street. Should I offer my help as the American white man did at the subway door placing the two children outside the subway car? Should I take care of the girl and the boy, take them by their hands until they reached the end of the steep long concrete stairs of the Atlantic Avenue station?

Courtesy is a characteristic of the Puerto Rican. And here I was— a Puerto Rican—hours past midnight, a valise, two white children and a white lady with a baby on her arm palpably needing somebody to help her at least until she descended the long concrete stairs.

But how could I, a Negro and a Puerto Rican approach this white lady who very likely might have preconceived prejudices against Negroes and everybody with foreign accents, in a deserted subway station very late at night?

What would she say? What would be the first reaction of this white American woman, perhaps coming from a small town with a valise, two children and a baby on her right arm? Would she say: Yes, of course, you may help me. Or would she think that I was just trying to get too familiar? Or would she think worse than that perhaps? What would I do if she let out a scream as I went toward her to offer my help?

Was I misjudging her? So many slanders are written every day in the daily press against the Negroes and Puerto Ricans. I hesitated for a long, long minute. The ancestral manners that the most illiterate Puerto Rican passes on from father to son were struggling inside me. Here was I, way past midnight, face to face with a situation that could very well explode into an outburst of prejudices and chauvinistic conditioning of the "divide and rule" policy of present day society.

It was a long minute. I passed on by her as if I saw nothing. As if I was insensitive to her need. Like a rude animal walking on two legs, I just moved on half running by the long subway platform leaving the children and the valise and her with the baby on her arm. I took the steps of the long concrete stairs in twos until I reached the street above and the cold air slapped my warm face.

This is what racism and prejudice and chauvinism and official artificial divisions can do to people and to a nation!

Perhaps the lady was not prejudiced after all. Or not prejudiced enough to scream at the coming of a Negro toward her in a solitary subway station a few hours past midnight.

If you were not that prejudiced, I failed you, dear lady. I know that there is a chance in a million that you will read these lines. I am willing to take that millionth chance. If you were not that prejudiced, I failed you, lady, I failed you, children. I failed myself to myself.

I buried my courtesy early on Memorial Day morning. But here is a promise that I make to myself here and now; if I am ever faced with an occasion like that again, I am going to offer my help regardless of how the offer is going to be received.

Then I will have my courtesy with me again.

WRITING ABOUT THE READING

5. Choose one of Colon's sketches in which he describes one of his experiences in New York. How and why was Colon changed by his experience as an immigrant?

6. Choose two of the sketches to compare. Why are these sketches similar or different in content, organization/structure, and/or tone?

7. Writers sometimes use the technique of irony, language involving discrepancy or incongruity, to suggest the complex nature of experience. Why do you think that the word "ironic" is used appropriately in discussing these sketches?

8. As a social critic, Colon had a serious intention in writing these sketches. What do you think was Colon's purpose and why do you think that these essays are effective (or not effective) in achieving his purpose?

WRITING FROM YOUR OWN EXPERIENCE

Note: In these assignments, write about your own experience or use that of someone you know, read about, or saw in a film/TV show.

9. Consider one of your own "dreams" for the future. After considering some of the steps you must take to achieve this goal, why would you argue that your dreams are attainable?

10. Colon describes the hardships of his early life as a poor immigrant trying to make a living in a big city. Recall a time when you had a difficult paid or unpaid work experience. Why was this work so difficult and what did you learn from this experience?

11. Has someone ever interviewed you for a job, a college application, a car loan, or a similar experience? What was the interview like and what was the outcome of this experience?

12. Colon describes a portrait of Bolivar that means a great deal to him. Choose one possession (such as a stuffed animal or an old baseball glove) to which you have a strong emotional attachment. Explain the reasons why this object means so much to you.

WRITING ABOUT RESEARCH

13. In his lifetime, Colon actively supported the Puerto Rican independence movement. Why do some Puerto Rican Americans today desire independence from the United States?

14. Puerto Ricans today do not agree about Puerto Rico becoming a state. What are some of the issues involved with statehood for Puerto Rico?

15. Choose an image of Hispanic Americans used in advertising (such as the Taco Bell dog, the Frito Bandito, or Chiquita Banana). Why do many people think that this ad sends an unfavorable message about Hispanics?

16. Choose a Hispanic American (such as a local or national figure) who has achieved success in a field such as education, government, or business. Why was this person successful? Some people to consider include:

   (a) Raul Castro, Governor of Arizona (1975)

   (b) Dr. Lauro F. Cavazos, Secretary of Education (1988)

   (c) Henry G. Cisneros (former Secretary of Housing and Urban Development)

   (d) Lincoln Diaz-Balart (Florida Congressman)

   (e) Jaime Escalante (teacher)

   (f) Luis V. Gutierrez (Congressman from Illinois)

   (g) Bob Martinez (Governor of Florida)

   (h) Gloria Molina (Los Angeles political figure)

   (i) Antonia Pantoja, founder of Aspira Inc., recipient of the Medal of Freedom (1996)

   (j) Federico Peña, Mayor of Denver and Secretary of Transportation

   (k) Bill Richardson (U.S. Secretary of Energy)

Selection 2

The Language Crusade

JOSEPH V. TORRES

Joseph V. Torres (also Joseph V. Torres-Metzgar) *(1933–) is a Mexican American whose family settled in the Southwest area in the 1700s. Growing up in Albuquerque, Torres became acquainted with its mixture of Hispanic, Anglo, and Native American cultures. He received B.A. (1960), MA. (1962), and Ph.D. (1965) degrees from the University of New Mexico.*

As a professor of history at the University of Nevada, Torres specializes in the study of the southwestern United States. Making use of his scholarly knowledge, Torres set his 1976 novel, Below the Summit, *in the Southwest, where "Anglo" discrimination against Mexican Americans has had a long history. The novel is about the impact of cultural pressures on a marriage between an "Anglo" rancher and a Mexican woman.*

As the Hispanic population of the United States has increased, states (such as California, Florida, and Texas) often have accepted Spanish as a second language. For example, in these states, public documents commonly are printed in both languages. Some people, alarmed by this tendency, have called for the recognition of English as the official language of the United States. Many Hispanic Americans view this effort to outlaw the use of Spanish as another example of discrimination. In "The Language Crusade," published in Hispanic *magazine (1996), Torres examines the reasons why some people have been attracted to the "English only" movement.*

PREPARING TO READ

1. How and why do people change their spoken or written language to adapt to different situations and/or to different audiences?
2. Why may a speaker/writer use a word to mean one thing and the listener/reader interpret the meaning differently? Consider words such as: "courage," "democracy," "freedom," "friendly," "liberty," or "responsible."

3. What do you think are some of the advantages and disadvantages of raising a child to be bilingual?

THE LANGUAGE CRUSADE

The great Chicano artist, poet, and writer Jose Antonio Burciaga once wrote about a dream he had in which English was declared the nation's official language. The names of familiar towns, cities, and famous landmarks were changed to their English translations. Puerto Rico became "Rich Port." Rio Piedras and Isla Caja de Muertos were called "Rock River" and "Dead Man's Casket Island." Alamo became "The Poplar," El Paso changed to "The Pass," Boca Raton was called "Rat's Mouth," and Yerba Buena became "Good Weed." Opponents of "Official English" have fun with Burciaga's translations, but clearly this issue of language isn't funny.

There was little humor in the Supreme Court's recent decision to review an Arizona case, *Yniquez* v. *Arizonans for Official English* this fall. In the case, a state Official English amendment passed in 1988 was found unconstitutional by a lower court. Presidential candidate and Senate majority leader Bob Dole (R-Kansas) wasn't laughing when he endorsed Official English while addressing the American Legion convention in Indianapolis last September. Dole said, "English should be acknowledged once and for all as the official language of the United States."

Dole's presidential bid and the upcoming Supreme Court review of the Yniquez case have moved the debate over language into uncharted territories. Official English critics have consistently labeled the attempt to legislate language as ridiculous. They call the language debate a non-issue. They point to the 1990 U.S. Census, which reports that 97 percent of all U.S. residents speak English. They admit, however, that these are dangerous times. The election of the Republican-controlled 104th Congress in 1994 has brought unprecedented support for Official English legislation, and Official English hearings have been held in both houses of Congress. "This year represents the greatest risk that an Official English bill will pass out of Congress," said Ed Chen, staff attorney for the American Civil Liberties Union in San Francisco.

Four major Official English bills were introduced in the first session of the 104th Congress last year. Bills have been sponsored by Senator Richard Shelby (R-Alabama) and Representative Bill Emerson

(R-Missouri) which call for making English the "official language" of government. Two bills sponsored in the House by Representatives by Peter King (R-New York) and Toby Roth (R-Wisconsin) go even further by calling for the elimination of bilingual education and bilingual ballots. Representative John Doolittle (R-California) also introduced an amendment which, if adopted, would amend the Constitution to declare English the official language of government of the United States.

Analyzing the increased momentum of this issue, Representative Esteban Torres (D-California) said that Official English is growing because of the political tenor that is predominant in the country. "This has become a very good tool to advocate against anybody who speaks a language other than English . . . and also conveys the concept of who really belongs here."

The debate has been brewing ever since former Senator S.I. Hayakawa (R-California) introduced an Official English constitutional amendment in 1981. At the time, the amendment found few supporters. In 1983 Hayakawa founded the Washington-based group U.S. English (a "national, nonpartisan, nonprofit citizen's action group") after retiring from the Senate. The organization, whose current chairman is Chile-born Mauro E. Mujica, has been instrumental in spearheading passage of Official English legislation through several state houses. Currently, 23 states have Official English laws on the book and at least 10 others, including California and Georgia, have legislation pending. Despite a General Accounting Office report released last year that said 99.94 percent of all federal government documents are produced in English, Official English proponents argue that more than 300 languages are spoken in the United States, and for the sake of cost-effectiveness and unity, the government needs to legislate and conduct its business in English. They also regularly stress that the overwhelming majority of U.S. citizens favors making English the official national language. A poll conducted by U.S. News and World Report last September showed that 73 percent of U.S. voters favored making English the official language of government.

Last August, U.S. English conducted its own poll, which asked 1,208 U.S. citizens the question: "Do you think English should be made the official language of the United States?" The poll revealed that 86 percent of all U.S. citizens and 81 percent of first-generation immigrants answered yes.

Some dispute the accuracy of such polls. Karen Hansen, an education policy analyst for the National Council of La Raza, said too often, polls are designed to elicit a specific response by not providing their respondents with enough information. While on speaking engagements, she often asks groups what percentage of the U.S. population speaks English. Typically, responses range from 50 to 75 percent. "They are shocked when they learn it's 97 percent," she said.

In 1986 the Virginia-based group English First was founded by Larry Pratt, who also started Gun Owners of America. (Pratt may best be remembered for having to step down earlier this year as co-chairman of GOP presidential candidate Patrick Buchanan's campaign for allegedly making public appearances with leaders of white supremacist organizations, including the Aryan Nation and Christian Identity.) Buchanan has also endorsed Official English.

With little demonstrated need to support Official English, opponents of the movement have labeled it xenophobic and racist. Chen says that Official English supporters play on the fears that many non-Hispanic white U.S. citizens have of the "browning of America." According to the U.S. Immigration and Naturalization Service, in the fifties, 53 percent of all legal immigrants in the United States were from Europe, with 22 percent from Latin America. Conversely, in the eighties, only 10 percent were from Europe and 47 percent were from Latin America. The U.S. Hispanic population has increased from 9 million in 1970 to 27 million in 1995, and the U.S. Census Bureau has projected that by 2050 the mainland U.S. Hispanic population will reach 88 million, 20 percent of the total population. Census figures reveal that in 1990, 32 million U.S. residents five years of age and older spoke a language other than English at home. More than 54 percent spoke Spanish. The majority, however, also spoke English "well" or "very well."

Jim Lyons, executive director of the National Association for Bilingual Education, criticizes U.S. English and English First for supporting bills over the years that do not increase the availability of programs that teach English. In New York, English as a Second Language (ESL) classes have waiting lists ranging from six to eighteen months, and in Los Angeles, ESL programs have waiting lists of 20,000 to 40,000 people. Jim Crawford, a Maryland-based author who has written several books on the language debate, including *Hold Your Tongue: Bilingualism and Politics of English Only*, said immigrants are learning English faster than previous generations because there are greater economic incentives to do so.

In his writings, Crawford documented the origins of the Official English movement. In its beginning form, it was a movement to curb immigration and then evolved into focusing on language. "It is absurd that English needs legal protection," said Crawford. "If you look at the facts—that immigrants are learning English—and then look at what's underneath the English-Only campaign, you will find that it's prejudice toward immigrants and fear that the nation is losing its cultural and racial identity." Indeed, literature from Official English groups and comments from its defenders appear to support Crawford's point that racism is the motivating factor.

A 1995 membership solicitation letter from U.S. English chairman Mujica sensationalized the issue and attempted to push the emotionally charged nationalism button. It began with a reference to the Arizona case being reviewed by the Supreme Court. It read, "Do you know Armando Ruiz? How about John Philip Evans or Rosie Garcia? Candido Mercado? James Padilla? Manuel Pena, Jr.? Peter Rios? Evangelina Rivas? Macario Saldate IV? Federico Sanchez? Victor Soltero? Let me give you clues: 1. They all live in Arizona. 2. They're all on the government payroll. 3. And, together they've filed a lawsuit that could change your life forever."

In 1988 U.S. English co-founder John Tanton resigned as chairman of U.S. English after a 1986 memo he wrote was disclosed. In it, he asked, "In this society, will the present majority peaceably hand over its political power to a group that is simply more fertile? . . . As whites see their power and control over their lives declining, will they simply go quietly into the night? Or will there be an explosion. . . We are building in a deadly disunity." The memo led to the resignation of its president, former Ronald Reagan appointee Linda Chavez, and advisory board member Walter Cronkite.

An early fund-raising letter from English First stated, "Tragically, many immigrants these days refuse to learn English! They never become productive members of society. They remain stuck in a linguistic and economic ghetto, many living off welfare and costing working Americans millions of tax dollars every year. Radical activists have been caught sneaking illegal aliens to the polls and using bilingual ballots to cast fraudulent votes. . . ." Jim Boulet, Jr., executive director of English First, has defended the group and its founder. When asked why legislation is needed for Official English when 97 percent of U.S. citizens speak English, he answered, "Most people in the country don't think murder is a good idea, but we have laws against it."

Hispanic organizations have protested that discrimination against Hispanics and non-English speakers is on the rise because of the Official English movement. Last year a Texas district court judge ruled that a Latina mother was abusing her daughter by speaking only Spanish to her. He ordered the mother to speak English to her daughter to ensure "she's not relegating her to a position of a housemaid."

Andy Banks, an international representative with the International Brotherhood of Teamsters, said that businesses are using the issue to exploit workers. In Miami, the Teamsters have helped employees of Fritz's Stair Cargo, a freight forwarding and logistics company, to file a complaint with the Equal Employment Opportunity Commission accusing the company of forcing workers to accept a three-tiered wage system that links an employee's salary with his or her ability to speak English. Banks said the company allegedly pays Spanish-speaking employees less than its English-speaking workers. Fritz's Stair Cargo has denied the charges.

Anticipating increased charges of discrimination in the workplace, the ACLU has initiated a hot-line so that employees all over the country can report when they have been discriminated against due to language restrictions. The Mexican American Legal Defense and Education Fund (MALDEF) began a national hot-line last year to register complaints against employers who prohibit Latino employees from speaking Spanish in the work place. MALDEF's hot-line received more than 88 calls in the first 48 hours it was up and running. The ACLU, according to Chen, ran local television public-service announcements in northern California about its language discrimination phone line earlier this year. The San Francisco office received 40 phone calls the week the spot ran. It normally averages 10 such calls per week.

Opponents of U.S. English and English First, such as the ACLU and MALDEF, have difficulty defusing the special interest groups' messages despite the tainted backgrounds of the organizations, their propaganda, and an increasing number of reported discrimination cases. The U.S. English and English First rely on catchy sound bites when describing programs they oppose. Bilingual education, for example, is called "linguistic welfare" in a brochure. Representative Roth, who testified at a December hearing on Shelby's Official English bill said, "I want to keep America one nation, one people. We must preserve the common bond that has kept this country of immigrants together for more than two centuries by making English our official language."

According to Chen, people respond to the Official English message because it is "simplistic" and "it seems like the right thing to do. It is a message that sounds non-racist and nice, which is why it's hard to fight. Our response is not a catchy one-line answer, but an explanation." When asked whether Hispanics support Official English, NABE's Lyons barked, "I don't know a Latino organization in the country that supports it." Most Latino organizations may agree on the issue, but not all Latinos do. Besides figureheads like Mujica and Chavez, some Hispanics do have conflicting views on the subject. Depending on the generation, some Mexican American parents encouraged immersion in English to protect their children from the ridicule they endured as Spanish speakers entering American schools. Other Hispanics believe English proficiency is a key factor for success in the U.S., while others, who understand the dominance English maintains in this country, simply consider the issue redundant.

With both the Democratic and Republican national conventions approaching in August, the political waters will get rougher as Dole and Clinton will each attempt to define each other and their candidacy with issues that appeal to the voters, or the lowest common denominator. The hot-button nature of the language issue means that it has the potential to ignite nationalist fervor in non-Hispanic America even more than it already has. Perhaps as the campaign drags on, a candidate who exposes the issue's true racist basis will emerge. Or maybe an observer like Burciaga would help by providing us with another of those Official English dreams that put the debate in its proper perspective.

WRITING ABOUT THE READING

4. Why does Torres begin the essay by suggesting the change of Spanish names to English?
5. Why does Torres say that those who support Official English use invalid or biased arguments?
6. Why does the writer say that the results of the U.S. English poll (which showed that 86 percent of U.S. citizens wanted English to be made the official language) are debatable?
7. Why do critics of Official English assert that this movement is connected to racism?
8. How would you describe the tone of this essay and what would be some of the details to support your position?

WRITING FROM YOUR OWN EXPERIENCE

Note: In these assignments, write about your own experience or use that of someone you know, read about, or saw in a film/TV show.

9. Have you ever had a problem because of misunderstanding what another person said? Why did this misunderstanding occur and how was it resolved?
10. What are some of the ways your use of language has changed since you entered college and what are the reasons for these changes?

11. Think over some of the ways you encounter Spanish in public (such as on the job, when using the telephone, reading a brochure, seeing an ad, etc.). How do you feel about the use of Spanish and what are the reasons for your reaction?

WRITING ABOUT RESEARCH

12. Why is learning a second language after adolescence often difficult for the student?

13. Using a thesaurus to find a group of synonyms for a word (or one of the following groups), explain the differences in connotations between these words. Consider groups such as:
    (a) drink, guzzle, imbibe, sip, swill, tipple
    (b) emaciated, gaunt, scrawny, skinny, slender
    (c) chore, drudgery, labor, toil, work
    (d) acquiesce, admit, agree, concede, give in, yield
    (e) brass, funds, greenback, money, moolah
    (f) bargain, cheap, inexpensive, nominal price, reduced
    (g) acquaintance, colleague, crony, friend, pal

14. Choose one of the many cities (or places) in which local names reflect its early history under Spain or Mexico (such as Los Angeles, San Francisco, El Paso, or St. Augustine). What was the history of the Hispanics in this city or region?

15. Investigate the conflict between Mexico and the United States over Texas in the nineteenth century. How and why did Texas become part of the United States?

16. Why was the Mexican American Legal Defense and Educational Fund (MALDEF) established and what are some of its goals and/or achievements?

Selection 3

Illegal Immigrants: Prophets of a Borderless World

RICHARD RODRIGUEZ

Richard Rodriguez *(1944–), journalist and essayist, is the son of Mexican American immigrants who spoke Spanish at home; Rodriguez first learned English when he entered school. Rodriguez earned a B.A. (1967) from Stanford and an M.A. from Columbia (1969). After graduate study at the University of California, Berkeley, and the Warburg Institute, London, Rodriguez decided to pursue a full-time career as a writer. His many awards include a Fulbright fellowship (1972–1973) and a National Endowment for the Humanities Fellowship (1976–1977).*

In 1982 Rodriguez received a Christopher Award for his book, Hunger of Memory: The Education of Richard Rodriguez. *The collection of essays depicts his struggles to learn English, which Rodriguez calls his "public language" as opposed to his "private language," Spanish. An advocate of Hispanic assimilation into the larger society, Rodriguez also writes of his opposition to both bilingual education and affirmative action. He argues that students should learn about things they do not know already, about how they are a link in a continuous flow of ideas from the past and from different cultures.*

In the following essay, Rodriguez turns his attention to the issue of illegal immigration from Mexico. He argues that in a world of global economies, these people show others the futility of national borders. "Illegal Immigrants: Prophets of a Borderless World" was originally published in NPQ: New Perspectives Quarterly *in 1995. Published by Center for the Study of Democratic Institutions,* NPQ *is an academic journal containing articles about social, economic, and political issues.*

PREPARING TO READ

1. Why would some people prefer to use the term "undocumented immigrants" to that of "illegal immigrants"?
2. Why do you agree (or disagree) that children of illegal immigrants should be permitted to attend public schools?

144

3. What would be some of the arguments for and against allowing children of illegal immigrants to receive public health services?

4. Why do you agree (or disagree) that today people live in a world of "overlapping economies"?

ILLEGAL IMMIGRANTS: PROPHETS OF A BORDERLESS WORLD

San Francisco—We might have expected it in France, in Germany or in Japan. But is America, the land built and sustained by immigrants, also becoming intolerant of them? Is that the message of the resounding vote in California last fall in favor of a measure that seeks to end illegal immigration by denying government services to illegal immigrants and their children?

Let's face it: America has never really like immigrants, at least not when the immigration is actually taking place. America ended up romanticizing the 19th-century immigrant, but only generations later.

Today, Americans insist that they are not anti-immigrant. "It is just the illegals we don't want," they say. American politicians warn that illegals are coming for our welfare dollars. But kids on the Mexican side of the border will tell you they are coming in search of a job. They are not coming because they have read Thomas Jefferson or because they know the Bill of Rights. They are coming because there is a rumor of work.

Illegals are an embarrassment to Mexico's government. They are an outrage to suburbanites in San Diego who each night see the Third World running through their rose garden. They are often adolescent, often desperate or reckless. They are disrespectful of American custom and law. They are also among the most modern people in the world.

Decades before wealthy Mexicans decided to enroll their children in Ivy League colleges in the U.S., Mexican peasants left their villages and trespassed across several centuries. They grew accustomed to thousands of miles of dirt roads and freeways, knew two currencies, and gathered a "working knowledge" of English to go along with their native Spanish.

Before professors in business schools were talking about global economics, the illegal knew all about it. Before fax machines punctured the Iron Curtain, coyotes [smugglers of illegal immigrants] knew the most efficient way to infiltrate Southern California. Before businessmen flew into Mexico City to sign big deals, the illegal was picking peaches in the fields of California or flipping pancakes at the roadside diner.

In 1994, we can say about them exactly what nativists a century ago said about the Ellis Island crowd: "They don't assimilate. They come to take, not to give. They are peasants who lower our national IQ."

The notion of the "legal immigrant" allows us to forget that all immigrants are outlaws. Immigrants violate custom; they assault convention. To be an immigrant is to turn your back on your father and your village. You break your mother's heart. The immigrant is as much a scandal to his ancient mountain village as to suburban Los Angeles.

Early in this century, Mexico passed laws to keep U.S. business interests out. Lately, Mexico's president, Carlos Salinas de Gortari, has begun to denationalize Mexican business and open his country to U.S. capital. Americans exclaim, "At last, Mexico has a truly modern leader!" But the Harvard-educated President of Mexico was preceded to the U.S. by several generations of peasants.

In the 1920's, when Mexico was trying to seal itself off from the U.S., Mexican peasants were illegally making their way north. Every few months, illegal workers would return, by choice or by deportation. They returned to their 16th-century villages with seductive rumors of America. More than Pancho Villa, more than Zapata, the illegal immigrants became the great revolutionaries of Mexico. They Americanized the tiniest villages of Mexico.

Today, jets make the world convenient to U.S. business executives and to middle-class tourists. We Americans assume our ability to roam where we will, making deals or taking pictures of each other in Bermuda shorts.

A Californian I know complains that a village in Ecuador is becoming more and more Americanized. Each year, he sees the change. I tell him, if he's so worried about the change, maybe he shouldn't travel so much.

We Americans have become like Shakespeare's dark lady of the sonnets. We stand at the window, we bat our eyelashes. We romance the world. We advertise our beauty and our sexy glamour. We display our happy white teeth. And then we wonder why the world is lined up at our door.

Although Californians voted for the anti-immigrant measure by a wide margin, it will not in the end decide illegal immigration. For the fact is that we all live in a world where economies overlap, where we no longer know where our automobiles are assembled, where billboards work their way into the adolescent imagination. We are headed for a century where the great question will be exactly this: What is a border?

The illegal immigrant is the bravest among us. The most modern among us. The prophet.

"The border, senor?" the illegal immigrant sighs. The border is an inconvenience, surely. A danger in the dark. But the border does not hold. The peasant knows the reality of our world decades before the California suburbanite will ever get the point.

WRITING ABOUT THE READING

5. Rodriguez compares the recent immigrants from Mexico to earlier immigrants. What are some of the similarities and differences between the two groups?
6. Why do you think (or disagree) that the writer is justified in labeling as "outlaws" both legal and illegal immigrants?
7. After summarizing Rodriguez's position about national borders, explain why you agree (or disagree) with his stand.
8. Rodriguez states that the United States is like a seductive lady who romances the world. Why do you think (or disagree) that this is a fair and effective comparison?
9. What do you predict would be the consequences of eliminating borders and allowing people to move freely between Mexico and the United States?

WRITING FROM YOUR OWN EXPERIENCE

Note: In these assignments, write about your own experience or use that of someone you know, read about, or saw in a film/TV show.

10. Suppose that you had to explain to a new immigrant the meaning of an unusual English word or phrase. Choose a word or phrase and define it. Consider a word such as: (a) hacker, (b) yuppie, (c) downsize, (d) clueless, or (e) hip hop.
11. Rodriguez writes that the Mexican immigrants enter the United States because they seek work. Even within the United States, people move to other cities or states in search of work. If you had to move to another city to find employment, which city would you choose and what would be the reasons for your choice?
12. Consider someone in your family who immigrated to the United States or moved to another city or state. Why did this person

move and what were some of the consequences of this person's actions?

13. Illegal immigrants usually are employed in low-paid, menial jobs (such as in agriculture) that are scorned by many Americans. Explain whether you think that Americans would take these jobs if illegal immigration were to be eliminated.

WRITING ABOUT RESEARCH

14. What was the "Operation Wetback" policy of the 1950s and why was it an effective or ineffective policy?

15. Why did the United States pass the National Origins Act in 1924 and what were some of the results of this act?

16. Evaluate some of the current efforts of the United States to control illegal immigration from Mexico. Why are these measures effective or ineffective?

17. Rodriguez states that Americans have "never really liked immigrants." Many people have argued that the 1927 execution of two Italian immigrant workers, Sacco and Vanzetti, was a result of this hostility towards immigrants rather than justice. After researching this case, explain why you think (or disagree) that Sacco and Vanzetti received a fair trial.

Arrival: 1960

PABLO MEDINA

Pablo Medina *(1948–), poet and novelist, was born in Havana, Cuba. At the age of 12, he immigrated with his family to New York City. He received both A.B. and M.A. degrees from Georgetown University in Washington, D.C. Medina, the author of several books of poetry and prose, has given readings and performances of his work throughout the United States, Latin America, and the Middle East. A recipient of numerous awards for his writing, including a National Endowment for the Arts Fellowship, Medina is currently on the faculty of the MFA Program for Writers at Warren Wilson College in Asheville, North Carolina, and teaches at the New School University in New York City.*

Medina often writes about the exile's experience. His recent novel, The Return of Felix Nogara *(2000), is the story of an exile who returns to his home, a fictional Caribbean island, to search for his lost happiness. In this excerpt from* Exiled Memories: A Cuban Childhood *(1990), Medina recalls his adjustment to his new life in the United States.*

PREPARING TO READ

1. What is "culture shock" and why do people often experience "culture shock" when they travel to a new city or country?
2. Why do you think that life in a big city (such as New York) often is portrayed as lonely, impersonal, and individualistic?
3. Why do Americans typically try to identify people as members of a particular group and what does this identification process indicate about U.S. culture?
4. Why is it helpful or harmful to label as "Hispanic" all people from the different countries where Spanish is spoken?

ARRIVAL: 1960

Snow. Everywhere the snow and air so cold it cracks and my words hang stiffly in the air like cartoons. After that first stunning welcome of the New York winter, I rush down the steps of the plane and sink my bare hands into the snow, press it into a ball, and throw it at my sister. I miss by a few yards. The snowball puffs on the ground. I make another and miss again. Then I can make no more, for my hands are numb. I look down at them: red and wet, they seem disembodied, no longer mine. A few flakes land on them, but these flakes are not the ones I know from *Little LuLu* or *Archie*; they are big lumpy things that melt soon after landing. On closer look, I can make out the intricate crystals, small and furry and short lived. As if from a great distance, I hear my mother calling. Her voice seems changed by the cold and the words come quicker, in shorter bursts, as if there might be a limited supply of them. I follow the family into the airport building. It is early February. It is El Norte.

The drive into Manhattan is a blur. We piled into a cab and took a wide and busy highway in, most probably the Grand Central Parkway. Once over the East River, my first impression was of riding down into a canyon, much of it shadowy and forbidding, where the sky, steel gray at the time, was a straight path like the street we were on, except bumpier and softer: old cotton swabbed in mercury. It seemed odd that out of that ominous ceiling came the pure white snow I had just touched.

But the snow on the ground did not stay white very long. Nothing does in New York. It started graying at the edges four days after our arrival when my father took my sister and me to school, Robert F. Wagner Junior High, on East 72nd Street. It was a long brick building that ran the length of the block. Inauspicious, blank, with shades half-raised on the windows, it could have been a factory or a prison. Piled to the side of the entrance steps was a huge mound of snow packed with children like fruit on supermarket ice. J.H.S. 167 was a typical New York school, a microcosm of the city where all races mingled and fought and, on occasion, learned. The halls were crowded, the classes were crowded, even the bathroom during recess was packed to capacity.

On that first day I was witness to a scene that was to totally alter my image of what school was. On my way from one class to the next, I saw a teacher—who, I later learned, was the prefect of discipline—dragging a girl away by the arm. The girl, trying to tug herself free, was screaming, "Mother fucker, mother fucker." He slapped her across the face several times. Most students, already practicing the indifference that is the keynote of survival in New York, barely turned their heads. I, however, stared, frozen by violence in a place previous experience had deluded me into thinking ought to be quiet and genteel and orderly. It was the loud ring of the bell directly overhead that woke me. I was late for English class.

When I entered the room, the teacher, a slightly pudgy lady with silver white hair, asked if I had a pass. I did not know what a pass was but I answered no anyway. It was my first day and I had gotten lost in the halls.

"Well, in that case, young man, you may come in."

She spoke with rounded vowels and smooth, slightly slurred *r*'s rolling out of her mouth from deep in the throat. Years later I was to learn to identify this manner of speech as an affectation of the educated.

"Next time, however, you must have a pass."

Not that it mattered if one was late to English class. Much of the time was spent doing reading or writing assignments while Mrs. Gall, whose appearance belied that she was close to retirement, did crossword puzzles. A few days later, in fact, something happened that endeared me to her for the rest of the term. Speaking to herself, not expecting any of the students to help her, she said, "A nine letter word for camel." Almost instantaneously, as if by magic, I responded, "Dromedary."

She looked up at me. "That's very good. You have a nice complexion. Where are you from?"

"Complexion?" I asked.

"Yes, skin."

Skin? What does skin have to do with any of this? I had never thought of my skin, let alone considered it a mark of foreignness.

"Cuba."

"Ah, I was there once."

Then she went off on a monologue of beaches and nightlife and weather.

Home for now was a two-bedroom apartment in a residential hotel on East 86th Street, which we would not have been able to afford were it not for the graces of the company my father worked for. We had few clothes, little money, and no possessions to speak of, yet I do not remember ever lacking anything, except perhaps good food, as my mother, who as a middle-class housewife had always relied on maids in Cuba, was just beginning to learn how to cook.

If there was no money for expensive restaurants or theater tickets, I always had thirty cents for the subway fare. From this building that glossed our poverty, I set out into the city that lay open like a geo-metric flower of concrete and steel. Its nectar was bittersweet, but it kept me, us, from wallowing in the self-pity and stagnation that I have seen among so many exiles. After a few months, realizing that a return to the island was not forthcoming, we looked on a future where the sun was rising again. Not the fierce tropical sun that made everything jump with life and set over the palm trees as quickly as it had risen, but a gentler, slower sun that yielded reluctantly to night and promised to renew itself. Constancy. It was blonde.

The New York sun is not ubiquitous. It hides behind buildings until well after eleven, then appears and disappears for a few hours in the grid sky. Eventually one does not see it at all, only its afterglow diffused by smog and its reflection on the windows of the tallest build-ings. Manhattan is an island without sunrise or sunset. If you want to witness the former, you go to the Long Island shore and look toward Europe; if you want the latter, you move west.

And so it was. I could go nowhere but into the city. Sometimes alone, sometimes with Sam, the one friend I made at school, I traveled from one end of the city to the other. At first boredom was the motiva-tor, but soon an intense curiosity that my parents not only tolerated but encouraged became the fire that fueled me.

Thus I discovered Washington Square, the source of Fifth Av-enue. Elegant, restrained, neo-Parisian, and ebbing southward from it, Greenwich Village, already in decadence but nevertheless glowing with an odd sort of peripheral, rebellious energy. Some seed had sprouted there I sensed, but it was years before I saw its vines spread throughout the land.

North I went, too, to find the Avenue's mouth and realized that this was no river of gold, but a snake that devoured its own and spewed them back to a place beyond light or hope or future. When one sees Harlem at 125th Street and Fifth Avenue, one comes face to face with the worst despair. The people there are fixed in a defeat not of their making, but rather the result of the color of their skins and a heritage imposed on them from the outside. Black you are and poor you shall remain; black you are and damned you shall be. The Avenue begins in Paris and ends in hell.

In six months we moved to 236th Street in the Upper Bronx, this time to a modest apartment in a modest building. The trees on the streets actually looked like trees, not like stunted saplings. They gave shade; there was enough room on their trunks to carve initials and love notes; the streets were not forever clogged with traffic; the sun was more visible, and from our sixth-floor windows the red blood of the sunset spilled over the Hudson a mile away.

Discovering the installment plan, my parents bought furniture and china and pictures to put on the walls. We even got a stereo. We met other families in the building, formed friendships. We were, suddenly, in middle-class mainstream America, Bronx style, and the past released its grip and ebbed far enough away so that only memory could reach it. Somehow luck had graced us: we had circumvented the snake.

WRITING ABOUT THE READING

5. Why does the family's arrival in New York give Medina culture shock?

6. How and why does Medina learn that he is "different" in the United States?

7. Why is it an important turning point in his memoir when Medina's family begins planning for the future?

8. What does Medina mean when he writes that "we had circumvented the snake" and why does he say this?

9. What does the writer's choice of descriptive words and phrases (such as "stiffly," "disembodied," "ominous," and "flower of concrete and steel") suggest about his experience?

10. How and why does the writer use the imagery of snow to symbolize his experience in New York City?

WRITING FROM YOUR OWN EXPERIENCE

Note: In these assignments, write about your own experience or use that of someone you know, read about, or saw in a film/TV show.

11. Like many other displaced peoples, Cubans had to go into exile and leave almost all of their possessions behind. Suppose that you were forced to go into exile in a new country within a few days. What preparations would you make for your exile and why would you make these preparations?

12. Medina describes an important turning point in his early life. Think of an experience you could describe as a "turning point" in your life. Why would you describe this experience this way and how did it affect your life?

13. Medina recounts an incident when students were indifferent as they watched a girl being slapped. This indifference, he states, is

the "keynote of survival in New York." Can you think of a time when you were indifferent or acted this way? What was the reason for your indifference and the outcome of your "not caring" attitude?

WRITING ABOUT RESEARCH

14. Choose a large city (such as Chicago, Dallas, Los Angeles, Miami, or New York) to investigate. Why would immigrants be attracted to this city?

15. What were the causes and results of the Cuban missile crisis of 1962?

16. Why did Cuban Americans react so strongly to the return of Elian Gonzales to Cuba?

17. What are some of the arguments for and against improving U.S. relations with Cuba?

Selection 5

Earth to Papi, Earth to Papi

GUSTAVO PEREZ FIRMAT

Gustavo Perez Firmat *(1949–), educator and writer, was born in Cuba and fled with his family to the United States when he was eleven. He received both B.A. (1972) and M.A. (1973) degrees from the University of Miami, and a Ph.D. from the University of Michigan (1979). Perez Firmat taught for many years at Duke University and currently is a professor of humanities at Columbia University. He was chosen as a Guggenheim Memorial Foundation fellow (1985) and National Endowment for the Humanities senior fellow (1985–1986).*

In Life-on-the-Hyphen *(1994), Perez Firmat studies the Cuban American culture of the exiles. Using the term the "one-and-a-half generation," he writes that the Cuban exiles willingly accommodated themselves to their new country, not holding on to their old traditions but instead "translating" them in the new setting. In one section of this book, Perez Firmat discusses the assimilation of Cuban-born Desi Arnaz (Lucille Ball's actor-singer husband in the 1950s I* Love Lucy *TV series). Perez Firmat describes Arnaz as accepting and open, a figure who, both in the TV show and in real life, made it clear that he willingly chose life in the United States.*

Next Year in Cuba, from which "Earth to Papi, Earth to Papi" is taken, was nominated for a Pulitzer Prize in 1995. In this book, Perez Firmat explores the culture of the next Cuban American generation, the children who have no firsthand knowledge of Cuba. He describes how the Americanization process has affected him and his family.

PREPARING TO READ

1. What is "nostalgia" and why do you suppose that many adults are nostalgic about earlier times or a place where they once lived?
2. What are some of the difficulties that immigrants face as they try to ensure that their children learn about their heritage and traditions?

3. What are some of the advantages and disadvantages of being a child of immigrants?

EARTH TO PAPI, EARTH TO PAPI

Today is Father's Day. My son is at a basketball camp and my daughter is spending the day with her mother. A few days ago David turned twelve, which makes him older than I was when I arrived in the United States. A couple of weeks before that, Miriam turned nine. Since the custodial arrangement with David and Miriam's mother, who still lives in Chapel Hill, is that I will celebrate their even-numbered birthdays, this year my son's birthday party was held at my house, while my daughter's took place at hers. If this pattern holds, Miriam will celebrate *los quince*, the traditional coming-out party for fifteen-year-old girls, with her Cuban mother, and her Sweet Sixteen with me and her American stepmother.

In the lives of exiles, as in the lives of the children of exiles, the personal and the cultural make a dense tangle. Almost all of the crucial decisions in my life—decisions about career, marriage, divorce, place of residence—have had cultural implications. When I decided to become an undergraduate English major, I embarked on a career that separated me from my native language. When I left Miami in order to attend graduate school in Ann Arbor, I exiled myself from Little Havana. When my first wife and I divorced and I later married Mary Anne, I took my distance from certain Cuban rituals and family traditions.

In my children's lives, too, the personal and the cultural intertwine, and not always by choice. If I lived in Miami, they would be growing up Cuban. If I were still married to their mother, they would be speaking Spanish at home, would see their Cuban relatives more often, and would have more Hispanic friends. For them, split parental custody has entailed split cultural custody. Although David and Miriam started on the road to assimilation long before I married Mary Anne, during the half of every week that they live with me, they're American in a way that they never were before.

Every American-born child of exiles or immigrants begins his or her life in the womb of a foreign country; it doesn't matter whether or not the baby comes into the world in the most American hospital of the most American city—at the moment of birth he's no different than he would have been had he been born in the old country. I know that David and Miriam were at their most Cuban when they were smallest.

Even afterward, during the early months of infancy, they remained swaddled in Cuban culture. The voices they heard, the faces they saw, the way they were coddled and cooed to—all of them spoke of Cuba. Yet even then David and Miriam had started a journey that would take them away from the culture of my birth.

I used to find it very hard to accept that my children would grow up and away from my homeland. For years after David and Miriam were born, the Cuban in me longed for the Cuban in them. I desperately needed them to be like me, to see the forests through my *árbol*-seeing eyes, to hear my *clave* rhythm in their souls. I even convinced myself that after having children I'd be more firmly linked to my past than ever before. I expected David and Miriam to secure my own, somewhat tenuous ties to my homeland. Once I had kids, I tried to make doubly sure that I remained faithful to old-country ways. I decided to speak Spanish in their presence, talk to them about our homeland, transmit Cuban attitudes and traditions. Never mind that I lived in Chapel Hill, a town with an insignificant Hispanic population, or that very early in their lives David and Miriam started addressing me sometimes as "Pop" rather than always as "Papi," or that their mother and I often caught ourselves speaking English to each other. And never mind, also, that from the moment they turned on the TV or stepped into a preschool class, what they heard was English. Since I was an exile, they had to be exiles too. Instead of seeing my children as a bridge to the future, I saw them as a tether to the past.

This way of thinking may sound crazy, but I wasn't all that unusual among my countrymen. For Cubans in this country, exile has been as much a spiritual legacy as a political status. Exile is our inheritance, like wealth or good looks. You're not born in exile, you're born into exile. By now, at least three generations of Cubans have regarded themselves in this way. One-and-a-halfers like me straddle the generational fence; in some ways we're exiles, while in others we're the children of exiles. But strictly speaking, the same person cannot be both an exile and the child of exiles. Just as the American-born daughter of immigrants is no longer an immigrant but an American, so it is with the children of exiles. The abbreviation for second-generation Cubans, ABCs (American-born Cubans), exposes the paradox. How can anyone truly be an American-born anything? If you're born in America, then you're American, whether your parents were Haitian, Bosnian, or Vietnamese. And yet there are many young Cubans who were born in Miami, who speak English more fluently than Spanish, who live according to American mores, who socialize with American friends, and who still look upon themselves as exiles.

Some time ago a Duke student that I had never had in a class came to my campus office. Wearing a baseball cap, a Polo shirt, and brand-new sneakers, he looked like many Duke undergraduates. After identifying himself as José Luis Costa, he proceeded to tell me in broken Spanish that he was a Cuban exile like me. But, unlike me, José Luis was born and raised in Miami, which made him an expatriate from a land he had never seen. His American birth didn't prevent him from asserting that, once Castro fell, he was planning to "return" to Cuba.

When my children were younger, I wanted them to be American-born Cubans like Joe (the name José Luis goes by among his friends). But since my kids lived in Chapel Hill rather than Coral Gables, in order to raise them Cuban I had to try to enclose them inside a time capsule; I had to create my own version of Old Havana. And so I undertook to do in my home in Chapel Hill what Cubans had done in a larger way in Little Havana. I believed that even if I "resided" in North Carolina, I could actually "live" in Miami. That's where my soul and my family were. That's where my food and my music came from. That's where my kids and I really belonged.

Had you walked inside my house during those years, the first thing you would have seen was a row of posters with Cuban motifs. The first and largest was a photograph of the interior of an old Cuban mansion, with its traditional *mediopuntos*, or stained-glass arches, over the doorways, giving visitors the feeling that they were walking into the living room in the picture rather than into my own. Another poster was a picture of *tinajones*, large terra-cotta planters typical of the Cuban province of Camagüey. Another was a picture of a cobblestoned street in Old Havana. And yet another showed an eighteenth-century map of the island. Of course, old maps and stained-glass arches and four-foot-tall planters had nothing to do with the house I actually lived in, a ranch-style home with cedar siding and hardwood floors. If you looked out my window, what you saw was gravel, not cobblestones; and instead of *tinajones* stuffed with hibiscus, the flower beds in the yard had rhododendron and azalea bushes. These incongruities tortured but did not deter me. My home was a piece of Cuba relocated in Chapel Hill; my home was a humidor full of Cuban-seed children and cigars. My home was truly a Little Havana.

What applied to the decor applied also to the way of life. The stereo constantly played Cuban music, usually younger Miami artists like Gloria Estefan and Willie Chirino. The pantry was always stocked with bottles of *mojo* seasoning and cans of Goya products and packages of Café Bustelo. The bar was stocked with Bacardi and Anís del Mono. Every night after dinner, I sat in my favorite chair and smoked a Padrón or Partagás cigar. During my visits to Miami, I recorded many hours of Cuban radio programming, which I listened to while I drove around in Chapel Hill. For the first three or four years of their lives, David and Miriam spoke and heard only Spanish. When we were at home, their mother and I used Spanish all the time, something we had not done before they were born. When we weren't at home, we found Hispanic or Spanish-speaking baby-sitters. As a result, David and Miriam's first words were the same as mine—*mami, papi, agua, galletica, abuela*. I even taught David the all-purpose Cuban expletive *coño*, roughly equivalent to dammit. Picture a restless two-year-old running up and down the house shouting, "*Coño, coño, coño.*" Although Rosa wasn't thrilled with her son's foreign language skills, my Cuban heart swelled with pride.

• • •

For the kids, the best parts of our Miami summers were the *cumpleaños*, or birthday parties, which we usually celebrated jointly. For David and Miriam, *cumpleaños* were as big a deal as Nochebuena was for me. If in our family Nochebuena was the nocturnal, adult winter celebration, *cumpleaños* were the diurnal, kid-oriented vernal equivalent. Like Nochebuena, *cumpleaños* are communal feasts, tribal pursuits of happiness. American birthday parties tend to be brief affairs for children only. With my children's friends, birthday celebrations barely produce a ripple in the family's routine. The birthday child invites four or five friends who spend a couple of hours at the pool or the skating rink, eat some cake, and go home. But Cuban birthday parties, the kind I grew up with and the kind we replicated in Miami, are prolonged affairs for the entire family. Although the focus is on the children with their *piñata* and birthday cake and games, the adults have their *pastelitos* and *cangrejitos*, their drinks and their music. While the children run around outside, the men play dominoes or watch a baseball game on TV. The party may begin at two or three in the afternoon and go until ten or eleven that night.

The idea behind the *cumpleaños* is that a child's birthday is a cause for rejoicing not just for the child but for parents, relatives, and friends. By limiting the celebration, the way Americans tend to, one asserts the child's separateness, his or her independence from a larger whole. This is why there is no Spanish expression analogous to "birthday child," which singles out one member from the rest of the family. The truth is that the birthday of every member of the family changes the whole family. Like deaths and weddings, birthdays are family events, causes for communal mourning or rejoicing. I was brought up to congratulate parents and grandparents on children's birthdays, to congratulate children on Mother's and Father's Day, and to buy presents not just for the birthday girl but for her brothers and sisters as well. When my kids were younger, and I was less assimilated, I used to congratulate the parents of David's or Miriam's friends in Chapel Hill on their child's birthday. Every time I did so, I was met with a quizzical stare. Eventually, it sank in that Americans don't expect to be congratulated for birthdays that are not their own.

• • •

But in spite of all the *coño* lessons, in spite of all the maps and posters, in spite of all the *cumpleaños* and Nochebuenas, in spite of all the shots of *salsa* and *picadillo*, I didn't succeed in making my children Cuban.

As David and Miriam got older, the language we used at home began to change. Gradually, almost imperceptibly at first, I found myself using more and more English with them. Once they began to spend most of each day at school, I could no longer assume that whatever they saw and felt they saw and felt in Spanish, and it seemed unfair to ask them to repeat in one language events and thoughts that had occurred in another. The choice was either to let them speak in English or limit the range of things they could talk about; having to pick between language and communication, I picked communication. I also became apprehensive that our Spanish-only household was creating too stark a contrast between our domestic and our public selves. In Miami, Spanish *is* a public language, but not in Chapel Hill, where if you say *qué hubo* the guy next to you thinks you're muttering in Chinese. I worried about the effect on my children of hearing their parents speaking one language and the rest of the world speaking another. I knew that until the day I died my first impulse on greeting someone would be to say *qué hubo* the way Cubans do, but I didn't want my kids to feel the same way. One side of me expected David and Miriam to be *cubanitos*; but another side of me cringed at the prospect of having a son and a daughter who, like me, didn't feel at home in their home.

What happened with language happened also with culture. As the years went by, the visits to Miami became less frequent or less prolonged, cousins were replaced by friends, *cumpleaños* were replaced by American sleep-overs, and the *boleros* on the stereo began to alternate with rock or rap. Although I didn't promote these changes, I didn't resist them either. I allowed myself to be carried along, half knowing that by so doing I was changing my own life. Finally, the day came when I realized that I had more or less given up on my project of re-creating Cuba in Chapel Hill. My campaign to raise *cubanitos* had slowed to a standstill. By the time David and Miriam were seven or eight years old, they spoke only English and felt mostly American. When I left their Cuban mother and married an American woman, my house became even less of a tiny Havana.

There are still times when I wish that I had tried harder to make my children preserve more of their Cuban heritage. Sometimes when their grandparents call from Miami and David or Miriam, after saying hello in Spanish, switch immediately to English, I feel like a traitor. At times like these I make up my mind to begin speaking in Spanish to them once again, but I never carry through. As the one-and-a-halfer, I'm supposed to be good at bridging generations, and yet instead of building a bridge between my parents and my children, I've dug a moat between them.

No, I didn't make my kids Cuban, and I'm sure that up there in Cuban heaven my uncles Pepe, Octavio, and Manolo are giving me the evil eye even now. But something else happened that I did not expect: David and Miriam helped to make me American. Before they were born, I thought I had little stake in the United States. I didn't read local newspapers, I paid little attention to current events, I never thought about voting. I saw myself as a transient, not a settler, as just a man passing through. My present was my future, my future was my past, and my past was Cuba.

After becoming a father, and especially after living with my children by myself for a couple of years when I was between marriages, I realized, first, that it's not good for children to be raised as exiles, and second, that it's also not good for children to have parents determined to remain exiles all their lives. Fortunately, children can help push even the most recalcitrant parents beyond themselves. David and Miriam have had no choice but to follow their father in his journey from language to language, from culture to culture, from wife to wife. But they have themselves, without knowing it, helped me along the way, made the trip worth the trouble.

• • •

Miriam and David, Chris and Jen, me and Mary Anne—ours is what is called a blended family. We blend diverse cultures, generations, and personal histories. Sometimes I wonder whether we're truly blended or merely mixed-up.

Chris and Jen, Mary Ann's children from her first marriage, are now twenty and twenty-four years old. Since Jen lives in D.C. and Chris goes to college, they have not lived with us for more than a few weeks at a time, yet through the years we have gotten to know each other fairly well. My relationship with them is guarded but intense. Given that I'm the man for whom their mother left their father (¡dominé!), they have reason to be wary. I'm the Cuban interloper, the Latin lover who swept Mary Anne off her feet and broke up their happy home (which wasn't all that happy). They can't quite figure me out, and I can't quite figure them out. Ultimately, we're ciphers to each other, though perhaps not more than I am to my own wife, or she is to me. I like their slim, healthy, clean looks and their casual, laid-back manner. Neither one is given to grand gestures; neither one of them struts or wears much jewelry. Jen gets her clothes at The Gap or Casual Corner, while Chris's tastes run to oversized T-shirts and baggy jeans that he buys for a dollar at the PTA thrift shop. Jen likes Jimmy Buffett and the Counting Crows; Chris is a Deadhead.

When their parents divorced, Jen and Chris took it in stride. They were always polite and civil. No hysterical middle-of-the-night calls, no accusations of abandonment, no threats of suicide. Unlike my mother, neither one lit a candle to Saint Jude, the patron saint of hopeless causes (but then again, my stepchildren wouldn't know about Saint Jude). Raised in the wake of the sixties, they were taught not to be judgmental. When Mary Anne and I finally got married, after years of storms and stresses, they gladly came to our wedding and acted as witnesses.

Not that Jen and Chris aren't mystified, and sometimes even a little miffed, by my values and habits. One of them once remarked to Mary Anne that I seemed always to be either working or dancing. I argue with Jen about politics, and I argue with Chris about women. Alas, my machismo seems to hold no more truck with him than it does with Miriam. Since by the time I crashed into their lives Jen and Chris were already grown, I'm not sure how much intimacy we will achieve. I suspect that in their eyes I'll always be their mother's husband rather than their stepfather, and that in mine they'll always be Mary Anne's kids rather than my stepchildren. Still, we try in unstated ways to reach out to one another. Chris likes tequila, so sometimes we get tipsy together. Jen likes to dance, so sometimes we party. Chris took up Spanish in college and won the school's Spanish award; Jen and her fiancé signed up for rumba lessons. Every once in a while, searching for common ground, they'll talk about some Cuban-related person or thing that they have come across. Jen will call to say that Jimmy Buffett has a song called "Everybody Has a Cousin in Miami" (now Jen has cousins in Miami too). Chris tells us about his Spanish friend Jaime and brings his girlfriends home to meet his mother's Cuban husband, who's always talking about sex. He calls me G-man, I call him C.

• • •

When I was born in a Havana hospital forty-some years ago, there were a lot of things that no one could have told my father. One of them is that his eldest son would end up married to an American woman who had grown children not by him and who spends her evenings scouring Cuban cookbooks in search of recipes for *quimbombó*. Another is that his own grandchildren would grow up eight hundred miles away (Cuba is about seven hundred miles from tip to tip), and that when he talked to them on the phone his grandson would exclaim, "Dang, Abuelo, wasn't Canseco awesome last night?"

After dinner is over, we all go our separate ways. David and Miriam head for the TV set, Chris and Kim disappear into the night, Jen and Jeff go upstairs to finish the fight they had begun that afternoon, and Mary Anne and I sit on the porch quietly scalping the last of the *mojitos*.

If I stick to the traditional Cuban idea of family, I'm not sure that my far-flung, osterized clan would count. For better and for worse, family has to be fierce, has to be love and hate and stickiness. This mellow blend of mine, it doesn't seem fiery enough. Most of the time we don't even attend each other's *cumpleaños*. Much like the clouds of smoke from my cigars, we come together for a little while and then we disperse. All the children at my table have another table, and tomorrow all four of them will be having dinner with other parents and stepparents. I find this disorienting, as I'm sure our children must. Sometimes when we're all together I have the impression that this is happening to somebody else; other times I have the impression that this could only happen to me. Is this what is meant by after-exile? Is mine a family or an after-family? Am I Gustavo or post-Gustavo?

As I sit on the porch with the fireflies flickering in the trees, I wonder how much of an impact I'll have on my stepchildren, or they on me. Given their age and our limited contact, we're not likely to change each other substantially, but if my marriage to Mary Anne has made David and Miriam and me more American, perhaps it will make Jen and Chris a little bit Latin. I kid them that in order to become honorary Cubans all they need to do is eat *quimbombó* and scream *qué rico* when they have sex. But Jen and Chris are not ABCs or CBAs but ABAs—American-born Americans. Why should I want these kids to be something other than what they are? For my loneliness I have my gallery of Cuban ghosts, who keep me company and sit on my shoulder at dinnertime. The truth is that when I'm with my American family, I enjoy the play of differences as much as the pleasure of recognition. It's crazy to expect to look at them and see myself; I'd rather look at them and see them.

And David and Miriam? How Cuban will they grow up to be? I'm not really sure, but I plan to do my darnedest so that we continue to understand and accompany each other. Like most parents, I recall vividly my children's first day in school. I remember seeing David get out of the car and walk up the ramp, a tiny desolate-looking figure in shorts and a T-shirt, carrying a Thundercats lunch box in one hand. I remember saying to myself, "This is it, I've lost him. Now he's going to be taken over by *los americanos*." When Miriam began school, I had the same sinking feeling, that she was going over to the enemy camp and leaving me for good. Both times my mind wandered to the boy on the dock, the Cuban boy that I was on the dock that morning in 1960, who had seen me board the ferry and leave. As Miriam walked away timidly, the way little kids do on the first day of school, it occurred to me that some sort of cycle was closing that day. The journey that began one October morning in Havana was ending on another morning, many years later, in Chapel Hill. So be it—sooner or later, everybody leaves on their journey. But what I want to believe, what I need to believe, what I cannot find peace without believing, is that when David and Miriam went up that ramp, they took me with them. I don't intend to stay behind again.

WRITING ABOUT THE READING

4. What do you think that the writer means when he states that in his life the "personal and the cultural intertwine" and why does he say this?

5. How and why does Perez Firmat choose "Chapel Hill" and "Miami" to show the contrast between cultures?

6. Contrast Perez Firmat at age twelve with his son at the same age. What probably accounts for many of these differences?

7. How and why does Perez Firmat contrast his own and his children's preferences in food and music?

8. Compare the differences in the ways Cuban Americans and "Anglos" celebrate birthdays (or other occasions). What do these differences reveal about the two cultures?

WRITING FROM YOUR OWN EXPERIENCE

Note: In these assignments, write about your own experience or use that of someone you know, read about, or saw in a film/TV show.

9. Suppose that you were asked to place in a time capsule, to be opened 100 years from now, one selection of music, food, or clothing to represent your generation's experience. What would be your choice and the reasons for this choice?

10. Perez Firmat describes his family as "blended," one in which both spouses have children from a previous marriage. Think of a similar family you know, or use one from a book or TV series, such as *The Brady Bunch*. Why was this "blended" family a happy or unhappy one?

11. Describe your most interesting birthday and explain why this birthday was so memorable.

WRITING ABOUT RESEARCH

12. Trace the origin and development of a musical or dance form of Hispanic origin (such as the conga, mambo, rumba, or tango) and explain why this music or dance has been popular in the United States.

13. One of the outcomes of the Hispanic presence in the United States has been a growth in media serving the Hispanic population. Research a Spanish-language newspaper, magazine, radio station, or TV station. What audience is it trying to reach and why has it been successful in reaching its audience?

14. Research the career of Desi Arnaz and explain how his success as a TV star influenced the dominant society's image of Cuban Americans.

15. After leaving Cuba, many exiles settled in Miami. How and why do you think that this immigrant population has benefited the Miami area?

16. Choose a notable Hispanic American (such as one of the following) and explain why this person is considered to be outstanding in his/her field of endeavor:
    (a) Luis Walter Alvarez (physicist)
    (b) Marlo Castillo (artist)
    (c) Gloria Estefan (singer)

(d) Carolina Herrera (fashion designer)

(e) Oscar Hijuelos, Pulitzer Prize for Fiction (1991)

(f) Ricardo Montalban (actor)

(g) Mario Molina, shared the Nobel Prize in chemistry (1995)

(h) Nicholas Mohr (novelist)

(i) Edward James Olmos (actor)

(j) Miguel Pinero (playwright)

(k) Jorge Ramos (journalist with Univision Spanish-language TV)

(l) Carlos Santana (musician)

(m) Cristina Saralegui (host of Emmy-award winning TV program *Cristina*)

The Myth of the Latin Woman

JUDITH ORTIZ COFER

Judith Ortiz Cofer *(1952–) comes from a military family that moved back and forth every few months from Puerto Rico to Paterson, New Jersey. She received a B.A. degree from Augusta College, Georgia (1974), an M.A. degree from Florida Atlantic University (1977), and a fellowship for study at Oxford University (1977). In 1994, she became a professor of English and creative writing at the University of Georgia. Her many awards include a fellowship from the National Endowment for the Arts (1989).*

Because she was constantly shuttled in her girlhood between Puerto Rico and the mainland, Cofer began to write as a way of helping her bridge the two cultures. The conflict between cultures is the theme of her collection of poetry and prose, entitled The Latin Deli *(1993), based on her life as a Latina in New Jersey. In "The Myth of the Latin Woman" from this collection, Cofer examines the stereotypes of Hispanic women in the dominant culture.*

PREPARING TO READ

1. What are some of the different cultural expectations (such as appearance, accepted behavior, career expectations, participation in activities, or expression of emotions) for a man or woman in U.S. society?

2. Support or refute the following statement: Depictions of Hispanic women as either very sexy or comic are common in ads, movies, and on TV.

3. Why do you think it is important (or not important) to present an authentic picture of Hispanic Americans (or other minorities) in ads, in the movies, and on TV?

4. What are some of the ways in which parents and schools can encourage young women (and/or young men) to be more self-reliant?

THE MYTH OF THE LATIN WOMAN

On a bus trip to London from Oxford University where I was earning some graduate credits one summer, a young man, obviously fresh from a pub, spotted me and as if struck by inspiration went down on his knees in the aisle. With both hands over his heart he broke into an Irish tenor's rendition of "María" from *West Side Story*. My politely amused fellow passengers gave his lovely voice the round of gentle applause it deserved. Though I was not quite as amused, I managed my version of an English smile: no show of teeth, no extreme contortions of the facial muscles—I was at this time of my life practicing reserve and cool. Oh, that British control, how I coveted it. But María had followed me to London, reminding me of a prime fact of my life: you can leave the Island, master the English language, and travel as far as you can, but if you are a Latina, especially one like me who so obviously belongs to Rita Moreno's gene pool, the Island travels with you.

This is sometimes a very good thing—it may win you that extra minute of someone's attention. But with some people, the same things can make *you* an island—not so much a tropical paradise as an Alcatraz, a place nobody wants to visit. As a Puerto Rican girl growing up in the United States and wanting like most children to "belong," I resented the stereotype that my Hispanic appearance called forth from many people I met.

Our family lived in a large urban center in New Jersey during the sixties, where life was designed as a microcosm of my parents' casas on the island. We spoke in Spanish, we ate Puerto Rican food bought at the bodega, and we practiced strict Catholicism complete with Saturday confession and Sunday mass at a church where our parents were accommodated into a one-hour Spanish mass slot, performed by a Chinese priest trained as a missionary for Latin America.

As a girl I was kept under strict surveillance, since virtue and modesty were, by cultural equation, the same as family honor. As a teenager I was instructed on how to behave as a proper señorita. But it was a conflicting message girls got, since the Puerto Rican mothers also encouraged their daughters to look and act like women and to dress in clothes our Anglo friends and their mothers found too "mature" for our age. It was, and is, cultural, yet I often felt humiliated when I appeared at an American friend's party wearing a dress more suitable to a semiformal than to a playroom birthday celebration. At Puerto Rican festivities, neither the music nor the colors we wore could be too loud. I still experience a vague sense of letdown when I'm invited to a "party" and it turns out to be a marathon conversation in hushed tones rather than a fiesta with salsa, laughter, and dancing—the kind of celebration I remember from my childhood.

I remember Career Day in our high school, when teachers told us to come dressed as if for a job interview. It quickly became obvious that to the barrio girls, "dressing up" sometimes meant wearing ornate jewelry and clothing that would be more appropriate (by mainstream standards) for the company Christmas party than as daily office attire. That morning I had agonized in front of my closet, trying to figure out what a "career girl" would wear because, essentially, except for Marlo Thomas on TV, I had no models on which to base my decision. I knew how to dress for school: at the Catholic school I attended we all wore uniforms; I knew how to dress for Sunday mass, and I knew what dresses to wear for parties at my relatives' homes. Though I do not re-call the precise details of my Career Day outfit, it must have been a composite of the above choices. But I remember a comment my friend (an Italian-American) made in later years that coalesced my impres-sions of that day. She said that at the business school she was attend-ing the Puerto Rican girls always stood out for wearing "everything at once." She meant, of course, too much jewelry, too many accessories. On that day at school, we were simply made the negative models by the nuns who were themselves not credible fashion experts to any of us. But it was painfully obvious to me that to the others, in their tai-lored skirts and silk blouses, we must have seemed "hopeless" and "vulgar." Though I now know that most adolescents feel out of step much of the time, I also know that for the Puerto Rican girls of my generation that sense was intensified. The way our teachers and class-mates looked at us that day in school was just a taste of the culture clash that awaited us in the real world, where prospective employers and men on the street would often misinterpret our tight skirts and jingling bracelets as a come-on.

Mixed cultural signals have perpetuated certain stereotypes—for example, that of the Hispanic woman as the "Hot Tamale" or sexual firebrand. It is a one-dimensional view that the media have found easy to promote. In their special vocabulary, advertisers have designated "sizzling" and "smoldering" as the adjectives of choice for describing not only the foods but also the women of Latin America. From conver-sations in my house I recall hearing about the harassment that Puerto Rican women endured in factories where the "boss men" talked to them as if sexual innuendo was all they understood and, worse, often gave them the choice of submitting to advances or being fired.

It is custom, however, not chromosomes, that leads us to choose scar-let over pale pink. As young girls, we were influenced in our decisions about clothes and colors by the women—older sisters and mothers who had grown up on a tropical island where the natural environment was a riot of primary colors, where showing your skin was one way to keep cool as well as to look sexy. Most important of all, on the island, women perhaps felt freer to dress and move more provocatively, since, in most cases, they were protected by the traditions, mores, and laws of a Spanish/Catholic system of morality and machismo whose main rule was: *You may look at my sister, but if you touch her I will kill you.* The extended family and church structure could provide a young woman with a circle of safety in her small pueblo on the island; if a man "wronged" a girl, everyone would close in to save her family honor.

This is what I have gleaned from my discussions as an adult with older Puerto Rican women. They have told me about dressing in their best party clothes on Saturday nights and going to the town's plaza to promenade with their girlfriends in front of the boys they liked. The males were thus given an opportunity to admire the women and to express their admiration in the form of *piropos*: erotically charged street poems they composed on the spot. I have been subjected to a few piropos while visiting the Island, and they can be outrageous, although custom dictates that they must never cross into obscenity. This ritual, as I understand it, also entails a show of studied indifference on the woman's part; if she is "decent," she must not acknowledge the man's impassioned words. So I do understand how things can be lost in translation. When a Puerto Rican girl dressed in her idea of what is attractive meets a man from the mainstream culture who has been trained to react to certain types of clothing as a sexual signal, a clash is likely to take place. The line I first heard based on this aspect of the myth happened when the boy who took me to my first formal dance leaned over to plant a sloppy overeager kiss painfully on my mouth, and when I didn't respond with sufficient passion said in a resentful tone: "I thought you Latin girls were supposed to mature early"—my first instance of being thought of as a fruit or vegetable—I was supposed to *ripen*, not just grow into womanhood like other girls.

It is surprising to some of my professional friends that some people, including those who should know better, still put others "in their place." Though rarer, these incidents are still commonplace in my life. It happened to me most recently during a stay at a very classy metropolitan hotel favored by young professional couples for their weddings. Late one evening after the theater, as I walked toward my room with my new colleague (a woman with whom I was coordinating an arts program), a middle-aged man in a tuxedo, a young girl in satin and lace on his arm, stepped directly into our path. With his champagne glass extended toward me, he exclaimed, "Evita!"

Our way blocked, my companion and I listened as the man half-recited, half-bellowed "Don't Cry for Me, Argentina." When he finished, the young girl said: "How about a round of applause for my daddy?" We complied, hoping this would bring the silly spectacle to a close. I was becoming aware that our little group was attracting the attention of the other guests. "Daddy" must have perceived this too, and he once more barred the way as we tried to walk past him. He began to shout-sing a ditty to the tune of "La Bamba"—except the lyrics were about a girl named María whose exploits all rhymed with her name and gonorrhea. The girl kept saying "Oh, Daddy" and looking at me with pleading eyes. She wanted me to laugh along with the others. My companion and I stood silently waiting for the man to end his offensive song. When he finished, I looked not at him but at his daughter. I advised her calmly never to ask her father what he had done in the army. Then I walked between them and to my room. My friend complimented me on my cool handling of the situation. I confessed to her that I really had wanted to push the jerk into the swimming pool. I knew that this same man—probably a corporate executive, well educated, even worldly by most standards—would not have been likely to regale a white woman with a dirty song in public. He would perhaps have checked his impulse by assuming that she could be somebody's wife or mother, or at least *somebody* who might take offense. But to him, I was just an Evita or a María: merely a character in his cartoon-populated universe.

Because of my education and my proficiency with the English language, I have acquired many mechanisms for dealing with the anger I experience. This was not true for my parents, nor is it true for the many Latin women working at menial jobs who must put up with stereotypes about our ethnic group such as: "They make good domestics." This is another facet of the myth of the Latin woman in the United States. Its origin is simple to deduce. Work as domestics, waitressing, and factory jobs are all that's available to women with little English and few skills. The myth of the Hispanic menial has been sustained by the same media phenomenon that made "Mammy" from *Gone with the Wind* America's idea of the black woman for generations; María, the housemaid or counter girl, is now indelibly etched into the national psyche. The big and the little screens have presented us with the picture of the funny Hispanic maid, mispronouncing words and cooking up a spicy storm in a shiny California kitchen.

This media-engendered image of the Latina in the United States has been documented by feminist Hispanic scholars, who claim that such portrayals are partially responsible for the denial of opportunities for upward mobility among Latinas in the professions. I have a

Chicana friend working on a Ph.D. in philosophy at a major university. She says her doctor still shakes his head in puzzled amazement at all the "big words" she uses. Since I do not wear my diplomas around my neck for all to see, I too have on occasion been sent to that "kitchen," where some think I obviously belong.

One such incident that has stayed with me, though I recognize it as a minor offense, happened on the day of my first public poetry reading. It took place in Miami in a boat-restaurant where we were having lunch before the event. I was nervous and excited as I walked in with my notebook in my hand. An older woman motioned me to her table. Thinking (foolish me) that she wanted me to autograph a copy of my brand new slender volume of verse, I went over. She ordered a cup of coffee from me, assuming that I was the waitress. Easy enough to mistake my poems for menus, I suppose. I know that it wasn't an intentional act of cruelty, yet of all the good things that happened that day, I remember that scene most clearly, because it reminded me of what I had to overcome before anyone would take me seriously. In retrospect I understand that my anger gave my reading fire, that I have almost always taken doubts in my abilities as a challenge—and that the result is, most times, a feeling of satisfaction at having won a convert when I see the cold, appraising eyes warm to my words, the body language change, the smile that indicates that I have opened some avenue for communication. That day I read to that woman and her lowered eyes told me that she was embarrassed at her little faux pas, and when I willed her to look up at me, it was my victory, and she graciously allowed me to punish her with my full attention. We shook hands at the end of the reading, and I never saw her again. She has probably forgotten the whole thing but maybe not.

Yet I am one of the lucky ones. My parents made it possible for me to acquire a stronger footing in the mainstream culture by giving me the chance at an education. And books and art have saved me from the harsher forms of ethnic and racial prejudice that many of my Hispanic *compañeras* have had to endure. I travel a lot around the United States, reading from my books of poetry and my novel, and the reception I most often receive is one of positive interest by people who want to know more about my culture. There are, however, thousands of Latinas without the privilege of an education or the entrée into society that I have. For them life is a struggle against the misconceptions perpetuated by the myth of the Latina as whore, domestic, or criminal. We cannot change this by legislating the way people look at us. The transformation, as I see it, has to occur at a much more individual level. My personal goal in my public life is to try to replace the old pervasive stereotypes and myths about Latinas with a much more interesting set of realities. Every time I give a reading, I hope the stories I tell, the dreams and fears I examine in my work, can achieve some universal truth which will get my audience past the particulars of my skin color, my accent, or my clothes.

I once wrote a poem in which I called us Latinas "God's brown daughters." This poem is really a prayer of sorts, offered upward, but also, through the human-to-human channel of art, outward. It is a prayer for communication, and for respect. In it, Latin women pray "in Spanish to an Anglo God/with a Jewish heritage," and they are "fervently hoping / that if not omnipotent, / at least He be bilingual."

WRITING ABOUT THE READING

5. Using some examples of "myths" that Cofer provides, explain why she calls these "myths."
6. Why does the writer compare the stereotype of "Maria" to that of "Mammy"?
7. How and why does the man reveal his assumptions about Hispanic women when he sings to the author?
8. What is Cofer's purpose in writing this essay?
9. How and why does she sometimes use humor to support her purpose?

WRITING FROM YOUR OWN EXPERIENCE

Note: In these assignments, write about your own experience or use that of someone you know, read about, or saw in a film/TV show.

10. Cofer explains how she practiced "reserve and cool" in a difficult social situation. Recall when you were in a similarly difficult social situation. Why was this situation difficult and what did you do about it?
11. In the past, girls were raised with limited opportunities. Think of a woman (such as a police officer, the head of a company or college, a judge, a mayor of a city, a senator, or an officer in the military) who has achieved far beyond the former expectations for women. Explain why you think (or disagree) her success shows that men and women have equal opportunities in today's society.

12. Today's ads and TV shows often feature a cultural ideal of extremely thin women. Explain whether you think that this ideal is harmful to young women.

13. Clothing has been studied as a "language" used to convey social position and attitudes. Reviewing your present wardrobe (or one that you would like to purchase), decide on the clothing that you would wear to a formal event (such as an interview or wedding) and an informal event (such as a class, concert, or a game). Compare your choice of clothing and explain what message you would send with each outfit.

WRITING ABOUT RESEARCH

14. Why were many Puerto Ricans upset about the U.S. Navy using Vieques for bombing exercises?

15. Research the concept of "machismo" (i.e., masculine courage and confidence) in Hispanic culture. Explain why you believe that the concept of "machismo" is harmful (or not harmful) to Hispanic women.

16. Many Puerto Ricans have settled in the New York area. Research their experience and explain why the word "Nuyorican" has been coined to describe this group.

17. Many recent books (such as the best-selling *Men Are from Mars, Women Are from Venus*) and articles express the writer's belief that the communication styles of men and women are different. Research this issue of communication differences and explain why you agree or disagree with this belief.

Selection 7

Like Mexicans

GARY SOTO

Gary Soto (1952–), *Mexican American poet and writer, was born in Fresno, California, and raised in the San Joaquin Valley. He received a B.A. degree from California State University, Fresno (1974) and an M.F.A. degree from the University of California, Irvine (1976). At the University of California, Berkeley (1979–1992), Soto taught in both the English and Chicano Studies Departments. He left teaching in 1993 to devote full-time to writing. Soto, who has received more prestigious awards for his poetry than any other Hispanic American writer, was awarded the Academy of American Poets Prize in 1974. His book of poetry,* The Tale of Sunlight *(1977), was nominated for the Pulitzer Prize in 1977.*

Based on his own early experience as a migrant worker, Soto writes about the everyday lives of working-class people. Although Soto draws from his Mexican American heritage, his poetry and prose transcend ethnicity to embrace all people. In "Like Mexicans" from Small Faces *(1993), Soto shows how he grew to appreciate the similarities and differences between his own and other ethnic cultures.*

PREPARING TO READ

1. Explain why you agree (or disagree) that today's young people have little to learn from their elders.
2. In the past, people often went to the elders of their community for advice. Where do people go today for advice and why do they go to these sources?
3. What are some of the ways friendships formed in childhood are similar to or different from those we form as adults?
4. Why does social class generally influence a person's choice of friends and/or romantic attachments?

LIKE MEXICANS

My grandmother gave me bad advice and good advice when I was in my early teens. For the bad advice, she said that I should become a barber because they made good money and listened to the radio all day. "Honey, they don't work como burros," she would say every time I visited her. She made the sound of donkeys braying. "Like that, honey!" For the good advice, she said that I should marry a Mexican girl. "No Okies, hijo"—she would say—"Look my son. He marry one and they fight every day about I don't know what and I don't know what." For her, everyone who wasn't Mexican, black, or Asian were Okies. The French were Okies, the Italians in suits were Okies. When I asked about Jews, whom I had read about, she asked for a picture. I rode home on my bicycle and returned with a calendar depicting the important races of the world. "Pues si, son Okies tambien!" she said, nodding her head. She saved the calendar away and we went to the living room where she lectured me on the virtues of the Mexican girl: first, she could cook and, second, she acted like a woman, not a man, in her husband's home. She said she would tell me about a third when I got a little older.

I asked my mother about it—becoming a barber and marrying Mexican. She was in the kitchen. Steam curled from a pot of boiling beans, the radio was on, looking as squat as a loaf of bread. "Well, if you want to be a barber—they say they make good money." She slapped a round steak with a knife, her glasses slipping down with each strike. She stopped and looked up. "If you find a good Mexican girl, marry her of course." She returned to slapping the meat and I went to the backyard where my brother and David King were sitting on the lawn feeling the inside of their cheeks.

"This is what girls feel like," my brother said, rubbing the inside of his cheek. David put three finger inside his mouth and scratched. I ignored them and climbed the back fence to see my best friend, Scott, a second-generation Okie. I called him and his mother pointed to the side of the house where his bedroom was a small aluminum trailer, the kind you gawk at when they're flipped over on the freeway, wheels spinning in the air. I went around to find Scott pitching horseshoes.

I picked up a set of rusty ones and joined him. While we played, we talked about school and friends and record albums. The horseshoes scuffed up dirt, sometimes ringing the iron that threw out a meager shadow like a sundial. After three argued-over games, we pulled two oranges apiece from his tree and started down the alley still talking school and friends and record albums. We pulled more oranges from the alley and talked about who we would marry. "No offense, Scott," I said with an orange slice in my mouth, "but I would never marry an Okie." We walked in step, almost touching, with a sled of shadows dragging behind us. "No offense, Gary," Scott said, "but I would *never* marry a Mexican." I looked at him: a fang of orange slice showed from his munching mouth. I didn't think anything of it. He had his girl and I had mine. But our seventh-grade vision was the same: to marry, get jobs, buy cars and maybe a house if we had money left over.

We talked about our future lives until, to our surprise, we were on the downtown mall, two miles from home. We bought a bag of popcorn at Penneys and sat on a bench near the fountain watching Mexican and Okie girls pass. "That one's mine," I pointed with my chin when a girl with eyebrows arched into black rainbows ambled by. "She's cute," Scott said about a girl with yellow hair and a mouthful of gum. We dreamed aloud, our chins busy pointing out girls. We agreed that we couldn't wait to become men and lift them onto our laps.

But the woman I married was not Mexican but Japanese. It was a surprise to me. For years, I went about wide-eyed in my search for the brown girl in a white dress at a dance. I searched the playground at the baseball diamond. When the girls raced for grounders, their hair bounced like something that couldn't be caught. When they sat together in the lunchroom, heads pressed together, I knew they were talking about us Mexican guys. I saw them and dreamed them. I threw my face into my pillow, making up sentences that were good as in the movies.

But when I was twenty, I fell in love with this other girl who worried my mother, who had my grandmother asking once again to see the calendar of the Important Races of the World. I told her I had thrown it away years before. I took a much-glanced-at snapshot from my wallet. We looked at it together, in silence. Then grandma reclined in her chair, lit a cigarette, and said, "Es pretty." She blew and asked with all her worry pushed up to her forehead: "Chinese?"

I was in love and there was no looking back. She was the one. I told my mother who was slapping hamburger into patties. "Well, sure if you want to marry her," she said. But the more I talked, the more concerned she became. Later I began to worry. Was it all a mistake? "Marry a Mexican girl," I heard my mother say in my mind. I heard it at breakfast. I heard it over math problems, between Western Civilization and cultural geography. But then one afternoon while I was hitchhiking home from school, it struck me like a baseball in the back: my mother wanted me to marry someone of my own social class—a poor girl. I considered my fiancee, Carolyn, and she didn't look poor, though I knew she came from a family of farm workers and pull-yourself-up-by-your-bootstraps ranchers. I asked my brother, who was marrying Mexican poor that fall, if I should marry a poor girl. He screamed "Yeah" above his terrible guitar playing in his bedroom. I considered my sister who had married Mexican. Cousins were dating Mexican. Uncles were remarrying poor women. I asked Scott, who was still my best friend, and he said, "She's too good for you, so you better not."

I worried about it until Carolyn took me home to meet her parents. We drove in her Plymouth until the houses gave way to farms and ranches and finally her house fifty feet from the highway. When we pulled into the drive, I panicked and begged Carolyn to make a U-turn and go back so we could talk about it over a soda. She pinched my cheek, calling me a "silly boy." I felt better, though, when I got out of the car and saw the house: the chipped paint, a cracked window, boards for a walk to the back door. There were rusting cars near the barn. A tractor with a net of spiderwebs under a mulberry. A field. A bale of barbed wire like children's scribbling leaning against an empty chicken coop. Carolyn took my hand and pulled me to my future mother-in-law who was coming out to greet us.

We had lunch: sandwiches, potato chips, and iced tea. Carolyn and her mother talked mostly about neighbors and the congregation at the Japanese Methodist Church in West Fresno. Her father, who was in khaki work clothes, excused himself with a wave that was almost a salute and went outside. I heard a truck start, a dog bark, and then the truck rattle away.

Carolyn's mother offered another sandwich, but I declined with a shake of my head and a smile. I looked around when I could, when I was not saying over and over that I was a college student, hinting that I could take care of her daughter. I shifted my chair. I saw newspapers piled in corners, dusty cereal boxes and vinegar bottles in corners. The wallpaper was bubbled from rain that had come in from a bad roof. Dust. Dust lay on lamp shades and window sills. These people are just like Mexicans, I thought. Poor people.

Carolyn's mother asked me through Carolyn if I would like a *sushi*. A plate of black and white things were held in front of me. I took one, wide-eyed, and turned it over like a foreign coin. I was biting into one when I saw a kitten crawl up the window screen over the sink. I chewed and the kitten opened its mouth of terror as she crawled higher, wanting in to paw the leftovers from our plates. I looked at Carolyn who said that the cat was just showing off. I looked up in time to see it fall. It crawled up, then fell again.

We talked for an hour and had apple pie and coffee, slowly. Finally, we got up with Carolyn taking my hand. Slightly embarrassed, I tried to pull away but her grip held me. I let her have her way as she led me down the hallway with her mother right behind me. When I opened the door, I was startled by a kitten clinging to the screen door, its mouth screaming "cat food, dog biscuits, *sushi.* . . . " I opened the door and the kitten, still holding on, whined in the language of hungry animals. When I got into Carolyn's car, I looked back: the cat was still clinging. I asked Carolyn if it were possibly hungry, but she said the cat was being silly. She started the car, waved to her mother, and bounced us over the rain-poked drive, patting my thigh for being her lover baby. Carolyn waved again. I looked back, waving, then gawking at a window screen where there were now three kittens clawing and screaming to get in. Like Mexicans, I thought. I remembered the Molinas and how the cats clung to their screens—cats they shot down with squirt guns. On the highway, I felt happy, pleased by it all. I patted Carolyn's thigh. Her people were like Mexicans, only different.

WRITING ABOUT THE READING

5. Why does the calendar figure so prominently in this essay?
6. Why has Soto included the episode about the oranges?
7. What are some of the similarities and differences between Soto and Scott?
8. Choose specific details from the description of Carolyn's home. What is suggested about Carolyn's family by these details?
9. What does Soto mean when he concludes that Carolyn's family are "like Mexicans, only different" and why does he say this?
10. Explain whether you think that Soto follows or disregards his grandmother's advice about marriage.

WRITING FROM YOUR OWN EXPERIENCE

Note: In these assignments, write about your own experience or use that of someone you know, read about, or saw in a film/TV show.

11. Soto's grandmother gave him advice about choosing a wife. Remember when an older person, such as a grandparent or teacher,

gave you some advice. Why did you accept or reject this advice and what were the consequences of your action?

12. What are the three to five most important characteristics you require in a friend and why are these traits so important?

13. Recall a time when you rebelled in some way against your family, school, church, or other organization. Why did you rebel and what was the outcome of your rebellion?

14. People sometimes need a sympathetic friend, as shown by the phrase "being there for me." Think of a difficult time when you were supportive of a friend or a friend was helpful to you. How and why was this support offered?

WRITING ABOUT RESEARCH

15. How and why has the United Farm Workers, organized by Cesar Chavez in 1965, been a leader in the movement for social and/or economic justice for Mexican American farmworkers?

16. How and why did events in California (such as the Gold Rush) lead to conflict with Mexico and the War of 1848?

17. In this selection, the grandmother uses the term "Okies." Why did many people ("Okies") move from Oklahoma to California in the 1930s?

Un Poquito de Tu Amor
[A Little Bit of Your Love]

SANDRA CISNEROS

Sandra Cisneros *(1954–), poet and writer, is the daughter of a Mexican father and a Chicana mother who frequently moved their family between Chicago and Mexico. She received a B.A. degree (1976) from Loyola University and an M.F.A. (1978) from the University of Iowa Writer's Workshop. Cisneros has been widely praised as the first major Chicana writer. She has received several fellowships and awards, including a National Endowment for the Arts grant, that have allowed her to devote herself full-time to writing.*

Drawing on her childhood experiences in Chicago, Cisneros's novel, The House on Mango Street *(1984), is narrated by a girl who describes the tragicomic lives of the women who live in her barrio. Her 1991 book,* Woman Hollering Creek and Other Stories, *set in San Antonio, Texas, uses interior monologues to reveal the contemporary lives of Mexican American women.*

In the following selection, Cisneros shows how her father's love taught her to feel life intensely. "Un Poquito de Tu Amor" is one of a collection of essays entitled Las Christmas: Favorite Latino Authors Share Their Holiday Memories *(1998).*

PREPARING TO READ

1. Explain whether you think that the media focus too much on news about disasters or violent events and not enough on positive events.
2. What do you use as your chief source of news (such as newspapers, news magazines, TV, or the Internet) and why do you prefer this source?
3. Why does a person often become more aware of a connection to all humanity after experiencing a tragedy, such as a relative or friend's death?

UN POQUITO DE TU AMOR
[A LITTLE BIT OF YOUR LOVE]

When my father died last year, a week before Valentine's Day, a piece of my heart died with him. My father, that supreme sentimental fool, loved my brothers and me to excess in a kind of over-the-top, rococo fever, all arabesques and sugar spirals, as sappy and charming as the romantic Mexican boleros he loved to sing. *Dame un poquito de tu amor siquiera, dame un poquito de tu amor nomás.* . . . Music from my time, Father would say proudly, and I could almost smell the gardenias and Tres Flores hair oil.

Before my father died, it was simple cordiality that prompted me to say, "I'm sorry," when comforting the bereaved. But with his death I am initiated into the family of humanity, I am connected to all deaths and to their survivors: *"Lo siento,"* which translates as both "I am sorry" and "I feel it" all at once.

Lo siento. Since his death, I feel life more intensely.

My father, born under the eagle and serpent of the Mexican flag, died beneath a blanket of stars and stripes, a U.S. World War II veteran. Like most immigrants, he was overly patriotic, exceptionally hardworking, and, above all, a great believer in family. Yet often I'm aware my father's life doesn't count, he's not "history," not the "American" politicians mean when they talk about "American."

I thought of my father especially this holiday season. The day before Christmas 1997, forty-five unarmed Mayas were slain while they prayed in a chapel in Acteal, Chiapas—twenty-one of them women, fourteen children. The Mexican president was shocked and promised to hold all those responsible accountable. The Mexican people aren't fools. Everybody knows who's responsible, but it's too much to wish for the Mexican president to fire himself.

I know the deaths in Chiapas are linked to me here in the United States. I know the massacre is connected to removing native people from their land, because although the people are poor the land is very rich and the government knows this. And the Mexican debt is connected to my high standard of living, and the military presence is necessary to calm U.S. investors, and the music goes round and round and it comes out here.

I have been thinking and thinking about all this from my home in San Antonio, Texas, as fidgety as a person with *comezón*, an itching, a hankering, an itch I can't quite scratch. What is my responsibility as a writer in light of these events? As a woman, as a mestiza? As a U.S.

citizen who lives on several borders? What do I do as the daughter of a Mexican man? Father, tell me. *Ayúdame*, help me, why don't you. *Lo siento*. I have been searching for answers. On Christmas, I am reverberating like a bell.

In my father's house, because my father was my father—*Hello, my friend!*—our Christmas dinners were a global feast, a lesson in history, diplomacy, and the capacity of the stomach to put aside racial grievances. Our holidays were a unique hybrid of cultures that perhaps could only happen in a city like Chicago, a bounty contributed by family and intermarriage, multiethnic neighborhoods, and the diversity of my father's upholstery-shop employees.

To this day, a typical Christmas meal at our home consists first and foremost of tamales, that Indian delicacy that binds us to the preconquest. Twenty-five dozen for our family is typical, the popular red tamales, the fiery green tamales, and the sweet, pink tamales filled with jam and raisins for the kids. Sometimes they're my mother's home-made batch—*This is the last year I'm going to make them!*—but more often they're ordered in advance from someone else willing to go through all the trouble, most recently from the excellent tamale lady in front of Carnicería Jiménez on North Avenue, who operates from a shopping cart.

Father's annual contribution was his famous *bacalao*, a codfish stew of Spanish origin, which he made standing in one spot like a TV chef—*Go get me a bowl, bring me an apron, somebody give me the tomatoes, wash them first, hand me that knife and chopping board, where are the olives?*

Every year we are so spoiled we expect—and receive—a Christmas tray of home-made pierogis and Polish sausage, sometimes courtesy of my sister-in-law's family, the Targonskis, and sometimes from my father's Polish upholsterers, who can hardly speak a word of English. We also serve Jamaican meat pies, a legacy from Darryl, who was once father's furniture refinisher, but has long since left. And finally, our Christmas dinner includes the Italian magnificence from Ferrara Bakery in our old neighborhood on West Taylor Street. Imagine if a cake looked like the Vatican. We've been eating Ferrara's pastries since I was in the third grade.

But this is no formal Normal Rockwell sit-down dinner. We eat when we're inspired by hunger or by *antojo*, literally "before the eye." All day pots are on the stove steaming and the microwave is beeping. It's common to begin a dessert plate of cannolis while someone next to you is finishing breakfast, a pork tamale sandwiched inside a piece of French bread, a mestizo invention thanks to the French intervention.

History is present at our table. The doomed Emperor Maximiliano's French bread as well as the Aztec corn tamales of the Americas, our Andalusian recipe for codfish, our moves in and out of neighbor-hoods where we were the brown corridor between Chicago communi-ties at war with one another. And finally a history of intermarriage, of employees who loved my father enough to share a plate of their home-made delicacies with our family even if our countries couldn't share anything else.

Forty-five are dead in Acteal. My father is gone. I read the news-papers and the losses ring in my heart. More than half the Mexican-American kids in this country are dropping out of high school—more than half—and our politicians' priority is bigger prisons. I live in a state where there are more people sentenced to death than anywhere else in the world. Alamo Heights, the affluent, white neighborhood of my city, values Spanish as a second language beginning in the first grade, yet elsewhere lawmakers work to demolish bilingual education for Spanish-dominant children. Two hours away from my home, the U.S. military is setting up camp in the name of bandits and drug lords. But I'm not stupid; I know who they mean to keep away. *Lo siento*. I feel it.

I'm thinking this while I attend a Latino leadership conference between the holidays. I don't know what I expect from this gathering of Latino leaders, exactly, but I know I don't want to leave without a statement about what's happened in Acteal. Surely at least the Latino community recognizes the forty-five are our family.

"It is like a family," one Arizona politico explains. "But understand, to you it may be a father who's died, but to me it's a distant cousin."

Is it too much to ask our leaders to lead?

"You're too impatient," one Latina tells me, and I'm so stunned I can't respond. A wild karaoke begins, and a Chicano filmmaker begins to preach—There's a season to play and a season to rage. He talks and talks till I have to blink back the tears. After what seems like an eter-nity, he finally finishes by saying, "You know what you have to do, don't you?"

And then it hits me, I do know what I have to do.

I will tell a story.

When we were in college my mother realized investing in real es-tate was the answer to our economic woes. Her plans were modest: to buy a cheap fixer-upper in the barrio that would bring us income. After months of searching, Mother finally found something we could afford, a scruffy building on the avenue with a store that could serve as Father's upholstery shop and two apartments above that would pay the mortgage. At last my mother was a respectable landlady.

Almost immediately a family on the third floor began paying their rent late. It wasn't an expensive apartment, something like a hundred dollars, but every first of the month, they were five or ten dollars short and would deliver the rent with a promise to pay the balance the next payday, which they did. Every month it was the same . . . the rent minus a few dollars promised for next Friday.

Mother hated to be taken advantage of. *Do they think we're rich or something, don't we have bills too?* She sent Father, who was on good terms with everybody. *You go and talk to that family, I've had it*!

And so Father went, and a little later quietly returned.

"I fixed it," Father announced.

"Already? How? What did you do?"

"I lowered the rent."

Mother was ready to throw a fit. Until Father said, "Remember when ten dollars meant a lot to us?"

Mother was silent, as if by some *milagro* she remembered. Who would've thought Father was capable of such genius? He was not by nature a clever man. But he inspires me now to be creative in ways I never realized.

I don't wish to make my father seem more than what he was. He wasn't Gandhi; he lived a life terrified of those different from himself. He never read a newspaper and was naive enough to believe history as told by *la televisión*. And, as my mother keeps reminding me, he wasn't a perfect husband either. But he was very kind and at some things extraordinary. He was a wonderful father.

Maybe I've looked to the wrong leaders for leadership. Maybe what's needed this new year are a few outrageous ideas. Something absurd and genius like those of my father, whose kindness and generosity teach me to enlarge my heart.

Maybe it's time to lower the rent.

Dame un poquito de tu amor siquiera, dame un poquito de tu amor nomás . . . ever since the year began that song runs through my head. My father just won't let up. *Lo siento*. I feel it.

Papá, Buddha, Allah, Jesus Christ, Yahweh, La Virgen de Guadalupe, the Universe, the God in us, help us. *Danos un poquito de tu amor siquiera, danos un poquito de tu amor nomás* . . . just a little bit of your love at least, just a little bit of your love, just that. . .

WRITING ABOUT THE READING

4. Choose one or more of the Spanish words or expressions used by Cisneros and explain what you think it means. Why do you think that she included some of the Spanish language in this essay?

5. Why does Cisneros begin the essay by associating her father's death with Valentine's Day?

6. What do the food and traditions of the Christmas celebration show about Cisneros's family?

7. Why does Cisneros see a connection between the massacre at Chiapas and her own life?

8. What does the story about the rent payment reveal about her father's character?

9. What has Cisneros learned from her father?

WRITING FROM YOUR OWN EXPERIENCE

Note: In these assignments, write about your own experience or use that of someone you know, read about, or saw in a film/TV show.

10. Cisneros is upset when she learns of the slaying of Mayas in Acteal. Can you recall some natural or man-made disaster (such as a bad storm, a flood, a power blackout, or a car accident) that you experienced or learned about? Why were you affected by this disaster and what did you learn from this experience?

11. Cisneros recalls her father's generosity to his tenants when they lacked money for the rent. Recall a time when you performed a similar, good-hearted act. Why did you act kindly and what was the result of this generous act?

12. Some people make an effort to perform at least one act of kindness every day. Think of some possible good-hearted acts you could undertake today. Which act is the most appealing to you and why would you choose this act of kindness?

13. Have you ever reached out to get to know someone of a different ethnic or racial background? Why was this attempt successful (or unsuccessful) and what were some of the consequences of this effort?

WRITING ABOUT RESEARCH

14. Choose an ethnic group (such as Mexican American) and research the celebration of a traditional holiday (New Year's, Christmas, Cinco de Mayo, carnival, etc.) in this group. How and why is this holiday celebrated?

15. Choose an ethnic group and research one of its observances of a major event in life (such as a birth, a "coming of age," a wedding,

or a funeral). What are the customs associated with this event and what do they represent?

16. How and why does your college celebrate a traditional event (such as homecoming or graduation)?

17. Choose an organization or business (such as the military, church, theater, or judicial system) and research some of its traditions. What do these traditions represent for this organization?

18. Cisneros mentions the famous Mexican shrine of "La Virgen de Guadalupe." What is the history of this shrine and why does it play such an important role in Mexican culture?

Turning Youth Gangs Around

LUIS J. RODRIGUEZ

Luis Rodriguez *(1954–) is a Mexican American poet and journalist who was born in El Paso, Texas, and grew up in South Central Los Angeles. In his early years, he worked as a truck driver, steel mill worker, carpenter, and chemical refinery worker. He attended California State University (1972–1973), East Los Angeles College (1978–1979), and the University of California, Berkeley (1980). Rodriguez's poetry and articles have been published in many journals.*

Rodriguez's memoir, Always Running: La Vida Loca—Gang Days in L.A. *(1993), was awarded the Carl Sandburg Award for a Non-Fiction Book. As a member of an East Los Angeles gang, Rodriguez participated in criminal activities and was imprisoned several times. Twenty-five of his friends died of gang violence before reaching the age of eighteen. Today, Rodriguez credits his love of writing as one of the factors that helped him escape from a life of crime.*

Rodriguez sees himself as a writer who speaks for the urban poor, those he describes as the socially ostracized children of workers in menial jobs. In "Turning Youth Gangs Around," Rodriguez, drawing from his own experience, explains why impoverished young men often become gang members. He believes that these young men have both a need to belong and a sense of powerlessness. The gang satisfies these needs by offering them friendship, protection, and a sense of power. His article was originally printed in 1994 in The Nation, *an academic journal of politics, economics, and social issues.*

PREPARING TO READ

1. The figure of the outlaw or criminal has been an appealing one in fiction and the movies. Take one famous fictional or media outlaw (such as "Robin Hood," "Gatsby," "Butch Cassidy," "Zorro," the "Godfather," or "Tony Soprano") and explain whether you find this character to be appealing.

2. Why do you think that generally young men but not young women become gang members?
3. Why do you think that today there seems to be an increase in violence committed by young people?
4. Why do you agree (or disagree) that poverty is an excuse or reason for criminal behavior?

TURNING YOUTH GANGS AROUND

Pedro is a thoughtful, articulate and charismatic young man; he listens, absorbs and responds. His movements are quick, well-developed during his years surviving in the streets of Chicago. Pedro is a 20-year-old gang leader. For most of his life, he has lived off and on between his welfare mother and an uncle. He has been kicked out of schools and has served time in youth detention facilities. He is also a great human being.

For four months in 1993, the courts designated me as his guardian under a house arrest sentence. He was respectful and polite. He meticulously answered all my messages. He was loved by my 6-year-old son. His best friend happens to be my 19-year-old son Ramiro.

During his stay, I gave Pedro books, including political books to help him become more cognizant of the world. One of these was *Palante*, a photo-text about the Young Lords Party of the 1970s. Pedro, whose family is from Puerto Rico, began to open up to an important slice of history that, until then, he'd never known about. Pedro read *Palante* from cover to cover—as he did other books, for the first time ever.

When Pedro was released from house arrest, he moved out of the neighborhood with his girlfriend and her small boy. He found a job. He remained leader of the gang, but was now talking about struggle, about social change, about going somewhere.

Last November, Pedro was shot three times with a .44. He was hit in his back, leg and hand. Ramiro and I visited him at the Cook County Hospital. He lived, but he was not the same after that. One day during Pedro's hospital stay, the same gang that had shot him ambushed and killed Angel, a friend of Ramiro and Pedro. Angel, an honor student at one of the best schools in the city, was on his way to school; a news account the next day failed to mention this, reporting only that he was a suspected gang member, as if this fact justified his death.

I tried to persuade Pedro to get his boys to chill. I knew that Ramiro and the others were all sitting ducks. Pedro went through some internal turmoil, but he decided to forbid retaliation. This was hard for him, but he did it.

Unfortunately, the story doesn't end there. Earlier this year, Pedro allegedly shot and killed one of the guys believed to be behind Angel's murder and his own shooting. Pedro is now a fugitive.

I tell you this to convey the complexity of working with youths like Pedro, youths most people would rather write off, but who are also intelligent, creative and even quite decent. The tragedy is that it is mostly young people like these who are being killed and who are doing the killing. I've seen them in youth prisons, hospitals and courts throughout the land; young people who in other circumstances might have been college graduates, officeholders or social activists. Unfortunately, many find themselves in situations they feel unable to pull out of until it's too late.

I've long recognized that most youths like Pedro aren't in gangs to be criminals, killers or prison inmates. For many, a gang embraces who they are, gives them the initiatory community they seek and the incipient authority they need to eventually control their own lives. These are things other institutions, including schools and families, often fail to provide. Yet without the proper guidance, support and means to contribute positively to society, gang involvement can be disastrous.

This August, a media storm was created when 11-year-old Robert Sandifer of Chicago, known as "Yummy" because he liked to eat cookies, allegedly shot into a crowd and killed a 14-year-old girl. A suspected member of a Southside gang, Yummy disappeared; days later he was found shot in the head. Two teenage members of Yummy's gang are being held in his death. Hours before his murder, a neighbor saw Yummy, who told her, "Say a prayer for me."

This is a tragedy, but without a clear understanding of the social, economic and psychological dynamics that would drive an 11-year-old to kill, we can only throw up our hands. Yet it isn't hard to figure out the motive forces behind much of this violence.

Sandifer, for example, was a child of the Reagan years, of substantial cuts in community programs, of the worst job loss since the Great Depression, of more police and prisons and of fewer options for recreation, education or work. Here was a boy who had been physically abused, shuttled from one foster home to another, one juvenile justice facility after another. At every stage of Robert's young life since birth, he was blocked from becoming all he could be. But there was nothing to stop him from getting a gun. From using it. And from dying from one.

No "three strikes, you're out," no trying children as adults, no increased prison spending will address what has created the Pedros and

Yummys of this world. Such proposals deal only with the end results of a process that will continue to produce its own fuel, like a giant breeder reactor. This is not a solution.

Gangs are not new in America. The first gangs in the early 1800s were made up of Irish immigrant youths. They lived as second-class citizens. Their parents worked in the lowest-paid, most menial jobs. These youths organized to protect themselves within a society that had no place for them. Other immigrants followed identical patterns. Today the majority of gang members are African-American and Latino, and they face the same general predicaments those early immigrants did. But today something deeper is also happening. Within the present class relations of modern technology-driven capitalism, many youths, urban and rural, are being denied the chance to earn a "legitimate" living. An increasing number are white, mostly sons and daughters of coal miners, factory workers or farmers.

Los Angeles, which has more gang violence than any other city, experienced the greatest incidence of gang-related acts during the 1980s and early 1990s, when 300,000 manufacturing jobs were lost in California. According to the Gang Violence Bridging Project of the Edmund G. "Pat" Brown Institute of Public Affairs at California State University, Los Angeles, the areas with the greatest impoverishment and gang growth were those directly linked to industrial flight.

At the same time, the state of California suffered deep cuts in social programs—most of them coming as a result of the passage in 1978 of Proposition 13, which decreased state funding for schools after a slash in property taxes. Since 1980, while California's population has jumped by 35 percent, spending for education has steadily declined. Yet there has been a 14 percent annual increase in state prison spending during the past decade; the state legislature has allocated $21 billion over the next ten years to build twenty new prisons.

Almost all areas in the United States where manufacturing has died or moved away are now reporting ganglike activity. There are seventy-two large cities and thirty-eight smaller ones that claim to have a "gang problem," according to a 1992 survey of police departments by the National Institute of Justice. Chicago, also hard hit by industrial flight, has many large multigenerational gangs like those in L.A.

What has been the official response? In Chicago "mob action" arrests have been stepped up (when three or more young people gather in certain proscribed areas, it is considered "mob action"), as have police sweeps of housing projects and "gang infested" communities. Recently there have been calls to deploy the National Guard against gangs, which is like bringing in a larger gang with more firepower against the local ones. This, too, is not a solution.

I agree that the situation is intolerable. I believe most people—from the Chicago-based Mothers Against Gangs to teachers who are forced to be police officers in their classrooms to people in the community caught in the crossfire—are scared. They are bone-tired of the violence. They are seeking ways out. First we must recognize that our battle is with a society that fails to do all it can for young people—then lays the blame on them.

It's time the voices for viable and lasting solutions be heard. The public debate is now limited to those who demonize youth, want to put them away, and use repression to curb their natural instincts to recreate the world.

I have other proposals. First, that we realign societal resources in accordance with the following premises: that every child has value and every child can succeed. That schools teach by engaging the intelligence and creativity of all students. That institutions of public maintenance—whether police or social services—respect the basic humanity of all people. That we rapidly and thoroughly integrate young people into the future, into the new technology. And finally, that we root out the basis for the injustice and inequities that engender most of the violence we see today.

Sound farfetched? Too idealistic? Fine. But anything short on imagination will result in "pragmatic," fear-driven, expediency-oriented measures that won't solve anything but will only play with people's lives.

Actually, the structural/economic foundation for such proposals as I've roughly outlined is already laid. The computer chip has brought about revolutionary shifts in the social order. The only thing that isn't in place is the non-exploitative, non-oppressive relations between people required to complete this transition.

I know what some people are thinking. What about being tough on crime? Let me be clear: I hate crime. I hate drugs. I hate children murdering children. But I know from experience that it doesn't take guts to put money into inhumane, punishment-driven institutions. In fact, such policies make our communities even less safe. It's tougher to walk these streets, to listen to young people, to respect them and help fight for their well-being. It's tougher to care.

For the past two years, I've talked to young people, parents, teachers and concerned officials in cities as far-flung as Hartford, Brooklyn, Phoenix, Seattle, Lansing, Denver, Boston, El Paso, Washington, Oakland, San Antonio and Compton. I've seen them grope with similar crises, similar pains, similar confusions.

Sometimes I feel the immensity of what we're facing—talking to Teens on Target in Los Angeles, a group made up of youths who have been shot, some in wheelchairs; or to teenage mothers in Tucson, one child caring for another; or to incarcerated young men at the maximum security Illinois Youth Center at Joliet. I felt it when a couple of young women cried in Holyoke, Massachusetts, after I read a poem about a friend who had been murdered by the police, and when I addressed a gym full of students at Jefferson High School in Fort Worth and several young people lined up to hug me, as if they had never been hugged before.

Because I have to deal with people like Yummy and Pedro every day, I decided this summer to do something more than just talk. With the help of Patricia Zamora from the Casa Aztlan Community Center in Chicago's Mexican community of Pilsen, I worked with a core of young people, gang and nongang, toward finding their own solutions, their own organizations, their own empowerment.

In the backyard of my Chicago home, some thirty people, mostly from the predominantly Puerto Rican area of Humboldt Park (my son's friends, and Pedro's homeys) and Pilsen, were present. They agreed to reach out to other youths and hold retreats, weekly meetings and a major conference. All summer they worked, without money, without resources, but with a lot of enthusiasm and energy. They hooked up with the National Organizing Committee, founded in 1993 by revolutionary fighters including gang members, welfare recipients, trade unionists, teachers and parents from throughout the United States. The N.O.C. offered them technical and educational assistance.

The young people's efforts culminated in the Youth '94 Struggling for Survival Conference, held in August at the University of Illinois, Chicago. More than a hundred young people from the city and surrounding communities attended. They held workshops on police brutality, jobs and education, and peace in the neighborhoods. A few gang members set aside deadly rivalries to attend this gathering.

Although there were a number of mishaps, including a power failure, the youths voted to keep meeting. They held their workshops in the dark, raising issues, voicing concerns, coming up with ideas. I was the only adult they let address their meeting. The others, including parents, teachers, counselors, resource people and a video crew from the Center for New Television, were there to help with what the young people had organized.

Then the building personnel told us we had to leave because it was unsafe to be in a building without power. We got Casa Aztlan to agree to let us move to several of their rooms to continue the workshops; I felt we would probably lose about half the young people in the fifteen-minute ride between sites. Not only did we hang on to most of the youths, we picked up a few more along the way. In a flooded basement with crumbling walls in Casa Aztlan we held the final plenary session. The youths set up a roundtable, at which it was agreed that only proposed solutions would be entertained. A few read poetry. It was a success, but then the young people wouldn't let it be anything else.

Youth Struggling for Survival is but one example of young people tackling the issues head-on. There are hundreds more across America. In the weeks before the November 8 elections in California, thousands of junior high and high school students, mostly Latino, walked out of schools in the Los Angeles area. Their target: Proposition 187, intended to deny undocumented immigrants access to education, social services, and non-emergency health care.

These young people need guidance and support; they don't need adults to tell them what to do and how to do it; to corral, crush or dissuade their efforts. We must reverse their sense of helplessness. The first step is to invest them with more authority to run their own lives, their communities, even their schools. The aim is to help them stop being instruments of their own death and to choose a revolutionary service to life.

We don't need a country in which the National Guard walks our children to school, or pizza-delivery people carry sidearms, or prisons outnumber colleges. We can be more enlightened. More inclusive. More imaginative.

WRITING ABOUT THE READING

5. People usually think of gang members as violent and threatening. How and why does Rodriguez's description of Pedro support or refute this stereotype?

6. Why do you think that it is effective (or ineffective) to begin the essay with the story of Pedro?

7. Based on this article, what would Rodriguez predict would happen if there were economic boom times and an increase in spending on social programs?

8. How and why does Rodriguez use the example of "Yummy" to support his argument?

9. Why does Rodriguez believe that dealing with young criminals more harshly is *not* an answer to the problem of gangs?

10. What evidence does Rodriguez use to support his statement that gangs are not new in the United States and why does he use this example?

WRITING FROM YOUR OWN EXPERIENCE

Note: In these assignments, write about your own experience or use that of someone you know, read about, or saw in a film/TV show.

11. Rodriguez tries to help Pedro because he is willing to "take a chance" that the young man will give up his life of violence. Recall a time when you "took a chance" on someone (or someone took a chance on you). Why did you (or the other person) take this risk and what were the consequences?

12. Pedro, despite his intelligence and desire for social change, continues to engage in gang life. Have you ever known anyone (or read about or seen on TV) who is in some way like Pedro, who has engaged in violent or harmful behavior? Why do you think that this person behaved in this way and what were the consequences of this person's actions?

13. Think of an organization (such as an honor society, social club, or boosters' club) that you would like to join. Why does this organization appeal to you?

14. Gang members often report enjoying violence and risky behavior. Recall a time when you engaged in an activity or sport that was risky (such as riding a motorcycle or bungee jumping). Why did you take this risk and what were the consequences of engaging in this behavior?

WRITING ABOUT RESEARCH

15. Rodriguez believes that there is a relationship between economic conditions and the choices made by young adults. How and why have recent changes in economic opportunity impacted young adults?

16. Rodriguez says that the children of poor immigrants often turn to crime. However, statistics reveal that the 1990s, when many immigrants came to the United States, was also a time when crime was on the decrease. Explain why there was a decrease (or increase or no change) in crime rates at this time.

17. How and why are law enforcement officials able to use modern technology (such as surveillance cameras or DNA testing) to catch and/or convict criminals?

Young, Single . . . and a Mom

CHRISTINE GRANADOS

Christine Granados *(1969–) was born and raised in El Paso, Texas, to a Mexican American father and mother. She received a B.A. degree (1992) from the University of Texas at El Paso. Formerly, Granados was editor of* Moderna *magazine and worked as a journalist for several daily newspapers. Granados now works as a freelance writer/columnist for publications including* People en Espanol, Latina, Hispanic, El Andar, *and the* Austin American-Statesman. *She also is pursuing an M.F.A. in creative writing at Southwest Texas State University in San Marcos, Texas, and working on a novel.*

Granados's article "Young, Single . . . and a Mom" describes the difficulties faced by many Latina single mothers in raising their children. The essay comes from Hispanic *(1997), a magazine with articles for and about Hispanic Americans.*

PREPARING TO READ

1. Explain whether or not you think that a mother's working outside the home hurts a child.
2. What do you think are some of the reasons that single mothers are more accepted today than in the past?
3. Parents often discuss spending "quality time" with their children. Give some examples of "quality time" and explain why you would use these examples to support your definition.
4. Explain whether you think that it is better to dissolve an unhappy marriage or to stay together "for the sake of the children."
5. What are some of the problems in raising their children faced by single fathers?

YOUNG, SINGLE . . . AND A MOM

> For Lupe, her mother was everything. She was the perfect gift given to her by God.
>
> —Victor Villasenor, *Rain of Gold*

Strength, honor, and comfort have forever been associated with Hispanic mothers. Their powerful mystique can be read and even felt in the lines of writers such as Victor Villasenor. In real life, Latina single mothers, abandoned by husbands or boyfriends, have been vilified as welfare moms and misunderstood. But in real life as in folklore, many single Hispanic mothers do prevail, successfully raising families and contributing to society.

Some single moms, such as Manuela Luna, of Austin, Texas, have had to survive tremendous challenges. Luna agreed to relate her experience in the hope that she can inspire others. After three years of living with her boyfriend, enduring one apartment eviction after another and not knowing where the next paycheck was coming from, Luna decided she needed to strike out on her own. The last straw came when Luna, then eight months pregnant, her one-year-old daughter, and Luna's boyfriend and father of her child were living in a car. "Andrea would sleep in the back, in a car seat; I was in the passenger seat, pregnant; and [my boyfriend] was in the driver's seat," she said matter-of-factly. "My heart and mind were telling me the same thing: This is not what I want my life to be." So, like millions of Hispanic single mothers, Luna decided to raise her children on her own.

Luna's road toward independence was a difficult one. At seventeen, she dropped out of school to have a baby and move in with her high school sweetheart. "I felt really guilty," said the 31-year-old Mexican American. "Because I'm Catholic, I believed we were supposed to stay together forever. Andrew and I split up because he was an irresponsible parent. He didn't know what it was going to be like to support a family. He couldn't hold a job." But she could, and after the split, she worked double shifts for minimum wage at a fastfood restaurant. She applied for government assistance to cover her family's grocery bills.

Her big break out of minimum-wage jobs came when she secured a clerical job at a weekly community newspaper in the city. She says the job gave her financial security and training. Now a successful administrative associate working for the City of Austin, Luna lives in her own apartment, supports her three children alone, has earned her general equivalency diploma, and plans to go to college. "I am going back to school when my youngest son turns ten—he's nine now," said Luna. "I want to learn more about computer programs."

Along with the acculturation of Latinas in the United States is a growing disregard of traditional family roles. As a consequence, along with the steady and large growth of the U.S. Hispanic population has come a rise in single motherhood. The 1990 U.S. Census figures show that 21 percent (4 million) of Hispanic households are fatherless compared with 12 percent of non-Hispanic white households. African Americans have the highest rate of fatherless homes, with 45 percent. "The Hispanic group is more likely not to be in a single-parent household," says Dr. Jane L. Delgado, 43, president and CEO of the National Coalition of Hispanic Health and Human Services, a Washington, D.C.-based nonprofit group. "We have a slightly higher rate [of single mothers] than the white community because Hispanics have strong Catholic roots whether we are practicing or not, and Catholicism states that the family should stay together." According to the 1990 census, 72 percent of Hispanics identify themselves as Roman Catholic. For many Latinas, abortion and adoption are not acceptable options. "[Hispanic women] do things very differently—we endure."

Single mothers, particularly teenagers, came under sharp scrutiny in 1996 as lawmakers volleyed the nagging question of welfare reform. After vetoing two bills, charging they were too severe on women and children, President Clinton did sign a welfare reform bill that ended the 61-year-old federal guarantee of cash for the nation's poor families with children. Sonia M. Perez, coauthor of *Untapped Potential: A Look at Hispanic Women in the U.S.*, said, "Politicians are trying to reform welfare or increase the socioeconomic status of people," but wind up attacking the people they are trying to help. "Their rhetoric says they don't really understand the issue of poverty. Unfortunately Latinos make up a segment of the population that those people are attacking."

Single moms may seem to have their hands full juggling the day-to-day running of their families, yet some mothers find that organization and their kids' cooperation keep them on top of things. Time is a precious commodity for Luz Rubio, 29, a single mother of three in Phoenix, Arizona. The executive director of the Arizona Society of Association Executives, Rubio says she could not have been a successful single mother for six years now if she didn't have such intelligent, understanding children. Sandra and Daniel, Rubio's older children (ages seven and five), are actively involved in planning the family schedule. Twenty-month-old Elizabeth gets her own day on the wall calendar in the master bedroom. "We have a calendar in our room with the dates laid out," said Rubio. "There is a day for Danny and one for Sandra." She says this ensures that each child is getting his or her mother's full attention. The family marks extra-curricular activities on the calendar as well. Sandra goes to cheerleading on certain days, and Danny goes to karate, while "Mommy has class on Thursday nights."

Rubio says her children make life easier on her by making their own arrangements when she can't be with them on Thursdays or on nights when she has to work late. "When my children have to come to the office with me, they fill their backpacks with stuff to do."

"Sometimes I feel guilty because I'm not the parent that picks them up after school," lamented Rubio. "I do feel bad because I can't do that." However, a single mother has to make do, and she compensates with quality instead of quantity. "The time we spend together is important to all of us. I don't spend a lot of time with them, but the time we do spend with each other is real quality time. For instance, we always sit down and have dinner together. Sandy feeds Elizabeth while I get dinner ready."

Gina Pinos, a 25-year-old promotions coordinator living in Yonkers, New York, also realized that a woman can succeed without a partner. Upon discovering she was pregnant in 1994, Pinos married her boyfriend. "We had talked about marriage before, but our main motivation was the baby," said Pinos about the marriage. "We did things for the wrong reasons." After the birth of Justin Benitez, who is now nineteen months old, Pinos and her husband split up. Although they shared a child, the couple realized they were incompatible and that the marriage could not be repaired.

"But I gave it a try, and I feel better because I tried," said Pinos, who claims her Ecuadorian roots may have influenced her decision to marry. "I learned that you shouldn't use marriage as a tool for a child's well-being. It's a religious institution for love. I'm glad I noticed early rather than later, when I wouldn't have had the courage to leave the marriage. [The baby will] be happy as long as I'm happy."

Family plays an important role in a single mother's success. Pinos says she couldn't have done it without the help of her friend and her mother. "I don't know what I'd do without my mom. If I didn't have my mom, sister, or aunt's help—forget it." One of the reasons Pinos says she moved to Yonkers was to be just five minutes away from her family.

Hope F. Calderone, a certified nurse midwife at the Mary's Center for Maternal and Child Care, Inc., based in Washington, D.C., believes in the "It takes a village" concept of childrearing. "The success of single mothers doesn't have anything to do with having a stable man in their life but much more to do with the extended family and support," said Calderone. "The Hispanic population is much better about having extended family to help them out. When the family is available they are generally very supportive." Delgado finds fault with the American definition of family. "The bottom line is that the concept of the nuclear family is false. We need an extended family, whether it be biological or friends. No one can do it alone."

A significant key to the success of Latina mothers is their own strong maternal role models. Successful Latinas consistently recognize their mothers or grandmothers for encouraging them by example. "My parents have been my salvation," said Jessica Alvarez, a teenage single mother of a ten-month-old baby boy. "I see my mom and dad as two very good role models. My mom's a very strong person. When my dad immigrated to the U.S., Mom kept the family going in Guatemala. She supported my dad's parents and her parents. [Today] she works from nine to six in the evening and supports everyone in the house—physically, mentally, and economically. She still supports her parents down in Guatemala. I think Hispanic families are very attached emotionally and morally. It all has to do with family values. My family is very united. If one of us is in danger of going down, we would rather all go down together. We're able to control our problems if we stick together."

Alvarez is not a single mother by choice. On September 9, 1995, a bullet changed the teenager's life forever. "My boyfriend was killed when I was six months pregnant. He got shot when he was coming home from work. Out of the blue somebody came and shot him." The high school senior is wise beyond her eighteen years. Throughout her many ordeals, her goals have never wavered. When she discovered she was pregnant, she and her boyfriend planned to get married, and she stayed in school. "I didn't see a point in stopping," said Alvarez resolutely. After the death of her fiance, she could have easily given up school altogether, but she persevered and although her grades dropped in the weeks after his death, she has managed to make the honor roll once again. She attends Bell Multicultural High School in Washington, D.C., during the day, takes classes at American University at night, and works part-time on weekends as a translator for a law office to help support herself and eighteen-month-old Anthony Alvarez-Sorto. She plans to study languages and eventually would like to be a translator at the United Nations.

The enduring strength and wisdom of Hispanic mothers is not a fiction—it is a reality. Although the American family dynamic may be changing, Latina single mothers, empowered by their culture, continue to forge ahead. With time, they will dispel any misconceptions about single mothers because they are caring, flexible, and strong.

WRITING ABOUT THE READING

6. How and why does Granados use the example of Manuela Luna to dramatize the plight of single Hispanic American women?
7. Based on this article, what are the traditional Hispanic expectations of women?
8. Why has acceptance of American values often resulted in a defiance of traditional roles by Hispanic American women?
9. What support in raising their children do single Hispanic women have?
10. What do you think is the author's attitude toward single women and what are the reasons for your conclusion?

WRITING FROM YOUR OWN EXPERIENCE

Note: In these assignments, write about your own experience or use that of someone you know, read about, or saw in a film/TV show.

11. Granados asserts that one of the positive qualities of Hispanic women is that they persist despite a difficult situation. Recall a time when you "endured" despite a difficult situation. Why did you endure and what was the result of this persistence?
12. Gina Pinos is Granados's example of a woman who chose to leave an unhappy marriage. Recall someone you know who had to make the same decision about his/her marriage. Why do you think that this person chose to remain in or leave the marriage and what were the consequences of this decision?
13. Granados uses the words like "caring," "flexible," and "strong" to characterize Hispanic American women. Choose one woman you know who can be described in the same way. Why are these words appropriately used to describe this woman?

WRITING ABOUT RESEARCH

14. In 1996, many single mothers were affected by welfare reforms. What were these reforms and why did they affect single mothers?
15. Many working mothers rely on the Head Start program for child care. Why was Head Start established and why has it been successful?

16. Choose a Hispanic actor, dancer, musician, or singer from the list below (or one of your own choice) and trace the person's rise to success. Suggestions:

    (a) Desi Arnaz (musician and actor)
    (b) Xavier Cugat (musician)
    (c) Cella Cruz (singer)
    (d) Gloria Estefan (singer)
    (e) Jose Feliciano (singer)
    (f) Carmen Miranda (singer and movie star)
    (g) Rita Moreno (actor)
    (h) Anthony Quinn (actor)
    (i) Chita Rivera (dancer)
    (j) Angel Cordero, jockey, Racing Hall of Fame (1988)
    (k) Roberto Duran, champion boxer (1989)
    (l) Rudy Galindo, National Figure Skating Championship (1996)
    (m) Richard Alonso "Pancho" Gonzales, U.S. Tennis Singles Championship (1948)
    (n) Rebecca Lobo, Olympic gold medal in basketball (1996)

COMPARING SELECTIONS: HISPANIC AMERICAN WRITERS

1. Compare the parent-child relationships in the readings by **Sandra Cisneros** and **Gustavo Perez Firmat**. Why do these selections support the belief that Hispanic Americans have strong family bonds?

2. Compare the discussion of American attitudes toward immigration by **Richard Rodriguez** and **Joseph Torres**. Why is there hostility toward immigrants and how is it manifested by members of the dominant culture?

3. Compare the reasons for and problems of immigrants past and present, as discussed by **Jesus Colon** and **Richard Rodriguez**. Why have the problems changed or remained much the same?

4. Compare the discussion of the Spanish language in the readings by **Gustavo Perez Firmat** and **Joseph Torres**. How do these authors feel about the retention or loss of the Spanish language and why do they feel this way?

5. Compare the importance of Hispanic foods and/or traditions in the readings by **Sandra Cisneros** and **Gustavo Perez Firmat**. How and why does the adoption of new or retention of familiar foods/traditions show the process of assimilation?

6. Contrast the picture of the Hispanic American woman in the readings by **Judith Ortiz Cofer** and **Gary Soto**. Explain whether you think that either stereotype is fair and accurate.

7. Compare the experience of arriving in America of **Jesus Colon** and **Pablo Medina**. What challenges did each writer have to face as he entered the U.S. society?

8. Compare the picture of friends in the selections by **Pablo Medina** and **Gary Soto**. Why and how did the friends help these writers understand American culture?

9. Consider **Luis Rodriguez's** discussion of gangs in light of **Richard Rodriguez's** discussion of immigration. Why is there a relationship between immigration and gang membership?

10. Compare the family structures shown in the essays by **Gustavo Perez Firmat** and **Sandra Granados**. Why do these selections show that there are changes in the traditional Hispanic family structure in the United States?

SELECTED BIBLIOGRAPHY—HISPANIC WRITERS

Abalos, David T. *La Comunidad Latina in the United States: Personal and Political Strategies for Transforming Culture.* Westport, CT: Praeger Publishers, 1998.

———. *Latinos in the United States: The Sacred and the Political.* Notre Dame: Univ. of Notre Dame Press, 1986.

Acuna, Rodolfo F. *Anything But Mexican: Chicanos in Contemporary Los Angeles.* New York: Verso, 1996.

———. *Sometimes There Is No Other Side: Chicanos and the Myth of Equality.* Notre Dame: Univ. of Notre Dame Press, 1998.

Babin, Maria Teresa, and Stan Steiner, eds. *Borinquen: An Anthology of Puerto Rican Literature.* New York: Alfred A. Knopf, 1974.

Bloom, Harold, ed. *Hispanic-American Writers. Modern Critical Views.* Philadelphia: Chelsea House Publishers, 1998.

Bonilla, Frank, Edwin Melendez, Rebecca Morales, and Maria de los Angeles Torres, eds. *Borderless Borders: U.S. Latinos, Latin Americans, and the Paradox of Interdependence.* Philadelphia: Temple Univ. Press, 1998.

Chavez, Linda. *Out of the Barrio: Toward a New Politics of Hispanic Assimilation.* New York: Basic Books/Harper Collins, 1991.

Cisneros, Sandra. *The House on Mango Street.* Houston, Texas: Arte Publico Press, 1984.

———. *Woman Hollering Creek and Other Stories.* New York: Random House, 1991.

Cofer, Judith Ortiz. *An Island Like You: Stories of the Barrio.* New York: Orchard Books, 1995.

———. *The Latin Deli.* Athens: Univ. of Georgia Press, 1993

———. *The Line of the Sun.* Athens: Univ. of Georgia Press, 1989.

———. *Silent Dancing.* Houston, Texas: Arte Publico Press, 1990.

Colon, Jesus. *A Puerto Rican in New York, and Other Sketches.* Mainstream Publishers, 1961. 2nd ed. New York: International Publishers, 1982.

Davis, Marilyn P. *Mexican Voices/American Dreams: An Oral History of Mexican Immigration to the United States.* New York: Henry Holt and Co., 1990.

Delgado, Richard, and Jean Stefancic. *The Latino/a Condition: A Critical Reader.* New York: New York Univ. Press, 1998.

Flores, William V., and Rina Benmayor. *Latino Cultural Citizenship: Claiming Identity, Space, and Rights.* Boston: Beacon Press, 1997.

Garcia, Maria Christina. *Havana USA: Cuban Exiles and Cuban Americans in South Florida, 1959–1994.* Berkeley: Univ. of California Press, 1996.

Garcia, Mario T. *Desert Immigrants: The Mexicans of El Paso, 1880–1920.* New Haven: Yale Univ. Press, 1981.

———. *Mexican Americans: Leadership, Ideology, and Identity, 1930–1960.* New Haven: Yale Univ. Press, 1989

Gonzalez-Pando, Miguel. *The Cuban Americans. The New Americans Series.* Westport, CT: Greenwood Press, 1998.

Hinojosa, Maria. *Raising Raul: Adventures Raising Myself and My Son.* New York: Viking, 1999.

Hospital, Carolina, ed. *Cuban American Writers: Los Atrevidos.* Princeton, NJ: Ediciones Ellas/Linden Lane Press, 1988.

Hospital, Carolina, and Jorge Cantera. *A Century of Cuban Writers in Florida: Selected Prose and Poetry.* Sarasota: Pineapple Press, 1996.

Kanellos, Nicolas, ed. *The Hispanic-American Almanac: A Reference Work on Hispanics in the United States.* Detroit: Gale Research, Inc., 1977.

Kornblum, William. *Sociology in a Changing World.* 4th ed. Fort Worth: Harcourt Brace, 1997.

Marger, Martin N. *Race and Ethnic Relations: American and Global Perspectives.* Belmont, CA: Wadsworth Pub. Co., 1997.

Martinez, Julio, and Francisco Lomeli. *Chicano Literature: A Reader's Encyclopedia.* Westport: Greenwood, 1985.

Medina, Pablo F. *Exiled Memories: A Cuban Childhood.* Univ. of Texas Press, 1990.

———. *The Floating Island.* Fredonia, New York: White Pine Press, 1999.

———. *The Marks of Birth.* New York: Farrar, Straus & Giroux, 1994.

———. *The Return of Felix Nogara.* New York: Persea Books, 2000.

Meier, Matt S., and Feliciano Ribera. *Mexican Americans/American Mexicans: From Conquistadors to Chicanos. America Century Series.* New York: Hill and Wang, 1993.

Olson, James S. *The Ethnic Dimension in American History.* 2nd ed. New York: St. Martin's Press, 1994.

Pedraza, Silvia, and Ruben G. Rumbaut, eds. *Origins and Destinies: Immigration, Race, and Ethnicity in America.* Belmont: Wadsworth, 1996.

Perez Firmat, Gustavo. *The Cuban Condition: Translation and Identity in Modern Cuban Literature.* New York: Cambridge Univ. Press, 1988.

———. *Life-on-the-Hyphen: The Cuban-American Way.* Austin: Univ. of Texas Press, 1994.

———. *Next Year in Cuba.* New York: Doubleday, 1995.

Portes, Alejandro, and R.L. Bach. *Latin Journey: Cuban and Mexican Immigrants in the United States.* Berkeley: Univ. of California Press, 1985.

Rodriguez, Luis J. *Always Running: La Vida Loca—Gang Days in L.A.* Willimantic, CT: Curbstone Press, 1993.

———. *The Concrete River.* Willimantic, CT: Curbstone Press, 1991.

Rodriguez, Richard. *Days of Obligation: An Argument with My Mexican Father*. New York: Viking Penguin, 1992.

——.*Hunger of Memory: An Autobiography*. Boston: David R. Godine, Publisher, 1982.

Rothenberg, Paula S. *Race, Class, and Gender in the United States*. New York: St. Martin's Press, 1998.

Ryan, Bryan, ed. *Hispanic Writers: A Selection of Sketches from Contemporary Authors*. Detroit: Gale Research, Inc., 1991.

Sandoval-Sanchez, Alberto. *Jose, Can You See?: Latinos On and Off Broadway*. Madison: Univ. of Wisconsin Press, 1999.

Sandoval-Sanchez, Alberto, and Nancy S. Sternbach, eds. *Puro Teatro: A Latina Anthology*. Tucson: Univ. of Arizona Press, 1999.

——.*Stages of Life: Transcultural Performance and Identity Formation in Latina Theatre*. Tucson: Univ. of Arizona Press, 2000.

Santiago, Esmeralda. *When I Was Puerto Rican*. New York: Random House, 1993.

Santiago, Esmeralda, and Joie Davidow. *Las Christmas: Favorite Latino Authors Share Their Holiday Memories*. New York: Alfred A. Knopf, 1998.

Shirley, Carl, and Paula Shirley. *Understanding Chicano Literature*. Columbia: Univ. of South Carolina Press, 1988.

Soto, Gary. *Baseball in April and Other Stories*. Harcourt, 1990.

——.*The Elements of San Joaquin*. Pittsburgh: Univ. of Pittsburgh Press, 1977.

——.*Living Up the Street: Narrative Recollections*. San Francisco: Strawberry Hill Pub., 1985.

——.*New and Selected Poems*. San Francisco: Chronicle Books, 1995.

——.*A Summer Life*. Hanover: Univ. Press of New England, 1990.

Torres-Metzgar, Joseph V. *Below the Summit*. Berkeley, CA: Tonatiuh International, 1976.

Turner, Faythe, ed. *Puerto Rican Writers at Home in the USA*. Seattle: Open Hand Publishing, 1991.

Velez-Ibanez, Carlos G. *Border Visions: Mexican Cultures of the Southwest United States*. Tucson: Univ. of Arizona Press, 1996.

SELECTED INTERNET RESOURCES—HISPANIC AMERICAN WRITERS

Note: Unless otherwise noted, all URL addresses listed begin with http://www.

Center for Latino Studies in the Americas.
   <usfca.edu/celasa/welcome/welcome.html>

Chicano/LatinoNet (CLNET). <latino.sscnet.ucla.edu/>

Chicano Studies Research Center (UCLA). <sscnet.ucla.edu/csrc/>

CLNet (Chicana/o Latina/o Communities Through Networking)
   (UCLA). <latino.sscnet.ucla.edu/>

Cuban Studies Institute (Tulane U.) <cuba.tulane.edu/>

Ethnic Studies at the University of Southern California.
   <usc.edu/isd/archives/ethnicstudies/ index.html>

HispanicDotCom. <hispanic.com/>

Hispanic Online. <hisp.com/>

IPRNET. The Information Services on Puerto Rican Issues.
   <iprnet.org/IPR/>

LatinoLink. <latinolink.com/>

Latino/Hispanic Resources (Texas Education Network).
   <tenet.edu/latino/latino.html>

National Latino Research Center (California State University San
   Marcos). <csusm.edu/nlrc/>

Stanford Center for Chicano Research (Stanford University).
   <stanford.edu/group/SCCR/>

U.S. Census Bureau. <census.gov>

Part 3

Asian American Writers

INTRODUCTION

The label "Asian Americans" includes writers, both native-born and immigrants, who have origins in one of the countries located in the Eastern Hemisphere. These Asian American writers (of Chinese, Filipino, Korean, Japanese, Asian Indian, Vietnamese, or Pacific Islander derivation) have significant differences in history, religion, and language. Furthermore, those from one country (such as China) are grouped as "Asian Americans" along with those from a traditional adversary (such as Japan). Thus, like the term "Hispanic," the label "Asian American" is a convenient, inclusive category that covers disparate subgroups.

The immigration of Asian Americans falls into two phases. During the first phase, lasting from the mid-nineteenth century through the early twentieth century, a few thousand immigrants, primarily from China and Japan, came to be workers in construction, agriculture, and service jobs. **Fae Myenne Ng** describes this early period. The first phase of immigration ended with the exclusionary acts and agreements of the early twentieth century that brought Asian American immigration to almost a near halt. In "Asian American Dreams," **Helen Zia** recounts her parents' experience as immigrants immediately after World War II.

Following this hiatus, the second wave of Asian American immigration began in the mid-1960s after changes in the immigration laws allowed people from the Eastern Hemisphere to immigrate to the United States. This change, along with America's involvement in the wars and political affairs of the East, led to dramatic increases in immigration from Asian countries by the twenty-first century.

Asian Americans (similar to members of other ethnic minority groups) often go through a four-stage process in a search for their ethnic identity. First, in the early school days children are not aware of their Asian American status. After these children become aware of their minority status, they often adopt the norms and behaviors of the dominant group (Stage 2). Ethnic emergence occurs in late adolescence or early adulthood (Stage 3) as Asian Americans begin exploring their ethnic heritage and considering the effects of ethnicity on their lives. Searching for a group with which to identify, they may look to the ethnic homeland group for acceptance. For example, **Fae Myenne Ng** visited her father's home in China, and **David Mura** lived in Japan for a year. After this exploratory period, Asian Americans may resolve their ethnic identity conflict (Stage 4) by coming to accept themselves as part American, part Asian.* This search for identity is reflected in several of the Asian American writers in this anthology and may be seen as well in writers from other minorities.

The following is a brief summary of the history of immigration of five of the major Asian American subgroups. Some of the research questions will lead the students to investigate further into the histories and cultures of these subgroups.

CHINESE AMERICANS

The Chinese Americans, comprising the largest group of Asian Americans, have a long history in the United States. In the nineteenth century, Chinese men came to the United States, leaving their women behind, to find temporary work, to save their earnings, and to return to China to marry and settle down. Many Americans viewed these unmarried men, living in tight, self-governing ethnic communities, forbidden to become naturalized citizens, as a threat. Americans treated these early immigrants with discrimination, hostility, and occasional violence. The anti-Chinese sentiments of Americans resulted in the Chinese Exclusion Act (1882–1943).

The Chinese population began to increase in the United States after 1943, when war refugees and families of Chinese American citizens were permitted to immigrate. After 1965, the Chinese American population grew dramatically with new immigration from China. By the beginning of the twenty-first century, the Chinese Americans had become a well-educated group, more integrated in American politi-

---

*Tse, Lucy. "Finding a Place to Be: Ethnic Identity Exploration of Asian Americans." *Adolescence*: 34 (Spring 1999): 121+. (Accessed 10 March 2001. EBSCOhost database online.)

cal and social institutions than in the past. Although they spoke English at school and followed typical U.S. customs, at home many Chinese Americans spoke their native language and retained some Chinese ways. Chinese American writers in this anthology include **Frank Chin, Shawn Wong, Amy Tan, Helen Zia, Fae Myenne Ng,** and **Eric Liu.**

JAPANESE AMERICANS

At the end of the nineteenth century, Americans at first felt that Japanese immigrants were less threatening than Chinese immigrants and welcomed Japanese as farm laborers in Hawaii and on the mainland. Unlike the bachelor Chinese immigrants, the Japanese brought their wives with them, established families, and became acculturated. However, because of growing anti-Japanese sentiment, a "gentleman's agreement" between the United States and Japan restricted Japanese immigration in the early twentieth century. Americans developed stronger anti-Japanese attitudes in the 1930s because of the Japanese invasion of China. Then, following the attack on Pearl Harbor (1941), anti-Japanese feeling escalated. Japanese Americans living in California were forced to move to relocation camps, where they remained until December 1945.

After World War II, several factors made other Americans again look favorably upon the Japanese Americans. First of all, many American soldiers serving in occupied Japan brought home Japanese wives. Then, the rapid economic recovery of Japan and the success of Japanese Americans made the dominant society view members of this group as hardworking, well educated, and law abiding. Because there has not been any massive immigration from Japan following the lifting of quotas, most Japanese Americans are not new immigrants but longtime, well-assimilated residents of the United States. **David Mura** is a representative Japanese American writer.

KOREAN AMERICANS

Although in the first half of the twentieth century a few thousand Koreans came to the United States as either agricultural workers or wives (following the Korean War), the greatest migration of Koreans came after the lifting of quotas in the mid-1960s. These immigrants (many of whom were Christian, middle-class, and well-educated) chose to emigrate because of economic conditions and political instability in Korea. In the United States, Korean Americans have been successful in establishing small, family-run businesses, often in areas abandoned by earlier immigrants. **Chang-rae Lee** is a Korean American writer who describes his family's experience in assimilating to the dominant culture.

FILIPINO AMERICANS

During the period following the Spanish-American War when the United States held the Philippine Islands, many Filipinos learned to speak English. As American nationals, Filipinos were free to move to the mainland, where they filled the need for farmworkers and low-paid service workers. Like the early Chinese immigrants, these Filipinos were chiefly single men with little education, who faced discrimination from the majority community. The post-1960 immigration has been comprised often of educated professionals seeking better economic opportunity.

VIETNAMESE AND OTHER SOUTHEAST ASIANS

The immigration of peoples from Southeast Asia came about as a result of U.S. involvement in the Vietnam War. The first wave of immigration (1966–1975) from Vietnam was comprised primarily of well-educated, English-speaking, political refugees. Feeling responsibility for their plight, Americans helped these immigrants with economic assistance. Following the defeat of South Vietnam (1975), a second wave of political refugees from Southeast Asia (including Vietnam, Laos, and Cambodia) fled to the United States. Speaking little English, without education or skills, those in this second wave had more difficulty in adapting to life in the United States. **Le Thi Diem Thuy** is a writer representative of these peoples from Southeast Asia.

ASIAN INDIANS

The immigration of Asian Indians has been facilitated by many factors, including their use of English as a major language in their native country, their high levels of education, and their long history of seeking work in other parts of the world. Because India could not provide sufficient employment for its college-educated population, thousands of highly educated professionals (including physicians, dentists, engineers, scientists, and businesspeople) moved to the United States after the mid-1960s. While occasionally encountering prejudice (because of their dark skins and their non-Christian faiths), these highly skilled Indians have been successful in the United States. **Bharati Mukherjee**, who came from a upper middle-class family, represents the immigrants from India.

IMPORTANT MILESTONES

1849–1882	Following the California Gold Rush, Chinese (almost all men) became temporary immigrants who hoped to make their fortunes and return to China.
1868	Japanese workers began emigrating to Hawaii and the mainland.
1882–1943	*Chinese Exclusion Act:* Congress passed an act forbidding Chinese to immigrate to the United States.
1898	The Philippine Islands became an American territory; as such, immigration laws did not apply to Filipinos.
1898	Hawaii was annexed by the United States.
1908	**"Gentleman's Agreement":** Theodore Roosevelt worked out an agreement by which Japan agreed to restrict emigration.
1913	*Alien Land Act:* The California state legislature passed a law prohibiting those ineligible for citizenship (such as Japanese emigrants) from purchasing land.
1924	*Oriental Exclusion Act:* All immigration from Japan was ended.
1924	*National Origins Act:* The act established each country's annual immigration quota. After 1929, a total of 150,000 emigrants per year was established for other than Western Hemisphere countries.
1935	The Philippines was granted commonwealth status, subjecting Filipinos to the National Origins Act.
1942–1945	Japanese Americans in California were sent to relocation camps after the Japanese attack on Pearl Harbor.
1950	**Korean War:** As a result of the war, Koreans began immigration to the United States. After the 1953 cease-fire, American troops remained in Korea.

1952	***McCarran-Walter Act:*** Ended the prohibition on Asian immigration.
1965	***The Immigration and Nationality Act of 1965:*** This act ended the old system of ethnic quotas based on national origins. The act permitted 170,000 people from the Eastern Hemisphere to emigrate each year, with preference going to refugees, those with family members in the United States, and professional and skilled workers. This act led to dramatic increases in immigration from Asian countries.
1970s–1980s	A series of wars and political disasters brought thousands of immigrants from Indochina (including peoples from Vietnam, Cambodia, and Laos) to the United States.

Confessions of a Chinatown Cowboy

FRANK CHIN .

Frank Chin *(1940–), writer, dramatist, and critic, attended the University of California, Berkeley (1958–1961) and the Writer's Workshop at the University of Iowa (1961–1963). After receiving a B.A. (1965) from the University of California, Santa Barbara, Chin worked in theater, film, and TV, and developed the Asian American Theater Workshop. He is a co-editor of* Aiiieeeee!: An Anthology of Asian American Writers, *one of the most important collections of Asian American literature. Chin's many awards include a Rockefeller grant (1975), National Endowment for the Arts grants (1975, 1980), and a Rockefeller American Generations grant (1991).*

Describing himself as a "fifth-generation Chinaman," Chin often challenges media stereotypes of passive and docile Chinese American men. He writes that Chinese American men have difficulty in establishing a personal identity because they are isolated from both their traditional and white cultures. He characterizes his writing as "Chinaman backtalk" to what he views as America's erroneous and racist stereotypes of Chinese Americans. Chin writes of the problems of Chinese American manhood in "Confessions of a Chinatown Cowboy" from his book, Bulletproof Buddhists and Other Essays *(1998).*

PREPARING TO READ

1. Why do you suppose many immigrants and their descendants continue to live in ethnic enclaves, such as Chinatowns?
2. What do you think would be some of the advantages and disadvantages of growing up in an ethnic neighborhood, such as Chinatown?
3. Why do ethnic groups, such as Chinese Americans, often establish schools to teach the language of the former homeland?
4. What are some of the ways you can think of in which Asian (and/or Asian American) culture has influenced U.S. society?

FROM *CONFESSIONS OF A CHINATOWN COWBOY*

Ben Fee

His hometown, Chinatown San Francisco, has forgotten the name of Ben Fee and the man he was, for its own good. In New York he's what he was in Frisco, but more so, a word-of-mouth legend, a bare-knuckled unmasked man, a Chinaman loner out of the old West, a character out of Chinese sword-slingers, a fighter. The kind of Chinaman we've been taught to ignore and forget if we don't want America to drive Chinatown out of town.

Ben Fee looks like a scaled-down Edward G. Robinson, a slightly shorter version of a short tough guy. An open, boyish smile on his face all the time and a Tiparillo in the right side of his mouth, all on top of a loose, careless, swaggering tough chubbiness that stops for nothing, not for moving cars, traffic jams, falling safes, nothing but the touch of Chinatown ladies, members of the International Ladies Garment Workers Union in the daytime, members of his English classes Friday nights, his friends all the time, who can't talk to him without touching his arm or hand, ". . . to see if I'm real," he says.

He's sixty-three years old, nearsighted, and on the move. I say that about him without any extra heart for an old man still going strong at sixty-three. He's from Chinatown. In Chinatown the old aren't expected to stop until they drop. What makes him a special old man is that he's not afraid of America, doesn't hate Chinese America, and likes himself enough to talk about a past that runs from China to San Francisco to New York. Unlike most of his generation, he hasn't given up memory and pride as the price for life in this country.

I looked to meet him researching "Chinaman's Chance—a Portrait of Changing Chinese America, " a documentary I did with Ene Riisna for WNET-TV. Ene Riisna, a tall, six-foot, skinny blonde braless filmmaker, wore a shrunken pullover sweater that reached to her waist with a stretch of the imagination and a skirt that hung around her hips. She tried to pull herself together, keep her navel covered, and look straight, responsible, objective, not knowing what to expect, and expecting the worst as we were over an hour late for our appointment with Fee. My hair was long, parted in the middle. My beard was long and as effective as a beard as needles are at making cactus look hairy, but it was me then, a kind of topping for me all in black: black cowboy boots, black denims, black leather belt with a tough, but not flashy, two-fanged buckle instead of the standard one-prong job, black western shirt with phoney pearl snaps, a silver vest, a toothpick in my mouth, and a Chinese wiseass beard making me solid affectation. Alice in Wonderland growing out of her clothes and a Chinaman dressed for a barn dance were on the scene. But we shared an attaché case.

Shirtsleeves rolled halfway up his forearms, tie loose, collar unbuttoned, waving his Tiparillo, he appeared out of too many old movies, a mobster ordering a hit, a cynical news-hawk stopping the presses, a labor organizer, sauntering, looking something like a teddy bear, and broadcasting all the instant charisma of a man wearing nothing but dynamite sticks, there he was, unmistakably nobody else but Ben Fee, wondering who the hell we were. Everything about him shifted into a "Who the hell are you?" when, suspecting this was Ben Fee, I said, "Ben Fee?"

He shifted his weight to the leg farthest from us, while appearing to stop slightly forward, coming out of the Chinese movies now and westerns at the Palace, put the Tiparillo in his mouth, passed a quick look over us, and took it out again. A sheathed sword in the right hand is a sign of trust. You can't draw your sword when it's sheathed in your fighting hand. Shifting it to your left hand is a warning. You can't shake hands with a burning cigar in your right hand. It's all a matter of language. He smiled, snapshot a quick album of us, then put the cigar back in his mouth, freeing his hand for a shake. Chinatown, Frisco all the way. He was from home. There was a moment of Chinatown manhood, not a kingdom of style, but a moment, at least a Frisco moment I had to come to New York to discover.

Now that we were home, I wondered how much home would get in our way.

In the code of Chinatown, only fools and finks took the English language, or the Chinese language, or words, written words, spoken words, seriously as language. Language as it was known in the world was emasculating, sissy stuff. That's how we compensated for the humiliation of all the time being heard talking in language lessons by Chinese folks and American people who never heard any sense from us when we opened up. Instead of real talk, we memorized phrases that worked, kept a stock of clichés we could string up in combos for any occasion and say nothing at all, no more. Polite, sort, and out. Out without being corrected, an "I'm fine, thank you," and swoop free. We'd pulled one on the *fan gwai* white man.

There were two kinds of talkers among us, two kinds of clowns, for only clowns talked. Talking made you a clown. On the street, if you kept your hands loose, not so down and tight as to look a chicken, but loose enough not to be mistaken for action, and kept everybody laughing, you wouldn't get beat up. "I'm going to beat the shit out of you," a big guy with a gang says. "Well, you better hurry up, man, cuz I gotta get to Chinese school," you say, making it a joke, making them busy with some fun. That was practical language skills of the here-and-now school.

There was something of a man in that clown act, but not the one where you talk college white. That college white in your mouth was the sound of shame on us, the sound of teachers calling us stupid, and you talking like a teacher grading papers meant you were too good for Chinatown and Chinamen. It meant if you weren't thinking of graduating the town for whiteness, you'd better. Hungry, all the time hungry, every sense was out whiffing for something rightly ours, chameleons looking for color, trying on tongues and clothes and hairdos, taking everyone else's, with none of our own, and no habitat, our manhood just never came home. Everything was copycat. Hunger and copycat. We had a lot of stutterers, thumb suckers. The sound of whiteness inevitably crept into our tongue, became the sound of good grades and making good, and Chinatown didn't want us anymore. The language I wrote (which Thom Gunn, the first real poet I ever met, and writer Phillip Roth told me wasn't English, making me go "huh?"), the sounds out of my mouth (which a black migrant worker giving me a lift in Florida told me were "pretty good language for a Chinese person"), is just good enough to turn off many in Chinatown. What they hear in the way I talk is a message white schools put in the sound, a message I don't mean—that I've turned my back on Chinatown and become white, worse than white. To become white, you shit in your blood, hate yourself and all your kind. For *juk sing* to become "Chinese" (pass for *juk kok*) means the same thing, a treatment, a session between electrodes, called an education.

Ben Fee and me, both from home, a generation between us, out of the town, working in white businesses that have done Chinese America bad in the past. The labor movement in California was formed to exclude Chinese labor and drive us out of the country. It led lynchings and made outlaws and scabs of every one of us who drove a truck, tended a bar, or worked at hundreds of other jobs until the fifties. My China brother was the first Chinaman to crack the bartender's union. I was the first Chinaman brakeman on the Southern Pacific Railroad. If I wasn't prejudiced against a Chinaman being into the union movement, I was at least suspected. Every Chinaman who ever wrote, came on proud of his education and English language, wrote a combination tour guide and cookbook—a clown act, showing Chinamen off as "Chinese American" fools. Educational TV served up a formula for being Chinese American: "I'm Chinese because I like chow mein, and I'm American because I like spaghetti," the "Chinese American" writer/reporter said on a program aired special to grades 3–6 in Frisco last year. Fee looked at me, Mr. TV in black and silver, wearing boots, from Oakland really, and an old Oakland at that—Oakland was never quite Frisco—affecting Oakland for TV, come to do a job on New York's Chinatown for TV, come to talk. Talk what? Talk how? We'd show in the talk whether we had anything to say to each other, other than "whiter than thou," "more Chinese than thou," "more assimilated than thou."

Between us was our awareness of our history, white racism's success with our people, and the new wave of writing calling white racism's success our success, off the pens of Tom Wolfe, explaining "why there is no National Association for the Advancement of Chinese Americans" ("Most Chinese who get college educations and good jobs leave Chinatown and the village life forever. But the Chinese heritage, the Chinese 'pride,' does mean that it is impossible for the Chinese in America, poor or rich, to picture themselves as a weak and helpless minority, hopelessly adrift in the tides of circumstances"), Kenneth LaMott, explaining "The Awakening of Chinatown" ("A central point at issue is that, whereas the blacks see the dominant white society as their chief enemy, the Chinese activists are primarily in rebellion against the older generation of their own people. . . . Perhaps it is an over-simplification, but I don't think it is far wrong to say these young men are more in rebellion against Confucius than they are against Mister Charley"), and others writing . . . on our preservation of culture, our assimilation, our "outwhiting the whites"—all of it penning love for us racistly. All of it making us look good at the expense of the blacks, all of it full of disturbing echoes of the Nazi anti-Semitist argument, all of it cunningly white.

Thanks to our lives in America I could call Ben "Chinese" and insult him. I could call him "American" and insult him. I could call him "black" and insult him. I could call him "Japanese" and insult him. Between Ben and me it was all a matter of language, whether or not we talked, because we were Chinamen in America—and the most suspicious kind of Chinamen. Each of us in his own way was something of a star or a pet in a bit of the white world, doing a white thing. He stepped forward, up close to me, grinned, and said, "Welcome, Chinatown Cowboy," and I was finally glad to see him. Thanks, Ben. Ride with this Chinatown cowboy a bit while I run off to rustle strange words and maverick up a language to write this mess in. Remember Burt Lancaster in *Vera Cruz*, a grinning gunfighter in black, always talking about some "Hannah" fellow who taught him everything he knew, a kind of foster father-priest of the badass good-time way of life, like the master in the Chinese movies, the old teacher? I come from your school. (It's an older school than you know.) My right hand is free. Tom Wolfe, I'm talking to you almost in your own language. And it hurts. We can only be wishy-washy in your mouth and untrue.

• • •

America doesn't want us as a visible native minority. They want us to keep our place as Americanized foreigners ruled by immigrant loyalty. But never having been anything else but born here, I've never been foreign and resent having foreigners telling me my place in America and America telling me I'm foreign. There's no denial or rejection of Chinese culture going here, just the recognition of the fact that Americanized Chinese are not Chinese Americans and that Chinese America cannot be understood in the terms of either Chinese or American culture, or some "chow mein/spaghetti" formula of Chinese and American cultures, or anything else you've seen and loved in Charlie Chan. A Chinese can take being told he speaks English pretty good and that he's pretty "Americanized and aggressive" as compliments, as English and being American are for him the results of conscious effort. The same things said to a Chinaman are insults. It's putting him in his place, not in the Chinatown a Chinese could see today, but in the Chinatown that's in the blood of all *juk sing*, the death camp Chinatown, Chinatown where the missionaries erected forty churches and church agencies and opened "Chinese schools" to teach us to be Chinese, the way NASA teaches Americans to be citizens of the moon playing on our fear of deportation by perpetuating, if not the fact, then the psychology of the Chinaman facing certain extinction by death or deportation. That Chinatown is our language. It's in our silence.

WRITING ABOUT THE READING

5. What details of appearance and behavior does Chin use to make Ben Fee "come alive" for the reader?

6. What are some of the differences between Ben Fee and the usual stereotype of a Chinese American man?

7. Why does the writer describe the ability to make a joke as a practical language skill?

8. Why is the writer ambiguous about the use of language that he calls "college white"?

9. Why does the writer use the term "chow mein/spaghetti" to describe the expected Americanization process?

10. Why does Chin accuse some writers, such as Kenneth LaMott, of making Chinese Americans look good at the expense of African Americans?

11. What words would you use to describe the tone of this essay and what would be the reasons for your choice?

WRITING FROM YOUR OWN EXPERIENCE

Note: In these assignments, write about your own experience or use that of someone you know, read about, or saw in a film/TV show.

12. The term "Chinaman's chance," used ironically by Chin as a title for his documentary, means to have little or no chance at all. Think of a time when you were faced with a situation in which you had little or no chance to win. Why were you faced with this situation and what was the result?

13. The writer likes to dress and think of himself as a kind of cowboy, a tough guy. Think of someone (male or female) you would describe as a "cowboy." Why would you describe the person in this way?

14. Choose one celebrity who has an image of a tough guy. Explain whether you think that this reputation helps or harms this celebrity.

WRITING ABOUT RESEARCH

15. Why did Chinese immigrants rely on their own social organizations (such as the tongs or the Six Companies of San Francisco) in the nineteenth century?

16. What was the contribution of Chinese immigrants to agriculture, mining, and/or railroads of the nineteenth century?

17. Research the "Chinatown" in a city in your area or that of a city such as San Francisco, New York, or Portland. Describing some aspect of Chinatown, such as the housing, businesses, or schools, explain why the Chinese influence remains here.

18. Choose one Chinese writer or philosopher and explain the writer's influence on traditional Chinese culture. Consider one of the following:

(Note: The spelling of Chinese names varies according to whether the editor uses the modern Pinyin or older Wade-Giles system for translating these names into English. The translation of book titles may vary as well.)

(a) Confucius (Kung-Fu-tzu) (551–479 B.C.E.): *The Analects*

(b) Laozi (Lao Tzu) (c. 520 B.C.E.): *The Way and Its Power*

(c) Zhuangzi (Chuang Tzu) (c. 369–286 B.C.E.): *On the Equality of Things*

(d) Qu Yuan (c. 340–278 B.C.E.): *Songs of the South*

(e) Mencius (Meng-tzu) (c. 371–289 B.C.E.)

(f) Gan Bao (fourth century): *In Search of the Supernatural*

(g) Wang Wei (701–761) poetry

(h) Li Bai (701–762) poetry

(i) Du Fu (712–770) poetry

(j) Yuan Zhen (779–831): *The Story of Ying-ying*

(k) Su Dongpo (1037–1101) poetry

(l) Wu Cheng'en (1506–1582): *Monkey*

(m) Cao Xuequn (1715–1763): *Dream of the Red Chamber*

(n) Shen Fu (1763–1808?): *Six Records of a Floating Life*

Selection 2

American Dreamer

BHARATI MUKHERJEE

Bharati Mukherjee *(1940–), writer and educator, was born in Calcutta, India, and came to the United States as a graduate student in 1961. In India, she earned a B.A. (1959) from the University of Calcutta and an M.A. (1961) from the University of Baroda. After she completed M.F.A. (1963) and Ph.D. degrees (1969) from the University of Iowa, Iowa City, Mukherjee became a professor of English at McGill University, Canada (1969–1980). After returning to the United States, Mukherjee taught at Montclair State College, New Jersey (1984–1987) and City University of New York (1987–1989). She became a naturalized U.S. citizen in 1988. Currently, she is a professor at the University of California, Berkeley. She was awarded Canada Arts Council Grants (1973, 1977), and received the 1989 National Book Critics Circle Award for* The Middleman and Other Stories.

Mukherjee has stated that she wants all people to be recognized as individuals, not as ethnic stereotypes. She emphasizes that the process of acculturation transforms both the individual and society. As she discusses in the selection "American Dreamer," Mukherjee herself underwent a profound transformation after she moved from India to the United States. She also notes in this essay that the wave of immigration since the 1960s has profoundly transformed America. This essay was first printed in Race: An Anthology in the First Person *(1997).*

PREPARING TO READ

1. How would you define "the American Dream" and why would you define it in this way?
2. Compare the diverse society of America today with the more homogeneous society of the 1950s. What are the advantages and disadvantages of each type of society?
3. Francis L. K. Hsu, a noted anthropologist, has pointed out that Americans believe both in the equality of all people and in the

superiority of U.S. society. How are these ideas inconsistent and why are Americans able to hold such conflicting ideas?

4. The writer states that today many "older" Americans are resentful against the new immigrants, such as those from Asia or Mexico. Explain why you think that these "older" Americans are justified (or not justified) in their hostility toward new immigrants?

AMERICAN DREAMER

The United States exists as a sovereign nation. "America," in contrast, exists as a myth of democracy and equal opportunity to live by, or as an ideal goal to reach.

I am a naturalized U.S. citizen, which means that, unlike native-born citizens, I had to prove to the U.S. government that I merited citizenship. What I didn't have to disclose was that I desired "America," which to me is the stage for the drama of self-transformation.

I was born in Calcutta and first came to the United States—to Iowa City, to be precise—on a summer evening in 1961. I flew into a small airport surrounded by cornfields and pastures, ready to carry out the two commands my father had written out for me the night before I left Calcutta: Spend two years studying creative writing at the Iowa Writers' Workshop, then come back home and marry the bridegroom he selected for me from our caste and class.

In traditional Hindu families like ours, men provided and women were provided for. My father was a patriarch and I a pliant daughter. The neighborhood I'd grown up in was homogeneously Hindu, Bengali-speaking, and middle-class. I didn't expect myself to ever disobey or disappoint my father by setting my own goals and taking charge of my future.

When I landed in Iowa 35 years ago, I found myself in a society in which almost everyone was Christian, white, and moderately well-off. In the women's dormitory I lived in my first year, apart from six international graduate students (all of us were from Asia and considered "exotic"), the only non-Christian was Jewish, and the only non-white an African-American from Georgia. I didn't anticipate then, that over the next 35 years, the Iowa population would become so diverse that it would have 6,931 children from non-English-speaking homes registered as students in its schools, nor that Iowans would be in the grip of a cultural crisis in which resentment against immigrants, particularly refugees from Vietnam, Sudan, and Bosnia, as well as unskilled Spanish-speaking workers, would become politicized enough to cause the Immigration and Naturalization Service to open an "enforcement" office in Cedar Rapids in October for the tracking and deporting of undocumented aliens.

In Calcutta in the '50s, I heard no talk of "identity crisis"—communal or individual. The concept itself—of a person not knowing who he or she is—was unimaginable in our hierarchical, classification-obsessed society. One's identity was fixed, derived from religion, caste, patrimony, and mother tongue. A Hindu Indian's last name announced his or her forefathers' caste and place of origin. A *Mukherjee* could only be a Brahmin from Bengal. Hindu tradition forbade intercaste, interlanguage, interethnic marriages. Bengali tradition even discouraged emigration: To remove oneself from Bengal was to dilute true culture.

Until the age of 8, I lived in a house crowded with 40 or 50 relatives. My identity was viscerally connected with ancestral soil and genealogy. I was who I was because I was Dr. Sudhir Lal Mukherjee's daughter, because I was a Hindu Brahmin, because I was Bengali-speaking, and because my desh—the Bengali word for homeland—was an East Bengal village called Faridpur.

The University of Iowa classroom was my first experience of coeducation. And after not too long, I fell in love with a fellow student named Clark Blaise, an American of Canadian origin, and impulsively married him during a lunch break in a lawyer's office above a coffee shop.

That act cut me off forever from the rules and ways of upper-middle-class life in Bengal, and hurled me into a New World life of scary improvisations and heady explorations. Until my lunch-break wedding, I had seen myself as an Indian foreign student who intended to return to India to live. The five-minute ceremony in the lawyer's office suddenly changed me into a transient with conflicting loyalties to two very different cultures.

The first 10 years into marriage, years spent mostly in my husband's native Canada, I thought of myself as an expatriate Bengali permanently stranded in North America because of destiny or desire. My first novel, *The Tiger's Daughter*, embodies the loneliness I felt but could not acknowledge, even to myself, as I negotiated the no man's land between the country of my past and the continent of my present. Shaped by memory, textured with nostalgia for a class and culture I had abandoned, this novel quite naturally became an expression of the expatriate consciousness.

It took me a decade of painful introspection to put nostalgia in perspective and to make the transition from expatriate to immigrant.

After a 14-year stay in Canada, I forced my husband and our two sons to relocate to the United States. But the transition from foreign student to U.S. citizen, from detached onlooker to committed immigrant, has not been easy.

The years in Canada were particularly harsh. Canada is a country that officially, and proudly, resists cultural fusion. For all its rhetoric about a cultural "mosaic," Canada refuses to renovate its national self-image to include its changing complexion. It is a New World country with Old World concepts of a fixed, exclusivist national identity. Canadian official rhetoric designated me as one of the "visible minority" who, even though I spoke the Canadian languages of English and French, was straining "the absorptive capacity" of Canada. Canadians of color were routinely treated as "not real" Canadians. One example: In 1985 a terrorist bomb, planted in an Air-India jet on Canadian soil, blew up after leaving Montreal, killing 329 passengers, most of whom were Canadians of Indian origin. The prime minister of Canada at the time, Brian Mulroney, phoned the prime minister of India to offer Canada's condolences for India's loss.

Those years of race-related harassments in Canada politicized me and deepened my love of the ideals embedded in the American Bill of Rights. I don't forget that the architects of the Constitution and the Bill of Rights were white males and slaveholders. But through their declaration, they provided us with the enthusiasm for human rights, and the initial framework from which other empowerments could be conceived and enfranchised communities expanded.

I am a naturalized U.S. citizen and I take my American citizenship very seriously. I am not an economic refugee, nor am I a seeker of political asylum. I am a voluntary immigrant. I became a citizen by choice, not by simple accident of birth.

Yet these days, questions such as who is an American and what is American culture are being posed with belligerence, and being answered with violence. Scapegoating of immigrants has once again become the politicians' easy remedy for all that ails the nation. Hate speeches fill auditoriums for demagogues willing to profit from stirring up racial animosity. An April Gallup poll indicated that half of Americans would like to bar almost all legal immigration for the next five years.

The United States, like every sovereign nation, has a right to formulate its immigration policies. But in this decade of continual, large-scale diasporas, it is imperative that we come to some agreement about who "we" are, and what our goals are for the nation, now that our community includes people of many races, ethnicities, languages, and religions.

The debate about American culture and American identity has to date been monopolized largely by Eurocentrists and ethnocentrists whose rhetoric has been flamboyantly divisive, pitting a phantom "us" against a demonized "them."

All countries view themselves by their ideals. Indians idealize the cultural continuum, the inherent value system of India, and are properly incensed when foreigners see nothing but poverty, intolerance, strife, and injustice. Americans see themselves as the embodiments of liberty, openness, and individualism, even as the world judges them for drugs, crime, violence, bigotry, militarism, and homelessness. I was in Singapore in 1994 when the American teenager Michael Fay was sentenced to caning for having spraypainted some cars. While I saw Fay's actions as those of an individual, and his sentence as too harsh, the overwhelming local sentiment was that vandalism was an "American" crime, and that flogging Fay would deter Singapore youths from becoming "Americanized."

Conversely, in 1994, in Tavares, Florida, the Lake County School Board announced its policy (since overturned) requiring middle school teachers to instruct their students that American culture, by which the board meant European-American culture, is inherently "superior to other foreign or historic cultures." The policy's misguided implication was that culture in the United States has not been affected by the American Indian, African-American, Latin-American, and Asian-American segments of the population. The sinister implication was that our national identity is so fragile that it can absorb diverse and immigrant cultures only by recontextualizing them as deficient.

Our nation is unique in human history in that the founding idea of "America" was in opposition to the tenet that a nation is a collection of like-looking, like-speaking, like-worshiping people. The primary criterion for nationhood in Europe is homogeneity of culture, race, and religion—which has contributed to blood-soaked balkanization in the former Yugoslavia and the former Soviet Union.

America's pioneering European ancestors gave up the easy homogeneity of their native countries for a new version of utopia. Now, in the 1990s, we have the exciting chance to follow that tradition and assist in the making of a new American culture that differs from both the enforced assimilation of a "melting pot" and the Canadian model of a multicultural "mosaic."

The multicultural mosaic implies a contiguity of fixed, self-sufficient, utterly distinct cultures. Multiculturalism, as it has been practiced in the United States in the past 10 years, implies the existence of a central culture, ringed by peripheral cultures. The fallout of official multiculturalism is the establishment of one culture as the norm and the rest as aberrations. At the same time, the multiculturalist emphasis on race- and ethnicity-based group identify leads to a lack of respect for individual differences within each group, and to vilification of those individuals who place the good of the nation above the interests of their particular racial or ethnic communities.

We must be alert to the dangers of an "us" vs. "them" mentality. In California, this mentality is manifesting itself as increased violence between minority, ethnic communities. The attack on Korean-American merchants in South Central Los Angeles in the wake of the Rodney King beating trial is only one recent example of the tragic side effects of this mentality. On the national level, the politicization of ethnic identities has encouraged the scapegoating of legal immigrants, who are blamed for economic and social problems brought about by flawed domestic and foreign policies.

We need to discourage the retention of cultural memory if the aim of that retention is cultural balkanization. We must think of American culture and nationhood as a constantly reforming, transmogrifying "we."

In this age of diasporas, one's biological identity may not be one's only identity. Erosions and accretions come with the act of emigration. The experience of cutting myself off from a biological homeland and settling in an adopted homeland that is not always welcoming to its dark-complexioned citizens has tested me as a person, and made me the writer I am today.

I choose to describe myself on my own terms, as an American, rather than as an Asian-American. Why is it that hyphenation is imposed only on nonwhite Americans? Rejecting hyphenation is my refusal to categorize the cultural landscape into a center and its peripheries; it is to demand that the American nation deliver the promises of its dream and its Constitution to all its citizens equally.

My rejection of hyphenation has been misrepresented as race treachery by some India-born academics on U.S. campuses who have appointed themselves guardians of the "purity" of ethnic cultures. Many of them, though they reside permanently in the United States and participate in its economy, consistently denounce American ideals and institutions. They direct their rage at me because, by becoming a U.S. citizen and exercising my voting rights, I have invested in the present and not the past; because I have committed myself to help shape the future of my adopted homeland; and because I celebrate racial and cultural mongrelization.

What excites me is that as a nation we have not only the chance to retain those values we treasure from our original cultures but also the chance to acknowledge that the outer forms of those values are likely to change. Among Indian immigrants, I see a great deal of guilt about the inability to hang on to what they commonly term "pure culture." Parents express rage or despair at their U.S.-born children's forgetting of, or indifference to, some aspects of Indian culture. Of those parents I would ask: What is it we have lost if our children are acculturating into the culture in which we are living? Is it so terrible that our children are discovering or are inventing homelands for themselves?

Some first-generation Indo-Americans, embittered by racism and by unofficial "glass ceilings," construct a phantom identity, more-Indian-than-Indians-in-India, as a defense against marginalization. I ask: Why don't you get actively involved in fighting discrimination? Make your voice heard. Choose the forum most appropriate for you. If you are a citizen, let your vote count. Reinvest your energy and re-sources into revitalizing your city's disadvantaged residents and neighborhoods. Know your constitutional rights, and when they are violated, use the agencies of redress the Constitution makes available to you. Expect change, and then it comes, deal with it!

As a writer, my literary agenda begins by acknowledging that America has transformed me. It does not end until I show that I (along with the hundreds of thousands of immigrants like me) am minute by minute transforming America. The transformation is a two-way process: It affects both the individual and the national-cultural identity.

Others who write stories of migration often talk of arrival at a new place as a loss, the loss of communal memory and the erosion of an original culture. I want to talk of arrival as gain.

WRITING ABOUT THE READING

5. Why did the writer's father make her promise to return home?
6. How and why did Mukherjee cut herself off from her previous life?
7. What is the author's attitude toward Canada and why does she feel this way?
8. What does the telephone call of Prime Minister Mulroney reveal about his attitude toward these Canadian citizens?
9. Suppose the people killed on the jet had been Canadians of Irish immigrant origin. How and why would the behavior of the Prime Minister likely be different?

10. Why do you think that Mukherjee's dislike of the term "multicultural mosaic" is justified (or unjustified)?

11. Why does Mukherjee write that there are some negative consequences of emphasis on race and ethnic identity?

12. Why does the writer celebrate what she calls "racial and cultural mongrelization"?

13. Explain whether you believe that Mukherjee gives good advice to immigrants.

WRITING FROM YOUR OWN EXPERIENCE

Note: In these assignments, write about your own experience or use that of someone you know, read about, or saw in a film/TV show.

14. Consider Mukherjee's arguments against "multicultural mosaic." Explain whether or not you agree with her position on multiculturalism and suggest another term that might be better than this one.

15. Mukherjee describes the time when she lived in Canada as a period of loneliness. Think of a time when you felt lonely. Why did you feel this way and what actions did you take to overcome loneliness?

16. Mukherjee recommends that immigrants take part in the political process. Even in college, students can participate in politics by voting for class or club officers. Recall a time when you voted, campaigned for a candidate, or ran for office yourself. Why did you participate in this experience and what was the result of your participation?

WRITING ABOUT RESEARCH

17. Like China, India has a long history and extensive literary heritage. Choose one important literary work and/or author from India. Explain why this work or person is significant. Consider: *(Note: Dates listed are approximate.)*

    Works:
    (a) "The Rig Veda" (1400 B.C.E.)
    (b) "The Uphanishads" (900–400 B.C.E.)
    (c) "The Bhagavad-Gita" (300–500 B.C.E.)

Poets and Writers:

(a) Gahlib (1797–1869)

(b) Mohandas K. Gandhi (1869–1948)

(c) Kalidasa (fifth century)

(d) Mirabai (sixteenth century)

(e) Ravidas (fifteenth century)

(f) Salman Rushdie (1947–)

(g) Rajee Seth (1935–)

(h) Rabindranath Tagore (1861–1941)

18. India is known for its emphasis on religion and spirituality. Choose one of the major religions of India (Buddhism, Hinduism, Islam, Jainism, Sikhism, and Sufism). Explain how and why the beliefs and/or practices of this religion influenced Indian culture and/or history.

19. Mukherjee states that she comes from a privileged group, the Brahmin caste. How and why does the caste system affect Indian culture and/or the lives of people?

The Chinese Man Has My Ticket

SHAWN WONG

Shawn Wong *(1949–) Chinese American writer, educator, and former professional drag racer, was born in Oakland, California. He received a B.A. (1971) from the University of California, Berkeley, and an M.A. (1974) from San Francisco State University. Wong currently is Chairman of the Department of English, University of Washington. He has received a Washington State Governor's Writers Day Award (1980), a National Endowment for the Arts fellowship grant (1981), and numerous other awards. The editor of several anthologies of Asian American and American multicultural writing, Wong is on the board of directors of several literary and arts organizations, including the Before Columbus Foundation. He is a co-editor of the book,* Aiiieeeee! An Anthology of Asian American Writers *(1974), which is credited with establishing the Asian American literary canon.*

Through his work in editing anthologies and other projects, Wong has long been involved in the rediscovery, preservation, and promotion of Asian American writing. Wong's 1979 novel, Homebase, *was only the third novel published by a Chinese American in the United States. The novel is the story of a descendant of the Chinese immigrants who built the railroads. The protagonist is exposed to racial stereotypes by both whites and African Americans. Similarly, in the selection, "The Chinese Man Has My Ticket," Wong shows how his identity often puzzles others. The essay is included in the anthology* How We Want to Live *(1998).*

PREPARING TO READ

1. Make a list of the three to five most important places in the United States for a visitor to see. Why would you recommend visiting these places?

2. Choose a foreign country to which you would like to travel. Explain why you would like to travel to this place.

3. If you were to choose one foreign language to know well, which would it be and why would you choose this language?
4. Explain whether you think that it is important for an English-speaking person to learn a foreign language today.

THE CHINESE MAN HAS MY TICKET

After President Nixon traveled to China in the early seventies, my friends kept asking me when I would visit China, the country of my ancestry. I was born in America and have never been to China. Over the years, the question of going has changed to a presumption, "Of course you've been there." Upon learning that I'm Chinese, strangers will describe their trip to China. Sometimes I let them assume that I've already seen what they describe. I nod with comprehension and even say, "Ah, yes." I feel guilty because these well-meaning people want to tell their stories to one who knows. I'm Chinese after all. "Been there, done that" should be my answer.

To complicate matters, I also tell people that I teach Asian American literature, which most people take to mean something from the Tang dynasty, rather than literature written in America by Americans of Asian ancestry. Sometimes I'm asked if the literature is translated, to which I usually respond, "Not yet." In my literature classes, most of the students are Asian, but even I have to look in my pronunciation guide to Asian names before the first day of class. When I was an undergraduate at Berkeley, Asian students accounted for only 6 percent of the student body and we were predominantly middle-class Chinese and Japanese Americans, born and raised in America. Today, on a large campus like Berkeley or the University of Washington, there might be 12 to 15 different Asian ethnic groups plus Asian students of mixed racial heritage, and they might account for 20 to 40 percent of the student body. In an attempt to remember my students' names on the first day of class, I write down who they look like next to their names—actors, musicians, friends, or former students. It doesn't do any good to write "black hair, brown eyes, glasses." Even the term *Asian American* is being contested by this new population. They want to know what it means and why my college generation from the late sixties named ourselves Asian Americans.

In the seventies, I tried to get my aunt to take me to China to find my roots and to show me where our family had lived. I saw it as an act of self-determination. A staunch anti-Communist, my aunt refused to go, saying, "I want to remember it the way it was." Aunt Ching-yi first arrived in America in 1938 when she came as a graduate student to attend Mills College, and she has never returned to China.

My parents arrived in America from China fifty years ago on October 31, 1947. My father and my aunt's younger brother, Peter Hsu, was thirty and my mother, Maria, was twenty-two. Like my aunt, they entered America with student visas. They were not poor immigrants. My father was a graduate student in civil engineering at the University of California at Berkeley and my mother was an art student at the California College of Arts and Crafts. Like my aunt, they were well educated; they could read, write, and speak English. They came from relatively wealthy families. My mother was a painter, photographer, dancer, and musician. She didn't know how to cook or even boil water. My father was an engineer who wrote beautiful letters and stories in English. In China, he was an award-winning athlete. He was tall, six-foot-two, and handsome; she was petite and truly beautiful. After the Communists took over China in 1949, they were granted permanent residency in America, the same year I was born in Oakland, California. With an American-born son, they realized that America was their home and there was no return to China. They never insisted that I learn Chinese. They were learning to be Americans; why would they teach me to be Chinese? My father wore double-breasted suits and drove a Buick Roadmaster, and my mother wore cashmere sweaters, silk scarves, and wool skirts. We went to Cal football games. They never did return to China; they both died here in America. I was supposed to be the best American son I could be, not to be Chinese. Assimilation and acculturation in the fifties were pervasive for all immigrants in America, the melting pot.

I've been to Hong Kong three times and to Japan once as a child, and to Hong Kong for a week to visit my grandmother when I was twenty-one, which was twenty-seven years ago. The irony is that my grandmother visited us in America every year rather than the other way around, then later moved to America. In 1996, she died at the age of ninety-nine in San Francisco. I lived in Taiwan for six months when I was seven and on the island of Guam for a year when I was six. I always felt out of place as an English-speaking Chinese kid in Hong Kong and Taiwan. During one of our longer stays, my mother dropped me off at a preschool in Hong Kong, but I came home after the first day and told my mother that I quit school because I couldn't understand anyone, because all the kids spoke Chinese. All this travel back and forth across the Pacific was the result of my father's work as a civilian engineer for the U.S. Navy. My mother has a picture of me dressed in full leather cowboy chaps and vest with hat and six guns standing in front of the Grand Hotel in Taipei, Taiwan. I remember singing "Home on the Range." In Taiwan, I was the only Chinese kid in an all-white American school. If there was ever a perfect time for an identity crisis, that was it.

I've never been comfortable in Asian countries. My face makes people assume that I belong. They speak their native tongues to me, expecting an answer. They are unwilling to believe that I'm a monolingual American, educated in a monolingual and monocultural public school system. When I was twenty-one I visited my grandmother in Hong Kong. Everyone on the street spoke Cantonese to me. I told them that I didn't speak Cantonese. To make matters worse, they then asked me in Mandarin if I spoke Mandarin. I can understand Mandarin, because my parents spoke Mandarin, but I can't speak it. When I was growing up my parents would often speak to me in Mandarin and I would answer in English. To the people in Hong Kong, I'm stupid because I don't know my own mother tongue, or worse, refuse to speak it. There's a word for Chinese like me: *jook sing,* "hollow bamboo." It means that we look Chinese, but are hollow and lack cultural substance on the inside. Sixty percent of the Asians in America are foreign born, which makes me the exception rather than the rule in the country of my birth. People in Asia know I'm foreign and people in America assume that I am foreign born. Sometimes I am asked how long I've been in this country; I always answer my age. Not getting the joke, some people have even replied, "No wonder I didn't hear an accent in your voice."

Like my father, my work defines my travel. So far I've been in every region of the United States from Hawaii and Alaska to Texas, North Carolina, and Florida, and in Europe to the United Kingdom, Ireland, Germany, France, and Italy. Ironically, my writing life is linked more to Germany and Italy than to any other country. My two novels have been translated and published in Germany and some of my short stories have been translated and published in Italy, but in no Asian countries, even though my books are about Asian America. I can read and speak German and some Italian. I am more comfortable in Italy than in any foreign country. Call it the revenge of Marco Polo.

I wrote my second novel, *American Knees,* while on a Rockefeller Foundation residency in Bellagio, northern Italy, in 1994. The novel is set, for the most part, in San Francisco's Asian American community. The dry cleaner in the little village of Bellagio didn't take my name when I left my clothes; she wrote *"cinese"* on a little tag and pinned it to my clothes. I was pleased that she at least got my ethnicity right. Sometimes being the only Asian for miles around is an advantage. In the afternoons, I learned to play bocce ball and the residents of Bella-gio would take it upon themselves to teach me Italian.

One day, tired of speaking Italian poorly, I walked down the hill to visit two dogs in the village, one a brown-and-white boxer who lived at the *gelateria* and the other a light brown cocker spaniel from the photo store. Whenever I petted one, the other competed for my af-fection. I knew they would always understand me. Later, I bought postcards from the man who owns the photo store and I said to him, "*Bella cane*, beautiful dog." That's the way I speak Italian. Having learned from phrase books and tapes, I say the whole phrase and the translation as if those I'm speaking to can't understand their own lan-guage. At other times I say, "*Va bene*, OK." Sometimes the Italians are drawn into my way of speaking and answer, "*Arrivederci*, good-bye." A little more of that dialogue and we'd be singing the Italian version of a Nat King Cole song sung in French.

By my third trip to Italy in 1997, I developed an uncanny fluency in all matters relating to Italian food, restaurants, markets, and public transportation. I also understand numbers, time, directions, weights, and measures. I am far more polite in Italian than I am in English. I am uncomfortable not knowing the language when I'm in Italy, but, unlike in Asia, no one expects me to know it. I feel helpless and stupid, be-cause I feel like the monolingual American that I am. The owner of the grocery store in Rome where I shopped declared one day that he wasn't going to speak English to me any more and that I must speak Italian from then on. "I am going to give you character," he told me. "I'm going to teach you past tense—you only know present tense." I was immensely grateful to this wonderful man, who spoke five languages.

Generally, people in Europe are more than happy to speak En-glish to me, because they don't think I'm an American. They think I'm a Japanese tourist. I know zero French and what French I do know, I dare not even pretend to pronounce, so I speak English to everyone. In Paris, everyone is very polite, unlike the stories Americans tell about rude Parisians who refuse to speak English. Most Parisians are re-lieved that I speak English so well. At Charles de Gaulle Airport, I'm directed to the flights to Tokyo before I ask about my flight to Chicago.

Whenever I'm in Europe I'm always curious as to whether or not I can discern the difference between mild racism and cultural confu-sion. In Rome, when people are rude to me, I try to figure out if they're being rude because I'm Asian, or American, or a Japanese tourist. This is very confusing for someone who, at home in America, can easily recognize a racist comment. In Europe I don't know if I need to stand up for my race or my country or my self-respect as a cash-spending tourist.

In the summer of 1997, I took fourteen of my University of Washington students, nine graduates and five undergraduates, to Rome for a month-long creative writing course, designed to reshape their thinking outside of the familiarity of their culture and language. We made a curious-looking group on the streets of Rome. Picture this: one Chinese American professor, twelve white women, one *hapa* (half-Asian woman), and one Chinese American male student. Prior to taking my students to Rome, I had only spent three days there in 1994, and probably knew of Rome no more than Audrey Hepburn did in the movie *Roman Holiday* (and I was no Gregory Peck). To say this was an experiment would be a gross understatement. It had the potential for gross chaos or fabulous discovery for all of us. This seemed like a good way to celebrate my twenty-fifth year of teaching. Why Rome?

How does one prepare for the twenty-first century? I tell my students to acknowledge the diversity of culture and language in this country and the world. I wanted to take my students and, more importantly, myself, out of our realm of cultural familiarity. Only then can we go forward and make real progress. "Let's get out of the classroom," I said to them. "You're writers."

My own writing has changed dramatically every time I've been away from my country. It was time to practice what I preached in the classroom about our responsibility to learn about other cultures. I wanted my students not only to write about Rome, but also to observe and document images that are completely foreign to their experience. I wanted them to also observe, in intricate detail, things that could be used in their writing even when it wasn't about Rome. Describe the light. Describe the interior space of the Pantheon. Learn the jargon of architecture. Examine the space and the quality of the light between buildings. Immerse ourselves in the images of antiquity and religion, the culture of contemporary Rome, the history of Italian art, and the language. Walk the Via Appia Antica, the ancient Roman road.

Outside of Rome, I took them to Tivoli to see the opulence of the Villa d'Este and to the sprawling expanse of the ruins of Hadrian's Villa; to Tarquinia to visit the Etruscan tombs where we gazed up from the pages of D.H. Lawrence's *Etruscan Places* and matched his words to the tombs we visited; to the dead city of Pompeii and to the luxurious vacation town of Sorrento where my students swam in the Gulf of Naples; and to the medieval hilltowns of Orvieto and Civita di Bagnoregio, the latter a magical town of the imagination, an Etruscan fortress perched on a rock and reachable only by foot-bridge. In Rome we saw everything from the underground necropolis of the Vatican, to the cloister of tiny Santi Quattro Coronati, to the bejeweled *il Bambino,* the Holy Infant of Aracoeli, to nearly every Caravaggio painting accessible to the public. Each day we bought food from the vendors in the Campo de' Fiori and cooked fabulous late evening dinners. My students taught themselves and taught me. On public transportation and entering museums my students had taught themselves this mantra without telling me, "*L'uomo cinese ha il mio biglietto.*" The Chinese man has my ticket. Train conductors accepted this explanation even though my students and I were sometimes separated by several crowded train cars while I held the only group ticket. I love them for their fearlessness, their adaptability, their acculturation, and their appetite for being a part of the world.

I believe we were all changed forever by the experience. After Rome, I returned home and nearly all of my students scattered across Italy and Europe to Siena, Florence, Venice, Milan, Prague, Paris, London, Dublin, Vienna, Barcelona, Jerusalem, and Istanbul. Not only did they all come home, but they came home with stories written with words I'd never seen on their pages before.

When I came home, my eighty-four-year-old aunt sent me an e-mail telling me that she had been writing her memoirs of her life in China and America. Since I'm the writer in the family, she wanted me to help her with her memoirs, over three hundred pages long. I was behind on my own writing projects, and meeting with her would involve flying from my home in Seattle to San Francisco, so all I could manage was a politely filial reply, "Sure, I'd be happy to look at it." She mailed it to me, along with her diaries, letters, and notes. Her three-hundred-page story begins with the following paragraph:

> When I was sixteen, my father fell in love with a prostitute and brought her home to live with us. Her name was Hsin Pao. We all hated her intensely, but she was only two years older than I and we had a lot to talk about. My study became her room. My brother called me "traitor." My mother eventually accepted her and was even glad to have someone to play mah-jongg with. Sometime later, my father took Hsin Pao to Tientsin to meet my father's other wife and family.

In Rome, I wanted my students to be prepared for the future, the multicultural world of the twenty-first century. Let's live in the world and move forward. That same month, my aunt was finally taking me into the past on that journey which has become our "return" to China. Self-determination is knowing the past as well as preparing for the future. My aunt tells me that, as a child, she once saw a book that documented sixty-four generations of our family. *Mama mia*, what a marvelous story she tells about the history of our family.

WRITING ABOUT THE READING

5. Often Americans assume that most immigrants are poor and uneducated. How and why do Wong's parents confound the usual expectations?
6. When Wong travels to Asian countries, what are the assumptions others make about him and why do they make these assumptions?
7. When Wong travels to Italy, what are the assumptions others make about him and why do they make these assumptions?
8. Why does the writer include the narrative about taking public transportation?
9. Why does Wong make a joke about how long he has been in the United States?
10. Why does Wong reply "Not yet" when he is asked if the literature he teaches is translated?
11. Why do Wong's students contest the use of the term "Asian American"?

WRITING FROM YOUR OWN EXPERIENCE

Note: In these assignments, write about your own experience or use that of someone you know, read about, or saw in a film/TV show.

12. Recall a time when your beliefs or assumptions about another person were confounded. How did you react and what were some of the consequences of finding your assumptions to be wrong?
13. Review your knowledge of U.S. history from high school and/or college courses. Would you agree (or disagree) that the contribution of Chinese Americans (and/or other Asian Americans) is almost invisible?
14. Suppose that you are going on a trip to China (or another faraway, non-Western country). You have been asked to pack a "cultural bag"—a suitcase with three or four objects/mementos showing who you are and what have been important moments in your life. What objects would you include and why would you take these objects?

WRITING ABOUT RESEARCH

15. Some writers think that China, not the United States, will be the dominant country in the twenty-first century. Explain why they believe this and whether you agree or not.

16. Visitors to China are usually taken to see the Great Wall, China's most famous historic site. Why and when did China build the Great Wall?

17. Choose another notable place in China that tourists might want to visit. Explain why this place is visited by tourists.

Where the Body
Meets Memory

DAVID MURA

David Mura (1952–), *poet and writer, was born in Great Lakes, Illinois. He received a B.A. (1974) from Grinnell College and an M.F.A. (1991) from Vermont College. His 1991 book,* Turning Japanese, *received a Josephine Miles Book Award and was cited as a New York Times Notable Book of the Year. His other awards include a National Endowment for the Arts Literature Fellowship (1985) and the Loft McKnight Award of Distinction for Poetry (1992). During recent years, Mura has taught creative writing and given readings from his poetry at several universities.*

A third-generation Japanese American, Mura lived for a year (1984) in Japan. During this time abroad, Mura became aware that, despite racist attitudes toward Asian Americans, despite the hostility shown toward his "mixed marriage" to a white woman, he felt more at home in the United States than in Japan.

Mura's writing focuses on the complexity and difficulties of being a member of this "model minority." He describes how the experience of being interned during World War II confused and humiliated second-generation Japanese Americans. Turning against their heritage, they became anxious to prove their loyalty to the United States, to show that they were assimilated, and to show that they were model citizens. In this selection from Where the Body Meets Memory *(1996), Mura shows how his father rejected his Japanese traditions and adopted the ways of the middle-class mainstream culture.*

PREPARING TO READ

1. Why do you think (or disagree) that today Asian Americans (in particular, Japanese Americans) are often stereotyped as a "model minority"?

2. Although in the United States marriages generally are based on love, in some societies, such as in Japan, the parents arrange marriages. What are the advantages or disadvantages of each system of marriage?

3. Explain whether you think that a couple's living together before getting married helps or harms a marriage.

4. What are some of the reasons that people are less likely today to have a lifelong, stable marriage than in the past?

WHERE THE BODY MEETS MEMORY

I have a friend whose father is a *hakujin* American and whose mother is Japanese. She says when you grow up in two cultures, you aren't split in half. Instead there are two distinct beings inside of you. If you're separated from one of the cultures, that being dies, at least for a time. It has no light to bathe in, no air, no soil. It can, like certain miraculous plants and seeds, come back to life, but the longer it dwells in that state of nonbeing, the harder it is to revive.

During that first year in college, my father lived with the two beings inside him, each struggling for existence, each with a voice, a vision of its own. There was the self that dressed each day in a V-neck and button-down, white socks and oxfords, that carried Shakespeare, Voltaire, *Principles of Economics, Biology,* in the crook of his arm, that sang "Long Ago and Far Away," under his breath. This self was beginning to study for confirmation at Professor Bigelow's Episcopalian church, was learning the names of the disciples, the gospels of Matthew and Mark, Luke and John. In the late spring, as the aroma of alfalfa crept up from the fields, and tiny green flecks of insects hopped on and pecked his lamp, this self could be heard reciting the Nicene Creed: ". . . and I believe in one holy Apostolic Church . . . in the resurrection of the dead . . . who died on the cross, was buried, and on the third day he rose again . . . " This self was writing for the school newspaper, articles on the Campus Carnival, the baseball team, a guest lecturer on the future of Europe after the war. This self was becoming addicted to Mrs. Bigelow's bran muffins and chocolate chip cookies, the smell of fresh-brewed coffee in the morning, was coming to at least know the names of the composers whose music Mr. Bigelow listened to on his phonograph. This self joined with the guys in the house when everyone went out to play softball or shoot baskets. This self was flourishing, growing in strength, finding each detail learned, each belief accepted, each conversation, caught a feeling of newness and hope, promises he had never known existed.

And the other self? Well, this was the self that once sang songs with the Issei in camp, in that quavering vibrato where the notes possess no Western definition and reliability, where over and over lovers are saying goodbye, someone is remembering their parents, their lover, weeping over the distance between them, where the hands in clapping sway from side to side with each clap. This self watched Mrs. Miyamoto do the *Buyō*, the classical dance, before the barracks, watched her dip back and forth in the dust, using her kerchief as a prop, first to show coyness, then to show interest, then to pull tight, one end clenched in her teeth, in a gesture that was both erotic and comic, causing laughter and delight to come cackling from the crowd. This was the self whose taste buds were formed from *shōyu* and *miso*, from steamed rice, from rolls of *norimaki*, from *tsukemono*, the puckery sweet pickles, a jar of which could disappear in the course of the meal were it not for the swift hand of his mother, slapping at the wrists of her children. This was the self that knew the names of everyone in his barracks, the Ogawas, Sones, Nishimuras, and Oshimas, who watched the bonfires spring up from the oil drums at night as the older people talked about Japan, about politics, about the issues of loyalty he barely understood, about traitors in their midst, spies for the government. This was the self for whom a birth, a death in the community was known by everyone. There was nowhere to keep a secret, no spaces for privacy. This was the self that went to Japanese school in L.A. and addressed the teacher as *"sensei,"* that struggled to learn the eighteen strokes of the *kanji* for *"kan"* (simplicity), that earned a brown belt by defeating Jimmy Honda, using a throw so simple, so pure, it took his opponent off guard and left him sprawling like a worm on the canvas mat. This self found comfort and closeness in his mother, who had little contact with anyone outside the Japanese community, and retained her Japaneseness in a way her husband could not. Because of his mother's quiet, gentle personality, my father sensed this Japaneseness not as a challenge or a criticism, but as a place he could find a stability, an ease, a conversation he could never have with his father.

But that was over now. He was becoming American.

All those years in Kalamazoo, my father's Japanese self seemed to be gasping for breath, its being gradually forgotten. This self believed in the quickness of spirits, the unspoken messages born of the silence that rests in the Japanese language, in the messages of gestures and hovering implications, in the visions that reside in dreams. This self, like his mother, was becoming a ghost.

• • •

A few years ago, I gave a reading at the Japanese American Community Center in San Francisco. As I was browsing through their small library, I came upon some issues of the *Nisei Vue,* a magazine about Nisei which came out for several years after World War II. I remembered my father had been the editor of the magazine for a while. I thought again of his early literary ambitions, the stories I had found in a suitcase in the basement during my twenties, the pages where he talked about the great Nisei novel, the one that would etch the lives of his generation into the memory of America.

Propelled by the Nisei's release from the camps and the boom of the postwar years, the magazine exuded a freshness and optimism, a sense of wondrous things to come. There were Nisei entering all types of jobs, from lawyers to nurses to business. There were beauty pageants and dancers, sports leagues with national tournaments, returning GIs with their war medals. Paging through one of the issues, I came upon an article on Nisei bobby-soxers in Hyde Park on the South Side of Chicago. These teens were in love with swing, they bobbed their hair and wore saddle shoes and pleated skirts and giggled and gossiped and organized dances like any American teenagers of that time. They swooned over Frank Sinatra, the biceps of William Holden, Richard Widmark's steely-eyed gaze.

And there, in one of the pictures, was someone who looked remarkably like my mother. Another picture showed this look-alike teenager at a slumber party. It must be my mother, I thought. She and her family did live in Hyde Park just after the war. (Later, when I ask her about this photo, she says it probably is her, she vaguely remembers the article.) Her face was pert, cute, with an emerging beauty that I'm sure must have been somewhat intimidating despite her small stature. At the time of the photos, she was probably just about to enter Frances Shimer, a woman's junior college.

A year later, in a story my father once told me, she will go to a Nisei mixer, probably on the South Side. My father, just arrived from Western Michigan University in Kalamazoo and now taking English graduate courses at the University of Chicago, will see her across the room. He nudges his friend and says, "That's the girl I'm going to marry." As in a fairy tale, it happens in an instant.

Several months later, at nineteen, she will marry my father, who has recently been drafted, and move with him to Virginia, where he is stationed. He will never go back to graduate school. Instead, in the Army, he will learn, as he put it, "how many stupid people there are in the world," and that his skills as a writer can separate him from the crowd, allow him to move into more interesting jobs.

In the diary my father keeps during their first month of marriage, March 1951, there's a tenderness and innocence I find touching and yet incredibly remote from my sense of the world. After describing their hotel room on his wedding night, he says to his diary, "I cannot tell any more, but I know I will remember last night all the rest of my life."

Struck by my mother's diminutive size and her beauty, my father wonders in the diary about taking her away from her family, from the city they have lived in since the end of the war. When he talks to my mother about this, she replies, "You're my husband now, and I go where you go. My place is with you," and my father's prose swells with love and gratitude for his new bride. He elaborately describes each meal she prepares for him in their small one-room house on the Virginia base, and if the type of food is ordinary, though with a hint of their background—fried chicken, rice balls, peas, and Jell-O—my father's praise for it is not. Then there is a first fight, prompted by what my father later perceives as his own crabbiness and displeasure with having to wake up so early for maneuvers. He worries about the consequences of their fight all day, till he returns and finds her forgiving and loving as ever.

To me, this portrait of their married life seems something out of *McCall's*. Yet I have no doubt that in many ways my father's diary is a fairly accurate description. Certainly, compared to many, my parents have had a steady, successful marriage, with few troubles. When their children grew up, my parents made a fairly easy transition into a new life, where tennis and golf and Nautilus became the center of their lives, learning to play together in a way that many couples, victims of the empty-nest syndrome, cannot. Both my parents' marriage and their selves can be characterized by the word "resilient," and in that, they mirror the rise of their generation of Japanese Americans after the experience of the camps.

And yet, I do know that my mother, at some point, made adjustments. On certain occasions when my father seemed to be working too much or when he seemed unaware of tensions between relatives or within our family, my mother let me know in casual remarks that this was part of marriage. "After a certain point you give up on changing someone, you realize you can't change them. You just learn to live with it."

She said this without anger or bitterness; at the same time I could tell this wasn't some traditional belief, a cultural code set in stone to uphold male privilege. Instead, her tone conveyed a sense of practicality, a sense that such accommodation was part and parcel of love. Such accommodation wasn't being unromantic or easy, but realistic; it involved a recognition of your own limitations as well as your partner's.

This lesson and her marriage have been, perhaps, my most valuable legacies from her. Whatever else happened in my childhood, I knew my parents loved each other. There was a lesson there in their perseverance, in their steadfastness.

And yet, it's one of the paradoxes of my life that out of their happy marriage should come a son so troubled about the relationships between women and men, so ill at ease with his own sexuality.

• • •

Today, holding my son in my arms, feeding him his bottle, rocking him to sleep, I suddenly felt there was something less selfless in a father's love for his son than for his daughter. When the son marries, there is not the sense that some cord must be broken, something let go. The son has already broken away by virtue of his being a male and a rival; the father can love the son without becoming a rival to his son's lover (though if the son is gay, all this changes slightly).

Then I looked at my Nikko's almost balding head, his long eyelashes that people tell me women will love, his button nose and chubby cheeks. As his body relaxed into the rhythm of sleep, his arms falling at his sides, I marveled at how intensely I love him. I though of how, in the future, the breakages of father and son, the almost inevitable cracking of bonds, might, perhaps must, take place. Fathers see in their sons a mirror of themselves; this is the selfish side of our love.

And what of a son's love for his father? Perhaps I feel that most when my father steps up to the tee, trying to settle himself, to aim his club. As he takes his backswing, at the very top he suddenly freezes, much too long; this hitch has hit him in old age, the sign that his muscles will not flow as smoothly or as powerfully as they once did, that his nerves have taken control. It tells of my father's growing fallibility and mortality, something I can barely stand to see, especially those times the hitch causes him to dub the ball only a few yards off the tee. This doesn't happen often yet, but each time it happens and I am there, I feel this deep and abiding sadness, this ache that wishes each of my father's shots to be picture perfect, to grant him this tiny bit of pleasure at this point in his life.

When the hitch first appeared, it was an embarrassment to my father and almost an affront to my mother. My father was ready to give up the game and he blamed my mother's critical eye in part for the decompensation of his swing. My mother said that for years she felt golf was my father's mistress, and she grew jealous of the time it took him away from her. Unlike with a mistress, there was simply no way for her to compete.

"I finally take up golf, like he wanted me to, and then this happens," she said. "And it's no fun anymore, for him or for me. I feel like I finally tried to do what he wanted, finally figured out a way to compete with this mistress, and then he gets this hitch and he can't perform."

The implications of this were not totally unapparent to my wife and me.

"It sounded so sexual," I said. "Do you think hypnotism might help?"

My wife often hypnotizes her oncology patients when they are suffering from the pains of chemotherapy or when she has to stick them with a needle. She's used it with others, including me, for dealing with psychological problems and tensions.

"I suppose so. It couldn't hurt."

The next day Susie went into my father's study with him. My mother paced downstairs in the kitchen. After the session, my father immediately went down to the basement, where he has built a driving net, and when he came back upstairs fifteen minutes later, he was overjoyed. My mother kept asking what Susie had done. She was amazed.

My father then had Susie make a tape that he could use to hypnotize himself when she was not there.

"You know," said Susie, "I suspect it's at least partly your mother that's causing the hitch. I'm sure she's part of the reason he keeps freezing up. So I told your father not to let anyone listen to the tape, that it was his alone."

"Did you tell him my mother couldn't listen to it?"

"I told him it was just for him." Pause. "And I told him that I thought it would be best for him not to golf with your mother for a while."

"Oh God," I said. I knew this would drive my mother insane.

The tape continued to work. My father's hitch disappeared, and my father was full of praises for Susie's hypnotic abilities. He told her that he had told an old Blue Cross/Blue Shield colleague about how hypnotism had helped his game. Later, the man came up to my father and asked him if his daughter-in-law had ever done any work with impotence.

Soon my mother became intensely curious about this tape. She would watch my father go into his study, lock the door, and listen to the tape, and something about this routine piqued her. She began to badger him about letting her listen to it.

"I just want to listen to it," she said. "Maybe it might help my game, did you ever think about that?"

He kept telling her that he didn't have time at that moment to let her listen to the tape or that he had left it in the car. He didn't feel he could tell what my wife had told him: *Don't let Terry listen to the tape. It's yours alone.*

"You told me I could listen to it yesterday," my mother would complain when he gave her one of his excuses.

"I'll let you listen to the tape. I will."

"I don't understand why you're making such a big thing about this."

"It's not a big thing. You're the one who's making a big thing about it."

Finally, he told her he would rewind the tape to let her listen to it. Instead, by mistake, he erased the tape.

"Freud would have a field day here," said my wife when she found out about this.

Gradually, my father's hitch came back. There was no more talk about hypnotism. He and my mother learned to live with his hitch and began to golf together again. One more adjustment to age.

I suppose, if this has been one of the testier episodes in their marriage, my father is indeed a lucky man.

Still, when I watch him swing, it is not my father's luck I think about, but mine, how he is poised on this precipice from which the body declines and never recovers. I am not on this precipice, and in this vanquishing of my rival, I feel a certain faint guilt, and beyond that an affection I have not let myself feel until now. My father pulls the club back, it freezes for what seems several seconds above his head, and I am no longer a child, I am no longer the one held in terror, no longer the one whom I pity. What I feel coursing through my body is a connection deeper than the years or memory and more basic than biology and duty, more mysterious than love. I am the son he has wanted me to be, standing beside him on the first tee, watching a moment later his ball soar off into the morning, landing softly on the dew-heavy grass, glistening almost as far as his failing sight can see.

WRITING ABOUT THE READING

5. Why does Mura assert that his father lived with "two beings" while in college?

6. What evidence does the writer supply to show that his father is now Americanized?

7. Why does the father's "hitch" when playing golf make the writer feel both affection and guilt?

8. Using evidence from the text, what can you infer about the writer's attitude toward his father?

9. Why did the mother's presence make the father uncomfortable when playing golf?
10. Why is it important to the writer to be the son that his father had wanted him to be?

WRITING FROM YOUR OWN EXPERIENCE

Note: In these assignments, write about your own experience or use that of someone you know, read about, or saw in a film/TV show.

11. Have you ever sensed a rivalry between yourself and your father, mother, brother, or sister? Why was there a rivalry and what were some of the results of this competition?
12. The writer's mother says that eventually you learn that you cannot change a person. Think of a time when you tried to change another person (or another person tried to change you). Why was this attempt made and what were the consequences of this attempt?
13. As children move into adulthood, adjustments often are made in the relationship between the child and the parent. How and why have you made adjustments in your relationship with your parents in recent years?

WRITING ABOUT RESEARCH

14. Choose one Japanese literary type, book, or writer and explain the work or writer's importance in traditional Japanese culture. Consider one of the following:
    (a) Early myths in (712) *Kojiki: (The Record of Ancient Matters)*
    (b) Izumi Shikibu (tenth century): *(The Diary of Lady Izumi Shikibu)*
    (c) Murasaki Shikibu (c. 978–1030): *The Tale of Genji*
    (d) Kamo No Chomei (twelfth century): *An Account of My Hermitage*
    (e) *Tales of the Heike* (thirteenth century)
    (f) No Theater (fourteenth–fifteenth centuries)
    (g) Matsuo Basho (1644–1694): *Narrow Road to the Deep North*
    (h) Haiku poetry
    (i) Natsume Soseki (1867–1916): *Three Cornered World (Kusamakura)*
    (j) Kawabata Yasunari (1899–1972) Nobel-prize winning novelist

15. How does a traditional Japanese art form (such as landscape gardening, the tea ceremony, paintings, or kimonos) reflect a love of beauty and a concern with form and balance?

16. Why did the U.S. government place Japanese Americans in relocation camps during World War II?

17. What efforts toward restitution has the U.S. government made to those Japanese Americans placed in relocation camps?

18. Thousands of Japanese Americans fought for the United States (in the 100th Infantry Battalion and the 442nd Regimental Combat Team) during World War II. What were some of the accomplishments of these units?

Selection 5

Mother Tongue

AMY TAN

Amy Tan (1952–), writer, the daughter of Chinese immigrants, was born in Oakland, California. She received B.A. (1973) and M.A. (1974) degrees from San Jose State University. After working as a reporter, editor, and freelance writer for several years, Tan became a full-time writer. She was nominated for a National Book Critics Circle award (1989) for The Joy Luck Club.

Tan's best-selling novels focus on the efforts of Chinese American women to understand their identity and their relationship to Chinese culture. The Joy Luck Club (1989), her first success, weaves together the stories of four immigrant women and their four Americanized daughters. The novel also explores the bond between mothers and daughters, who often misunderstand each other because of generational and cultural differences.

Tan's relationship with her mother also is the subject of "Mother Tongue," which first appeared in The Threepenny Review (1990). Tan believes that she did not do well in school in English because she had learned substandard, "broken" English at home. Partly out of rebellion, Tan became a writer to show others that she had mastery of the language.

PREPARING TO READ

1. Why do you agree (or disagree) that achievement tests are "culturally biased" against students who come from families in which standard English is not spoken?
2. Why do you suppose that many immigrants from Asian countries might find speaking English to be more difficult than did the older immigrants from Europe?
3. What are some of the generational or cultural differences that cause conflict between mothers and daughters today?

MOTHER TONGUE

I am not a scholar of English or literature. I cannot give you much more than personal opinions on the English language and its variations in this country or others.

I am a writer. And by that definition, I am someone who has always loved language. I am fascinated by language in daily life. I spend a great deal of my time thinking about the power of language—the way it can evoke an emotion, a visual image, a complex idea, or a simple truth. Language is the tool of my trade. And I use them all—all the Englishes I grew up with.

Recently, I was made keenly aware of the different Englishes I do use. I was giving a talk to a large group of people, the same talk I had already given to half a dozen other groups. The nature of the talk was about my writing, my life, and my book, *The Joy Luck Club*. The talk was going along well enough, until I remembered one major difference that made the whole talk sound wrong. My mother was in the room. And it was perhaps the first time she had heard me give a lengthy speech, using the kind of English I have never used with her. I was saying things like, "The intersection of memory upon imagination" and "There is an aspect of my fiction that relates to thus-and thus"—a speech filled with carefully wrought grammatical phrases, burdened, it suddenly seemed to me, with nominalized forms, past perfect tenses, conditional phrases, all the forms of standard English that I had learned in school and through books, the forms of English I did not use at home with my mother.

Just last week, I was walking down the street with my mother, and I again found myself conscious of the English I was using, the English I do use with her. We were talking about the price of new and used furniture and I heard myself saying this: "Not waste money that way." My husband was with us as well, and he didn't notice any switch in my English. And then I realized why. It's because over the twenty years we've been together I've often used that same kind of English with him, and sometimes he even uses it with me. It has become our language of intimacy, a different sort of English that relates to family talk, the language I grew up with.

So you'll have some idea of what this family talk I heard sounds like, I'll quote what my mother said during a recent conversation which I videotaped and then transcribed. During this conversation, my mother was talking about a political gangster in Shanghai who had the same last name as her family's, Du, and how the gangster in his early years wanted to be adopted by her family, which was rich by comparison. Later, the gangster became more powerful, far richer than my mother's family, and one day showed up at my mother's wedding to pay his respects. Here's what she said in part:

"Du Yusong having business like fruit stand. Like off the street kind. He is Du like Du Zong—but not Tsung-ming Island people. The local people call putong, the river east side, he belong to that side local people. That man want to ask Du Zong father take him in like become own family. Du Zong father wasn't look down on him, but didn't take seriously, until that man big like become a mafia. Now important person, very hard to inviting him. Chinese way, came only to show respect, don't stay for dinner. Respect for making big celebration, he shows up. Mean gives lots of respect. Chinese custom. Chinese social life that way. If too important won't have to stay too long. He come to my wedding. I didn't see, I heard it. I gone to boy's side, they have YMCA dinner. Chinese age I was nineteen."

You should know that my mother's expressive command of English belies how much she actually understands. She reads the *Forbes* report, listens to *Wall Street Week*, converses daily with her stockbroker, reads all of Shirley MacLaine's books with ease—all kinds of things I can't begin to understand. Yet some of my friends tell me they understand 50 percent of what my mother says. Some say they understand 80 to 90 percent. Some say they understand none of it, as if she were speaking pure Chinese. But to me, my mother's English is perfectly clear, perfectly natural. It's my mother tongue. Her language, as I hear it, is vivid, direct, full of observation and imagery. That was the language that helped shape the way I saw things, expressed things, made sense of the world.

Lately, I've been giving more thought to the kind of English my mother speaks. Like others, I have described it to people as "broken" or "fractured" English. But I wince when I say that. It has always bothered me that I can think of no way to describe it other than "broken," as if it were damaged and needed to be fixed, as if it lacked a certain wholeness and soundness. I've heard other terms used, "limited English," for example. But they seem just as bad, as if everything is limited, including people's perceptions of the limited English speaker.

I know this for a fact, because when I was growing up, my mother's "limited" English limited *my* perception of her. I was ashamed of her English. I believed that her English reflected the quality of what she had to say. That is, because she expressed them imperfectly her thoughts were imperfect. And I had plenty of empirical evidence to support me: the fact that people in department stores, at banks, and at restaurants did not take her seriously, did not give her good service, pretended not to understand her, or even acted as if they did not hear her.

My mother has long realized the limitations of her English as well. When I was fifteen, she used to have me call people on the phone to pretend I was she. In this guise, I was forced to ask for information or even to complain and yell at people who had been rude to her. One time it was a call to her stockbroker in New York. She had cashed out her small portfolio and it just so happened we were going to go to New York the next week, our very first trip outside California. I had to get on the phone and say in an adolescent voice that was not very convincing, "This is Mrs. Tan."

And my mother was standing in the back whispering loudly, "Why he don't send me check, already two weeks late. So mad he lie to me, losing me money."

And then I said in perfect English, "Yes, I'm getting rather concerned. You had agreed to send the check two weeks ago, but it hasn't arrived."

Then she began to talk more loudly. "What he want, I come to New York tell him front of his boss, you cheating me?" And I was trying to calm her down, make her be quiet, while telling the stockbroker, "I can't tolerate any more excuses. If I don't receive the check immediately, I am going to have to speak to your manager when I'm in New York next week." And sure enough, the following week there we were in front of this astonished stockbroker, and I was sitting there redfaced and quiet, and my mother, the real Mrs. Tan, was shouting at his boss in her impeccable broken English.

We used a similar routine just five days ago, for a situation that was far less humorous. My mother had gone to the hospital for an appointment, to find out about a benign brain tumor a CAT scan had revealed a month ago. She said she had spoken very good English, her best English, no mistakes. Still, she said, the hospital did not apologize when they said they had lost the CAT scan and she had come for nothing. She said they did not seem to have any sympathy when she told them she was anxious to know the exact diagnosis, since her husband and son had both died of brain tumors. She said they would not give her any more information until the next time and she would have to make another appointment for that. So she said she would not leave until the doctor called her daughter. She wouldn't budge. And when the doctor finally called her daughter, me, who spoke in perfect English—lo and behold—we had assurances the CAT scan would be found, promises that a conference call on Monday would be held, and apologies for any suffering my mother had gone through for a most regrettable mistake.

I think my mother's English almost had an effect on limiting my possibilities in life as well. Sociologists and linguists probably will tell you that a person's developing language skills are more influenced by peers. But I do think that the language spoken in the family, especially in the immigrant families which are more insular, plays a large role in shaping the language of the child. And I believe that it affected my re-sults on achievement tests, IQ tests, and the SAT. While my English skills were never judged as poor, compared to math, English could not be considered my strong suit. In grade school I did moderately well, getting perhaps B's, sometimes B-pluses, in English and scoring per-haps in the sixtieth or seventieth percentile on achievement tests. But those scores were not good enough to override the opinion that my true abilities lay in math and science, because in those areas I achieved A's and scored in the ninetieth percentile or higher.

This was understandable. Math is precise; there is only one cor-rect answer. Whereas, for me at least, the answers on English tests were always a judgment call, a matter of opinion and personal experi-ence. Those tests were constructed around items like fill-in-the-blank sentence completion, such as, "Even though Tom was _____, Mary thought he was _____." And the correct answer always seemed to be the most bland combinations of thoughts, for example, "Even though Tom was shy, Mary thought he was charming," with the grammatical structure "even though" limiting the correct answer to some sort of se-mantic opposites, so you wouldn't get answers like, "Even though Tom was foolish, Mary thought he was ridiculous." Well, according to my mother, there were very few limitations as to what Tom could have been and what Mary might have thought of him. So I never did well on tests like that.

The same was true with word analogies, pairs of words in which you were supposed to find some sort of logical, semantic rela-tionship—for example, "*Sunset* is to *nightfall* as _____ is to _____." And here you would be presented with a list of four possible pairs, one of which showed the same kind of relationship: *red* is to *stoplight, bus* is to *arrival, chills* is to *fever, yawn* is to *boring*. Well, I could never think that way. I knew what the tests were asking, but I could not block out of my mind the images already created by the first pair, "*sunset* is to *nightfall*"—and I would see a burst of color against a darkening sky, the moon rising, the lowering of a curtain of stars. And all the other pairs of words—red, bus, stoplight, boring—just threw up a mass of confusing images, making it impossible for me to sort out something as logical as saying: "A sunset precedes nightfall" is the same as "a chill precedes a fever." The only way I would have gotten that answer right would have been to imagine an associative situation, for example, by being disobedient and staying out past sunset, catching a chill at night which turns into feverish pneumonia as punishment, which indeed did happen to me.

I have been thinking about all this lately, about my mother's English, about achievement tests. Because lately I've been asked, as a writer, why there are not more Asian Americans represented in American literature. Why are there few Asian Americans enrolled in creative writing programs? Why do so many Chinese students go into engineering? Well, these are broad sociological questions I can't begin to answer. But I have noticed in surveys—in fact, just last week—that Asian students, as a whole, always do significantly better on math achievement tests than in English. And this makes me think that there are other Asian-American students whose English spoken in the home might also be described as "broken" or "limited." And perhaps they also have teachers who are steering them away from writing and into math and science, which is what happened to me.

Fortunately, I happen to be rebellious in nature and enjoy the challenge of disproving assumptions made about me. I became an English major my first year in college, after being enrolled as pre-med. I started writing nonfiction as a freelancer the week after I was told by my former boss that writing was my worst skill and I should hone my talents toward account management.

But it wasn't until 1985 that I finally began to write fiction. And at first I wrote using what I thought to be wittily crafted sentences, sentences that would finally prove I had mastery over the English language. Here's an example from the first draft of a story that later made its way into The Joy Luck Club, but without this line: "That was my mental quandary in its nascent state." A terrible line, which I can hardly pronounce.

Fortunately, for reasons I won't get into today, I later decided I should envision a reader for the stories I would write. And the reader I decided upon was my mother, because these were stories about mothers. So with this reader in mind—and in fact she did read my early drafts—I began to write stories using all the Englishes I grew up with: the English I spoke to my mother, which for lack of a better term might be described as "simple"; the English she used with me, which for lack of a better term might be described as "broken"; my translation of her Chinese, which could certainly be described as "watered down"; and what I imagine to be her translation of her Chinese if she could speak in perfect English, her internal language, and for that I sought to preserve the essence, but neither an English nor a Chinese structure. I wanted to capture what language ability tests can never reveal: her intent, her passion, her imagery, the rhythms of her speech and the nature of her thoughts.

Apart from what any critic had to say about my writing, I knew I had succeeded where it counted when my mother finished reading my book and gave me her verdict: "So easy to read."

WRITING ABOUT THE READING

4. What do you think Tan means when she refers to "all the Englishes" she grew up with?
5. What are some of the possible meanings suggested by the title "Mother Tongue"?
6. Why does Tan's mother have difficulty communicating over the telephone?
7. Why does Tan think math tests were easier for her than were English tests?
8. Why does Tan believe many Asian American students major in math and science rather than English and humanities?
9. How and why did Tan's choice of an intended reader influence her writing?
10. Why was it important to Tan that her mother like her book?

WRITING FROM YOUR OWN EXPERIENCE

Note: In these assignments, write about your own experience or use that of someone you know, read about, or saw in a film/TV show.

11. Tan believes that the limited English spoken at home made taking achievement tests difficult for her. Recall a time when you were anxious about taking a difficult test. Why were you anxious and how did this anxiety affect your achievement on this test?
12. Tan decides to become a writer to show those people who said she could not write. Have you ever decided to be defiant and do something because someone told you were not able to do it or that it was forbidden? Why did you rebel and what were the consequences of your defiance?
13. The level of English used with friends or at home is often more informal than the language spoken in public. What are some examples of situations in which you would use more formal language and why would you speak more formally?

14. Humor often comes from some sort of discrepancy, such as the difference between the mother's spoken English and Tan's formal "translation" of her mother's words. Choose a comedian, sitcom, or movie that you find to be humorous. Explain how and why you find this humor to be appealing.

15. Sometimes people do not agree about the humor in a situation. Although the mother does not intend to be humorous, her "broken" English appears funny to the reader. Provide an example of a time when you "tried to be funny" and another person failed to find the humor in the joke or situation. How and why did each person react in this situation?

WRITING ABOUT RESEARCH

16. Describe one or more of the holidays and traditions (such as New Year's Celebrations, Feng Shui, acupuncture, and I Ching) that Asian Americans have introduced to the United States.

17. Tan's mother came to the United States because of wars and political changes in China. Choose an important twentieth century Chinese leader and explain this person's role in the development of modern China. Consider:

    (a) Chiang Kai Shek (Jiang Jieshi)
    (b) Chiang Ch'ing (wife of Mao Zedong)
    (c) Deng Ziaoping
    (d) Mao Zedong (Mao Tse-tung) (1893–1976)
    (e) Sun Yat Sen (1866–1925)
    (f) Zhou Enlai

Beyond Our Shadows:
From Nothing a Consciousness

HELEN ZIA

Helen Zia *(1952–), activist, journalist, and editor, is a second-generation Chinese American, who was born in Newark, New Jersey. She received a B.A. (1973) from Princeton, attended the Tufts University School of Medicine (1975), and then took graduate studies in industrial relations at Wayne State University. She has worked as a journalist for a variety of newspapers and periodicals, including* Ms *magazine. Zia was one of the cofounders of American Citizens for Justice (ACJ), an organization founded after the 1982 "hate crime" murder of Vincent Chin, a Chinese American. She has served as the president of the New York Chapter of Asian American Journalists Association (AAJA), which fights against media stereotyping of Asian Americans.*

Zia has been a leading voice protesting discrimination against the Asian American community. In this excerpt from Asian American Dreams: The Emergence of an American People *(2000), Zia writes of the discrimination that she and other members of her family met because they were Chinese Americans.*

PREPARING TO READ

1. Why could asking an Asian American "Where do you come from?" be interpreted as discriminatory?
2. Why do many first-generation immigrants often start their own small businesses, like a grocery store?
3. During World War II and the Korean conflict, many Americans treated Asian Americans with suspicion and hostility. Consider the present representation of similarly unpopular groups in the media. Explain whether you think that there are some similarities in the two situations.

BEYOND OUR SHADOWS:
FROM NOTHING A CONSCIOUSNESS

"Little China doll, what's your name?"

This question always made me feel awkward. I knew there was something unwholesome in being seen as a doll, and a fragile china one at that. But, taught to respect my elders at all times, I would answer dutifully, mumbling my name.

"Zia," they would cluck and nod. "It means 'aunt' in Italian, you know?"

To me, growing up in New Jersey, along the New York–Philadelphia axis, it seemed almost everyone was a little Italian, or at least had an Italian aunt.

One day in the early 1980s, the routine changed unexpectedly. I was introduced to a colleague, a newspaper editor. Making small talk, he said, "Your name is very interesting . . ." I noted his Euro-Anglo heritage and braced myself for yet another Italian lesson.

"Zia, hmm," he said. "Are you Pakistani?"

I nearly choked. For many people, Pakistan is not familiar geography. In those days it was inconceivable that a stranger might connect this South Asian, Pakistani name with my East Asian, Chinese face.

Through the unscientific process of converting Asian names into an alphabetic form, my romanized Chinese last name became identical to a common romanized Pakistani name. In fact, it was homonymous with a much despised ruler of Pakistan. Newspaper headlines about him read: "President Zia Hated by Masses" and "Pakistanis Cry, Zia Must Go." I'd clip out the headlines and send them to my siblings in jest. When President Zia's plane mysteriously crashed, I grew wary. After years of being mistaken for Japanese and nearly every other East Asian ethnicity, I added Pakistani to my list.

I soon discovered this would be the first of many such incidents. Zia Maria began to give way to Mohammad Zia ul-Haq. A new awareness of Asian Americans was emerging.

• • •

The abrupt change in my name ritual signaled my personal awakening to a modern-day American revolution in progress. In 1965, an immigration policy that had given racial preferences to Europeans for nearly two hundred years officially came to an end. Millions of new immigrants to America were no longer the standard vanilla but

Hispanic, African, Caribbean, and—most dramatically for me—Asian. Though I was intellectually aware of the explosive growth in my community, I hadn't yet adjusted my own sense of self, or the way I imagined other Americans viewed me.

Up until then, I was someone living in the shadows of American society, struggling to find some way into a portrait that was firmly etched in white and, occasionally, black. And there were plenty of reminders that I wasn't relevant. Like the voices of my 1960s high school friends Rose and Julie. Rose was black, and Julie was white. One day we stood in the school yard, talking about the civil rights movement swirling around us, about cities engulfed in flames and the dreams for justice and equality that burned in each of us.

As I offered my thoughts, Rose abruptly turned to me and said, "Helen, you've got to decide if you're black or white." Stunned, I was unable to say that I was neither, that I had an identity of my own. I didn't know the words "Asian American." It was a concept yet to be articulated.

Somewhere between my school yard conversation and the confrontation with my Pakistani namesake, Asian Americans began to break through the shadows. By then we had already named ourselves "Asian American" and we were having raging debates and fantastic visions of an America *we* fit into. But few outside of Asian America cared about our shadow dreams.

Gradually we began to be visible, although not necessarily seen the way we wished. Then we had to discover what it meant to be in the light.

When I was growing up in the 1950s and 1960s, there were barely a half-million Asian Americans in the nation. Of those, only 150,000 were Chinese Americans—not enough to populate a small midwestern city. We made up less than 0.1 percent of the population. Most of us lived on the islands of Hawaii or in a few scattered Chinatown ghettoes.

My parents met in New York City's Chinatown in 1950. They were among the new wave of Northern Chinese who fled China as a result of the Japanese occupation, the devastation of World War II, and the rise of the Chinese Communist Party. My father, Yee Chen Zia, was a poet and scholar from the canaled, garden city of Suzhou, known as the Venice of China. Like many Chinese of his generation, he had been a patriotic warrior against Japan, later becoming a newspaper editor and a member of the Chinese diplomatic corps in the United States. After the war, he decided to settle in New York, taking on various odd jobs—cabdriver, Fuller Brush salesperson, Good Humor ice cream truck driver.

My mother, Beilin Woo, was raised not far from Suzhou, in the metropolis of Shanghai. She fled its postwar chaos as a tubercular teenager aboard the *General Gordon*, the last American ship to leave Shanghai before the Communist government took power. Her first task upon arrival at the port of San Francisco was to find a husband who could not only ensure her continued stay in the United States but also help her repay her sister for the cost of the passage to America.

Finding marriageable suitors was not a problem for women from Asia. For more than half a century before World War II, several racially discriminatory laws prohibited Asian men from becoming U.S. citizens or marrying outside their race. The United States also barred women from China, India, and the Philippines from immigrating. The combined impact of these prohibitions created generations of lonely Asian bachelor societies in America. But World War II forced the United States to change such policies, so obviously offensive to its allies in Asia as well as to the thousands of Asian and Asian American GIs fighting for America. The shameful citizenship laws were eventually repealed and women like my mother gained entry into the country.

Among the many Chinese American men who courted my mother at her boardinghouse near San Francisco's Chinatown was a bank clerk who had come all the way from New York City in search of a wife. His jovial disposition and stable job appealed to her, even though he said he was forty years old. They were married in Reno, Nevada, on October 31, 1949. My twenty-year-old mother was on her way to New York as Mrs. John Yee.

Communicating with her new husband, however, was not easy. Like the vast majority of Chinese in America at that time, he was from Canton Province, a thousand miles away from Shanghai. The language, customs, and even facial features of the regions' peoples were different. Their local Chinese dialects of Shanghainese and Cantonese were unintelligible to each other. Cantonese people were considered more easygoing, lighthearted in spirit and darker in complexion, while Northern Chinese were taller and thought to be arrogant and hot-tempered. To get around in Chinatown, my mother had to learn some Cantonese. In the meantime she and her husband communicated in a mixture of pidgin English and pidgin Cantonese.

They settled into a dank tenement on Henry Street, where many new arrivals made their first home in New York. It stands today, with the shared bathroom down the hall and the bathtub in the kitchen, still home to new generations of Chinese immigrants. A year later, my older brother was born. They named him Henry, after the street. Had he been a girl, they planned to name him Catherine, after the nearby cross street. During the day, Henry's father worked a few blocks away in Chatham Square, at the Bank of China, while my mother found new friends. New York's Chinatown had only 15,000 residents in 1950, compared to more than 100,000 in 1990; a tiny but growing number came from Shanghai and its neighboring cities of Hangzhou, Ningbo, Suzhou, and Nanjing. Bound by their similar dialects and regional cuisine, which were so unlike those of the larger Cantonese community surrounding them, the Shanghainese speakers congregated at the curio shop of a Mrs. Fung, on the corner of Doyers and Pell. That's where my mother met my father.

When Henry was still an infant, his father suffered a massive stroke and died. From his death certificate my mother learned that her husband was ten years older than he had disclosed. The young widow was eligible for marriage again in the Chinatown society, with my father in pursuit. Months later they wed and moved to Newark, New Jersey, where my father was trying, unsuccessfully, to run a small furniture store. I soon came on the scene, another member of the post–World War II Asian American baby boom.

On a clear day the Manhattan skyline is visible from Newark, but the insular familiarity of Chinatown was worlds away. Outside of Chinatown it was rare to encounter another person of Chinese or other Asian descent. In Newark and the various New Jersey communities where we later moved, the only way to meet Asians was to stop complete strangers on the street, while shopping, or at the bus stop—anywhere that we happened to see the occasional person who looked like us. At an A&P supermarket checkout counter, my mother met her friend Sue, who came to the United States as a war bride, having married a GI during the postwar occupation of Japan. The animosity between China and Japan that brought both women to New Jersey was never an issue. Each was so thrilled to find someone like herself.

Auntie Sue and her son Kim, who was of mixed race, white and Japanese, were regular visitors to our home. Though our mothers bonded readily, it was harder for their Asian American kids to connect simply because we looked alike. Mom and Auntie Sue had the shared experience of leaving their war-ravaged Asian homes for a new culture, but Kim and I shared little except for our Asian features; we stuck out like yellow streaks on a white-and-black canvas. Outside of Chinatown, looking Asian meant looking foreign, alien, un-American. The pressure on us was to fit in with the "American" kids we looked so unlike, to conform and assimilate. Why would we want to be around other Asian kids who reminded us of our poor fit? At the tender age of six, I already felt different from the "real" Americans. I didn't feel comfortable with Kim and sensed his ambivalence to me. But the joke was on us, because no matter how hard we might try to blend in with the scenery, our faces gave us away.

Still, I was proud to be Chinese. Mom and Dad filled us with stories about their childhoods in China. Dad was born in 1912, one year after the founding of the Chinese Republic, and was imbued with a deep love for his native country. He was the second son of a widow who was spurned by her in-laws. His mother sold her own clothes to pay for his schooling. She beat my father every day so that he would study harder—this he told us proudly whenever we slacked off. Dad modeled his life after the ideal of the Confucian scholar-official: by studying assiduously he won academic honors and scholarships and achieved recognition as a poet and writer. China's system of open examinations was the foundation of the civil service—a Chinese creation, Dad pointedly reminded us as he turned the TV off. Studying hard, he said, was a time-honored route to advancement for even the poorest Chinese.

Mom grew up in Shanghai under the Japanese occupation. From the time she was a small child she lived with a fear and dislike of Japanese soldiers. Because of the war, her education was disrupted and she never went beyond the fourth grade—a source of regret that made her value education for her children. Mom's childhood memories were of wartime hardships and days spent picking out grains of rice from the dirt that had been mixed in as a way to tip the scales. Her stories taught me to be proud of the strength and endurance of the Chinese people.

Dad told us about our heritage. When other children made fun of us, or if news reports demeaned China, he reminded us that our ancestors wore luxurious silks and invented gunpowder while Europeans still huddled naked in caves. Of course, I knew that Europeans had discovered clothing, too, but the image was a reassuring one for a kid who didn't fit. My father wanted us to speak flawless English to spare us from ridicule and the language discrimination he faced. He forbade my mother to speak to us in Chinese, which was hard, since Mom spoke little English then. We grew up monolingual, learning only simple Chinese expressions—*che ve le,* "Come and eat"—and various Shanghainese epithets, like the popular phrase for a naughty child—*fei si le,* or "devilish to death." Dad also expected us to excel in school, since, he said, our Asian cranial capacities were larger than those of any other race. Pulling out the *Encyclopaedia Britannica* to prove his point, he'd make us study the entry, then test us to make sure we got the message. He told us about the Bering Strait and the land bridge from Asia to America, saying that we had a right to be in this country because we were cousins to the Native Americans.

These tidbits were critical to my self-esteem. In New Jersey, it was so unusual to see a person of Asian descent that people would stop what they were doing to gawk rudely at my family wherever we went. When we walked into a store or a diner, we were like the freak show at Barnum & Bailey's circus, where Chinese were displayed as exotic creatures in the late 1800s, along with the two-headed dog. A sense of our own heritage and worth gave us the courage and cockiness to challenge their rudeness and stare down the gawkers.

What Mom and Dad couldn't tell us was what it meant to be Chinese in America. They didn't know—they were just learning about America themselves. We found little help in the world around us. Asians were referred to most often as Orientals, Mongols, Asiatics, heathens, the yellow hordes, and an assortment of even less endearing terms. Whatever the terminology, the message was clear: we were definitely not Americans.

There is a drill that nearly all Asians in America have experienced more times than they can count. Total strangers will interrupt with the absurdly existential question "What are you?" Or the equally common inquiry "Where are you from?" The queries are generally well intentioned, made in the same detached manner that you might use to inquire about a pooch's breed.

My standard reply to "What are you?" is "American," and to "Where are you from?" "New Jersey." These, in my experience, cause great displeasure. Eyebrows arch as the questioner tries again. "No, where are you really from?" I patiently explain that, really, I am from New Jersey. Inevitably this will lead to something like "Well then, what country are your people from?" Sooner or later I relent and tell them that my "people" are from China. But when I turn the tables and ask, "And what country are your people from?" the reply is invariably an indignant "I'm from America, of course."

The sad truth was that I didn't know much about my own history. I knew that Chinese had built the railroads, and then were persecuted. That was about it. I didn't know that in the 1700s a group of Filipinos settled in Louisiana, or that in 1825 the first Chinese was born in New York City. I didn't know that Asian laborers were brought to the Americas as a replacement for African slaves—by slave traders whose ships had been rerouted from Africa to Asia. I didn't even know that Japanese Americans had been imprisoned only a decade before my birth. Had I known more about my Asian American history I might have felt less foreign. Instead, I grew up thinking that perhaps China, a place I had never seen, was my true home, since so many people didn't think I belonged here.

I did figure out, however, that relations between America and any Asian nation had a direct impact on me. Whenever a movie about

Japan and World War II played at the local theater, my brothers and I became the enemy. It didn't matter that we weren't Japanese—we looked Japanese. What's worse, by now my family had moved to a new housing development, one of the mass-produced Levittowns close to Fort Dix, the huge army base. Most of our neighbors had some connection to the military.

At the Saturday matinee, my brothers and I would sit with all the other kids in town watching the sinister Zero pilots prepare to ambush their unsuspecting prey, only to be thwarted by the all-American heroes—who were, of course, always white. These movies would have their defining moment, that crescendo of emotion when the entire theater would rise up, screaming, "Kill them, kill them, kill them!"—them being the Japanese. When the movie was over and the lights came on, I wanted to be invisible so that my neighbors wouldn't direct their patriotic fervor toward me.

As China became the evil Communist menace behind the Bamboo Curtain, and the United States was forced to deal with its stalemate in the Korean War, the Asian countries seemed interchangeable. Back when Japan was the enemy, China was the good ally—after all, that's how my mom and dad got to come to America. But now, quixotically, Japan was good and China was evil.

Chinese in America were suspected to be the fifth column of Chinese Communists, as J. Edgar Hoover frequently said before Congress and throughout the McCarthy era witch-hunts. In the 1950s, while Japanese American families attempted to return to normalcy after their release from American concentration camps during the war, the FBI switched its surveillance eye onto hundreds of Chinese Americans. My father was one.

Our mail routinely arrived opened and damaged, and our phone reception was erratic. I thought everyone's mail service and phone lines were bad. Polite FBI agents interviewed our neighbors, asking if my father was up to anything suspicious. What attracted the attention of the FBI was Dad's tendency to write letters to newspapers and politicians when he disagreed with their views on China or anything else. Nothing ever came of the FBI investigations of my father, nor was a ring of Chinese American spies ever found—but I later learned that the probes succeeded in intimidating the Chinese American communities of the 1950s, creating a distrust of and inhibiting their participation in politics.

The FBI queries hardly bolstered our acceptance in our working-class housing tract. Neighbor kids would nose around and ask, "So what *does* your father do?" It didn't help that my father had instructed us to say, "He's self-employed." This only added to our sense of foreignness.

Like so many Asian immigrants unable to break into the mainstream American labor market, my father had to rely on his own resourcefulness and his family's labor. In the back room of our house we made "baby novelties" with little trinkets and baby toys and pink or blue vases that my father then sold to flower shops. Every day, in addition to doing our schoolwork, we helped out in the family business.

Our home was our workplace, the means to our livelihood, and therefore the center of everything. This conveniently matched the Confucian notion of family, whereby the father, as patriarch, is the master of the universe. In our household it was understood that no one should ever disobey, contradict, or argue with the patriarch, who, in the Confucian hierarchy, is a stand-in for God. My mother, and of course the children, were expected to obey God absolutely.

This system occasionally broke down when my mother and father quarreled, usually about my father's rigid expectations of us. But in the end, God always seemed to win. Growing up female, I could see the Confucian order of the Three Obediences in action: the daughter obeys the father, the wife obeys the husband, and, eventually, the widow obeys the son. The Confucian tradition was obviously stacked against me, as a girl.

I found similar lessons in the world beyond our walls. Mom's best friend from the Chinatown Shanghainese clique had followed us to New Jersey, attracted by the low home costs and the fact that we already lived there. Auntie Ching and her husband opened a Chinese restaurant at a major intersection of the highway. In those days, there were few places outside Chinatown to get real Chinese food. After they had spent their own money to upgrade the kitchen and remodel the restaurant, business was booming. But Auntie Ching had no lease for the restaurant—and the German American owner, sensing an opportunity for himself, evicted the Chings and set up his own shop.

Our tiny Chinese American community was horrified that the Chings would be treated so unjustly. My cantankerous dad urged them to fight it out in court. But they chose not to, believing that it would be better not to make waves. Chinese cannot win, they said, so why make trouble for ourselves? Such defeatism disturbed my father, who would often say in disgust, "In America, a 'Chinaman's chance' means no chance." He felt that the Chinese way of dealing with obstacles—to either accept or go around them, but not to confront them directly—would never get us very far in the United States.

As a child, I didn't see Chinese or other Asian Americans speaking up to challenge such indignities. When my parents were denied the right to rent or buy a home in various Philadelphia neighborhoods, they had to walk away despite my father's outrage. We could only internalize our shame when my mother and her troop of small children were thrown out of supermarkets because we were wrongly accused of opening packages and stealing. Or when Henry was singled out of a group of noisy third graders for talking and he alone was expelled from the lunchroom for the rest of the year. Or when my younger brother Hoyt and the few other Asian boys in school were rounded up because another kid said he thought he saw an "Oriental" boy go into his locker.

Other times the discomfort was less tangible. Why did my fifth-grade teacher, a Korean War veteran, become so agitated when topics of China and Asian culture came up? Was there a reason for his apparent dislike of me and my brothers, who also had him as a teacher? After my Girl Scout troop leader asked all the girls to state their religions, what caused her to scowl in disgust at me when I answered Buddhist? My family didn't practice an organized religion, so I didn't know what else to say.

Absorbing the uncertainty of my status in American society, I assumed the role that I observed for myself—one of silence and invisibility. I enjoyed school and, following my father's example, studied hard and performed well academically, but I consciously avoided bringing attention to myself and rarely spoke up, even on matters related to me.

WRITING ABOUT THE READING

4. Why does the editor ask Zia if she is Pakistani and what does it reveal about him?
5. What does the writer mean when she says that Chinese Americans "began to be visible although not necessarily seen the way we wished"?
6. Why do you think that Zia's mother married as soon as possible after arrival?
7. Why does Zia's mother have difficulty communicating with her first husband?
8. Why is it surprising that Zia's mother became friends with Auntie Sue?
9. Why does the writer's father stress the long history and cultural heritage of the Chinese?
10. What are some of the ways in which Zia and her family are made to feel "outsiders" in U.S. society?
11. Why did the family come under surveillance by the FBI?

WRITING FROM YOUR OWN EXPERIENCE

Note: In these assignments, write about your own experience or use that of someone you know, read about, or saw in a film/TV show.

12. Zia's father runs his own small business out of his home. Suppose you had to choose between owning your own small business or working in a large corporation. Which would you choose and why would you make this choice?

13. Although they are treated unjustly by the owner of the property, Auntie Ching and her husband refuse to fight back. Have you ever been treated unjustly? Why were you treated this way and what action did you take?

14. Zia writes that the relations between the United States and any Asian nation had a direct impact on the way she was regarded. Suppose the United States were to get into a conflict with China, or another Asian nation. Explain why you think (or disagree) that Asian Americans would again face suspicion and hostility.

WRITING ABOUT RESEARCH

15. Zia tells how her life was affected by the changes in immigration policy after 1965. Choose one of the newer immigrant groups that have come to the United States in large numbers since 1965. What were some of the reasons that motivated these people to come to the United States? Consider immigrants from Haiti, Pakistan, India, Malaysia, the Middle East, Russia, the Balkans, and the West Indies.

16. How and why did the Communist takeover of China in 1949 affect Chinese immigration to the United States?

17. How and why did the Chinese Cultural Revolution (1966–1976) affect immigration?

18. Why were the shops of Korean Americans destroyed in the Los Angeles riots of 1992?

False Gold

FAE MYENNE NG

Fae Myenne Ng *(1957–), writer, was born in the United States. She attended the University of California, Berkeley, and earned an M.F.A. from Columbia University. She also has received a National Endowment for the Arts Grant. For several years, Ng has been a contributor to periodicals.*

The central event of Ng's first novel, Bone *(1993), is the suicide of one of the three daughters of a Chinese American immigrant family. The novel reveals the hardship faced by immigrants and the guilt that they feel about abandoning their homeland and their traditions. The novel also dramatizes the cultural confusion of their American-born children about their position in relation to the two cultures. These issues also can be seen in "False Gold," which was originally published in* The New Republic *magazine (1993). In this reading, Ng writes of her father's immigration to the United States and her visit to his home in China. Note: The surname is pronounced "Ing."*

PREPARING TO READ

1. Today, many middle-class Americans adopt unwanted children (usually girls) from Asian countries, such as China or Korea. What do you think are some of the arguments for and against such adoptions?

2. Often college graduates are offered well-paying jobs that would take them far away from their home. Explain whether you would leave your family and move far away (to a distant city, state, or country) for such a good job.

3. Suppose you could "meet" either an ancestor of yours or a famous person from the past. Which person would you choose to "meet" and why would you choose this person?

FALSE GOLD

It's that same old, same old story. We all have an immigrant ancestor, one who believed in America; one who, daring or duped, took sail. The Golden Venture emigrants have begun the American journey, suffering and sacrificing, searching for the richer, easier life. I know them; I could be one of their daughters. Like them, my father took the sacrificial role of being the first to venture. Now, at the end of his life, he calls it a bitter, no-luck life. I have always lived with his question, Was it worth it? As a child, I saw the bill-by-bill payback and I felt my own unpayable emotional debt. Obedience and Obligation: the Confucian curse.

For $4,000 my father became the fourth son of a legal Chinese immigrant living in San Francisco. His paper-father sent him a coaching book, detailing complicated family history. It was 1940; my father paid ninety more dollars for passage on the *s.s. Coolidge*. He had little hand luggage, a change of clothes, herbs and seeds and a powder for soup. To soothe his pounding heart during the fifteen-day voyage he recited the coaching book over and over again. It was not a floating hell. "The food was Chinese. We traveled third-class. A bunk was good enough space." He was prepared for worse. He'd heard about the Peruvian ships that transported Chinese coolies for plantation labor in the 1850s. (Every generation has a model.) One hundred and twenty days. Two feet by six for each man. Were these the first ships to be called floating hells?

Gold Mountain was the name of my father's America. In February, when the Golden Venture immigrants sailed from Bangkok, they were shouting, Mei Guo! Mei Guo! "Beautiful Country" was the translation they preferred. America is the land of light and hope. But landing here is only the beginning of a long tale. When I saw the photos of the shipwrecked Chinese on the beach, I was reminded of the men kept on Angel Island, the detention center in the middle of San Francisco Bay. A sea of hats on the deck of the ship. Triple-decked bunkers. Men in loose pants playing volleyball. "Was volleyball fun?" I wanted to know. My father shrugged, "Nothing else to do. It helped pass the day." Our fathers spent months detained on Angel Island. Their name for it was Wooden House. What, I wonder, are the Chinese calling the detention center in Bethlehem, Pennsylvania?

After his release from Angel Island, my father lived at a bachelor hotel on Waverly Place with a dozen other bachelors in one room, communal toilets, no kitchen. He had breakfast at Uncle's Cafe, dinners at the Jackson Cafe, midnight noodles at Sam Wo's. Drinks at the Li Po Bar or Red's Place, where fat burlesque queens sat on his lap. Marriage for duty. Sons for tradition. My father left the hotel but kept the habits. He still eats like a mouse, in the middle of the night, cooking on a hot plate in his room. (I do my version of the same.) He keeps his money under the floorboard. When I have it, I like to have a grip, bill by bill. Like everyone, too little money upsets me; but more money than I can hold upsets me too. I feel obliged to give it away. Is it a wonder that money has a dirty feel? Get it and get it fast. Then get rid of it.

I remember this Angel Island photograph. Thirty bare-chested Chinese men are waiting for a medical examination. The doctor, a hunching man with a scraping stare, sits at a small desk, elbows and thick hands over a black book. At his side, a guard in knee-high boots measures a boy's forehead. Arranged by height, baby-eyed boys stand stoop-shouldered on the outer edge. The men, at least a head taller, stand toward the center of the room, staring at the examiner. Those eyes scare me. Bold and angry and revengeful. Eyes that owe. Eyes that will make you pay. Humiliation with a vengeance.

As boldly, the Golden Venture men have looked into American cameras. (If they believed a foot on soil would make them legal, a photo in an American newspaper would be as good as a passport.) There was a "See me!" bounce in their faces. They'd arrived, and now they wanted to send their news back home. And back home, a grateful father jumped when he picked out his son as one of the survivors, "He's alive! My son made it."

Another photo. A Golden Venture man looks out from a locked door, his face framed by a tight window. He has a jail-view of the Beautiful Country. How would he describe his new world? I imagine he'd use his own body as a measure. "Window, two head high. Sun on both ears." Can we forget the other "face" photograph taken earlier this century? The sold and smuggled prostitute, demoted from brothel to a crib, a wooden shack with barred windows that barely fits a cot. Looking out from her fenced window, she has the same downcast eyes, the same bitter-strange lips that seem to be smiling as well as trembling. The caption quotes her price: "Lookie two bits, feelee floor bits, doee six bits."

Life was and still is weighed in gold. People buy people. Sons and wives and slaves. There was the imperial edict that forbade Chinese to leave China; there was China's contribution to France during World War I, in which tens of thousands of Chinese lived horrible lives as indentured slaves. I've heard parents threaten to sell children who misbehave. (Mine threatened to throw me into the garbage can where they claimed they found me.) There's the story of

Old Man Jeong, the one on Beckett Alley. Lonely after his wife died, fearful no one would care for him in his senile retirement, he went back to his home village and bought himself a wife. A woman born in 1956.

Listen to the animal names. Snakes sneak into America. The Golden Venture was a snake ship. The emigrants are snake cargo; the middleman, a snakehead. In my father's time, a pig was sold to America. A pig gets caught, a pig gets cheated. My father feels cheated, sold, on an easy story.

• • •

On a recent visit to my father' s house in Guangzhou, I found his original coaching book. I knew it had been untouched since he last held it. In my hand, the loosely bound papers felt like ashes. I thought about how when he committed everything to memory, he became another man's son. There's an elaborate map of the family compound; each page is lined with questions and answers, some marked with red circles. Tedious questions and absurd details. How much money did Second Brother send to Mother? How much farmland did Mother have and what vegetables were harvested? Third Brother's wife's feet, were they big or bound? The book has a musty smell that reaches into my throat.

One out of every four relations let me know they wanted to come to America. At the end of my visit, a distant relation and her 13-year-old daughter followed me into the rice paddies. "I'm selling her," the mother told me.

"What did you say? Say again?" I replied.

She held a palm over her (golden) lower teeth, and said it again, "Don't you know what I'm saying? Sell. We sell her."

I stared at her. She laughed some more and then just walked away, back toward the village. The girl followed me, quiet till we got to the river, where she posed for some pictures and then asked for my address. I wrote it on the back of a business card. (I considered giving her my post office box.) I hope never to be surprised. I hope never to see this child at my door holding the card like a legal document.

"Don't add and don't take away" was the advice of an uncle who heard that I wrote things. Stay safe. Keep us safe. How right that "China" is written with the character "middle." Obedience is a safe position. The Golden Venture men trusted the stories they heard. Their clansmen entrusted their dreams to them. The question is not how bad it is in China. The question is how good it can be in America. My father believes the Golden Venturers have only passed through the first hell. In coming to America, he laments (there is no other word) that he trusted too much. Ironic that in Chinese he bought a name that reads, To Have Trust.

WRITING ABOUT THE READING

4. Why does the father have to pretend to be the son of another family in order to immigrate?

5. Why does the writer use the term "sacrificial role" to describe the father's immigration to the United States?

6. What emotions do the photographs of the people on Angel Island evoke for the writer and why does she feel this way?

7. Based on what you learn in this reading, what can you infer about the father's life once he arrived in the United States?

8. What do you think the writer means when she says that "Life was and still is weighed in gold"?

9. What is the writer's reaction when her relative wants to sell her daughter and why do you think the writer feels this way?

10. What connotations do the words "gold" and "golden" come to have in this reading?

11. What words would you use to describe the tone of this essay and why would you describe the reading this way?

WRITING FROM YOUR OWN EXPERIENCE

Note: In these assignments, write about your own experience or use that of someone you know, read about, or saw in a film/TV show.

12. Ng mentions the traditional Confucian virtue of obligation to one's parents. In Chinese culture, even adult children are expected to obey their parents; disobedience is expected to result in shame. Have you ever had a sense of shame or guilt because you disobeyed someone or failed to live up to the person's expectations? Why did you feel this way and what were the consequences resulting from your emotions?

13. From the reading, it appears that the father was sadly disappointed by his experience in the United States. Have you ever eagerly anticipated a trip or other event, only to be disappointed? Why were you disappointed and what were the results of this experience?

14. Ng calls her father's move to America a sacrifice. Can you think of someone who sacrificed him-/herself for family, friend, or country? Explain why you think this person was motivated to do this and the consequences of this action.

WRITING ABOUT RESEARCH

15. What are some of the highlights of the history of the Chinese in the United States following the Gold Rush of 1849?
16. What were some of the traditional beliefs of Confucianism that Chinese immigrants brought with them?
17. As Ellis Island was the entry site for Europeans, so Asian Americans entered through Angel Island. Describe the experience of Asian Americans at Angel Island or the history of this entry port.

Coming Home Again

CHANG-RAE LEE

Chang-rae Lee *(1965–), writer, was born in Korea and moved to the United States at the age of three with his family. After completing a B.A. (1987) at Yale, Lee received an M.F.A. (1993) from the University of Oregon. He has taught creative writing at the University of Oregon and Hunter College, New York. Currently, Lee teaches at the University of Oregon, Eugene. Lee's 1995 novel* Native Speaker *earned several awards, including the American Book Award from the Before Columbus Foundation and the American Library Association Notable Book of the Year Award.*

Native Speaker *concerns the search for identity of Korean Americans who, despite their financial success, feel alienated from both the American and Korean cultures. In this reading, Lee examines how his going away to an elite boarding school affected his mother. "Coming Home Again" was originally published in* The New Yorker *(1995).*

PREPARING TO READ

1. Explain whether you think that it is advantageous to board at college rather than living at home.

2. What are some Asian American foods that have been adopted in the United States and what is the effect of "mainstreaming" these foods?

3. In recent years, Americans have turned away from traditional cooked meals to microwave dinners, fast foods, and ready-cut salads and vegetables. What do you think these foods show about American values?

COMING HOME AGAIN

When my mother began using the electronic pump that fed her liquids and medication, we moved her to the family room. The bedroom she shared with my father was upstairs, and it was impossible to carry the machine up and down all day and night. The pump itself was attached to a metal stand on casters, and she pulled it along wherever she went. From anywhere in the house, you could hear the sound of the wheels clicking out a steady time over the grout lines of the slate-tiled foyer, her main thoroughfare to the bathroom and the kitchen. Sometimes you would hear her halt after only a few steps, to catch her breath or steady her balance, and whatever you were doing was instantly suspended by a pall of silence.

I was usually in the kitchen, preparing lunch or dinner, poised over the butcher block with her favorite chef's knife in my hand and her old yellow apron slung around my neck. I'd be breathless in the sudden quiet, and, having ceased my mincing and chopping, would stare blankly at the brushed sheen of the blade. Eventually, she would clear her throat or call out to say she was fine, then begin to move again, starting her rhythmic *ka-jug*; and only then could I go on with my cooking, the world of our house turning once more, wheeling through the black.

I wasn't cooking for my mother but for the rest of us. When she first moved downstairs she was still eating, though scantily, more just to taste what we were having than from any genuine desire for food. The point was simply to sit together at the kitchen table and array ourselves like a family again. My mother would gently set herself down in her customary chair near the stove. I sat across from her, my father and sister to my left and right, and crammed in the center was all the food I had made—a spicy codfish stew, say, or a casserole of gingery beef, dishes that in my youth she had prepared for us a hundred times.

It had been ten years since we'd all lived together in the house, which at fifteen I had left to attend boarding school in New Hampshire. My mother would sometimes point this out, by speaking of our present time as being "just like before Exeter," which surprised me, given how proud she always was that I was a graduate of the school.

My going to such a place was part of my mother's not so secret plan to change my character, which she worried was becoming too much like hers. I was clever and able enough, but without outside pressure I was readily given to sloth and vanity. The famous school—

which none of us knew the first thing about—would prove my mettle. She was right, of course, and while I was there I would falter more than a few times, academically and otherwise. But I never thought that my leaving home then would ever be a problem for her, a private quarrel she would have even as her life waned.

Now her house was full again. My sister had just resigned from her job in New York City, and my father, who typically saw his psychiatric patients until eight or nine in the evening, was appearing in the driveway at four-thirty. I had been living at home for nearly a year and was in the final push of work on what would prove a dismal failure of a novel. When I wasn't struggling over my prose, I kept occupied with the things she usually did—the daily errands, the grocery shopping, the vacuuming and the cleaning, and, of course, all the cooking.

When I was six or seven years old, I used to watch my mother as she prepared our favorite meals. It was one of my daily pleasures. She shooed me away in the beginning, telling me that the kitchen wasn't my place, and adding, in her half-proud, half-deprecating way, that her kind of work would only serve to weaken me. "Go out and play with your friends," she'd snap in Korean, "or better yet, do your reading and homework." She knew that I had already done both, and that as the evening approached there was no place to go save her small and tidy kitchen, from which the clatter of her mixing bowls and pans would ring through the house.

I would enter the kitchen quietly and stand beside her, my chin lodging upon the point of her hip. Peering through the crook of her arm, I beheld the movements of her hands. For *kalbi*, she would take up a butchered short rib in her narrow hand, the flinty bone shaped like a section of an airplane wing and deeply embedded in gristle and flesh, and with the point of her knife cut so that the bone fell away, though not completely, leaving it connected to the meat by the barest opaque layer of tendon. Then she methodically butterflied the flesh, cutting and unfolding, repeating the action until the meat lay out on her board, glistening and ready for seasoning. She scored it diagonally, then sifted sugar into the crevices with her pinched fingers, gently rubbing in the crystals. The sugar would tenderize as well as sweeten the meat. She did this with each rib, and then set them all aside in a large shallow bowl. She minced a half-dozen cloves of garlic, a stub of ginger-root, sliced up a few scallions, and spread it all over the meat. She wiped her hands and took out a bottle of sesame oil, and, after pausing for a moment, streamed the dark oil in two swift circles around the bowl. After adding a few splashes of soy sauce, she thrust her hands in and kneaded the flesh, careful not to dislodge the bones. I asked her why it mattered that they remain connected. "The meat needs the bone nearby," she said, "to borrow its richness." She wiped her hands clean of the marinade, except for her little finger, which she would flick with her tongue from time to time, because she knew that the flavor of a good dish developed not at once but in stages.

Whenever I cook, I find myself working just as she would, readying the ingredients—a mash of garlic, a julienne of red peppers, fantails of shrimp—and piling them in little mounds about the cutting surface. My mother never left me any recipes, but this is how I learned to make her food, each dish coming not from a list or a card but from the aromatic spread of a board.

I've always thought it was particularly cruel that the cancer was in her stomach, and that for a long time at the end she couldn't eat. The last meal I made for her was on New Year's Eve, 1990. My sister suggested that instead of a rib roast or a bird, or the usual overflow of Korean food, we make all sorts of finger dishes that our mother might fancy and pick at.

We set the meal out on the glass coffee table in the family room.

I prepared a tray of smoked-salmon canapés, fried some Korean bean cakes, and made a few other dishes I thought she might enjoy. My sister supervised me, arranging the platters, and then with some pomp carried each dish in to our parents. Finally, I brought out a bottle of champagne in a bucket of ice. My mother had moved to the sofa and was sitting up, surveying the low table. "It looks pretty nice," she said. "I think I'm feeling hungry."

This made us all feel good, especially me, for I couldn't remember the last time she had felt any hunger or had eaten something I cooked. We began to eat. My mother picked up a piece of salmon toast and took a tiny corner in her mouth. She rolled it around for a moment and then pushed it out with the tip of her tongue, letting it fall back onto her plate. She swallowed hard, as if to quell a gag, then glanced up to see if we had noticed. Of course we all had. She attempted a bean cake, some cheese, and then a slice of fruit, but nothing was any use.

She nodded at me anyway, and said, "Oh, it's very good." But I was already feeling lost and I put down my plate abruptly, nearly shattering it on the thick glass. There was an ugly pause before my father asked me in a weary, gentle voice if anything was wrong, and I answered that it was nothing, it was the last night of a long year, and we were together, and I was simply relieved. At midnight, I poured out glasses of champagne, even one for my mother, who took a deep sip. Her manner grew playful and light, and I helped her shuffle to her mattress, and she lay down in the place where in a brief week she was dead.

• • •

My mother could whip up most anything, but during our first years of living in this country we ate only Korean foods. At my harangue-like behest, my mother set herself to learning how to cook exotic American dishes. Luckily, a kind neighbor, Mrs. Churchill, a tall, florid young woman with flaxen hair, taught my mother her most trusted recipes. Mrs. Churchill's two young sons, palish, weepy boys with identical crew cuts, always accompanied her, and though I liked them well enough, I would slip away from them after a few minutes, for I knew that the real action would be in the kitchen, where their mother was playing guide. Mrs. Churchill hailed from the state of Maine, where the finest Swedish meatballs and tuna casserole and angel food cake in America are made. She readily demonstrated certain techniques—how to layer wet sheets of pasta for a lasagna or whisk up a simple roux, for example. She often brought gift shoeboxes containing curious ingredients like dried oregano, instant yeast, and cream of mushroom soup. The two women, though at ease and jolly with each other, had difficulty communicating, and this was made worse by the often confusing terminology of Western cuisine ("corned beef," "deviled eggs"). Although I was just learning the language myself, I'd gladly play the interlocutor, jumping back and forth between their places at the counter, dipping my fingers into whatever sauce lay about.

I was an insistent child, and, being my mother's firstborn, much too prized. My mother could say no to me, and did often enough, but anyone who knew us—particularly my father and sister—could tell how much the denying pained her. And if I was overconscious of her indulgence even then, and suffered the rushing pangs of guilt that she could inflict upon me with the slightest wounded turn of her lip, I was too happily obtuse and venal to let her cease. She reminded me daily that I was her sole son, her reason for living, and that if she were to lose me, in either body or spirit, she wished that God would mercifully smite her, strike her down like a weak branch.

In the traditional fashion, she was the house accountant, the maid, the launderer, the disciplinarian, the driver, the secretary, and, of course, the cook. She was also my first basketball coach. In South Korea, where girls' high school basketball is a popular spectator sport, she had been a star, the point guard for the national high school team that once won the all-Asia championships. I learned this one Saturday during the summer, when I asked my father if he would go down to the schoolyard and shoot some baskets with me. I had just finished the fifth grade, and wanted desperately to make the middle school team the coming fall. He called for my mother and sister to come along. When we arrived, my sister immediately ran off to the swings, and I recall being annoyed that my mother wasn't following her. I dribbled clumsily around the key, on the verge of losing control of the ball, and flung a flat shot that caromed wildly off the rim. The ball bounced to my father, who took a few not so graceful dribbles and made an easy layup. He dribbled out and then drove to the hoop for a layup on the other side. He rebounded his shot and passed the ball to my mother, who had been watching us from the foul line. She turned from the basket and began heading the other way.

"*Um-mah*," I cried at her, my exasperation already bubbling over, "the basket's over *here*!"

After a few steps she turned around, and from where the professional three-point line must be now, she effortlessly flipped the ball up in a two-handed set shot, its flight truer and higher than I'd witnessed from any boy or man. The ball arced cleanly into the hoop, stiffly popping the chain-link net. All afternoon, she rained in shot after shot, as my father and I scrambled after her.

When we got home from the playground, my mother showed me the photograph album of her team's championship run. For years I kept it in my room, on the same shelf that housed the scrapbooks I made of basketball stars, with magazine clippings of slick players like Bubbles Hawkins and Pistol Pete and George (the Iceman) Gervin.

It puzzled me how much she considered her own history to be immaterial, and if she never patently diminished herself, she was able to finesse a kind of self-removal by speaking of my father whenever she could. She zealously recounted his excellence as a student in medical school and reminded me, each night before I started my homework, of how hard he drove himself in his work to make a life for us. She said that because of his Asian face and imperfect English, he was "working two times the American doctors." I knew that she was building him up, buttressing him with both genuine admiration and her own brand of anxious braggadocio, and that her overarching concern was that I might fail to see him as she wished me to—in the most dawning light, his pose steadfast and solitary.

In the year before I left for Exeter, I became weary of her oft-repeated accounts of my father's success. I was a teenager, and so ever inclined to be dismissive and bitter toward anything that had to do with family and home. Often enough, my mother was the object of my derision. Suddenly, her life seemed so small to me. She was there, and sometimes, I thought, *always* there, as if she were confined to the four walls of our house. I would even complain about her cooking. Mostly, though, I was getting more and more impatient with the difficulty she encountered in doing everyday things. I was afraid for her. One day, we got into a terrible argument when she asked me to call the bank, to question a discrepancy she had discovered in the monthly statement. I asked her why she couldn't call herself. I was stupid and brutal, and I knew exactly how to wound her.

"Whom do I talk to?" she said. She would mostly speak to me in Korean, and I would answer in English.

"The bank manager, who else?"

"What do I say?"

"Whatever you want to say."

"Don't speak to me like that!" she cried.

"It's just that you should be able to do it yourself," I said.

"You know how I feel about this!"

"Well, maybe then you should consider it *practice*," I answered lightly, using the Korean word to make sure she understood.

Her face blanched, and her neck suddenly became rigid, as if I were throttling her. She nearly struck me right then, but instead she bit her lip and ran upstairs. I followed her, pleading for forgiveness at her door. But it was the one time in our life that I couldn't convince her, melt her resolve with the blandishments of a spoiled son.

•   •   •

When my mother was feeling strong enough, or was in particularly good spirits, she would roll her machine into the kitchen and sit at the table and watch me work. She wore pajamas day and night, mostly old pairs of mine.

She said, "I can't tell, what are you making?"

"*Mahn-doo* filling."

"You didn't salt the cabbage and squash."

"Was I supposed to?"

"Of course. Look, it's too wet. Now the skins will get soggy before you can fry them."

"What should I do?"

"It's too late. Maybe it'll be OK if you work quickly. Why didn't you ask me?"

"You were finally sleeping."

"You should have woken me."

"No way."

She sighed, as deeply as her weary lungs would allow.

"I don't know how you were going to make it without me."

"I don't know, either. I'll remember the salt next time."

"You better. And not too much."

We often talked like this, our tone decidedly matter-of-fact, chin up, just this side of being able to bear it. Once, while inspecting a potato fritter batter I was making, she asked me if she had ever done anything that I wished she hadn't done. I thought for a moment, and told her no. In the next breath, she wondered aloud if it was right of her to have let me go to Exeter, to live away from the house while I was so young. She tested the batter's thickness with her finger and called for more flour. Then she asked if, given a choice, I would go to Exeter again.

I wasn't sure what she was getting at, and I told her that I couldn't be certain, but probably yes, I would. She snorted at this and said it was my leaving home that had once so troubled our relationship. "Remember how I had so much difficulty talking to you? Remember?"

She believed back then that I had found her more and more ignorant each time I came home. She said she never blamed me, for this was the way she knew it would be with my wonderful new education. Nothing I could say seemed to quell the notion. But I knew that the problem wasn't simply the *education*; the first time I saw her again after starting school, barely six weeks later, when she and my father visited me on Parents Day, she had already grown nervous and distant. After the usual campus events, we had gone to the motel where they were staying in a nearby town and sat on the beds in our room. She seemed to sneak looks at me, as though I might discover a horrible new truth if our eyes should meet.

My own secret feeling was that I had missed my parents greatly, my mother especially, and much more than I had anticipated. I couldn't tell them that these first weeks were a mere blur to me, that I felt completely overwhelmed by all the studies and my much brighter friends and the thousand irritating details of living alone, and that I had really learned nothing, save perhaps how to put on a necktie while sprinting to class. I felt as if I had plunged too deep into the world, which, to my great horror, was much larger than I had ever imagined.

I welcomed the lull of the motel room. My father and I had nearly dozed off when my mother jumped up excitedly, murmured how stupid she was, and hurried to the closet by the door. She pulled out our old metal cooler and dragged it between the beds. She lifted the top and began unpacking plastic containers, and I thought she would never stop. One after the other they came out, each with a dish that traveled well—a salted stewed meat, rolls of Korean-style sushi. I opened a container of radish kimchi and suddenly the room bloomed with its odor, and I reveled in the very peculiar sensation (which perhaps only true kimchi lovers know) of simultaneously drooling and gagging as I breathed it all in. For the next few minutes, they watched me eat. I'm not certain that I was even hungry. But after weeks of pork parmigiana and chicken patties and wax beans, I suddenly realized that I had lost all the savor in my life. And it seemed I couldn't get enough of it back. I ate and I ate, so much and so fast that I actually went to the bathroom and vomited. I came out dizzy and sated with the phantom warmth of my binge.

And beneath the face of her worry, I thought, my mother was smiling.

From that day, my mother prepared a certain meal to welcome me home. It was always the same. Even as I rode the school's shuttle bus from Exeter to Logan airport, I could already see the exact arrangement of my mother's table.

I knew that we would eat in the kitchen, the table brimming with plates. There was the *kalbi*, of course, broiled or grilled depending on the season. Leaf lettuce, to wrap the meat with. Bowls of garlicky clam broth with miso and tofu and fresh spinach. Shavings of cod dusted in flour and then dipped in egg wash and fried. Glass noodles with onions and shiitake. Scallion-and-hot-pepper pancakes. Chilled steamed shrimp. Seasoned salads of bean sprouts, spinach, and white radish. Crispy squares of seaweed. Steamed rice with barley and red beans. Homemade kimchi. It was all there—the old flavors I knew, the beautiful salt, the sweet, the excellent taste.

After the meal, my father and I talked about school, but I could never say enough for it to make any sense. My father would often recall his high school principal, who had gone to England to study the methods and traditions of the public schools, and regaled students with stories of the great Eton man. My mother sat with us, paring fruit, not saying a word but taking everything in. When it was time to go to bed, my father said good night first. I usually watched television until the early morning. My mother would sit with me for an hour or two, perhaps until she was accustomed to me again, and only then would she kiss me and head upstairs to sleep.

During the following days, it was always the cooking that started our conversations. She'd hold an inquest over the cold leftovers we ate at lunch, discussing each dish in terms of its balance of flavors or what might have been prepared differently. But mostly I begged her to leave the dishes alone. I wish I had paid more attention. After her death, when my father and I were the only ones left in the house, drifting through the rooms like ghosts, I sometimes tried to make that meal for him. Though it was too much for two, I made each dish anyway, taking as much care as I could. But nothing turned out quite right—not the color, not the smell. At the table, neither of us said much of anything. And we had to eat the food for days.

I remember washing rice in the kitchen one day and my mother's saying in English, from her usual seat, "I made a big mistake."

"About Exeter?"

"Yes. I made a big mistake. You should be with us for that time. I should never let you go there."

"So why did you?" I said.

"Because I didn't know I was going to die."

I let her words pass. For the first time in her life, she was letting herself speak her full mind, so what else could I do?

"But you know what?" she spoke up. "It was better for you. If you stayed home, you would not like me so much now."

I suggested that maybe I would like her even more.

She shook her head. "Impossible."

Sometimes I still think about what she said, about having made a mistake. I would have left home for college, that was never in doubt, but those years I was away at boarding school grew more precious to her as her illness progressed. After many months of exhaustion and pain and the haze of the drugs, I thought that her mind was beginning to fade, for more and more it seemed that she was seeing me again as her fifteen-year-old boy, the one she had dropped off in New Hampshire on a cloudy September afternoon.

I remember the first person I met, another new student, named Zack, who walked to the welcome picnic with me. I had planned to eat with my parents—my mother had brought a coolerful of food even that first day—but I learned of the cookout and told her that I should probably go. I wanted to go, of course. I was excited, and no doubt fearful and nervous, and I must have thought I was only thinking ahead. She agreed wholeheartedly, saying I certainly should. I walked them to the car, and perhaps I hugged them, before saying goodbye. One day, after she died, my father told me what happened on the long drive home to Syracuse.

He was driving the car, looking straight ahead. Traffic was light on the Massachusetts Turnpike, and the sky was nearly dark. They had driven for more than two hours and had not yet spoken a word. He then heard a strange sound from her, a kind of muffled chewing noise, as if something inside her were grinding its way out.

"So, what's the matter?" he said, trying to keep an edge to his voice.

She looked at him with her ashen face and she burst into tears. He began to cry himself, and pulled the car over onto the narrow shoulder of the turnpike, where they stayed for the next half hour or so, the blank-faced cars droning by them in the cold, onrushing night.

Every once in a while, when I think of her, I'm driving alone somewhere on the highway. In the twilight, I see their car off to the side, a blue Olds coupe with a landau top, and as I pass them by I look back in the mirror and I see them again, the two figures huddling together in the front seat. Are they sleeping? Or kissing? Are they all right?

WRITING ABOUT THE READING

4. Why is cooking the traditional Korean foods so important to Lee?
5. How and why does the writer use different experiences with food to link this reading together?
6. Why does the writer's mother fit (or not fit) the stereotype of an Asian woman?
7. Why does the writer's mother become upset when he presses her to call the bank about a discrepancy in the monthly statement?
8. Why does the word "ambivalent" characterize the mother's attitude toward Lee's going to Exeter?
9. Why is it so important to the mother that Lee eats her cooking?
10. How does the concluding paragraph relate to the opening paragraph?

WRITING FROM YOUR OWN EXPERIENCE

Note: In these assignments, write about your own experience or use that of someone you know, read about, or saw in a film/TV show.

11. When Lee was a child, he enjoyed standing in the kitchen, learning to cook from his mother. Recall a similar situation when you watched your mother or father work on a household task. Why do you remember this situation in particular and what did you learn?
12. Many people have "comfort foods," such as ice cream or hot chocolate. These may be foods remembered from their childhood. What are your favorite "comfort foods" and why do you choose these foods?
13. Lee takes over the cooking because his mother is seriously ill. Have you ever had to take on some responsibilities because of the illness of a relative, coworker, or friend? What did you do to help this person and what were the consequences of your actions?

14. Lee came from a family that stressed the importance of a good education. What would you say to support the statement: "Multicultural education is just good education. Period."

WRITING ABOUT RESEARCH

15. How and why did the United States become involved in the Korean War?
16. What are some of the major differences (such as government and/or economic conditions) between North and South Korea?
17. Why do many economists consider South Korea to be one of the strongest economic powers in Asia?

Song for My Father

ERIC LIU

Eric Liu *(1968–), writer, editor, and television commentator, was born in Poughkeepsie, New York. He received a B.A. (1990) from Yale and a J.D. (1999) from Harvard University. Liu worked as a speechwriter during President Clinton's administration.*

The reading, "Song for My Father," is an excerpt from The Accidental Asian: Notes of a Native Speaker *(1998). The book is a collection of essays on questions of identity for "Asian Americans," a label that Liu believes is based on race, on shared physical characteristics, rather than ethnicity. In this selection, Liu reveals how his father's assimilation included a penchant for using colorful American expressions.*

PREPARING TO READ

1. Why do you agree (or disagree) that success in the business world requires the ability to read people and play office politics more than the ability to do the job well?
2. Explain whether you agree with the common belief that first-generation immigrants are harder working and/or more ambitious than people born in the United States.
3. Why is a good command of spoken and written English critical to success?

SONG FOR MY FATHER

1.

By my bed, gathering a little dust now, I'm afraid, is a small paperback book. I've kept it there ever since it was published four or five years ago, and it's become one of those things in my apartment that I see every day without seeing anymore.

• • •

So it's no accident that in this stack of salves I've included this slender paperback. It is unlike any other book I own. On the cover, set against a faded backdrop of his own handwriting, is a color photograph of my father. In the photograph, taken sometime in the 1960s, my father's head is turned to his left, his mouth slightly open in a relaxed smile. Even behind heavy-framed glasses, his eyes appear to be seeing something clearly. It seems he might be saying something soon, something thoughtful, or maybe playful. A lock of his black hair, bunched like wet grass, has fallen out of place, sweeping across his forehead. His skin, still smooth and full, tells me he was a young man not that many years before the picture was taken. But his visage— knowing, kind, self-aware—tells me he has already become the man I knew as Baba. That picture is why I keep the paperback at my bedside. It keeps my father close, sets his gaze upon me as I sleep.

The book was compiled by several of my father's childhood friends after he died in 1991. This wasn't, as far as I know, some sort of Chinese tradition, publishing a memorial book for a departed chum. It was just an act of loyalty; of love, if I may say that. In part, the book is a record of grief, containing the obituary from the *Poughkeepsie Journal*, my eulogy, an elegiac essay by my mother. But for most of its 198 pages, it is actually a prose reunion, a memoir of the idyllic adolescence of a band of boys in postwar Taiwan.

There are pieces in the book, written by my father and his brothers and his classmates, about high school life, about a favorite teacher, about camping and fishing trips, about picaresque adventures where nary an adult appears. There are photographs too; in many of them, Dad and his friends are wearing their school uniforms, baggy and vaguely military. One snapshot I remember vividly. Eight or nine of them are walking up a dirt road, jesting and smiling. And there's my father at the end of this happy phalanx—khaki hat a bit too big, arm pumping jauntily and foot raised in mid-march, singing a song. The face is my father's, but the stance, so utterly carefree, is hardly recognizable. I stared at that picture for a long time when I first got the book.

It's through these photographs that I'll read the book every so often, searching the scenes for new revelations. That's partly because the photographs are so wonderful, soft black-and-white images of an innocence beyond articulation. But it's also, frankly, because I do not understand the text. Almost all the entries, you see, are written in

Chinese—a language that I once could read and write with middling proficiency but have since let slip into disuse. Though I know enough to read from top to bottom, right to left, and "back" to "front," I recognize so few of the characters now that perusing the text yields little more than frustration, and shame. I know what the book contains only because Mom has told me. And she's had to tell me several times.

On one or two occasions I've sat down with my pocket Chinese-English dictionary, determined to decipher at least the essays that my father wrote. This was painstaking work and I never got very far. For each Chinese character, I first had to determine the ideographic root, then count the brush strokes, then turn to an index ordered by root and by number of strokes, then match the character, then figure out its romanized spelling, then look up its definition. By the time I solved one word, I'd already forgotten the previous one. Meaning was hard enough to determine; context was even more elusive.

So it is, I sometimes think, with my father's life. On the one hand, it's easy to locate my father and my family in the grand narrative of "the Chinese American experience." On the other hand, it doesn't take long for this narrative to seem more like a riddle than a fable. Leafing through the pages of the memorial book, staring dumbly at their blur of ideographs, I realize just how little I know about those years of Baba's life before he arrived in America, and before I arrived in the world. I sense how difficult it is to be literate in another man's life, how opaque an inheritance one's identity truly is. I begin to perceive my own ignorance of self.

When Chao-hua Liu came to the United States in 1955, at the age of eighteen, he was Chinese. When he died thirty-six years later, he was, I'd say, something other than Chinese. And he had helped raise a son who was Chinese in perhaps only a nominal sense. But what, ultimately, does all this mean? Where does this Chineseness reside? In the word? In the deed? In what is learned—or what is already known? And how is it passed from one generation to the next? Some of the answers lie, I know, in a book I am still unable to read. But there are other answers, I suspect, in a book I must now begin to write.

2.

If I could render as a painting the image I have of my father as a young man, it would be a post-impressionist work, late Cezanne, rather than a work of realist precision. Actually, it would be more like an unfinished Cezanne: blocks of color; indistinct shapes; and then, suddenly, great swaths of blank canvas. The scraps of knowledge I have of my father's pre-American life come from letters he wrote, from my mother's secondhand memories, from family lore. They aren't random fragments, exactly. But they aren't full-fledged stories either. They're more like scenes, symbolic images that can be arranged in rough sequence yet still resist narration.

Here is some of what I know about my Chinese father: That he was the second of six brothers, born in Nanjing in 1936. That his father was a pilot and a general whose given name, Goo Yun, translates roughly as Deliverance of the Nation. That he fled in the night with his family to Taiwan when Communist forces had advanced too close. That when he was a boy, he raised pigeons in a cage on the roof of his house and then one day set them all free. That he was ill for a lengthy period as a child, but took the opportunity of being bedridden to read the Chinese classics over and over again. That the medication he took would prove, years later, to have damaged his kidneys. That his father's driver taught him how to drive a jeep at age twelve, or maybe thirteen. That his family's cook taught him how to make dumplings. That he was an outstanding student and mischievous, though mischievous in the safe, authority-affirming way of an outstanding student. That he left his home and his country after high school.

It is typical, I suppose, that the second generation forgets to ask the first generation why it became the first. But is it typical, as well, to accept without comment what few recollections the first generation offers? Or was it simply my own lack of curiosity? I never knew, for instance, that Baba was born in Nanjing until I was applying to college and needed to fill in the space for "Father's Birthplace." I never knew whether he, the son of a general, felt pressure to join the military. I never knew why he set those pigeons free. I never knew how Confucius and Mencius had influenced him, although he told my mother that they had. I never knew whether he was bitter about the bad medicine. I never knew where he drove once he learned to drive. I never knew what ambitions he packed with him when he sailed across the Pacific. I never knew whether he was homesick when he cooked his first meal in America.

My knowledge of Baba's years in China and Taiwan is like a collection of souvenirs, but of souvenirs that don't belong to me. They evoke a milieu; they signify something. But sifting through them, I cannot be sure whether the story they tell is simply the story I've chosen to imagine. If I were a fiction writer, I could manipulate these scenes a hundred different ways. I could tell you a tale and pass it off as emblematic of Baba's childhood, of wartime China, of the Chinese condition. Even as an essayist, I impute significance to the scenes in a way that reveals as much about my own yearnings as it does about my father's. It is the Heisenberg principle of remembrance: the mere act of observing a memory changes that memory's meaning.

This truth, that we unwittingly mold other people's pasts to our own ends, is easy to grasp on an individual level—especially when the individual is a son searching sentimentally for his father. On a collective level, though, it becomes rather less obvious. Nation, race, diaspora—all these are communities of collective memory, and the greater the community, the more occluded are its motives for remembering. For people who think of themselves as "a people," the hard facts of history tend to melt into folklore, which dissolves into aesthetic, which evaporates like mist into race-consciousness. What matters, after a while, is not the memory of shared experience so much as the shared experience of memory.

Consider the mythology of the Overseas Chinese, which is how people in China and Taiwan refer to the thirty million or so ethnic Chinese who live elsewhere. The idea is simple: there is China, which is filled with Chinese; and there is the rest of the world, which, to varying degrees, is sprinkled with Chinese. The ethnocentrism is manifest, the essentialism unapologetic: "You can take a Chinese out of China, but you can't take the China out of a Chinese."

But just what is it that binds together these millions of Chinese outside China? Well, it's their Chineseness. And what is Chineseness? That which binds together the Chinese. Entire conferences and scholarly tomes have been devoted to this catechism, with roughly the same results. Granted, there exists, in the form of a rich culture and history, what political scientist Samuel Huntington would call a "core Sinic civilization." That civilization, however, isn't intrinsic to people of Chinese genotype; it is transmitted—or not. And whether it is transmitted to the Overseas Chinese depends, ultimately, on consent rather than descent. Chineseness isn't a mystical, more authentic way of being; it's just a decision to act Chinese.

Which, of course, only raises more questions. Though my father, in the first eighteen years of his life, was Chinese and nothing but Chinese; though his were the actions of a Chinese person, it is difficult to isolate which aspects of his values and behavior you would specifically call "Chinese." True, he believed in the importance of family and the value of education. He was respectful toward his elders. He was self-disciplined and intellectually rigorous. He was even-tempered, not a rebellious spirit. He appreciated the beauty of Chinese painting and the wisdom of Chinese poetry. He loved reading and writing Chinese. He enjoyed eating Chinese food.

This is beginning to sound, though, like a piece of inductive reasoning: working in reverse from a general notion of what it means to "act Chinese" in order to identify a particular personality as Chinese.

One problem with such backward reasoning is that it views colorless attributes through a tinted lens, turning a trait like even-temperedness into a sure sign of Chineseness. Another is that it filters out evidence that contradicts the conclusion: there was plenty about Dad, after all, that didn't fit anybody's stereotype of "Chinese character." That may be hard to tell when my indistinct image of him is set against a faded Chinese backdrop. It becomes more apparent in the context I knew him in: the context of America.

3.

Another photograph, this one dated April 1962. It's a black-and-white shot, slightly out of focus, set in a spare apartment. There is no art on the walls, not even a calendar. The curtains are thin, a diaphanous membrane that can't quite contain the light outside. In the center of the picture is my father, sitting at a desk with stacks of papers and books. He is leaning back slightly in a stiff wooden chair, his left leg crossed, and he is reading a book that rests easily on his knee. He is wearing a sweatshirt emblazoned with ILLINOIS and a Stars and Stripes shield. He is smoking a pipe, which he holds to his mouth absently with his right hand.

When I first saw this picture, it put me in mind of a daguerreotype image I'd once seen of an 1890s Yale student sitting in his room. The settings, of course, couldn't have been more different. That Yale room, with its dark wood paneling and clubby leather chairs, walls adorned with undergraduate paraphernalia, was the domain of a Gilded Age heir. My father's room was the kind of place one rightly calls a flat. Yet for all the obvious differences in scene, there was, in both my father and that long-ago Yalie, the same self-conscious manner. We are Serious Young Men, their contemplative poses announce, and we are preparing for the Future.

Maybe it's just the pipe and the college sweatshirt, or the posture. Still, I can't help thinking that my father in this photograph looks—what? Not quite so Chinese, I suppose. When this shot was taken, he'd already been in the United States for over seven years. He'd worked odd jobs to save money. One of them, my personal favorite, was painting the yellow line down the middle of a South Dakota highway. He had become, during this period, a devotee of Hank Williams and Muhammad Ali. He'd earned a degree in philosophy—Western philosophy—from the University of Illinois, and had become fascinated with Camus and existentialism. He had finished a master's in mathematics. He had been dating my mother, whom he'd met at a picnic with other students from Taiwan, for three years. They would be married a year later.

Their wedding, from what my mother has told me, was a fairly accurate measure of where they were in life then: not quite in the mainstream, but so happy to have each other's company, so much in a world of their own, that little else mattered. The ceremony took place in a church, because that was where weddings took place in America. Except for the officiant and a few others, almost everyone there was Chinese. Still, there were no traditional Chinese rituals; no ancestor worship or kowtowing or burning of incense. They spoke their vows in English. The bride wore white, the groom a rented black tuxedo. The reception was in the church basement. The honeymoon, in rural Michigan. It was the end of November.

I wonder how people regarded them, these young newlyweds. To your average citizen of rural Michigan, this slight, black-haired couple probably looked like exchange students or tourists: like foreigners. To me, they look heartbreakingly American. Indeed, this hopeful phase—this period of composing a life to the rhythms of a new country—is far easier for me to conjure up than their years in China and Taiwan. There are more photographs, for one thing, more anecdotes to help sharpen my impressions. There are familiar names and places too, like Ann Arbor, Millbrook, Bennett College. But more than all that, there is the familiar idiom of progress—the steady sense of climbing, and climbing higher; of forgetting, and forgetting more.

In our archetype of the immigrant experience, it is the first generation that remains wedded to the ways of the Old Country and the second generation that forsakes them. This, we learn, is the tragedy of assimilation: the inevitable estrangement between the immigrant father who imagines himself still in exile and the American son who strains to prove his belonging. There is, I'll admit, a certain dramatic appeal to this account. There is also, unfortunately, a good deal of contrivance. In search of narrative tension, we let ourselves forget that the father, too, is transformed. We let ourselves think of the first generation's life as a mere chrysalis, an interlude between the larval existence of the homeland and the fully formed Americanness of the second generation. But the truth is that the father can sometimes become his own form of butterfly.

In Baba's case, the metamorphosis found its most vivid expression in language. Even as a teenager in Taiwan he had excelled in his English classes. Once he came to the States he picked up jargon, slang, and idiom with a collector's enthusiasm. IBM, which he joined after grad school and where he worked for twenty-seven years, was both a great source and a constant testing ground for his American vernacular. It gave him, for instance, his favorite acronym—SNAFU—which, he loved to remind us, stood for Situation Normal: All Fucked Up.

I think Baba's facility with English is part of what gave me such a powerful sense when I was growing up that he wasn't quite like other Chinese immigrants. Other Chinese immigrants, it seemed, spoke English as if it was Chinese, using he and she interchangeably, ignoring the conjugation of verbs, not bothering to make nouns plural. My father's English was several tiers better than that; more important, he spoke the language with relish, as if he owned it.

He did have an accent, although for the life of me now, I can't describe it or reproduce it. In fact, I remember being surprised once when a friend said something about the Chinese inflection of my father's English: the same sense of surprise I'd had as a boy when I saw myself and my friends in a mirror and realized how much shorter I was than they were. I simply didn't hear his accent.

What I heard was the way he was fluent in American small talk, the way he got a kick out of backhanded compliments and cornball humor. What I heard was the way he would fixate delightedly on phrases that he'd pick up here and there. "What a joke" was a refrain he learned from my friend George. "I mean business!" he got from an auto-repair ad on television. "I yield to the congresswoman from Old English Way" was how, after watching the parliamentary theater of the Iran-Contra hearings, he would pass the phone to Mom when I called home. What I heard too was how well he could argue in English, angrily, when a repairman tried to rip him off.

His command of written English was also surprisingly good. When I was in high school Baba would edit my writing assignments for clarity and logic. When my sister Andrea was in high school, and was editor of the newspaper, he would actually write short unsigned columns just to help her fill up ink space. He would opine for 300 words about the death penalty or student apathy or some such pressing topic with sincerity and just a touch of goofiness.

4.

My mother says that Baba's Chinese, actually, was first-rate, as good as that of any Confucian gentleman-scholar. This doesn't surprise me, considering his linguistic aptitude and all the time he spent as a boy reading classic Chinese texts. Even to my untrained eye, the quick and elegant strokes of his calligraphy reveal just how supple a material this language was in his hands. I imagine Baba took great pride in his talent. I wonder, then, why he never insisted that I be able to read the Chinese canon—alas, that I be able to read even a Chinese menu.

Over the years, my knowledge of Chinese has ebbed and flowed; at its highest tides, it has never been more than shallow. At home, my parents communicated with each other almost entirely in Chinese, but they spoke to me in an amalgam that was maybe two-thirds Chinese, and I replied almost entirely in English. From second to seventh grade, I went to Chinese school every Sunday afternoon. But the program ended after seventh grade, and I made little effort to keep up my studies. When I got to college, I took two years of intensive Chinese to replenish my knowledge from grade school. But then I graduated, and I haven't studied Chinese since.

Not once during the ebb periods did my father ever pressure me to become more fluent. There was one time he sent me a letter in Chinese, and I thought it might be a solemn message about the importance of preserving my heritage. It turned out to be a gag, a string of silly Chinese puns. This, it seemed, was his attitude toward my dissipating Chineseness: studied nonchalance. Whenever my grandmother called us from Taiwan, I'd stumble through a few pleasantries in fractured Mandarin, and Baba would feel obliged to offer a half-serious apology for my pitiful performance. After hanging up, though, he'd never say a word to me about it.

I wish he had. Today, I am far from bilingual. In written Chinese, I am functionally illiterate; in spoken Chinese, I am 1.5-lingual at best, more suited to following conversations than joining them. True, some of the things that come hardest to non-native Mandarin speakers—an ear for the four different tones, the ability to form certain sounds— come easily to me, because I've heard the language all my life. I also, as a result, have an instinctive feel for the proper construction of Chinese sentences. What I don't have, alas, is much of a vocabulary. I can sense that thinking in Chinese yields a unique, ineffable way of perceiving the world. I can sense how useful Chinese is for filling the interstitial spaces of English. But I sense these things and express them only as a child might, since I have, really, only a child's mastery of Chinese.

When I contrast my father's possession of English with my forfeiture of Chinese, I feel like something of a fool; as if I had squandered an inheritance and not even realized its magnitude until I was left with only spare change. Yet I know that in a fundamental way it was my father's possession of English that had made possible my forfeiture of Chinese. You could say, indeed, that I merely completed his assimilation. He might have preferred deep down that I be literate in his first language. But he preferred above all that I have unimpeded access to every avenue of American life. So long as I appeared to have that, any Chinese I might have was just a bonus.

I understand this attitude, even if I regret some of its consequences now. I recognize, as well, what a luxury it is to express such regret. As he made his way in this country, my father piled up more misgivings than I may ever know. Yet he could only file them away: there was no time for such indulgences; no reason to do an honest accounting of his losses and gains. Now I attempt such an accounting. And I find myself perhaps too willing to extend the lines of the ledger: to count the first quarter of my own life as the fifth quarter of his.

Baba would not have expected, or even wanted, such a grace period. If there was one dominant theme in his life, it was that he didn't want to be treated differently—better or worse—just because he was different. This principle, and the pride that upheld it, made for a selective kind of assimilation. He did not want to be a square peg in a round hole. But he realized at a certain point that, like a chopstick, he had both a square end and a round end; that he could find ways to fit in without whittling down his integrity.

What he did with his name is a good example. Unlike some of his Chinese immigrant peers, my father never took on an "American" first name like Charlie or Chet. His concession to convention was to shorten "Chao-hua" to "Chao" and to pronounce his surname as loo instead of leeoo—so that to the white world, he was, phonetically, chow loo. I suppose that still sounds pretty foreign to many people (including his own mother). But by carrying himself as if the name "Chao Liu" was as American as "Chuck Lewis," he managed, in effect, to make it so.

How did he carry himself? My father had several roles when he was in public, by which I mean, in mostly white environments. One was the savvy manager. As he climbed the ranks of middle management at IBM, Dad became ever more adept at the intangibles of corporate life—the ability to read people and play internecine politics; to conform and yet distinguish himself. He knew how the system worked: knew it well enough to become one of the few Chinese faces in the upper tiers of IBM's Poughkeepsie operation; knew it well enough also to sense the leveling of his trajectory during his last years. At dinner, he and Mom would spend what seemed like hours deconstructing the latest office maneuverings, mixing gossipy news of intrigue with bits of bureaucratese. As Andrea and I sat there, bored by the grown-up talk, Dad would suddenly break out of Chinese and toss an observation our way: "'A' students end up working for 'C' students." And then back to Chinese.

Another role he took on, probably not unrelated, was that of the pushy underdog. Dad didn't have a chip on his shoulder; he was good-natured, didn't play the victim. But in the many small transactions of our daily lives—with mechanics, teachers, salesmen, doctors, repair-men, and any other figures who might hold momentary leverage over us—Dad was not going to be taken advantage of. He wasn't shy about asking for documentation, explanation, and the fine print. He had no qualms about being assertive in defense of household interests. Some-times his willingness to get in people's faces would embarrass me. Other times, I'll admit, it delighted me.

I remember being awed by Baba whenever he and Mom hosted parties for our neighbors. On those occasions he was the social dynamo: outgoing, loud, backslapping, playful. In conversation, he had a bantam energy and a penchant for running jokes that simultaneously charmed his guests and kept them from getting too personal. Every few minutes, it seemed, his high-pitched laugh would rip through the house, fol-lowed, like a wave, by the louder, more resonant guffaws of Jim, Gil, Jack, and the other big white guys he was leaning into. What were they talking about? Sports? Neighborhood scuttlebutt? Off-color jokes? I didn't know; I knew only how exciting it was to see Dad in action.

To be sure, my father was just as energetic and jocular at all-Chinese parties. That was simply his personality. But I'd never seen a Chinese immigrant of his generation behave so exuberantly with white folks. In the presence of yangren ("foreigners"), most of my par-ents' Chinese friends, whether or not they were naturally gregarious, became more reserved and formal. As they switched to English, their guard went up. Baba's expressiveness, his bouncy self-assurance, was quite a contrast.

Of course, in the quarters of his private self, there was more to my father, more than even his own son knew. There was the same geniality and humor that he showed in public. But there was also sub-tlety, in the thoughtful way he gave me advice. There was gentleness, in the way he would come into my room after I'd fallen asleep to close the window and kiss me by the ear. There was an agility of spirit, in the way he happily dropped the work he was doing when Mom called him to the porch one summer evening: "Come see the moon!" They sat there, smiling and talking, while my sister and I rode our bikes past. There was grace, in the way he and Mom danced to "Hooked on Clas-sics" on the linoleum kitchen floor. There was an omnivorous intellect that won him the family sobriquet of Walking Encyclopedia. There was ambition, impatience: he'd started a doctorate, then abandoned it. There was also, in my father, an inner turmoil that revealed itself only in his fitful, twitchy naps. There was a pensiveness that would bring him into the study on Sunday afternoons just to sit by the window, rub his eyes, and smoke a cigarette. There was sadness, I now realize, a deep and silent current of existential sadness.

About a year after his death, I tried on one of the casual blazers Baba had owned, a tan Haggar herringbone. It didn't quite fit me, which I knew would be the case, but which disappointed me nonetheless. As I took it off, I found two sheets of paper folded in the interior pocket that made me think suddenly, and sharply, about my father's interior life. Scribbled on one sheet, in his distinctive hand, were the lyrics from a mournful Hank Williams ballad he used to listen to: "I'm so lonesome I could cry." On the other sheet were some notes to himself, meditations in a dense Chinese scrawl. I wondered: What do those Chinese notes say? Why did he carry this song with him? Why, to the end, did he hold it so close?

WRITING ABOUT THE READING

4. How and why does the writer compare his understanding of his father to a post-impressionist painting or a collection of souvenirs?

5. What does the photograph of the writer's father at college suggest about the role he was playing?

6. Why does the son say that because he does not know Chinese well, he lacks the ability to perceive the world as Chinese do?

7. Why does Liu's father assume the role of "pushy underdog" in some situations?

8. Why do you think Liu's father played the part of an energetic "social dynamo" at parties?

9. Why does the son compare his father to a chopstick with both a square and a round end?

10. Explain why you think that the writer ends this selection with a discussion of the Hank Williams's song?

WRITING FROM YOUR OWN EXPERIENCE

Note: In these assignments, write about your own experience or use that of someone you know, read about, or saw in a film/TV show.

11. Liu, who worked as a speechwriter for many years, emphasizes the importance of speaking well in this essay. Think of a time that you had to speak before a class or in public. Explain how you felt about giving this speech and how the speech turned out.

12. Characteristic ways of behaving or thinking often can be attributed to family influence. Think of a trait (such as friendliness,

generosity, or frugality) that is characteristic of members of your family. How and why do you show this trait?

13. As part of the Americanization process, Liu's father adopted colorful American expressions. Choose three slang terms that you would use (or choose from the following list). Explain what these terms mean and under what circumstances you would use this language. Consider:

(a) give it 110 percent

(b) This is bugging me.

(c) go with the flow

(d) his old lady

(e) megabuck

(f) momentum

(g) check out the scene

(h) one in a million

(i) She dissed me.

(j) phat

(k) some dude

(l) That's cool.

(m) We messed up.

(n) split before class

(o) totally awesome

(p) weather-wise

(q) work up a sweat

(r) got busted

(s) get bummed out

(t) They're hung up on it.

WRITING ABOUT RESEARCH

14. Why was it important (up to the modern era) for a person aspiring to a high position in the Chinese government to become a well-educated scholar (a mandarin)?

15. Why is there a controversy between the United States and China over the independence of Taiwan?

16. What have been some of the consequences of China's repossession of Hong Kong at the end of the twentieth century?

17. Choose an Asian American who has achieved success in the United States. Why was this person successful? Some people to consider include:

(a) Subrahmanyan Chandrasekhar (Nobel Prize in physics)

(b) Elaine L. Chao (Labor Secretary)

(c) Paul Ching-wu Chu (expert in superconductivity technology)

(d) Lance Ito (judge)

(e) Hat Gobind Khorana (Nobel Prize in medicine)

(f) Tsung Dao Lee (Nobel Prize in physics)

(g) Wing Luke (political leader for whom the Wing Luke Asian Museum in Seattle was named)

(h) Patsy Mink (political leader)

(i) Constance Tom Noguchi (sickle cell disease researcher)

(j) Tsutomo Shimormura (computers)

(k) Samuel Chao Chung Ting (Nobel Prize in physics)

(l) Susumu Tonegawa (Nobel Prize in medicine)

(m) Hen Ning Yang (Nobel Prize in physics)

(n) Chien-shiung Wu (physicist)

The Gangster We Are All Looking For

LE THI DIEM THUY

Le Thi Diem Thuy *(1972–), writer and solo performance artist, was born in Vietnam and raised in California. She is the recipient of a 1997 Bridge Residency at the Headlands Center for the Arts. Her writings have appeared in many periodicals, including* Harper's Magazine. *Her solo performance works have been presented at the Whitney Museum of American Art at Philip Morris, the International Women Playwright's Festival in Ireland, and the New World Theater at the University of Massachusetts, Amherst.*

In "The Gangster We Are All Looking For," the writer tells of her childhood experiences of leaving Vietnam by boat in 1979, living in a Singapore refugee camp, and immigrating to the United States. This essay was originally printed in The Massachusetts Review *(1996), an academic journal of literature, the arts, and public affairs.*

PREPARING TO READ

1. Why do you suppose people enjoy watching frightening movies, such as horror movies or those with violence?
2. Explain whether you think that America should serve as a "peacekeeper" for the world by becoming militarily involved in regional conflicts, such as those in Asia, the Mideast, or the Balkans.
3. Why do you agree (or disagree) that human beings will always engage in wars?

THE GANGSTER WE ARE ALL LOOKING FOR

Vietnam is a black-and-white photograph of my grandparents sitting in bamboo chairs in their front courtyard. They are sitting tall and proud, surrounded by chickens and roosters. Their feet are separated from the dirt by thin sandals. My grandfather's broad forehead is shining. So too are my grandmother's famed sad eyes. The animals are obliviously pecking at the ground. This looks like a wedding portrait, though it is actually a photograph my grandparents had taken late in life, for their children, especially for my mother. When I think of this portrait of my grandparents in the last years of their life, I always envision a beginning. To what or where, I don't know, but always a beginning.

• • •

When my mother, a Catholic schoolgirl from the South, decided to marry my father, a Buddhist gangster from the North, her parents disowned her. This is in the photograph, though it is not visible to the eye. If it were, it would be a deep impression across the soft dirt of my grandparents' courtyard. Her father chased her out of the house, beating her with the same broom she had used every day of her life, from the time she could stand up and sweep to the morning of the very day she was chased away.

• • •

The year my mother met my father, there were several young men working at her house, running errands for her father, pickling vegetables with her mother. It was understood by everyone that these men were courting my mother. My mother claims she had no such understanding.

She treated these men as brothers, sometimes as uncles even, later exclaiming in self-defense, "I didn't even know about love then."

• • •

Ma says love came to her in a dark movie theater. She doesn't remember what movie it was or why she'd gone to see it, only that she'd gone alone and found herself sitting beside him. In the dark, she couldn't make out his face but noticed he was handsome. She wondered if he knew she was watching him out of the corner of her eye. Watching him without embarrassment or shame. Watching him with a strange curiosity, a feeling that made her want to trace and retrace his silhouette with her fingertips until she'd memorized every feature and could call his face to her in any dark place she passed through. Later, in the shadow of the beached fishing boats on the blackest nights of the year, she would call him to mind, his face a warm companion for her body on the edge of the sea.

• • •

In the early days of my parents' courtship, my mother told stories. She confessed elaborate dreams about the end of war: foods she'd
eat (a banquet table, mangoes piled high to the ceiling); songs she'd
make up and sing, clapping her hands over her head and throwing her
hair like a horse's mane; dances she'd do, hopping from one foot to the
other. Unlike the responsible favorite daughter or sister she was to her
family, with my father, in the forest, my mother became reckless,
drunk on her youth and the possibility of love. Ignoring the chores to
be done at home, she rolled her pants up to her knees, stuck her bare
feet in puddles, and learned to smoke a cigarette.

• • •

She tied a vermilion ribbon in her hair. She became moody.
She did her chores as though they were favors to her family, forgetting that she ate the same rice and was dependent on the same supply of food. It seemed to her the face that stared back at her from
deep inside the family well was the face of a woman she had never
seen before. At night she lay in bed and thought of his hands, the
way his thumb flicked down on the lighter and brought fire to her
cigarette. She began to wonder what the forests were like before the
trees were dying. She remembered her father had once described to
her the smiling broadness of leaves, jungles thick in the tangle of
rich soil.
One evening, she followed my father in circles through the forest, supposedly in search of the clearing that would take them to his
aunt's house. They wandered aimlessly into darkness, never finding
the clearing or the aunt she knew he never had.
"You're not from here," she said.
"I know."
"So tell me, what's your aunt's name?"
"Xuan."
"Spring?"
"Yes."
She laughed. I can't be here, she thought.
"My father will be looking for me—"
"I'll walk you home. It's not too late."
In the dark, she could feel his hand extending toward her, filling
the space between them. They had not touched once the entire evening
and now he stood offering his hand to her. She stared at him for a long
time. There was a small scar on his chin, curved like her fingernail. It
was too dark to see this. She realized she had memorized his face.

• • •

My first memory of my father's face is framed by the coiling barbed wire of a prison camp in South Vietnam. My mother's voice crosses through the wire. She is whispering his name and, in this utterance, caressing him. Over and over she calls him to her: "Anh Minh, Anh Minh." His name becomes a tree she presses her body against. The act of calling blows around them like a warm breeze, and when she utters her own name, it is the second half of a verse that began with his. She drops her name like a pebble is dropped into a well. She wants to be engulfed by him. "Anh Minh, em My. Anh Minh. Em, em My."

She is crossing through barbed wire the way some people step through open windows. She arrives warm, the slightest film of sweat on her bare arms. She says, "It's me, it's me." Shy and formal and breathless, my parents are always meeting for the first time. Savoring the sound of a name, marveling at the bone structure.

I trail behind them, the tip of their dragon's tail. I am suspended like a silk banner from the body of a kite. They flick me here and there. I twist and turn in the air, connected to them by this fabric that worms spin.

• • •

For a handful of pebbles and my father's sharp profile my mother left home and never returned. Imagine a handful of pebbles. The casual way he tossed them at her as she was walking home from school with her girlfriends. He did this because he liked her and wanted to let her know. Boys are dumb that way, my mother told me. A handful of pebbles, to be thrown in anger, in desperation, in joy. My father threw them in love. Ma says they touched her like warm kisses, these pebbles he had been holding in the sun. Warm kisses on the curve of her back, sliding down the crook of her arm, grazing her ankles and landing around her feet in the hot sand.

• • •

What my father told her could have been a story. There was no one in the South to confirm the details of his life. He said he came from a semi-aristocratic Northern family. Unlacing his boot, he pulled out his foot and told her to pay close attention to how his second toe was significantly longer than his other toes. "A sure sign of aristocracy," he claimed. His nose was high, he said, because his mother was French, one of the many mistresses his father kept. He found this out when he was sixteen. That year, he ran away from home and came south.

"There are thieves, gamblers, drunks I've met who remind me of people in my family. It's the way they're dreamers. My family's a garden full of dreamers lying on their backs, staring at the sky, drunk and chok-ing on their dreaming." He said this while leaning against a tree, his arms folded across his bare chest, his eyes staring at the ground, his shoulders golden.

She asked her mother, "What does it mean if your second toe is longer than your other toes?"

"It means . . . your mother will die before your father," her mother said.

"I heard somewhere it's a sign of aristocracy."

"Huh! What do we know about aristocracy?"

•   •   •

My father's toes fascinated my mother. When she looked at his bare feet she saw ten fishing boats, two groups of five. Within each group, the second boat ventured ahead, leading the others. She would climb a tree, stand gripping the branch with her own toes, and stare down at his. She directed him to stand in the mud. There, she imag-ined what she saw to be ten small boats surrounded by black water, a fleet of junks journeying in the dark.

She would lean back and enjoy this vision, never explaining to him what it was she saw. She left him to wonder about her senses as he stood, cigarette in hand, staring at her trembling ankles, not mov-ing until she told him to.

•   •   •

I was born in the alley behind my grandparents' house. At three in the morning my mother dragged herself out of the bed in the small house she and my father lived in after they married.

He was in prison, so, alone, she began to walk. She cut a crooked line on the beach. Moving in jerky steps, like a ball tossed on the waves, she seemed to be thrown along without direction. She walked to the schoolhouse, sat on the sand, and leaned against the first step. She felt grains of sand pressing against her back. Each grain was a minute pinprick that became increasingly painful to her. She felt as though her back would break out in a wash of blood. She thought, I am going to bleed to death. We are going to die.

In front of the schoolhouse lay a long metal tube. No one knew where it came from. It seemed always to have been there. Children hid in it, crawled through it, spoke to one another at either end of it, marched across it, sat on it, and confided secrets beside it. There had been so little to play with at the school recesses. This long metal tube became everything. A tarp was suspended over it, to shield it from the sun. The tube looked like a blackened log that sat in a room without walls. When the children sat in a line on the tube, their heads bobbing this way and that in conversation, it seemed they were sitting under a canopied raft.

The night I was born, my mother looked at this tube and imagined it to be the badly burnt arm of a dying giant whose body was buried in the sand. She could not decide if he had been buried in the sand and was trying to get out or if he had tried to bury himself in the sand but was unable to pull his arm under in time. In time for what? She had heard a story about a girl in a neighboring town who was killed during a napalm bombing. The bombing happened on an especially hot night when this girl had walked to the beach to cool her feet in the water. They found her floating on the sea. The phosphorus from the napalm made her body glow like a lantern. In her mind, my mother built a canopy for this girl. She started to cry, thinking of the buried giant, the floating girl, these bodies stopped in midstep, on their way somewhere.

· · ·

She began to walk toward the tube. She had a sudden urge to be inside it. The world felt dangerous to her and she was alone. At the mouth of the tube she bent down; her belly blocked the opening. She tried the other side, the other mouth. Again her belly stopped her. "But I remember," she muttered out loud, "as a girl I sometimes slept in here." This was what she wanted now, to sleep inside the tube.

· · ·

"Tall noses come from somewhere—"
"Not from here."
"Not tall noses."

· · ·

Eyes insinuate, moving from her nose to mine then back again. Mouths suck air in, form it into the darkest shade of contempt, then spit it at her feet as she walks by. I am riding on her hip. I am the new branch that makes the tree bend, but she walks with her head held high. She knows where she pulled me from. No blue eye.

· · ·

Ma says war is a bird with a broken wing flying over the countryside, trailing blood and burying crops in sorrow. If something grows in spite of this, it is both a curse and a miracle. When I was born, she cried when I cried, knowing I had breathed war in and she could never shake it out of me. Ma says war makes it dangerous to breathe, though she knows you die if you don't. She says she could have thrown me against the wall, breaking me until I coughed up this war which is killing us all. She could have stomped on it in the dark and danced on it like a madwoman dancing on gravestones. She could have ground it down to powder and spit on it, but didn't I know? War has no beginning and no end. It crosses oceans like a splintered boat filled with people singing a sad song.

• • •

Every morning Ahn wakes up in the house next to mine, a yellow duplex she and I call a townhouse because we found out from a real estate ad that a townhouse is a house that has an upstairs and a downstairs. My father calls Ahn the "chicken-egg girl." Each morning Ahn's mother loads a small pushcart with stacks of eggs and Ahn walks all over Linda Vista selling eggs. Her back yard is full of chickens and roosters. Sometimes you can see a rooster fly up and balance itself on the back gate, and it will crow and crow, off and on, all day long until dark comes.

• • •

We live in the country of California, the province of San Diego, the village of Linda Vista. We live in old Navy Housing, bungalows that were built in the 1940s and '50s. Since the 1980s these bungalows have housed Vietnamese, Cambodian, and Laotian refugees from the Vietnam War. When we moved in, we had to sign a form promising not to push fish bones down the garbage disposal.

We live in a yellow row house on Westinghouse Street. Our house is one story, made of wood and plaster. We are connected to six two-story houses and another one-story house at the other end. Across from our row of houses, separated by a field of brown dirt, sits another row of yellow houses, same as ours and facing us like a sad twin. Linda Vista is full of houses like ours, painted in peeling shades of olive green, baby blue, and sunbaked yellow.

There's new Navy Housing on Linda Vista Road, the long street that takes you out of here. We see the people there watering their lawns, the children riding pink tricycles up and down the cul-de-sacs. We see them in Victory Supermarket, buying groceries with cash. In Kelley Park they have picnics and shoot each other with water guns. At school their kids are Most Popular, Most Beautiful, Most Likely to Succeed. Though there are more Vietnamese, Cambodian, and Laotian kids at the school, we are not Most of anything in the yearbook. They call us Yang because one year a bunch of Laotian kids with the last name Yang came to our school. The Navy Housing kids started calling all the refugee kids Yang.

Yang. Yang. Yang.

• • •

Ma says living next to Ahn's family reminds her of Vietnam because the blue tarp suspended above Ahn's back yard is the bright blue of the South China Sea. Ma says isn't it funny how sky and sea follow you from place to place as if they too were traveling and not just the boat that travels across or between them. Ma says even Ahn reminds her of Vietnam, the way she sets out for market each morning.

Ba becomes a gardener. Overnight. He buys a truck full of equipment and a box of business cards from Uncle Twelve, who is moving to Texas to become a fisherman. The business cards read "Tom's Professional Gardening Service" and have a small, green embossed picture of a man pushing a lawn mower. The man's back is to the viewer, so no one who doesn't already know can tell it's not Ba. He says I can be his secretary because I speak the best English. If you call us on the business phone, you will hear me say: "Hello, you have reached Tom's Professional Gardening Service. We are not here right now, but if you leave us a message, we will get back to you as soon as possible. Thank you."

• • •

It is hot and dusty where we live. Some people think it's dirty, but they don't know much about us. They haven't seen our gardens full of lemongrass, mint, cilantro, and basil. They've only seen the pigeons pecking at day-old rice and the skinny cats and dogs sitting in the skinny shade of skinny trees as they drive by. Have they seen the berries we pick which turn our lips and fingertips red? How about the small staircase Ba built from our bedroom window to the back yard so I would have a short cut to the clothesline? How about the Great Wall of China which snakes like a river from the top of the steep Crandall Street hill to the slightly curving bottom? Who has seen this?

• • •

It was so different at the Green Apartment. We had to close the gate behind us every time we came in. It clanged heavily, and I imagined a host of eyes, upstairs and downstairs, staring at me from behind slightly parted curtains. There were four palm trees planted at the four far corners of the courtyard and a central staircase that was narrow at the top and fanned out at the bottom. The steps were covered in fake grass, like the set of an old Hollywood movie, the kind that stars an aging beauty who wakes up to find something is terribly wrong.

• • •

We moved out of the Green Apartment after we turned on the TV one night and heard that our manager and his brother had hacked a woman to pieces and dumped her body into the Pacific Ocean in ten-gallon garbage bags that washed onto the shore. Ma said she didn't want to live in a place haunted by a murdered lady. So we moved to Linda Vista, where she said there were a lot of Vietnamese people like us, people whose only sin was a little bit of gambling and sucking on fish bones and laughing hard and arguing loudly.

• • •

Ma shaved all her hair off in Linda Vista because she got mad at Ba for gambling her money away and getting drunk every week watching *Monday Night Football*. Ba gave her a blue baseball cap to wear until her hair grew back, and she wore it backward, like a real bad-ass.

After that, some people in Linda Vista said that Ma was crazy and Ba was crazy for staying with her. But what do some people know?

• • •

When the photograph came, Ma and Ba got into a fight. Ba threw the fish tank out the front door and Ma broke all the dishes. They said they never should've been together.

Ma's sister had sent her the photograph from Vietnam. It came in a stiff envelope. There was nothing inside but the photograph, as if anything more would be pointless. Ma started to cry. "Child," she sobbed, over and over again. She wasn't talking about me. She was talking about herself.

Ba said, "Don't cry. Your parents have forgiven you."

Ma kept crying anyway and told him not to touch her with his gangster hands. Ba clenched his hands into tight fists and punched the walls.

"What hands?! What hands?!" he yelled. "Let me see the gangster! Let me see his hands!" I see his hands punch hands punch hands punch blood.

• • •

Ma is in the kitchen. She has torn the screen off the window. She is punctuating the pavement with dishes, plates, cups, rice bowls. She sends them out like birds gliding through the sky with nowhere in particular to go. Until they crash. Then she exhales "'Huh!'" in satisfaction.

I am in the hallway gulping air. I breathe in the breaking and the bleeding. When Ba plunges his hands into the fish tank, I detect the subtle tint of blood in water. When he throws the fish tank out the front door, yelling, "Let me see the gangster!" I am drinking up spilled water and swallowing whole the beautiful colored tropical fish before they hit the ground, caking themselves in brown dirt until just the whites of their eyes remain, blinking at the sun.

All the hands are in my throat, cutting themselves on broken dishes, and the fish swim in circles; they can't see for all the blood.

Ba jumps in his truck and drives away.

When I grow up I am going to be the gangster we are all looking for.

• • •

The neighborhood kids are standing outside our house, staring in through the windows and the open door. Even Ahn, our chicken-egg seller. I'm sure their gossiping mothers sent them to spy on us. I run out front and dance like a crazy lady, dance like a fish, wiggle my head and throw my body so everything eyes nose tongue comes undone. At first they laugh but then they stop, not knowing what to think. Then I stop and stare each one of them down.

"What're you looking at?" I ask.

"Lookin' at you," one boy says, half giggling.

"Well," I say, with my hand on my hip and my head cocked to one side, "I'm looking at you too," and I give him my evil one-eye look, focusing all my energy into one eye. I stare at him hard like my eye is a bullet and he can be dead.

I turn my back on them and walk into the house.

• • •

I find Ma sitting in the windowsill. The curve of her back is inside the bedroom while the rest of her body is outside, on the first step Ba built going from the bedroom to the garden. Without turning to look at me, she says, "Let me lift you into the attic."

"Why?"

"We have to move your grandparents in."

I don't really know what she is talking about, but I say O.K. anyway.

• • •

We have never needed the attic for anything. In fact, we have never gone up there. When we moved my grandparents in, Ma simply lifted me up and I pushed the attic door open with one hand, while with the other I slipped in the stiff envelope containing the photograph of my grandparents. I pushed it the length of my arm and down to my fingertips. I pushed it so far it was beyond reach, but Ma said it was enough, they had come to live with us, and sometimes you don't need to see or touch people to know they're there.

Ba came home drunk that night and asked to borrow my blanket. I heard him climbing the tree in the back yard. It took him a long time. He kept missing the wooden blocks that run up and down the tree like a ladder. Ba put them in when he built the steps going from the bedroom window into the garden. If you stand on the very top block, your whole body is hidden by tree branches. Ba put those blocks in for me, so I could win at hide-and-go-seek.

When Ba finally made it onto the roof, he lay down over my room and I could hear him rolling across my ceiling. Rolling and crying. I was scared he would roll off the edge and kill himself, so I went to wake Ma.

She was already awake. She said it would be a good thing if he rolled off. But later I heard someone climb the tree, and all night two bodies rolled across my ceiling. Slowly and firmly they pressed against my sleep, the Catholic schoolgirl and the Buddhist gangster, two dogs chasing each other's tails. They have been running like this for so long, they have become one dog one tail.

• • •

Without any hair and looking like a man, my mother is still my mother, though sometimes I can't see her even when I look and look and look so long all the colors of the world begin to swim and bob around me. Her hands always bring me up, her big peasant hands with the flat, wide nails, wide like her nose and just as expressive. I will know her by her hands and her walk which is at once slow and urgent, the walk of a woman going to the market with her goods securely bound to her side. Even walking empty-handed, my mother suggests invisible bundles whose contents no one but she can unravel. And if I never see her again, I will know my mother by the smell of sea salt and the prints of my own bare feet crossing sand, running to and away from, to and away from, family.

• • •

When the eviction notice came, we didn't believe it so we threw it away. It said we had a month to get out. The houses on our block had a new owner who wanted to tear everything down and build better housing for the community. It said we were priority tenants for the new complex, but we couldn't afford to pay the new rent so it didn't matter. The notice also said that if we didn't get out in time, all our possessions would be confiscated in accordance with some section of a law book or manual we were supposed to have known about but had never seen. We couldn't believe the eviction notice so we threw it away.

• • •

The fence is tall, silver, and see-through. Chainlink, it rattles when you shake it and wobbles when you lean against it. It circles the block like a bad dream. It is not funny like a line of laundry whose flying shirts and empty pants suggest human birds and vanishing acts. This fence presses sharply against your brain. We three stand still as posts. Looking at it, then at each other—this side and that—out of the corners of our eyes. What are we thinking?

At night we come back with three uncles. Ba cuts a hole in the fence and we step through. Quiet, we break into our own house through the back window. Quiet, we steal back everything that is ours. We fill ten-gallon garbage bags with clothes, pots and pans, flip-flops, the porcelain figure of Mary, and our wooden Buddha.

• • •

In the arc of four flashlights we find our favorite hairbrushes behind bedposts. When we are done, we are clambering and breathless. We can hear police cars coming to get us, though it's quiet.

We tumble out the window like people tumbling across continents. We are time traveling, weighed down by heavy furniture and bags of precious junk. We find ourselves leaning against Ba's yellow truck. Ma calls his name, her voice reaching like a hand feeling for a tree trunk in darkness.

In the car, Ma starts to cry. "What about the sea?" she asks. "What about the garden?" Ba says we can come back in the morning and dig up the stalks of lemongrass and fold the sea into a blue square. Ma is sobbing. She is beating the dashboard with her fists. "I want to know," she says, "I want to know, I want to know . . . who is doing this to us?" Hiccupping, she says, "I want to know why, why there's always a fence. Why there's always someone on the outside wanting someone . . . something on the inside and between them . . . this . . . sharp fence. Why are we always leaving like this?"

Everyone is quiet when Ma screams.

"Take me back!" she says. "I can't go with you. I've forgotten my mother and father. I can't believe . . . Anh Minh, we've left them to die. Take me back."

Ma wants Ba to stop the car, but Ba doesn't know why. The three uncles, sitting in a line in the back of the truck, think Ma is crazy. They yell in through the window, "My, are you going to walk back to Vietnam?"

"Yeah, are you going to walk home to your parents' house?"

In the silence another laughs.

Ba puts his foot on the gas pedal. Our car jerks forward, then plunges down the Crandall Street hill. Ma says, "I need air, water . . . " I roll the window down. She puts her head in her hands. She keeps crying, "Child." Outside, I see the Great Wall of China. In the glare of the streetlamps, it is just a long strip of cardboard.

• • •

In the morning, the world is flat. Westinghouse Street is lying down like a jagged brushstroke of sunburnt yellow. There is a big sign inside the fence that reads

COMING SOON:
CONDOMINIUMS   TOWNHOUSES   FAMILY HOMES

Beside these words is a watercolor drawing of a large, pink complex.

• • •

We stand on the edge of the chainlink fence, sniffing the air for the scent of lemongrass, scanning this flat world for our blue sea. A wrecking ball dances madly through our house. Everything has burst wide open and sunk down low. Then I hear her calling them. She is whispering, "Ma/Ba, Ma/Ba." The whole world is two butterfly wings rubbing against my ear.

Listen . . . they are sitting in the attic, sitting like royalty. Shining in the dark, buried by a wrecking ball. Paper fragments floating across the surface of the sea.

Not a trace of blood anywhere except here, in my throat, where I am telling you all this.

WRITING ABOUT THE READING

4. Why did the writer's grandparents object to the marriage of her mother and father?

5. Why does the writer use the term "gangster" to describe her father?

6. Why does the writer describe herself as "the tip of their dragon's tail"?

7. What does the writer suggest about herself when she writes that "my eye is a bullet"?

8. How and why was the writer's family so influenced by the Vietnam War?

9. Why does the writer's family have to break into the house and steal their possessions?

10. What do they leave behind when the family breaks into the house and why is the mother so upset about this?

11. The writer asks why there is always a fence separating people. What are some of the examples of "fences" in this reading and why are these fences erected?

12. Explain what the writer means when she says, "War has no beginning and no end. It crosses oceans like a splintered boat filled with people singing a sad song."

WRITING FROM YOUR OWN EXPERIENCE

Note: In these assignments, write about your own experience or use that of someone you know, read about, or saw in a film/TV show.

13. Choose someone whose life has been disrupted in some way by a violent experience, or a war, or by the consequences of war. Explain how this person's life was disrupted and why the person was able to "pick up the pieces" after this experience.

14. Choose a book, TV show, or movie about war. Explain whether you think that this work gives a glamorous or realistic picture of war.

15. The writer states that there is always a fence separating people. Choose a "fence," something that you think separates people today. How and why does this fence keep people apart?

WRITING ABOUT RESEARCH

16. How and why did the United States become involved in the Vietnam War?

17. How and why did the war in Southeast Asia stimulate the immigration of people from countries such as Cambodia, Laos, Vietnam, or Thailand?

18. Choose an Asian American who has achieved success in a field such as sports, art, music, movies, theater, or literature. Why was this person successful? Some people to consider include:

   (a) Miran Ahn (artist)
   (b) Michael Chang (tennis star)
   (c) Hisako Hibi (artist)
   (d) David Henry Kwang (playwright)
   (e) Bruce Lee (martial arts expert)
   (f) Maya Lin (architect)
   (g) Hung Liu (artist)
   (h) Yong Soon Min (artist)
   (i) Norine Nishimura (artist)
   (j) M. Pei (architect)
   (k) Hanh Thi Pham (artist)
   (l) Vera Wang (designer)
   (m) Kristy Yamaguchi (Olympic figure skater)
   (n) Lawrence Yep (writer)

COMPARING SELECTIONS: ASIAN AMERICAN WRITERS

1. Compare the Americanization process of the fathers discussed in the readings by **David Mura** and **Eric Liu**. Why would you agree (or disagree) that these two fathers are assimilated into U.S. society?

2. Contrast the marriages shown in the readings by **Chang-rae Lee** and **Le Thi Diem Thuy**. Which is the more traditional, stable marriage and why is this so?

3. Compare the relationship between parent and child in the readings by **Chang-rae Lee** and **Eric Liu**. What accounts for the strong bond between parent and child in each essay?

4. Compare the difficulties of the immigrant experience in the readings by **Fae Myenne Ng** and **Le Thi Diem Thuy**. What are some of the similarities and differences of the immigration experience past and present?

5. Compare the effects of prejudice toward Asian Americans on the families of **David Mura** and **Helen Zia**. How and why did each family suffer discrimination because of military and political conflicts?

6. The question "Who Am I?" is asked by many writers in this anthology. What are some of the similarities and differences in the treatment of this question in the readings by **David Mura** and **Shawn Wong**?

7. Compare the family pressures on the writer to achieve success in the readings by **Chang-rae Lee** and **Eric Liu**. How and why did the families encourage their sons' achievement?

8. Compare and contrast the way each writer responds to stereotypes in the readings by **Frank Chin** and **Shawn Wong**. Explain which method you prefer and why you think this is the better way to handle discrimination.

9. Consider the assimilation of **Eric Liu's** father in light of the recommendations in **Bharati Mukherjee's** essay. Would Mukherjee consider him to be assimilated?

10. Many immigrants, especially those who arrive in the United States as adults, have difficulty in mastering English. Compare the difficulties in learning English discussed in the selections by **Chang-rae Lee** and **Amy Tan**. How and why did their parent's use of English influence the writers?

11. Contrast the attitude toward the American Dream shown in the essays by **Bharati Mukherjee** and **Fae Myenne Ng**. Why do you think that Mukherjee has a more positive attitude toward the immigration experience than does Ng?

SELECTED BIBLIOGRAPHY—ASIAN AMERICAN WRITERS

Bloom, Harold, ed. *Asian-American Writers.* Philadelphia: Chelsea House Publishers, 1999.

Brown, Wesley, and Amy Ling, eds. *Visions of America: Personal Narratives from the Promised Land.* New York: Persea Books, 1993.

Brownstone, David M. *The Chinese-American Heritage. America's Ethnic Heritage Series.* New York: Facts on File, 1988.

Chen, Da. *Colors of the Mountain.* New York: Random House, 2000.

Chin, Frank. *Bulletproof Buddhists and Other Essays.* Honolulu: Univ. of Hawaii Press, 1998.

———. *The Chickencoop China and The Year of the Dragon.* Seattle: Univ. of Washington Press, 1981.

———. *Donald Duk.* St. Paul, MN: Coffee House Press, 1991.

———. *Gunga Din Highway.* St. Paul, MN: Coffee House Press, 1994.

Chin, Frank, Jeffery Paul Chan, Lawson Fusao Inada, and Shawn Hsu Wong, eds. *Aiiieeeee!: An Anthology of Asian-American Writers.* Washington: Howard Univ. Press, 1974.

Fong, Timothy, and Larry Shinagawa. *Asian Americans: Experiences and Perspectives.* Upper Saddle River, NJ: Prentice Hall, 2000.

Hong, Maria, ed. *Growing Up Asian American: An Anthology.* New York: William Morrow and Co., Inc., 1993.

Hsu, Francis L.K. *Americans and Chinese: Passages to Differences.* Honolulu: Univ. of Hawaii Press, 1981.

———. *Americans and Chinese: Two Ways of Life.* New York: H. Schuman, 1953.

———. *The Challenge of the American Dream: The Chinese in the United States.* Belmont, CA: Wadsworth Publishing, 1971.

———. *Under the Ancestors' Shadow.* Garden City, NY: Anchor Books, 1967. Reprinted Stanford Univ. Press, 1971.

Hutner, Gordon, ed. *Immigrant Voices: Twenty-four Narratives on Becoming an American.* New York: Signet Classic, 1999.

Jen, Gish. *Typical American.* Boston: Houghton Mifflin, 1991.

Kim, Elaine H. *Asian American Literature: An Introduction to the Writings and Their Social Context.* Philadelphia: Temple Univ. Press, 1982.

Kingston, Maxine Hong. *The Woman Warrior.* New York: Vintage Books, 1977.

———. *China Men.* New York: Ballantine Books, 1981.

Kornblum, William. *Sociology in a Changing World.* 4th ed. Fort Worth: Harcourt Brace, 1997.

Lee, Chang-rae. *A Gesture Life.* New York: Riverhead, 1999.

———. *Native Speaker.* New York: Putnam, 1995.

Lim, Shirley Geok-lin. *Among the White Moon Faces: An Asian-American Memoir of Homelands.* New York: Feminist Press at CUNY, 1996.

———, ed. *Asian American Literature: An Anthology.* Lincolnwood, IL: NTC/Contemporary Publishing Group, 2000.

Lim, Shirley Geok-lin, Mayumi Tsutakawa, and Margarita Donnelly, eds. *The Forbidden Stitch: An Asian American Women's Anthology.* Corvallis, OR: Calyx Books, 1989.

Ling, Amy. *Between Worlds: Women Writers of Chinese Ancestry.* New York: Pergamon Press, 1990.

Liu, Eric. *The Accidental Asian: Notes of a Native Speaker.* New York: Random House, 1998.

———, ed. *Next: Young American Writers on the New Generation.* New York: Norton, 1994.

Making Waves: An Anthology of Writings by and about Asian American Women. Boston: Beacon Press, 1989.

Marger, Martin N. *Race and Ethnic Relations: American and Global Perspectives.* Belmont, CA: Wadsworth Pub. Co., 1997

Min, Anchee. *Becoming Madame Mao.* Boston: Houghton Mifflin, 2000.

———. *Red Azalea.* New York: Pantheon Books, 1994.

Mukherjee, Bharati. *Jasmine.* New York: Fawcett Crest, 1989.

———. *The Middleman and Other Stories.* New York: Grove Press, 1988.

Mura, David. *Turning Japanese: Memoirs of a Sansei.* Anchor Books/Doubleday, 1991.

———. *Where the Body Meets Memory.* New York: Anchor Books/Doubleday, 1996.

Ng, Fae Myenne. *Bone.* New York: Hyperion, 1993.

Ng, Franklin, ed. *The Asian American Encyclopedia.* New York: Marshall Cavendish, 1995.

O'Hearn, Claudine Chiawei. *Half and Half. Writers on Growing Up Biracial and Bicultural.* New York: Pantheon, 1998.

Olson, James S. *The Ethnic Dimension in American History.* 2nd ed. New York: St. Martin's Press, 1994.

Rothenberg, Paula S. *Race, Class, and Gender in the United States.* New York: St. Martin's Press, 1998.

Saito, Leland. *Race and Politics: Asian Americans, Latinos, and Whites in a Los Angeles Suburb.* Urbana: Univ. of Illinois Press, 1998.

Scarborough, Jack. *The Origins of Cultural Differences and Their Impact on Management.* Westport, CT: Quorum Books, 1998.

Spence, Jonathan D. *The Chan's Great Continent: China in Western Minds.* New York: Norton, 1998.

Sugimoto, Etsu Inagaki. *A Daughter of the Samurai.* Garden City, NY: Doubleday, 1947.

Takaki, Ronald T. *A Different Mirror: A History of Multicultural America.* Boston: Little, Brown, 1993.

———. *Double Victory: A Multicultural History of America in World War II.* Boston: Little, Brown, 2000.

———. *Strangers at the Gates Again: Asian American Immigration after 1965.* New York: Chelsea House, 1995.

———. *Strangers from a Different Shore: A History of Asian Americans.* Boston: Little, Brown, 1993.

———, ed. *From Different Shores: Perspectives on Race and Ethnicity in America.* New York: Oxford Univ. Press, 1994.

———. *From Exiles to Immigrants: The Refugees from Southeast Asia.* New York: Chelsea House, 1995

Tan, Amy. *The Hundred Secret Senses.* New York: Putnam, 1995.

———. *The Joy Luck Club.* New York: Putnam, 1989.

———. *The Kitchen God's Wife.* New York: Putnam, 1991.

Wagner-Martin, Linda, and Cathy N. Davidson. *The Oxford Book of Women's Writing in the United States.* New York: Oxford Univ. Press, 1995.

Wong, Shawn. *American Knees.* New York: Simon & Schuster, 1995.

———. *Homebase: A Novel.* New York: Reed Books, 1979.

———, ed. *Asian American Literature: A Brief Introduction and Anthology.* New York: HarperCollins, 1996.

Wong, Shawn, Ishmael Reed, and Kathryn Trueblood, eds. *The Before Columbus Foundation Fiction Anthology: Selections from the American Book Awards, 1980–1990.* New York: Norton, 1992.

Wu, William. *The Yellow Peril: Chinese Americans in American Fiction 1850–1940.* Hamden, CT: Archon, 1982.

Yang, Jeff et al. *Eastern Standard Time: A Guide to Asian Influence on American Culture from Astro Boy to Zen Buddhism.* Boston: Houghton Mifflin, 1997.

Zia, Helen. *Asian American Dreams: The Emergence of an American People.* New York: Farrar, Straus and Giroux, 2000.

SELECTED INTERNET RESOURCES—ASIAN AMERICAN WRITERS

Note: Unless otherwise noted, all URL addresses listed begin with http://www.

Asian American Association.

Asian American Net.

Asian American Resources (Asian American Policy Review, Harvard University). <http://ksgwww.harvard.edu/~aapr/resources.htm>

Asian American Studies (California State University, Northridge). <csun.edu/~hfaas002/aas.html>

Asian American Studies (University of California, Davis). <cougar.ucdavis.edu/asa/>

Asian American Studies Center (UCLA). <sscnet.ucla.edu/aasc/content.html>

AsianAvenue. <AsianAvenue.com>

Asian Community Online Network. <igc.apc.org/acon/>

Asian Studies Resources. <http://sunsite.unc.edu/ucis/Asian.html>

AsianWeek Magazine. <asianweek.com>

Chinatown Resource Guide. <kqed.org/tv/productions/hood/chinatown/resourceguide/>

Ethnic Studies at the University of Southern California. <usc.edu/isd/archives/ethnicstudies/index.html>

National Clearinghouse for U.S.-Japan Studies. <lux.ucs.indiana.edu/~japan/>

National Japanese American Historical Society.

U of Texas Asian Studies Network Information Center. <http://asnic.utexas.edu/asnic/index.html>

U.S. Census Bureau. <census.gov>

Part 4

Native American Writers

INTRODUCTION

Native Americans, unlike members of other minorities, are not immigrants, but the descendants of conquered peoples, the original inhabitants of lands that later became the United States. The "Indians" also were not one uniform ethnic group, although European Americans often regarded them as such. Instead, Native Americans were members of approximately 600 separate groups who spoke 200 different languages, encompassed a variety of cultures, and varied in their use of technology and agricultural practices. This indigenous population was nearly totally eradicated, either through military defeat, the devastation of disease, or destruction of the native culture. In her essay "America's Oldest Racism," **Elizabeth Cook-Lynn** decries the "theft" of the lands and the "deliberate murder" of the indigenous peoples.

By the end of the nineteenth century, after the Native American population had been almost totally eradicated, the survivors were forced to assimilate to the dominant culture. Those who resisted assimilation were relocated to reservations where the federal government decided what was best for them. Vacillating back-and-forth in its handling of Native Americans, the federal government sometimes interacted with the individual person; at other times, the government dealt with the entire tribe as one nation. For many years, the government followed a "termination" policy designed to integrate Native Americans into the white culture and to destroy tribal affiliations and cultures. However, since the 1970s, the federal government has supported a more enlightened policy of "self-determination" and has allowed tribes to negotiate directly with federal agencies. In his essay, **Vine Deloria, Jr.**, discusses the present conditions of life for those Native Americans living on the reservation.

In the past, facing a hostile dominant culture, many Native Americans, especially those of mixed ancestry, denied any "Indian" heritage. **Joseph Bruchac's** grandfather was one who denied his heritage. However, by the beginning of the twenty-first century, in a culture more sympathetic to Native Americans, there was a growing tendency for Americans to research their family tree, to locate an ancestor, and to proclaim their Native American ancestry and culture. Today, many Native American writers are of mixed ancestry. The selections from several authors, including **Joseph Bruchac, Louis Owens, N. Scott Momaday, Inez Petersen**, and **Gerald Vizenor** show these writers trying to preserve their Native American heritage, language, and traditions while living in the dominant society.

Unlike Europeans (who often have a conqueror's attitude toward nature), Native Americans traditionally have great respect and reverence for what writer **Simon Ortiz** refers to as the "holy earth." Therefore, a strong "sense of place," of the influence of the environment on human life, is a common theme in many of these readings. For example, **Linda Hogan** emphasizes the connection she feels to all of nature while participating in a traditional ritual.

Native Americans also emphasize language and storytelling as a way to connect to their traditions. Two writers who deal with the importance of language are **Simon J. Ortiz** and **Leslie Marmon Silko**. In addition, many other writers, such as **Joseph Bruchac** and **Scott Momaday**, are respected as "storytellers" who have preserved the oral traditions and myths of their people.

Although from different tribes, many Native Americans today have joined together in a common cause, a "Pan-Native American" movement. They often protest negative stereotypes (the drunken, savage Native American) and the use of racist terms (such as "Redskins" or "Braves"). Native American writers emphasize the dignity of their identity and try to bring into sharper focus the experience they face in the two cultures of the dominant society and the Native American tradition. Two of the writers included here, **Vine Deloria** and **Simon J. Ortiz**, have been politically active in these causes.

As Native Americans begin to make economic gains, they often seek to reclaim some of their land or to receive compensation for its loss. Because tribes are not subject to federal taxes, Native Americans have been able to establish successful businesses, including legalized gambling, and use the profits to buy back their land. Other tribes, after going to court over the loss of their lands, have been awarded large judgments. Finally, some Native Americans have begun to share in the profits of the valuable mineral resources discovered on reservation lands formerly thought to be worthless.

WHO WERE THE INDIGENOUS PEOPLES?

At the time the Europeans came to North America, the Native Americans lived in seven areas, each one containing several different tribes. The great variety of cultures in the United States can be seen by the following partial listing.

The Northeastern Woodlands area encompassed the land between the Mississippi and the Atlantic, north of the Carolinas and the Ohio River valley. Here, the Native Americans lived in wigwams or bark houses in agricultural villages protected by stockades. Tribes included: **Chippewas, Iroquois, Massachusetts, Mohawks, and Mohegans.**

The Southeastern tribes lived between the Mississippi and the Atlantic Ocean, south of the Ohio River Valley. These peoples practiced agriculture and lived in mud-plaster homes in towns. Tribes included: **Calusas, Cherokees, Creeks, and Seminoles.**

The Great Plains groups lived in an area covering present-day Montana, the Dakotas, western Kansas, and Oklahoma. Using horses descended from those originally brought to the Americas by the Spaniards, these peoples were nomadic hunters of buffalo. Tribes included: **Comanches, Crows, Dakotas, and Sioux.**

The Great Basin groups lived in the area of present-day Utah, Nevada, and eastern California. Because of the lack of water, it was difficult to grow crops, and these peoples subsisted on small game, berries, seeds, and insects. Tribes included: **Shoshones, Paiutes, and Utes.**

The Northern Plateau tribes lived in present-day western Montana, Idaho, and eastern Washington. They fished for salmon, hunted for small game, and gathered berries and roots. They included: **Flatheads, Nez Perces, and Spokanes.**

The Southwestern Desert included Arizona, Colorado, and New Mexico. One group of tribes consisted of nomadic hunters who lived in tepees. They included **Apaches and Navajos.** The other group lived in towns of adobe buildings and practiced agriculture. They included: **Hopi, Pueblo, and Zuni** tribes.

The Pacific Coast group lived in California, Oregon, and Washington. In the south, they lived in nomadic villages and subsisted on roots and berries. They included: **Chumosh, Miwoks, and Salinas.** In the northern area, they had abundant fish and game. They included: **Chinooks and Tolowas**.

IMPORTANT MILESTONES

1830	*The Native American Removal Act:* This act called for relocation of all Native Americans to lands west of the Mississippi River.
1887	*Dawes Act/General Allotment Act:* Embarking on a policy of forced assimilation, the federal government ceased to treat each tribe as a foreign nation. Instead the federal government broke up the tribes and dealt with individual Native Americans, who were given citizenship and made wards of the government. As part of this process, the federal government allotted a portion of tribal lands to individual Native Americans. The result was the loss of reservation lands.
1889	The government allowed homesteaders in Oklahoma.
1898	*Curtis Act:* Members of the Five Civilized Tribes were made subject to allotment.
1902	*Dead Indian Land Act:* This act permitted Native Americans to sell to whites land that they had inherited from dead relatives.
1906	*Burke Act:* This act authorized Native Americans to sell their allotted lands. As a result, whites bought 27 million acres from Native Americans.
1924	*Pueblo Lands Board Act:* A government commission was empowered to mediate a dispute between whites and Native Americans in New Mexico.
1928	**Meriam Report:** This report detailed the appalling conditions of life on the reservations and showed how Native Americans had been tricked out of their allotted lands.
1934	*Indian Reorganization Act:* Reversing its stand on tribal organization, the federal government encouraged Native Americans to form self-governing tribal groups. In addition, the government reduced efforts to force Native Americans to assimilate.

1946	**Indian Claims Commission:** Native Americans were allowed to file claims against the federal government for lands lost through fraudulent treaties.
1953–1956	**"Termination" policy:** Again trying to deal with Native Americans on an individual rather than a tribal basis, the federal government attempted to get rid of the reservation system and to eliminate recognition of the tribe.
1960s	**American Indian Movement (AIM):** Impacted by the Civil Rights Movement, Native Americans began to organize. Looking beyond tribal affiliation, they came to recognize the common plight of all Native Americans and to regain lands that they felt were theirs.
1972	***Native American Education Act*** and ***The Education Amendments Act of 1978:*** Supporting efforts for "self-determination," the federal government allowed Native Americans to decide how their children should be educated.
1974	***Native American Self-Determination and Education Assistance Act:*** The federal government permitted tribes to negotiate directly with federal agencies (such as the Bureau of Native American Affairs). Tribal governments could restructure or reject federal programs to make sure that these programs met tribal needs.

Selection 1

America's Oldest Racism: The Roots of Inequality

ELIZABETH COOK-LYNN

Elizabeth Cook-Lynn *(1930–), a member of the Crow Creek Sioux tribe, received a B.A. (1952) and M.A. (1972) degrees from South Dakota State College. An educator, poet, and writer, Cook-Lynn is professor emerita of English and Native American studies at Eastern Washington University. She also is a trustee of the Association for American Indian Research and managing editor of* Wicazo Sa Review: A Journal of Native American Studies.

In the 1960s, Cook-Lynn was active in what came to be known as the Native American Literary Renaissance. Before this time, literary critics generally ignored Native American writers whose writing often was classified as anthropology rather than literature. However, after the award of the 1969 Pulitzer Prize to N. Scott Momaday, other Native American writers began to be recognized. Cook-Lynn participated in the formation of this Native American literary community and in 1977 published her book Then Badger Said This.

When Native Americans began to be militant in the 1960s, they combined political activism with a concern for preservation of their traditions, their spirituality, and the environment. Dedicated to her people's cause, Cook-Lynn views her writing as an act of survival, a weapon against the dominant society that tries to make the Native American population invisible.

In 1996, Cook-Lynn published a collection of essays Why I Can't Read Wallace Stegner and Other Essays *in which she used Wallace Stegner as representative of the many writers who have presented a false picture of Native Americans. In the following persuasive essay, taken from this collection, Cook-Lynn refutes a contemporary academic writer who justifies the European take-over of the Native American lands and a policy of "rational discrimination." Calling the historical treatment of Native Americans "colonial genocide," Cook-Lynn argues that Native Americans today continue to have the right to self-determination and sovereignty.*

PREPARING TO READ

1. Using information from the notes on the author and the title of the work, what do you predict will be the subject of this essay and the author's attitude toward this topic?
2. Explain what you think that the terms "colonial" and "genocide" mean and why they are appropriate (or not appropriate) to use in discussing the treatment of Native Americans by European Americans.
3. Compare what you know of the treatment of Native Americans with that of African Americans (or another minority group) and explain why there are similarities and differences.

AMERICA'S OLDEST RACISM:
THE ROOTS OF INEQUALITY

In spite of many positive experiences in the academic world, America's oldest racism remains as troubling as ever.

A young East Indian-American scholar by the name of Dinesh D'Souza who is now a John M. Olin Scholar at the American Enterprise Institute in Washington, D.C., has called up the memory of an awful history by giving contemporary voice to the idea of "prudent/rational discrimination" as a virtuous practice for a democracy like America. It is for some a good idea, the last word; for others, the new racism. For Indians the argument is an old idea that they know well, an idea which has been defended in America since the landing of Columbus.

Though I admit to being a little confused concerning D'Souza's particular stance on American Indians (they do not take a central position in any of his arguments), it is my understanding that he believes Europeans were quite justified in thinking themselves superior to Indians and implementing a firm policy to take over their lands. The right of one group to dominate another, he suggests, was not the result of biological racism but the result of "ethnocentric theories of cultural difference," and this reality, he says, makes the "progress" toward civilization which has characterized Western U.S. history a good and inevitable thing. His debatable point that the concept of race in the modern biological sense did not exist when the enslavement of Africans originally occurred in the fifteenth and sixteenth centuries has little connection to what happened to Indians during the nineteenth and twentieth centuries when two-thirds of their treaty-protected lands were stolen by America, nor does it connect with the continued colonial power exercised by the United States over Indian populations. Thus, if one looks at D'Souza's argument and the results of five hundred years of European occupation of native lands on this continent from the point of view of decimated native populations reduced to beggary in the country they occupied for thousands of years, the distinction hardly matters.

In suggesting that affirmative action as a national policy and civil rights activism as a social agenda are no longer necessary, D'Souza says that biological racism, which really raised its ugly head ideologically when Europeans first encountered non-Western peoples, is declining as a social force in America and that discrimination is a good thing if it is based on evidence rather than ideology. He wonders if we should define racism as a "doctrine of *intrinsic* superiority and inferiority" between groups. Before he convinces anyone of what that would mean in terms of actual behavior, he goes on to argue that, in the 1990s and beyond, there are circumstances in which discrimination, at least in the black/white context, makes sense and, furthermore, that prejudice may not be the result of ignorant predisposition (i.e., stereotype), as had once been thought; but rather, it may be one citizen's prudent judgment of another. It is a muddled argument, to be sure. Nevertheless, for the better part of the current decade, ever since D'Souza finished graduate studies at America's elitist institutions and began writing about "illiberal education," he has been touted by editors, scholars, and politicians alike as a new voice, a meritorious scholar of contemporary conservative thinking. The *Free Press* publishes his books; the *Atlantic Monthly* publishes his essays.

For the indigenous populations of this continent, from the Maya to the Cree, there is nothing new about D'Souza's thinking, nor does he bring substantive new evidence to his argument concerning the history and the consequences of racism in America. His argument is that affirmative action and the liberal civil rights programs have failed as social policy because their underlying ideas have not been based on the "reality of traits" attributed to specific racial groups. African Americans, he points out, do have a substantially higher crime rate than whites; therefore, for whites to fear them is not racist—just practical. Women do get pregnant and leave their jobs; therefore, it is sensible for employers to discriminate in favor of men in hiring practices. It is economically justified. He says that affirmative action treats competent individuals as incompetent and thus should be scrapped as social policy. He uses the prejudices of one group toward another to bolster his notion that it is not just whites who notice and discriminate. For example, he says that "49 percent of blacks and 68 percent of Asians say that Hispanics tend to have bigger families than they can support." This means, one supposes, that if Hispanics are poor, it is their own fault. He says virtually nothing about social policies toward indigenous populations which amount to colonial genocide, Termination/Relocation, jurisdiction, coercive assimilation, and so on.

One of the major flaws in almost all of D'Souza's discussion on race and equality in America is that it is based, as is all of the race discourse in this country since the Civil War, on the black/white paradigm almost exclusively. This exclusive and narrow look at American society has skewed the discourse on cause and effect to which we are all now subjected. D'Souza's contention is that the civil rights model as we know it, based as it is on prejudice and stereotype, would be denounced by Martin Luther King as wrong, even immoral. His interpretation of King's ideology on race, whether it is sensible or not, is convenient, because such a conclusion allows all of us to put aside the historical violence of the economic policies of a capitalistic democracy which are at the root of inequality in America. Such an argument is specious, also, because America's oldest racial act, the deliberate theft of a continent from its original inhabitants, could never have been accomplished without government intervention. If any acts in history have demonstrated the triumph of government regulation over the free market, the thefts of Indian lands do so. It was never a free market for the Sioux, who said to potential buyers, "The Black Hills are not for sale." They consented neither to the sale itself nor to the terms. Indeed, the federal government and the state governments have conspired in Indian land thefts for more than a hundred years. If the argument about race and equality in America is ever to be understood, the Indian experience in economics must become part of the discourse.

The rationale for America's oldest racism was never about slavery. It was never about the color of one's skin. The oldest racism in America was about the economically motivated, government-sponsored theft of lands occupied by others and the subsequent, deliberate murder of millions of Indians by the U.S. citizens and military. While one could argue that such activities would give support to D'Souza's call for the removal of government from the process, this has never been a reasoned interpretation of the American Indian experience, because the U.S. government has also represented a democratic "free market" based on the exploitation of resources for profit, an ideology which has always been anathema to native cultures on this continent.

The historical and deep-seated rationale for historical theft, dispossession, and inequality is exemplified by a Horatio Greenough sculpture called "Rescue Group," which was commissioned in 1837

and placed in the East Portico of the Capitol in Washington, D.C.,
some twenty years later. The sculpture has remained in the hearts and
minds of Americans as an example of the intellectual ideals of a superior civilization. It shows the savage menacing white society, represented by a helpless woman and child, and a pioneer man towering
over a dark Indian. According to D'Souza's thinking, this art could be
said to be based on experience, not racial ideology. Indians did kill
white pioneer families, so they deserved to be defeated and colonized.
They did carry tomahawks in one hand and scalps in the other. This
art, then, is not racist. It is very simply a logical image arising out of a
realistic historical experience.

It is worth noting that at the same time Greenough was modeling
his clay—indeed, as early as 1827—the Cherokee Nation, in an effort
to save itself and its treaty-protected lands from American democracy,
was adopting a constitution with the express purpose of establishing a
national Cherokee government modeled upon American principles. It
did them little good. Like the Jews who contributed to German culture
for hundreds of years and then faced Hitler in the twentieth century,
their efforts at participating as Indians in American culture in the middle of the nineteenth century were not only futile, they were considered absurd. The Georgia state legislature, while it did not send them
to the ovens, wrote as follows:

> Resolved, That all the lands appropriated and unappropriated
> within the conventional limits of Georgia, belong to her ab-
> solutely, that the title is in her; that the Indians are tenants at her
> will; that she may at any time she pleases determine their ten-
> ancy, by taking possession of the premises; and that Georgia has
> the right to extend her authority and laws over the whole terri-
> tory, and to coerce obedience to them from all descriptions of
> people, be they white, red, or black, within her limits.

While many contemporary Americans believe the Jewish holo-
caust stands alone in the annals of racist crime, Indians who have
survived in America are not so sure. D'Souza's argument seems to be
trying to convince us that the action of the State of Georgia, which
typifies hundreds of such actions across this land, was based on "rational discrimination"—that racism probably had little or nothing to
do with it and was, in any case, efficacious. The Cherokees were "removed." The Supreme Court modified the "removal" and allowed
the Cherokees to live subject to American law and power. America
and the State of Georgia ascended, and the Cherokee Nation today
like all of the Indian nations of this land, considers itself among the

bare survivors of racist America. Contrarily, D'Souza might suggest that to absorb and assimilate the unwilling Cherokees for the purpose of colonization was only "Amer-centric," not racist. Thus, to confer American citizenship (in 1924) upon a population that neither wanted it nor requested it, can't be considered anti-Indian or racist, since their "agreement" was documented. The people of the white power structures of America who managed social policy during this removal era were as driven by the ideals of market capitalism as are D'Souza's colleagues today. To steal Indian lands for profit then was simply an economic issue, and today it continues to be a matter of good economics to defend these policies and, in the process, transcend ethnic cultures.

The argument in defense of this kind of Indian history is the same defense D'Souza advocates for the continued well-being of America. It is not racism to discriminate, his argument says, because "people's perceptions of others are always filtered through the lens of their own prior experiences," the "distilled product of many years of experience." Moreover, these acts are efficient; they make economic and common sense.

If you agree that such discrimination "forces a choice in which the claims of morality are on one side, and the claims of rationality and productivity are on the other," so be it, says D'Souza's argument. The choices he gives simply leave out Indians who even today, through some miracle or unaccountable oversight, continue to possess thousands of acres of land and historical rights as citizens of Indian nations. He puts everything into a civil rights mode, ignoring the treaty rights model which is the true basis for American Indian history. For Americans of the future, D'Souza suggests, the choices are threefold: first, racial preference could be treated as an essential remedy (one wonders if this could mean the defense of native nationhood); second, all discrimination, including rational discrimination, could be considered illegal in both the public and private sectors (one wonders if this means the federal government and state governments would be forced to stop colonial practices on Indian lands); or, third— clearly D'Souza's preference—rational discrimination could be made legal and civil rights legislation be repudiated. What would become of two hundred years of agonized defense of Indian rights, property, and sovereignty under the contrived paradigm of these three choices is left to the imagination.

The modern dialogue and the history of Indians on this continent leads one to cynicism about the possibility that the average American and the average Indian can define the world in terms of mutually acceptable ideals. Because the debate on race and society in America, at least since the Civil War, has been almost entirely about black and white, the end of slavery, and the new immigrants and diversity, the hope of the American public was for a time that desegregation would bring the end of racism. Some say the end of racism as a widespread phenomenon has, indeed, come to pass. Though others say the hopes for solutions to racial conflict under present circumstances are getting more and more difficult, optimists like D'Souza believe that harmony is possible and that there is no longer any need for public policy in desegregating blacks and whites, nor any federal intervention of any kind. People today are in regular contact with each other, these optimists say, and they no longer have false views of one another; their newly formulated, clear images of one another promote racial harmony, and *continued assimilation will make oppression of one group by another group impossible.*

Such idealization of a long and troubled racial history has made any modern civil rights debate almost meaningless to the Native Americans who are citizens of Indian nations in this country. Because these debates are based on the experiences of blacks, whites, and new immigrants, the result has been a failure to understand that for equality and democracy to be defined according to the original constitutional and aboriginal intent, Indians must be seen as Indians, not as ethnic individuals in America. They must be seen as the original peoples, possessing dual citizenship in their own tribal nation(s) as well as in the United States. They must be seen as nations of people who occupied this continent for thousands of years with personal and national rights and who still do.

The problem with much of what D'Souza writes is not that it is ahistorical; rather, it is a return to a failed history of justice for America's first peoples. Of course, D'Souza readily admits that he is not a historian of either society or ideas. His point is that affirmative action as public policy and the repeal of the Civil Rights Act of 1964 are necessary if the black/white dialogue is to improve and if blacks are ever to achieve parity. Indians are not in this discourse, nor have they ever been his concern.

His argument, however, for the return of individual rights unfettered by government and his enthusiastic defense of the traditions of the West and of progress toward civilization are frightening. They deny again the right of Native America to see its Indianness as separate from mainstream Americanism, and they put at risk much of the work done by native scholars in academia over the past thirty years in the development of Native American Studies as a defensive mechanism for unique tribal experience and knowledge. It excludes participation by Indians as anything but "ethnic minorities."

For Indian country today, D'Souza's argument seems to defend colonization by economics and conquest by assimilation. What's new about that?

WRITING ABOUT THE READING

4. Using evidence from the text, explain why Cook-Lynn disagrees with the statement that biological racism "is declining as a social force in America."

5. Using examples of emotionally laden words from the text (such as "touted" or "futile"), explain whether or not you think that the tone of Cook-Lynn's essay is appropriate for an argumentative essay.

6. Why does Cook-Lynn call it a "major flaw" to focus exclusively on the "black/white paradigm"?

7. In the issue of racism, why does the author see economics as important (or more significant) than biological differences?

8. How and why does the author use the example of the Cherokee tribe to support her position on sovereignty and self-determination?

WRITING FROM YOUR OWN EXPERIENCE

Note: In these assignments, write about your own experience or use that of someone you know, read about, or saw in a film/TV show.

9. Cook-Lynn wrote this essay because she disagreed with another writer. Have you ever disagreed with another person's beliefs? Why did you disagree and what were the consequences of this disagreement?

10. Cook-Lynn is unhappy with those writers who have presented unfavorable stereotypes of Native Americans. Most Americans are acquainted with a book, film, TV show, or advertisement that used some Native American characters. What was your reaction to this work and/or character and the reason for your reaction?

11. Choose a sports team (such as the "Indians," "Braves," or "Seminoles") that uses a Native American name or mascot. What would be some of the arguments for and against changing the name or mascot of this team?

12. Cook-Lynn often seems angry about what she calls the "theft" of the Native American lands. Has anyone ever tried to take something away from you or harm you? What was your response and why did you react this way?

WRITING ABOUT RESEARCH

13. What were the reasons that the government moved the Cherokees to Oklahoma in the 1830s and what were the results of this policy?
14. Why and how did the Native Americans eventually lose their Oklahoma lands?
15. What were the causes and results of the 1835–1842 war of the Seminoles (under Chief Osceola) against the United States?
16. Research some depictions of Native Americans in works of visual art such as paintings, photographs, cartoons, or sculptures. Why would you evaluate this representation as favorable or unfavorable to Native Americans?

Selection 2

The Reservation Conditions

VINE DELORIA, JR.

Vine Deloria, Jr. *(1933–), a Standing Rock Sioux, is a lawyer, writer, educator, and a prominent spokesman for Native Americans. He received a B.S. degree (1958) from Iowa State University, an M.Th. (1963) from Lutheran School of Theology, Illinois, and a J.D. (1970) from the University of Colorado. From 1972–1974, Deloria taught at the University of California, Los Angeles. From 1978–1991, he was professor of American Indian Studies, political science, and history of law at the University of Arizona. In 1991, Deloria joined the faculty of the Center for Studies of Ethnicity and Race in America at the University of Colorado, Boulder. He has served as executive director of the National Congress of American Indians and chairman of the Institute for the Development of Indian Law (1970–1978). His best-selling 1969 book,* Custer Died for Your Sins: An Indian Manifesto, *a strong indictment of the treatment of Native Americans by whites, was awarded the Anisfield-Wolf Award (1970).*

A prominent spokesman for Native American nationalism, Deloria opposes the assimilation of Native Americans to contemporary technological society. Instead, Deloria believes that traditional tribal social organization is necessary for the survival of Native Americans. He often criticizes the U.S. government for its failure to live up to treaties and to provide adequately for the needs of the Native Americans under its supervision. In recent years, Deloria has stated that he is somewhat encouraged by the tendency for all Americans to show an interest in the environment and in spiritual beliefs.

Deloria discusses contemporary life for many Native Americans in his essay "The Reservation Conditions," which appeared in 1991 in an academic journal, National Forum. *This journal, published by Phi Kappa Phi Honor Society, features articles by scholars on prominent issues of the day. In this essay, Deloria first discusses the causes of some of the economic-social problems of those Native Americans living on the reservation. He then compares these problems to those of "mainstream" people who remain in rural areas. Although he offers no specific remedies for these problems, Deloria does recommend that Native Americans return to their cultural traditions.*

PREPARING TO READ

1. Although Deloria discusses the social-economic situation of those Native Americans who choose to live on reservations, the majority of Native Americans prefer to move to urban areas. What do you suppose would be some of the reasons for each choice?
2. Deloria believes that an increase in the use of modern technology results in a decrease in the sense of community on the reservation. Explain whether you think that modern technology (such as ATMs, faxes, telephones, cell phones, e-mail, and Internet) serves to isolate people from one another.
3. Although Deloria is concerned with the erosion of the traditional culture of Native Americans, many writers describe a loss of traditional values in all of American society. What is an example of a "traditional value" (such as "modesty," "hard work," or "polite manners") that you think has been lost in contemporary society and why do you think that this value has disappeared?

THE RESERVATION CONDITIONS

Indian-reservation life today has only the slightest resemblance to the conditions of three decades ago, and the current situation has elements of hope and portents of disaster. The major change during this period has been the linkage of reservations with the outside world through access to electricity and modern communications and entertainment conveniences. The result has been a rapid individualizing of the Indian family and community and the corresponding loss of personal and communal identity. The inner core of Indian life has shifted dramatically from shared experiences of local conditions to quasi-shared experiences of the larger world, and only in the last few years have we seen a counteracting movement among Indians to deal with this condition.

Electricity is the ultimate individualizing factor. People now have their own lights and appliances; they need no longer share these things with others. All forms of communication and entertainment are personal and individual, and they isolate people from each other. Families may watch television together; the medium does not communicate a sense of belonging, but an experience of observing promotes individual rather than group values and beliefs. The group values that modern media does communicate are whimsical, ahistorical, and arbitrary, wholly degenerative of traditions and all forms of social control. As traditions vanish, behavior is replaced by institutional controls, and individuals and communities are subjected to external patterns of action that have no other purpose than to move large numbers of people back and forth between politically acceptable activities.

In the old days, before television, telephone, radio, and the fax machine, Indian children took as their examples for behavior the other people in the village or community. Traditional songs and customs formed the core of childhood experiences, and external information and experiences were the anomalies of life—disconnected from the centrality of the world in which children lived. Today each Indian child has a variety of information and entertainment sources. With the VCR available as a babysitting device, the child is virtually isolated from learning through interaction with other people. Thus, in order to do something specifically "Indian," individuals within the reservation must make a special effort to carve out of their use of time certain periods in which Indian things are done. So the very idea of being an Indian has become something external to many people; in a fundamental sense, Indians are quickly becoming consumers and hobbyists of their own culture.

Modern communications also suggest that individuals are an interchangeable commodity in society, and that age, experience, wisdom, and gender provide no special insights into life; publicity alone provides an individual with the platform from which to speak and endorses whatever the individual represents as a valid interpretation of the world. Thus, a pop singer with a cause is often the public equivalent of cadres of knowledgeable and experienced professionals in a field. When this attitude is transferred into Indian communities, it produces a disdain for elders, a drastic decline in traditional virtues of politeness and gentility, and a tendency to elevate the demagogue to a position of power within the community. This new social mix dominates and controls all actions in and by Indian communities.

The federal government unwittingly produced this situation by emphasizing the development of a cash economy during the 1960s in the programs of the Office of Economic Opportunity. Indians were encouraged to adopt the values and attitudes of the urban consumer society and were assured that the federal government was intent on bringing immense financial resources to the reservations. Although most of the programs that dealt with people stressed employment skills, there was no major capital investment in reservations in the nature of supporting a permanent business community. Thus, cash income for the past three decades has been derived from training and educational programs that have seen drastic reductions during the same period. In short, the two curves of available income and consumer needs have been moving in contradictory and opposite directions.

Two stop-gap measures have been introduced to alleviate the tremendous financial pressures in Indian communities. During the Reagan years, tribes were encouraged to develop gambling activities on the reservations with the hope that the income from these games, primarily bingo, would substitute for reduced federal expenditures. Rapid development of big-stakes bingo games has placed the tribes on a collision course with state and local governments which have also seen gambling as a means of raising funds and avoiding the political liabilities of raising taxes. Most of the jurisdictional battles between tribes and states inevitably involve a determination of which political entity has the edge in collecting taxes or deriving income from non-tax sources.

The second source of alternative income has been the increased use of reservation natural resources, including, very recently, the leasing of reservation lands for use as hazardous-waste disposal sites—a practice in absolute contrast with traditional tribal values. Use of tribal lands for industrial development, mineral extraction, and waste disposal means pushing tribal members from a self-sufficient use of lands to the status of welfare recipient and unemployed worker, requiring therefore a much larger social-welfare program for reservation residents. Tribes generally receive only a small percentage of royalties for mineral extraction; but in spite of promises and contractual obligations to provide employment for tribal members, they rarely see any real jobs opened up for Indians by energy and timber industries.

For more than a century, education has been understood as the first and most fundamental service provided by the federal government to Indian tribes—originally as a means of destroying tribal culture and substituting Western values and, more recently, as a means of providing Indian children with the necessary skills to find good employment in American society. In 1934, Congress authorized special assistance for Indian children through the Johnson-O'Malley Act, and during the 1960s a great variety of special programs were added through amendments to basic national education laws. But the impact of these programs has been minimal, because the funds have been channeled to public-school districts, which are then encouraged to include Indians in their student bodies. Indians are valuable for a head count for purposes of receiving federal funds, but they generally experience systematic discrimination after the count has been taken. The result is a high school dropout rate approximately twice that of other minorities and nearly three times that of non-Indian whites.

Federal on-reservation education has not improved during this period but for different reasons. There is virtually no monitoring of federal employees. Hearings in 1989 showed widespread sexual abuse of children by Bureau of Indian Affairs employees who acted with impunity toward their Indian wards. Because child abuse was not an offense listed among the major crimes on Indian reservations, there has been great debate about whether someone committing child abuse can even be indicted for incidents occurring there. Over the past three decades, most day schools have been consolidated on the reservations, and gigantic educational plants have been constructed that handle up to two thousand students each. Children are sometimes bused as much as an hour each way from home to school, and many Indian children are up before the sun, standing on dirt roads waiting for their buses. The situation continues to deteriorate in spite of the best efforts of parents and the local community to make changes.

Traditionally, most people on the large western reservations lived in isolated places in small communities that were as often composed of an extended family as of groups of smaller families. The housing programs of the 1960s and 1970s were designed around traditional urban and suburban housing patterns, so that most of the larger communities on the reservations now have special suburban street layouts with reasonably new housing. Families are placed in homes according to financial need and capability. People who would not have chosen to live near each other now find themselves as neighbors, and instances of domestic violence and family feuds have skyrocketed in these housing developments. People who did not drink when living in isolated areas now engage in perpetual drinking when confined within the suburban housing patterns. Loss of ability to speak the tribal language is another characteristic of the new tribal housing, because English is the language of the bureaucracy and of the entertainment media available in the housing developments. Tribal elections now mirror the candidate's ability to reflect the specific needs of housing-development residents who perceive themselves as a special clientele deserving of special privileges.

Relations with states and federal agencies have notably deteriorated in recent decades. Most of the discussion of areas of tribe-state/federal-agency friction have focused on natural-resource use and ownership; but, in fact, the conflict revolves around control of rules and regulations for use of resources. State fish and game agencies, while allowing game resources to decline in some areas of the state, have been overly aggressive against tribes on the basis of conservation arguments. It would be instructive to do a study of the length of open seasons at or near game and vacation resorts in comparison with game populations. Federal agencies intent on giving public resources to private operators often view Indian resources as their own, because of the federal trust responsibility for the reservation lands. They unnecessarily encumber tribal governments with complex reporting and organizational responsibilities in order to have a voice in tribal decision-making.

The reservation populations continue to explode, straining existing services and natural resources to the limit. Even with the expanded housing programs of the last three decades, there is a serious housing shortage on most reservations as new families are being formed more rapidly than housing becomes available. The average age of the reservation population is below twenty-one years, forecasting a major crisis in all kinds of services and opportunities within the decade. This increase in population is occurring at a time when local non-Indian, off-reservation communities are suffering major population and employment losses. Some areas of the West are now at the critical stage of population loss, where existing county and small-town institutions—such as schools and transportation facilities—may collapse. Many parts of western America threaten to become federally subsidized rural slums with vast stretches of uninhabited land owned by various federal agricultural and land agencies.

The imaginary "mainstream" American society is rapidly disappearing. In all previous decades of American existence, the image of the Norman Rockwell rural community served as the benchmark toward which government programs were supposed to be bringing the Indians. Social-service and welfare programs are now losing their focus as assistance designed to upgrade poverty-stricken people, and they seem to be concentrating on simply a continuance of certain kinds of economic status: the well-subsidized white farmer, the partially subsidized white rancher who uses federal lands for a pence, and the chronically unemployed reservation and small-town poor. Until a major revision in the way the states and federal government understand rural American life is accomplished, very little can be done to correct the problems of the reservations.

The most hopeful sign in Indian country is the increasing appreciation of traditional ways. Many Indians now seek to make their lives less complicated, and traditional practices are noted for their simplicity and humanity. Giveaways are increasingly working to recycle existing resources through the reservation communities, and the sense of family created by these customs is on the rise. Religious factionalism, as represented by missionary efforts by Christian denominations, is declining as clientele of the mainstream Protestant churches is increasingly restricted to an older population of long-time members. Younger people are now embracing pan-tribal versions of traditional religion or remaining unchurched and fringe participants of traditional ceremonies.

When examined in isolation, Indian reservations seem to be hopeless pockets of poverty; when compared with equivalent non-Indian rural communities, reservations are not atypical and have both natural and human resources to deal with their problems. When modern reservation communities are seen in the light of a century of development, it is clear that Indians will move forward through the present difficulties to much better conditions as they simplify their lives by returning to their cultural traditions.

WRITING ABOUT THE READING

4. What do you think that Deloria means when he says that "individuals are an interchangeable commodity in society" and why does he state this?
5. How and why are the modern ways these Native American children learn to be "Indians" different from the traditional ways Native American children learned their culture?
6. Why does Deloria believe that the development of new housing has been harmful to Native Americans?
7. Why is the writer critical of the educational services provided to Native Americans by the federal government?
8. Using evidence from the reading, explain whether you think that the intended audience for this essay would be favorable, neutral, or hostile.

WRITING FROM YOUR OWN EXPERIENCE

Note: In these assignments, write about your own experience or use that of someone you know, read about, or saw in a film/TV show.

9. Deloria points out that the need for increased income has led some Native Americans to institute legalized gambling on the reservation. In addition, lotteries (which are a type of gambling) have become common as many states try to raise revenues. Using examples from your own knowledge or experience, support or refute one of the following statements:
   (a) States should raise money for education through the use of lotteries.
   (b) Lotteries are a form of taxes that hurt the poor the most.

(c) Native Americans should be allowed to use gambling activities as a source of revenue.

10. Have you ever gambled in some way, such as buying a lottery ticket or placing a bet on the outcome of a football game? What were some of the reasons for and the results of this gambling?

11. Deloria, concerned about the environment, is critical of the use of reservation lands for purposes such as mineral extraction or waste disposal. Have you become interested in protecting the environment? How did you become concerned about this issue and what was the outcome of this involvement?

WRITING ABOUT RESEARCH

12. Choose one Native American reservation to research and describe. Are there the same socioeconomic problems on this reservation that Deloria discusses in his essay?

13. How and why have Native Americans benefited from legalized gambling activities on the reservation?

14. How and why have tribal lands been used for industrial development, mineral extraction, and/or waste disposal?

15. What has been the role of the Council of Energy Resources Tribes (CERT) in protecting reservation lands and resources and why has this council assumed this role?

16. What have been some of the results of the leasing arrangements between the Crows in Montana and one or more of the following companies: Westmoreland Resources Company, Shell Oil Company, Peabody Coal Company, and/or Gulf Oil Corporation?

Selection 3

The Names: A Memoir

N. SCOTT MOMADAY

N. Scott Momaday *(1934–), of Kiowa heritage, grew up on the reservations of the Southwest. He received an A.B. from the University of New Mexico (1958), and A.M. (1960) and Ph.D. (1963) degrees from Stanford. From 1972–1980, he was professor of English at Stanford. Since 1980, he has been professor of English and Comparative Literature at the University of Arizona. In addition to being an educator, poet, and writer, Momaday is a painter whose works have been exhibited in various galleries. Momaday is a trustee of the Museum of the American Indian, New York, and a consultant for both the National Endowment for the Humanities and National Endowment for the Arts.*

Momaday was awarded the Pulitzer Prize (1969) for House Made of Dawn, *a work that is acknowledged as inaugurating the Native American Literary Renaissance. In this novel, a Native American soldier, returning to the United States after World War II, has to choose between the traditional ways and those of the modern world. Momaday uses the oral traditions of his tribe and an episodic narrative to capture the essence of the Native American experience.*

Momaday's writing often intertwines three ideas. First, Momaday affirms the power of words, of imaginative language and stories, as the means by which people shape their reality. Second, he envisions language as means by which people can relate to the natural environment. Through stories and imagination, people become aware of the beauty and sacredness of the land that sustains all life. Finally, using these stories and sacred places, people can come to know who they are and how they relate to their heritage. These ideas can be found in the following excerpt from his 1976 memoir, The Names. *Here, Momaday uses sacred places and his imagination to recall scenes from his boyhood and to envision his Kiowa grandfather, Mammedaty.*

PREPARING TO READ

1. Even in the modern world, people are excited by the power and beauty of nature. Choose an outdoor scene that you consider moving and explain why you were impressed by this scene.

2. Think of some of the myths and stories you have heard about historical figures (such as George Washington) or more contemporary figures (such as John Kennedy or Martin Luther King). What do you believe this story reveals about the values of American culture?

3. Why is there often a conflict between those who want economic growth and those who want preservation of the wilderness?

4. What do you think is the most important ecological problem today and why should people be concerned about this problem?

THE NAMES: A MEMOIR

Children trust in language. They are open to the power and beauty of language, and here they differ from their elders, most of whom have come to imagine that they have found words out, and so much of magic is lost upon them. Creation says to the child: Believe in this tree, for it has a name.

• • •

If you say to a child, "The day is almost gone," he will take you at your word and will find much wonder in it. But if you say this to a man whom the world has disappointed, he will be bound to doubt it. *Almost* will have no precision for him, and he will mistake your meaning. I can remember that someone held out his hand to me, and in it was a bird, its body broken. *It is almost dead.* I was overcome with the mystery of it, that the dying bird should exist entirely in its dying.

• • •

I can almost see into the summer of a year in my childhood. I am again in my grandmother's house, where I have come to stay for a month or six weeks—or for a time that bears no common shape in my mind, neither linear nor round, but it is a deep dimension, and I am lonely in it. Earlier in the day—or in the day before, or in another day— my mother and father have driven off. Somewhere on a road, in Texas, perhaps, they are moving away from me, or they are settled in a room away, away, thinking of me or not, my father scratching his head, my mother smoking a cigarette and holding a little dog in her lap. There is a silence between them and between them and me. I am thoughtful. I see into the green, transparent base of a kerosene lamp; there is a still circle within it, the surface of a deeper transparency. Do I bring my hands to my face? Do I turn or nod my head? Something of me has just now moved upon the metal throat of the lamp, some distortion of my-self, nonetheless recognizable, and I am distracted. I look for my image then in the globe, rising a little in my chair, but I see nothing but my ghost, another transparency, glass upon glass, the wall beyond, another distortion. I take up a pencil and set the point against a sheet of paper and define the head of a boy, bowed slightly, facing right. I fill in quickly only a few details, the line of the eye, the curve of the mouth, the ear, the hair—all in a few simple strokes. Yet there is life and ex-pression in the face, a conjugation that I could not have imagined in these markings. The boy looks down at something that I cannot see, something that lies apart from the picture plane. It might be an animal, or a leaf, or the drawing of a boy. He is thoughtful and well-disposed. It seems to me that he will smile in a moment, but there is no laughter in him. He is contained in his expression—and fixed, as if the founda-tion upon which his flesh and bones are set cannot be shaken. I like him certainly, but I don't know who or where or what he is, except that he is the inscrutable reflection of my own vague certainty. And then I write, in my child's hand, beneath the drawing, "This is someone. Maybe this is Mammedaty. This is Mammedaty when he was a boy." And I wonder at the words. *What are they?* They stand, they lean and run upon the page of a manuscript—I have made a manuscript, rude and illustrious. The page bears the likeness of a boy—so simply crude the likeness to some pallid shadow on my blood—and his name con-sists in the letters there, the words, the other likeness, the little, jumbled drawings of a ritual, the nominal ceremony in which all homage is re-turned, the legend of the boy's having been, of his going on. I have said it, I have set it down. I trace the words; I touch myself to the words, and they stand for me. My mind lives among them, moving ever, ever going on. I lay the page aside, I imagine. I pass through the rooms of the house, slowly, pausing at familiar objects: a quiver of arrows on the wall, old photographs in oval frames, beaded emblems, a Bible, an iron bedstead, a calendar for the year 1942. Mammedaty lies ten years in the ground at Rainy Mountain Cemetery. What is there, *just there*, in the earth, in the bronze casket, under Keahdinekeah's shawl? I go out into the yard; the shadows are long to the east, and the sunlight has deep-ened and the red earth is darkened now to umber and the grasses are burnished. Across the road, where the plain is long and undulant and bears the soft sheen of rose gentian and rose mallow, there are figures like fossils in the prisms of the air. I see a boy standing still in the dis-tance, only his head and shoulders visible above the long, luminous grass, and from the place where he stands there comes the clear call of a meadowlark. It is so clear, so definite in the great plain! I believe that it circles out and out, that it touches like ancient light upon the thistles at

Saddle Mountain, upon the broken floor of Boke's store, upon the thin shadows that follow on the current of the Washita. And round on the eastern shelves I see the crooked ravines which succeed to the sky, a whirlwind tracing a red, slanting line across the middle distance, and there in the roiling dust a knoll, a gourd dance and give-away, and Mammedaty moves among the people, answers to his name; low thunder rolls upon the drum. A boy leads a horse into the circle, the horse whipping its haunches around, rattling its blue hooves on the hard earth, rolling its eyes and blowing. There are eagle feathers fixed with ribbons in the braided mane, a bright red blanket on the back of the black, beautiful hunting horse. The boy's arms are taut with the living weight, the wild will and resistance of the horse, swinging the horse round in a tight circle, to the center of the circle where Mammedaty stands waiting to take the reins and walk, with dignity, with the whole life of the hunting horse, away. It is good and honorable to be made such a gift—the gift of this horse, this hunting horse—and honorable to be the boy, the intermediary in whose hands the gift is passed. My fingers are crisped, my fingertips bear hard upon the life of this black horse. *Oh my grandfather, take hold of this horse. It is good that you should be given this horse to hold in your hands, that you should lead it away from this holy circle, that such a thing should happen in your name.* And the southern moon descends; light like phosphorus appears in the earth, blue and bone, clusters of blue-black bunch grass, pocks in pewter. Flames gutter momently in the arbor and settle to the saffron lamps; fireflies flicker on the lawn; frogs begin to tell of the night; and crickets tell of the night, but there is neither beginning nor end in their telling. The old people arrive, the thin-limbed, deep-eyed men in their hats and braids, the round-faced women in their wide half sleeves and fringed shawls, apron-bound, carrying pots and pans and baskets of food—fried bread, boiled cracked corn, melons, pies and cakes—and for hours my grandmother has been cooking meat, boiled beef, fried chicken, chicken-fried beefsteaks, white and brown gravies. *Cohn' Tsotohah, Tsoai-talee, come here; I want to tell you something.* I sit at an old man's knee. I don't know who he is, and I am shy and uncomfortable at first; but there is delight in his eyes, and I see that he loves me. There are many people in the arbor; everyone listens. *Cohn', do you see the moon?* The full, white moon has receded into the southeast; it is a speckled moon; through the arbor screen it shimmers in the far reaches of the night. *Well, do you see?— there is a man in the moon. This is how it happened: Saynday was hungry. Oh, everyone was hungry then; the buffalo were keeping away, you know. Then Saynday's wife said to him, "Saynday, tomorrow the men are going on a hunt. You must go with them and bring back buffalo meat." "Well, yes," said Saynday. And the next day he went out on the hunt. Everyone found buffalo, except*

Saynday. Saynday could find no buffalo, and so he brought some tomatoes home to his wife. She was angry, but she said to him, "Saynday, tomorrow the men are going hunting again. Now I tell you that you must go with them, and you must bring back buffalo meat." "Well, yes," said Saynday. And again he went on the hunt. Everyone found buffalo, except Saynday. He could find no buffalo, and so he brought tomatoes home to his wife again. She was very angry, but she said to him, "Saynday, tomorrow the men are going hunting again. You must go with them, and you must bring back buffalo meat." "Well, yes," said Saynday. And Saynday went out on the hunt for the third time. And it was just the same: everyone found Buffalo, except Saynday. Saynday could find no buffalo, and so he brought tomatoes home to his wife again. She was so angry that she began to beat him with a broom. Saynday ran, but she ran after him, beating him with the broom. He ran faster and faster, until he got away, and then he wanted to hide. He hid in the moon. There he is now in the moon, and he will not come down because he is afraid of his wife. My people laugh with me; I am created in the old man's story, in his delight. There is a black bank and lightning in the north, the moon higher and holding off, the Big Dipper on a nail at the center of the sky. I lie down on the wide bench at my grandmother's back. The prayer meeting goes on, the singing of Christian hymns in Kiowa, now and then a gourd dance song.

There would be old men and old women in my life.

I invented history. In April's thin white light, in the white landscape of the Staked Plains, I looked for tracks among the tufts of coarse, brittle grass, amid the stones, beside the tangle of dusty hedges. When I look back upon those days—days of infinite promise and steady adventure and the certain sanctity of childhood—I see how much was there in the balance. The past and the future were simply the large contingencies of a given moment; they bore upon the present and gave it shape. One does not pass through time, but time enters upon him, in his place. As a child, I knew this surely, as a matter of fact; I am not wise to doubt it now. Notions of the past and future are essentially notions of the present. In the same way an idea of one's ancestry and posterity is really an idea of the self. About this time I was formulating an idea of myself.

• • •

But I was yet a child, and I lay low at Hobbs, feeling for the years in which I should find my whole self. And I had the strong, deceptive patience of a child, had not to learn it as patience but only to persist in it. Patience is what children have; it is especially theirs to have. I grew tall, and I entered into the seventh grade. I sat looking into books; there were birds on the lawn, chirping. Girls ambled in the dark corridors in white socks and saddle oxfords, and there were round, sweet syllables on their tongues. Time receded into Genesis on an autumn day in 1946.

West of Jemez Pueblo there is a great red mesa, and in the folds of the earth at its base there is a canyon, the dark red walls of which are sheer and shadow-stained; they rise vertically to a remarkable height. You do not suspect that the canyon is there, but you turn a corner and the walls contain you; you look into a corridor of geologic time. When I went into that place I left my horse outside, for there was a strange light and quiet upon the walls, and the shadows closed upon me. I looked up, straight up, to the serpentine strip of the sky. It was clear and deep, like a river running across the top of the world. The sand in which I stood was deep, and I could feel the cold of it through the soles of my shoes. And when I walked out, the light and heat of the day struck me so hard that I nearly fell. On the side of a hill in the plain of the Hissar I saw my horse grazing among sheep. The land inclined into the distance, to the Pamirs, to the Fedchenko Glacier. The river which I had seen near the sun had run out into the endless ether above the Karakoram range and the Plateau of Tibet.

WRITING ABOUT THE READING

5. Why is Momaday's vision of his grandfather so important in formulating an idea of his own identity?
6. What do you think Momaday means when he says: "an idea of one's ancestry and posterity is really an idea of the self"?
7. How and why does the storyteller's narrative about Saynday affect Momaday's decision to become a writer?
8. What evidence is there in this memoir of Momaday's reverence for the land?

WRITING FROM YOUR OWN EXPERIENCE

Note: In these assignments, write about your own experience or use that of someone you know, read about, or saw in a film/TV show.

9. Momaday imagines walking through the rooms of a house and looking at some familiar objects from his childhood. Imagine that you were walking through a house you lived in as a child. What

objects would you remember and why would these objects stand out in your memory?

10. Think of an important event in your childhood that helped to give you a sense of who you are. Why did this event make you more aware of your identity?

11. Momaday imagines that he gives his grandfather the gift of a horse. Recall when you received a significant gift. Why was this gift so important and what did you do after receiving this gift?

12. Choose someone who is important in your life. Suppose you decided to give a significant gift to this person. What would be your present and why would you give this gift to this person?

WRITING ABOUT RESEARCH

13. Who were the Kiowa people and how did they live before the arrival of the Europeans?

14. Momaday includes a myth told by one of the elders. Research another story or myth of Native Americans and explain why it is significant or compare it to another myth that you know.

15. Momaday's memoir describes a gift-giving ceremony of the Kiowa peoples. What is another ceremony associated with a Native American tribe and why is this ceremony so important?

16. Explain why dance and music are so important in the traditions of one or more groups of Native Americans.

Selection 4

Measuring My Blood

from *Interior Landscapes: Autobiographical Myths and Metaphors*

GERALD VIZENOR

Gerald Vizenor *(1934–), of Anishinabe, Ojibwa, and Chippewa heritage, is an acclaimed novelist, poet, and educator. While serving with the U.S. Army in Japan in the early 1950s, Vizenor became interested in Japanese literature. He obtained a B.A. from the University of Minnesota (1960) and undertook graduate study at the University of Minnesota and Harvard. Following this, Vizenor became a social worker, civil rights activist, and journalist. He organized the Indian Studies program at Bemidji State University and taught literature and tribal history at several universities. He is currently professor, Native Studies program, at the University of California, Berkeley. Vizenor has won many awards for his books, including the American Book Award (1988) for his novel* Griever: An American Monkey King in China.

One of the most prolific Native American writers, Vizenor is concerned primarily with the themes of mixed racial heritage and the conflict between tribal and nontribal worlds. To dramatize these themes, Vizenor often employs the traditional Native American figure of the trickster. Playful, comic, and disruptive, the trickster forces people to break out of formulaic ways of thinking and behaving. Vizenor envisions the adventure of life as essentially mysterious and comic because of the role of chance.

The trickster figure and chance are central to Vizenor's memoir, "Measuring My Blood" from Interior Landscapes: Autobiographical Myths and Metaphors *(1990). Here, Vizenor narrates the story of his trickster father who is killed by chance in the city. But his story about his grandmother and her secrets reveals that she, too, is a trickster, a trait that runs through the family. As a writer, Vizenor has been described by literary critics as a "compassionate trickster," who uses his often satirical writing as a disruptive activity to bring about changes in the reader and in society.*

PREPARING TO READ

1. Explain whether you agree or disagree that it is cruel to play "practical jokes" on other people and the reasons for your stand.

2. Choose a recent violent crime that has caught the attention of the media. Explain why you think that the media focused on this particular crime.
3. Explain whether you agree or disagree that the media give too much attention to violent crimes and give your reasons for this position.

MEASURING MY BLOOD
FROM *INTERIOR LANDSCAPES:*
AUTOBIOGRAPHICAL MYTHS AND METAPHORS

Alice Beaulieu, my grandmother, told me that my father was a tribal trickster with words and memories; a compassionate trickster who did not heed the sinister stories about stolen souls and the evil gambler. Clement William must have misremembered that tribal web of protection when he moved to the cities from the White Earth Reservation.

Nookomis, which means grandmother, warned her trickster grandson that the distant land he intended to visit, in search of his mother who had been stolen by a wind spirit, was infested with hideous humans, "evil spirits and the follower of those who eat human flesh." Naanabozho was the first tribal trickster on the earth. He was comic, a part of the natural world, a spiritual balance in a comic drama, and so he must continue in his stories. "No one who has ever been within their power has ever been known to return," she told her grandson. "First these evil spirits charm their victims by the sweetness of their songs, then they strangle and devour them. But your principal enemy will be the great gambler who has never been beaten in his game and who lives beyond the realm of darkness." The trickster did not heed the words of his grandmother.

Naanabozho paddled by canoe to the end of the woodland and took a path through the swamps and over high mountains and by deep chasms in the earth where he saw the hideous stare of a thousand gleaming eyes. He heard groans and hisses of countless fiends gloating over their many victims of sin and shame. The trickster knew that this was the place where the great gambler had abandoned the losers, the spirits of his victims who had lost the game.

The trickster raised the mat of scalps over the narrow entrance to the wiigiwaam. The evil gambler was inside, a curious being, a person who seemed almost round; he was smooth, white, and wicked.

"So, Naanabozho, you too have come to try your luck," said the great gambler. His voice was horrible, the sound of scorn and ridicule. Round and white, he shivered. "All those hands you see hanging around the wiigiwaam are the hands of your relatives who came to gamble. They thought as you are thinking, they played and lost their lives in the game. Remember, I demand that those who gamble with me and lose, give me their lives. I keep the scalps, the ears, and the hands of the losers; the rest of the body I give to my friends the wiindigoo, the flesh eaters, and the spirits I consign to the world of darkness. I have spoken, and now we will play the game."

Clement William Vizenor lost the game with the evil gambler and did not return from the cities. He was a house painter who told trickster stories, pursued women, and laughed most of his time on earth. He was murdered on a narrow street in downtown Minneapolis.

"Giant Hunted in Murder and Robbery Case," appeared as a headline on the front page of the *Minneapolis Journal*, June 30, 1936. The report continued: "Police sought a giant Negro today to compare his fingerprints with those of the rifled purse of Clement Vizenor, 26 years old, found slain yesterday with his head nearly cut off by an eight-inch throat slash.

"Vizenor, an interior decorator living at 320 Tenth Street South, had been beaten and killed in an alley. . . . He was the second member of his family to die under mysterious circumstances within a month. His brother, Turban Vizenor, 649 Seventeenth Avenue Northeast, was found in the Mississippi river June 1, after he had fallen from a railroad bridge and struck his head.

"Yesterday's slashing victim, who was part Indian, had been employed by John Hartung, a decorator. One pocket had been ripped out of the slain man's trousers. His purse lay empty beside him. Marks in the alley showed his body had been dragged several feet from the alley alongside a building."

The *Minneapolis Tribune* reported that the arrest of a "Negro in Chicago promised to give Minneapolis police a valuable clue to the murder of Clement Vizenor, 26-year-old half-breed Indian, who was stabbed to death in an alley near Washington Avenue and Fourth street early June 27. Vizenor's slaying was unsolved." The murder was never solved, and no motive was ever established. Racial violence was indicated in most of the newspaper stories, but there was no evidence in the investigations that race was a factor in the murder. My father could have been a victim of organized crime. There was no evidence of a struggle; he had not been robbed; the police would not establish a motive for the crime. There were several unsolved homicides at that time in Minneapolis.

The picture of my father published in the newspaper was severed from a photograph that shows him holding me in his arms. This is the last photograph, taken a few weeks before his death, that shows us together. Clement wore a fedora and a suit coat; he has a wide smile. We are outside, there is a tenement in the background; closer, a heap of used bricks. I must remember that moment, my grandmother with the camera, our last pose together.

The *Minneapolis Tribune* reported later that the police had "arrested a half-breed Indian in a beer parlor near Seventh Avenue South and Tenth Street and are holding him without charge for questioning in connection with the slaying, early Sunday, of Clement Vizenor. . . . The man who, according to police, was drunk, was picked up after making statements that indicated he might know who Vizenor's assailant was. He is alleged to have claimed knowledge of who Vizenor's friends were, and of many of the murdered man's recent activities. The murder was blamed by police upon any one of a growing number of drunken toughs roaming the Gateway district almost nightly, armed with knives and razors.

"The killing of Vizenor climaxes a series of violent assaults upon Gateway pedestrians in recent weeks by robbers who either slugged or slashed their victims."

In another report, the police "sought the husband of a former New York showgirl for questioning in connection with the knife murder of Clement Vizenor. The man sought is believed to be the same who left with Vizenor from a cafe at 400 Tenth Street South about five hours before the murder. Alice Finkenhagen, waitress at the Tenth Street cafe, gave police a good description of the man who called Vizenor to come outside. Detectives partially identified the showgirl's husband as that man. Also they learned this man had resented Vizenor's attentions to his showgirl wife.

"Vizenor was called from the cafe at about 12:30 a.m. Sunday. Later he appeared at his home, then left again. His body was found at 5:30 a.m., his throat slashed, in an alley near Washington and Fifth Avenues South. Police also were holding three half-breed Indians for questioning in the case. Vizenor was a half-breed."

The report continues: "A former New York showgirl and her husband were released by Minneapolis police Thursday after questioning failed to implicate them as suspects in the knife murder. . . . Police learned that Vizenor's attentions to the showgirl had been resented by her husband. But that difference was amicably settled long ago, detectives found out."

The *Minneapolis Tribune* reported later that "Captain Paradeau said he was convinced Clement had been murdered but that robbery was not the motive. The slain youth was reported to have been mild tempered and not in the habit of picking fights. Police learned he had no debts and, as far as they could ascertain, no enemies."

THE LAST PHOTOGRAPH

clement vizenor would be a spruce
on his wise return to the trees
corded on the reservation side
he overturned the line
colonial genealogies
white earth remembrance
removed to the cities at twenty three

my father lived on stories
over the rough rims on mason jars
danced with the wounded shaman
low over the stumps on the fourth of july

my father lied to be an indian
he laughed downtown
the trickster signature to the lights

clement honored tribal men at war
uniforms undone
shadows on the dark river
under the nicollet avenue bridge

tribal men burdened with civilization
epaulets adrift
ribbons and wooden limbs
return to the evangelists
charities on time

catholics on the western wire
threw their voices
treaties tied to catechisms
undone in the woodland

reservation heirs on the concrete
praise the birch
the last words of indian agents
undone at the bar

clement posed in a crowded tenement
the new immigrant
painted new houses pure white
outback in saint louis park
our rooms were leaded and cold
new tribal provenance

histories too wild in the brick
shoes too narrow

clement and women
measured my blood at night

my father holds
me in the last photograph
the new spruce
with a wide smile
half white
half immigrant
he took up the cities and lost at cards

"Clement Vizenor was survived by his mother, Alice Beaulieu; his wife, LaVerne Peterson; three brothers, Joseph, Lawrence, and Everett; two sisters, Ruby and Lorraine; and his son, Gerald Robert Vizenor, one year and eight months old." When my father was murdered, I was living with my grandmother, aunts, and uncles in a tenement at 320 Tenth Street South in Minneapolis.

Twenty-five years later I met with Minneapolis police officials to review the records of their investigation. I was, that summer, the same age as my father when he was murdered.

There was some resistance, some concern that my intentions were not personal but political; the police must be defensive about crimes they have never solved. A thin folder was recovered from the archives. The chief of detectives was surprised when he examined the file; he saw his name on a report and remembered that he was the first officer called to investigate the crime. He explained that he was a new police officer then and defended his trivial report. "We never spent much time on winos and derelicts in those days. . . . Who knows, one Indian vagrant kills another."

"Clement Vizenor is my father."

"Maybe your father was a wino then," he said, and looked to his watch. "Look kid, that was a long time ago. Take it on the chin, you know what I mean?"

I knew what he meant and closed the investigation on an unsolved homicide. The detective must have been the same person who told my mother to move out of town and forget what had happened. She tried to forget and left me with my grandmother in the tenement. Later, my mother placed me in several foster homes.

I hear my father in that photograph and imagine his touch, the turn of his hand on my shoulder, his warm breath on my cheek, his word trickeries, and my grandmother behind the camera. My earliest personal memories are associated with my grandmother and my bottle. She would hide my bottle to wean me in the trickster manner because, she said later, I carried that bottle around all day clenched between my front teeth. She reconsidered the trickster method, however, when I learned the same game and started to hide her bottles of whiskey. She might have forgotten where she placed the bottles, mine and hers, and then told stories, compassionate reunions of our past. I remember the moment, the bottles, and the stories, but not the camera. My father and that photograph hold me in a severed moment, hold me to a season, a tenement, more than we would remember over the dark river.

Alice Beaulieu continued her career in a tenement, poor but never lonesome. She was in her sixties when she married a blind man in his forties. I was eighteen, home on leave from the military at the time, and proud to wear my new uniform to a reception. My grandmother was in the kitchen, in the arms of her new husband. "He's a lusty devil," she whispered to me, "and he thinks I'm beautiful, so don't you dare tell him any different." She was a lover, favored in imagination, and she was plump and gorgeous that afternoon.

Alice and Earl Restdorf lived in a narrow dark apartment on LaSalle Avenue near Loring Park. Earl was pale, generous, and sudden with his humor. He repaired radios, a sacrament to sound, and collected radios that needed repair. Cabinets, chassis, tubes, and superheterodynes were stacked at the end of the small dining room. My grandmother would sit on the side of a double bed, because she had never had a secured, private bedroom in the tenement, and chew snuff when she was older. Earl did not approve of her tobacco habits. Alice stashed soup cans in secret places to catch her brown spit; she pretended that her husband could not smell the snuff or hear the juice. He smiled, folded in a chair near his radios.

My grandmother paid my son a dollar each time we visited to hold her pinches of snuff a secret. Robert was two and three years old when he learned the pleasures of secrets. She loved to tease and praise children, her grandchildren and great-grandchildren, and when she laughed on the side of the bed her cheeks bounced and her stomach leapt under the worn patch pockets on her plain print dresses. Alice Beaulieu was gorgeous. Robert has never told a soul about her juice cans at the side of the bed.

WRITING ABOUT THE READING

4. Why does Vizenor use the story about Naanabozho as an introduction to his narrative about his father?

5. Why was it important for Vizenor to try to find out what had happened to his father?

6. How would you describe the attitude of the chief of detectives to the murder of Clement Williams and what would account for this attitude?

7. Why can Vizenor's grandmother also be described as a trickster?

8. Why does the writer include the poem "The Last Photograph"?

WRITING FROM YOUR OWN EXPERIENCE

Note: In these assignments, write about your own experience or use that of someone you know, read about, or saw in a film/TV show.

9. Have you ever had to keep an important secret? Why did you keep or reveal the secret and what were some of the results of keeping (or disclosing) this secret?

10. Recall a time when you played a trick on someone (or had a trick played on you). How did the person on whom the trick was played react and what was the reason for this reaction?

11. Choose someone you know who could be described as a trickster. Why would you call this person a trickster?

12. Recall a time when you carried on a long search for a person, animal, and/or object. Why did you carry on this search and what was the result of your search?

WRITING ABOUT RESEARCH

13. What is the history and/or current status of the Anishinabe, Ojibwa, and/or Chippewa tribes?

14. Research the training law enforcement officers in one city or region receive in dealing with minorities, such as Native Americans. Explain whether you think that this training is adequate (or insufficient).

15. Many cultures, as well as that of Native Americans, have a body of literature about a "trickster" figure. How and why is this figure important to this culture? Consider one of the following characters:

(a) Brer Rabbit (African American)

(b) Bugs Bunny (American film)

(c) Coyote (Native American)

(d) Loki (Norse mythology)

(e) Monkey (Chinese)

(f) Reynard the Fox (European)

(g) The Fool (Shakespeare)

16. Choose a contemporary comedian or comic actor and explain how and why this person embodies many of the characteristics of the trickster.

The Language We Know

SIMON J. ORTIZ

Simon J. Ortiz *(1941–), born and raised in the Acoma Pueblo homeland, is a storyteller, poet, translator, reporter, and political leader. After service in the U.S. Army, Ortiz attended the University of New Mexico (1966–1968). He then received a fellowship for writing from the University of Iowa (1968–1969). Ortiz was one of forty writers published in the first anthology of contemporary Native American writing,* The American Indian Speaks *(1969). His many awards include a National Endowment for the Arts Fellowship (1981) and Humanitarian Award for Literary Achievement, New Mexico Humanities Council, 1989. Ortiz also has taken a leadership role in the Acoma community, becoming the First Lieutenant Governor for Acoma Pueblo in New Mexico (1989).*

As a political activist, Ortiz stresses the need for Native Americans to "fight back" against the social, economic, and political forces which keep them in poverty and seek to destroy their culture. Viewing words as a powerful weapon in this ongoing struggle, Ortiz's works often focus on the dignity of Native Americans in the contemporary world. In the following excerpt from I Tell You Now: Autobiographical Essays by Native American Writers *(1987), Ortiz describes the world of his Acoma boyhood, his boarding school education, and his development as a writer.*

PREPARING TO READ

1. Suppose you were asked to choose one political cause to support. What would be this cause and why would you choose it?
2. What are some of the probable reasons that young adults today are or are not interested in politics?
3. How and why did you become aware that words have the power to help or harm?
4. Why is it that obtaining an education often puts a person in conflict with some of the beliefs and traditions learned at home?

THE LANGUAGE WE KNOW

I don't remember a world without language. From the time of my earliest childhood, there was language. Always language, and imagination, speculation, utters of sound. Words, beginnings of words. What would I be without language? My existence has been determined by language, not only the spoken but the unspoken, the language of speech and the language of motion. I can't remember a world without memory. Memory, immediate and far away in the past, something in the sinew, blood, ageless cell. Although I don't recall the exact moment I spoke or tried to speak, I know the feeling of something tugging at the core of the mind, something unutterable uttered into existence. It is language that brings us into being in order to know life.

• • •

My childhood was the oral tradition of the Acoma Pueblo people—Aaquumeh hano—which included my immediate family of three older sisters, two younger sisters, two younger brothers, and my mother and father. My world was our world of the Aaquumeh in McCartys, one of the two villages descended from the ageless mother pueblo of Acoma. My world was our Eagle clan-people among other clans. I grew up in Deetziyamah, which is the Aaquumeh name for McCartys, which is posted at the exit off the present interstate highway in western New Mexico. I grew up within a people who farmed small garden plots and fields, who were mostly poor and not well schooled in the American system's education. The language I spoke was that of a struggling people who held ferociously to a heritage, culture, language, and land despite the odds posed them by the forces surrounding them since 1540 A.D., the advent of Euro-American colonization. When I began school in 1948 at the BIA (Bureau of Indian Affairs) day school in our village, I was armed with the basic ABC's and the phrases "Good morning, Miss Oleman" and "May I please be excused to go to the bathroom," but it was an older language that was my fundamental strength.

In my childhood, the language we all spoke was Acoma, and it was a struggle to maintain it against the outright threats of corporal punishment, ostracism, and the invocation that it would impede our progress towards Americanization. Children in school were punished and looked upon with disdain if they did not speak and learn English quickly and smoothly, and so I learned it. It has occurred to me that I learned English simply because I was forced to, as so many other Indian children were. But I know, also, there was another reason, and this was that I loved language, the sound, meaning, and magic of language. Language opened up vistas of the world around me, and it allowed me to discover knowledge that would not be possible for me to know without the use of language. Later, when I began to experiment with and explore language in poetry and fiction, I allowed that a portion of that impetus was because I had come to know English through forceful acculturation. Nevertheless, the underlying force was the beauty and poetic power of language in its many forms that instilled in me the desire to become a user of language as a writer, singer, and storyteller. Significantly, it was the Acoma language, which I don't use enough of today, that inspired me to become a writer. The concepts, values, and philosophy contained in my original language and the struggle it has faced have determined my life and vision as a writer.

• • •

In Deetziyamah, I discovered the world of the Acoma land and people firsthand through my parents, sisters and brothers, and my own perception, voiced through all that encompasses the oral tradition, which is ageless for any culture. It is a small village, even smaller years ago, and like other Indian communities it is wealthy with its knowledge of daily event, history, and social system, all that make up a people who have a many-dimensioned heritage. Our family lived in a two-room home (built by my grandfather some years after he and my grandmother moved with their daughters from Old Acoma), which my father added rooms to later. I remember my father's work at enlarging our home for our growing family. He was a skilled stoneworker, like many other men of an older Pueblo generation who worked with sandstone and mud mortar to build their homes and pueblos. It takes time, persistence, patience, and the belief that the walls that come to stand will do so for a long, long time, perhaps even forever. I like to think that by helping to mix mud and carry stone for my father and other elders I managed to bring that influence into my consciousness as a writer.

Both my mother and my father were good storytellers and singers (as my mother is to this day—my father died in 1978), and for their generation, which was born soon after the turn of the century, they were relatively educated in the American system. Catholic missionaries had taken both of them as children to a parochial boarding school far from Acoma, and they imparted their discipline for study and quest for education to us children when we started school. But it was their indigenous sense of gaining knowledge that was most meaningful to me. Acquiring knowledge about life was above all the most important item; it was a value that one had to have in order to be fulfilled personally and on behalf of his community. And this they insisted upon imparting through the oral tradition as they told their children about our native history and our community and culture and our "stories." These stories were common knowledge of act, event, and behavior in a close-knit pueblo. It was knowledge about how one was to make a living through work that benefited his family and everyone else.

Because we were a subsistence farming people, or at least tried to be, I learned to plant, hoe weeds, irrigate and cultivate corn, chili, pumpkins, beans. Through counsel and advice I came to know that the rain which provided water was a blessing, gift, and symbol and that it was the land which provided for our lives. It was the stories and songs which provided the knowledge that I was woven into the intricate web that was my Acoma life. In our garden and our cornfields I learned about the seasons, growth cycles of cultivated plants, what one had to think and feel about the land; and at home I became aware of how we must care for each other: all of this was encompassed in an intricate relationship which had to be maintained in order that life continue. After supper on many occasions my father would bring out his drum and sing as we, the children, danced to themes about the rain, hunting, land, and people. It was all that is contained within the language of oral tradition that made me explicitly aware of a yet unarticulated urge to write, to tell what I had learned and was learning and what it all meant to me.

My grandfather was old already when I came to know him. I was only one of his many grandchildren, but I would go with him to get wood for our households, to the garden to chop weeds, and to his sheep camp to help care for his sheep. I don't remember his exact words, but I know they were about how we must sacredly concern ourselves with the people and the holy earth. I know his words were about how we must regard ourselves and others with compassion and love; I know that his knowledge was vast, as a medicine man and an elder of his kiva, and I listened as a boy should. My grandfather represented for me a link to the past that is important for me to hold in my memory because it is not only memory but knowledge that substantiates my present existence. He and the grandmothers and grandfathers before him thought about us as they lived, confirmed in their belief of a continuing life, and they brought our present beings into existence by the beliefs they held. The consciousness of that belief is what informs my present concerns with language, poetry, and fiction.

• • •

My first poem was for Mother's Day when I was in the fifth grade, and it was the first poem that was ever published, too, in the Skull Valley School newsletter. Of course I don't remember how the juvenile poem went, but it must have been certain in its expression of love and reverence for the woman who was the most important person in my young life. The poem didn't signal any prophecy of my future as a poet, but it must have come from the forming idea that there were things one could do with language and writing. My mother, years later, remembers how I was a child who always told stories—that is, tall tales—who always had explanations for things probably better left unspoken, and she says that I also liked to perform in school plays. In remembering, I do know that I was coming to that age when the emotions and thoughts in me began to moil to the surface. There was much to experience and express in that age when youth has a pre-cociousness that is broken easily or made to flourish. We were a poor family, always on the verge of financial disaster, though our parents always managed to feed us and keep us in clothing. We had the problems, unfortunately ordinary, of many Indian families who face poverty on a daily basis, never enough of anything, the feeling of a denigrating self-consciousness, alcoholism in the family and community, the feeling that something was falling apart though we tried desperately to hold it all together.

My father worked for the railroad for many years as a laborer and later as a welder. We moved to Skull Valley, Arizona, for one year in the early 1950s, and it was then that I first came in touch with a non-Indian, non-Acoma world. Skull Valley was a farming and ranching community, and my younger brothers and sisters and I went to a one-room school. I had never really had much contact with white people except from a careful and suspicious distance, but now here I was, totally surrounded by them, and there was nothing to do but bear the experience and learn from it. Although I perceived there was not much difference between *them* and *us* in certain respects, there was a distinct feeling that we were not the same either. This thought had been inculcated in me, especially by an Acoma expression—*Gaimuu Mericano*—that spoke of the "fortune" of being an American. In later years as a social activist and committed writer, I would try to offer a strong positive view of our collective Indianness through my writing. Nevertheless, my father was an inadequately paid laborer, and we were far from our home land for economic-social reasons, and my feelings and thoughts about that experience during that time would become a part of how I became a writer.

Soon after, I went away from my home and family to go to boarding school, first in Santa Fe and then in Albuquerque. This was in the 1950s, and this had been the case for the past half-century for Indians: we had to leave home in order to become truly American by joining the mainstream, which was deemed to be the proper course of our lives. On top of this was termination, a U.S. government policy which dictated that Indians sever their relationship to the federal government and remove themselves from their lands and go to American cities for jobs and education. It was an era which bespoke the intent of U.S. public policy that Indians were no longer to be Indians. Naturally, I did not perceive this in any analytical or purposeful sense; rather, I felt an unspoken anxiety and resentment against unseen forces that determined our destiny to be un-Indian, embarrassed and uncomfortable with our grandparents' customs and strictly held values. We were to set our goals as American working men and women, singlemindedly industrious, patriotic, and unquestioning, building for a future which ensured that the U.S. was the greatest nation in the world. I felt fearfully uneasy with this, for by then I felt the loneliness, alienation, and isolation imposed upon me by the separation from my family, home, and community.

Something was happening; I could see that in my years at Catholic school and the U.S. Indian school. I remembered my grandparents' and parents' words: educate yourself in order to help your people. In that era and the generation who had the same experience I had, there was an unspoken vow: we were caught in a system inexorably, and we had to learn that system well in order to fight back. Without the motive of a fight-back we would not be able to survive as the people our heritage had lovingly bequeathed us. My diaries and notebooks began then, and though none have survived to the present, I know they contained the varied moods of a youth filled with loneliness, anger, and discomfort that seemed to have unknown causes. Yet at the same time, I realize now, I was coming to know myself clearly in a way that I would later articulate in writing. My love of language, which allowed me to deal with the world, to delve into it, to experiment and discover, held for me a vision of awe and wonder, and by then grammar teachers had noticed I was a good speller, used verbs and tenses correctly, and wrote complete sentences. Although I imagine that they might have surmised this as unusual for an Indian student whose original language was not English, I am grateful for their perception and attention.

• • •

During the latter part of that era in the 1950s of Indian termination and the Cold War, a portion of which still exists today, there were the beginnings of a bolder and more vocalized resistance against the current U.S. public policies of repression, racism, and cultural ethnocide. It seemed to be inspired by the civil rights movement led by black people in the U.S. and by decolonization and liberation struggles worldwide. Indian people were being relocated from their rural homelands at an astonishingly devastating rate, yet at the same time they resisted the U.S. effort by maintaining determined ties with their heritage, returning often to their native communities and establishing Indian centers in the cities they were removed to. Indian rural communities, such as Acoma Pueblo, insisted on their land claims and began to initiate legal battles in the areas of natural and social, political and economic human rights. By the retention and the inspiration of our native heritage, values, philosophies, and language, we would know ourselves as a strong and enduring people. Having a modest and latent consciousness of this as a teenager, I began to write about the experience of being Indian in America. Although I had only a romanticized image of what a writer was, which came from the pulp rendered by American popular literature, and I really didn't know anything about writing, I sincerely felt a need to say things, to speak, to release the energy of the impulse to help my people.

My writing in my late teens and early adulthood was fashioned after the American short stories and poetry taught in the high schools of the 1940s and 1950s, but by the 1960s, after I had gone to college and dropped out and served in the military, I began to develop topics and themes from my Indian background. The experience in my village of Deetziyamah and Acoma Pueblo was readily accessible. I had grown up within the oral tradition of speech, social and religious ritual, elders' counsel and advice, countless and endless stories, everyday event, and the visual art that was symbolically representative of life all around. My mother was a potter of the well-known Acoma clayware, a traditional art form that had been passed to her from her mother and the generations of mothers before. My father carved figures from wood and did beadwork. This was not unusual, as Indian people know; there was always some kind of artistic endeavor that people set themselves to, although they did not necessarily articulate it as "Art" in the sense of Western civilization. One lived and expressed an artful life, whether it was in ceremonial singing and dancing, architecture, painting, speaking, or in the way one's social-cultural life was structured. When I turned my attention to my own heritage, I did so because this was my identity, the substance of who I was, and I wanted to write about what that meant. My desire was to write about the integrity and dignity of an Indian identity, and at the same time I wanted to look at what this was within the context of an America that had too often denied its Indian heritage.

To a great extent my writing has a natural political-cultural bent simply because I was nurtured intellectually and emotionally within an atmosphere of Indian resistance. Aacquu did not die in 1598 when it was burned and razed by European conquerors, nor did the people become hopeless when their children were taken away to U.S. schools far from home and new ways were imposed upon them. The *Aaquumeh hano*, despite losing much of their land and surrounded by a foreign civilization, have not lost sight of their native heritage. This is the factual case with most other Indian peoples, and the clear explanation for this has been the fight-back we have found it necessary to wage. At times, in the past, it was outright armed struggle, like that of present-day Indians in Central and South America with whom we must identify; currently, it is often in the legal arena, and it is in the field of literature. In 1981, when I was invited to the White House for an event celebrating American poets and poetry, I did not immediately accept the invitation. I questioned myself about the possibility that I was merely being exploited as an Indian, and I hedged against accepting. But then I recalled the elders going among our people in the poor days of the 1950s, asking for donations—a dollar here and there, a sheep, perhaps a piece of pottery—in order to finance a trip to the nation's capital. They were to make another countless appeal on behalf of our people, to demand justice, to reclaim lost land even though there was only spare hope they would be successful. I went to the White House realizing that I was to do no less than they and those who had fought in the Pueblo Revolt of 1680, and I read my poems and sang songs that were later described as "guttural" by a Washington, D.C., newspaper. I suppose it is more or less understandable why such a view of Indian literature is held by many, and it is also clear why there should be a political stand taken in my writing and those of my sister and brother Indian writers.

• • •

The 1960s and afterward have been an invigorating and liberating period for Indian people. It has been only a little more than twenty years since Indian writers began to write and publish extensively, but we are writing and publishing more and more; we can only go forward. We come from an ageless, continuing oral tradition that informs us of our values, concepts, and notions as a native people, and it is amazing how much of this tradition is ingrained so deeply in our contemporary writing, considering the brutal efforts of cultural repression that was not long ago outright U.S. policy. We were not to speak our languages, practice our spiritual beliefs, or accept the values of our

past generations; and we were discouraged from pressing for our natural rights as Indian human beings. In spite of the fact that there is to
some extent the same repression today, we persist and insist in living,
believing, hoping, loving, speaking, and writing as Indians. This is
embodied in the language we know and share in our writing. We have
always had this language, and it is the language, spoken and unspoken, that determines our existence, that brought our grandmothers
and grandfathers and ourselves into being in order that there be a continuing life.

WRITING ABOUT THE READING

5. What is the role of art in the Acoma culture and why does this heritage contribute to Ortiz's becoming a writer?
6. How and why did the civil rights and resistance movements affect
   Ortiz's decision to become a writer?
7. What is Ortiz's attitude toward the government's termination policy and the reasons for his stand?
8. What does the section about speaking at the White House reveal
   about the writer's attitude toward the invitation and his audience?
9. Why was it so important for the Acoma Pueblo people to be able
   to retain their language?

WRITING FROM YOUR OWN EXPERIENCE

*Note: In these assignments, write about your own experience or use that of
someone you know, read about, or saw in a film/TV show.*

10. Ortiz's life was shaped partly by the historical events (the Civil
    Rights Movement) and the times in which he lived. Choose an im-
    portant historical event during your lifetime. Explain whether this
    historical event or movement has affected your life or that of
    someone you know.
11. When Ortiz went to school, his family said that he must educate
    himself in order to help his people. What is your purpose in ob-
    taining an education and why is this your purpose?
12. At school, Ortiz was embarrassed about his family's customs and
    values. Choose a time when you felt embarrassed about your
    home and/or a family member. Why were you ashamed and what
    were some of the results of your feelings?

13. At school, Ortiz resented being urged to abandon his traditional customs and values. Recall a time when you were pressured to give up a belief or behavior. What was your reaction and the results of your being so pressured?

WRITING ABOUT RESEARCH

14. During World War II, the U.S. military used Navaho "code talkers" to transmit secret communications. How and why was the Navaho language used for this purpose?

15. Ortiz writes of the need for Native Americans to "fight back" in order to survive as a people. In the past, there were many efforts by Native Americans to resist the European encroachment. Research one such effort (such as one of the conflicts listed below). Why did it occur and what was its outcome?

    (a) The Pequot tribe of New England attacked a white settlement (the Pequot War of 1637).

    (b) King Philip, chief of the Wampanoags, attacked white settlements in New England (King Philip's War of 1675).

    (c) Chief Pontiac led Ottawas, Delawares, Miamis, Kickapoos, and Shawnees against settlements in the Ohio valley (Pontiac's Rebellion of 1763).

    (d) At the Battle of The Fallen Timbers (1794), the Shawnees battled the forces led by Major General "Mad Anthony" Wayne.

16. Research the traditional architecture and/or houses of the Pueblos. What is unusual about these structures and why were they well adapted to the environment?

17. Choose one of the arts and crafts of Native Americans living in the Southwest. How were these objects made and what was their purpose? Consider:

    (a) baskets

    (b) beadwork

    (c) carvings

    (d) Hopi Kachinas

    (e) jewelry

    (f) Navajo rugs

    (g) Navajo sandpainting

    (h) pottery

Selection 6

Notes of a Translator's Son

JOSEPH BRUCHAC

Joseph Bruchac *(1942–), of Abenaki heritage, is an educator, writer, editor, and publisher. He received a B.A. (1965) from Cornell University, an M.A. (1966) from Syracuse University, and Ph.D. (1975) from Union Graduate School. Following three years of teaching in Ghana, West Africa, Bruchac taught at Skidmore College. He also established creative writing workshops in prisons throughout the country. As an outcome of his interest in multicultural literature, Bruchac founded the Greenfield Review Press (1970); he is now director of the Greenfield Review Literary Center. His many awards include a Rockefeller Foundation fellowship, several National Endowment for the Arts grants, and a PEN Syndicated Fiction Award. He has written many prize-winning books for children, young adults, and adults.*

Bruchac believes that Native American culture is more humanistic than that of European Americans. For example, he has stated that children are better off with caring elders in the extended Native American family than in the isolated, nuclear family of Western culture. He also believes that the Native American tradition is superior in its greater emphasis on the importance of the heart and spirit, in its recognition of the balance between men and women, and in its acknowledgment of the connection of people to the land. He sees the Native American as caught between two cultures, a dilemma he believes is representative of all contemporary experience, particularly that of members of minorities. Finally, Bruchac stresses the need to understand others and the common humanity of all people.

Bruchac emphasizes that one way to learn about others is an understanding of their myths and stories. He feels that literature has a dual role; it should both entertain and instruct. In his writing, Bruchac seeks to preserve the traditional stories of Native Americans. He incorporates stories in his essay "Notes of a Translator's Son," which was first printed in I Tell You Now: Autobiographical Essays by Native American Writers *(1987). In this excerpt from his memoir, Bruchac explains how his grandfather, facing prejudice, concealed his Native American heritage. As Bruchac grew to manhood, he learned to reconcile the various aspects of his "confused heritage."*

PREPARING TO READ

1. For Bruchac, a good story should both entertain and instruct. Choose a story, book, or film that you feel meet these two criteria and explain why you chose this work. Consider such classics as *Charlotte's Web* or *Mary Poppins*.

2. After completing college, Bruchac spent three years living in Ghana, West Africa. Many young people have joined the Peace Corps or undertaken other work to help people in underdeveloped countries. What would be the reasons that someone would take a job that is personally fulfilling even if not high paying?

3. Explain whether you agree that people learn a lesson from making mistakes.

NOTES OF A TRANSLATOR'S SON

The best teachers have showed me that things have to be done bit by bit. Nothing that means anything happens quickly—we only think it does. The motion of drawing back a bow and sending an arrow straight into a target takes only a split second, but it is a skill many years in the making. So it is with a life, anyone's life. I may list things that might be described as my accomplishments in these few pages, but they are only shadows of the larger truth, fragments separated from the whole cycle of becoming. And if I can tell an old-time story now about a man who is walking about, *waudjoset ndatlokugan,* a forest lodge man, *alesakamigwi udlagwedewugan,* it is because I spent many years walking about myself, listening to voices that came not just from the people but from animals and trees and stones.

Who am I? My name is Joseph Bruchac. The given name is that of a Christian saint—in the best Catholic tradition. The surname is from my father's people. It was shortened from *Bruchacek*—"big belly" in Slovak. Yet my identity has been affected less by middle European ancestry and Christian teachings (good as they are in their seldom-seen practice) than by that small part of my blood which is American Indian and which comes to me from a grandfather who raised me and a mother who was almost a stranger to me. I have other names, as well. One of those names is Quiet Bear. Another, given me by Dewasentah, Clan Mother at Onondaga, is *Gah-neh-go-he-yo.* It means "the Good Mind." There are stories connected to those names, stories for another time.

What do I look like? The features of my face are big: a beaked nose, lips that are too sensitive, and sand-brown eyes and dark eyebrows that lift one at a time like the wings of a bird, a low forehead that looks higher because of receding brown hair, an Adam's apple like a broken bone, two ears that were normal before wrestling flattened one of them. Unlike my grandfather's, my skin is not brown throughout the seasons but sallow in the winter months, though it tans dark and quickly when the sun's warmth returns. It is, as you might gather, a face I did not used to love. Today I look at it in the mirror and say, *Bruchac, you're ugly and I like you.* The face nods back at me and we laugh together.

The rest of me? At forty-two I still stand 6'2" tall and weigh the 195 pounds I weighed when I was a heavyweight wrestler at Cornell University. My arms and hands are strong, as strong as those of anyone I've met, though my two sons—Jim who is sixteen and 6'4", and Jesse who is thirteen and close to 6'—smile when I say that. When they were little their games included "Knock Papa Down." Each year they've found it a little easier to do. My physical strength, in part, is from my grandfather, who was never beaten in a fight. Like his, the fingers of my hands are short and thick. I hold them out and see the bulges in the knuckles, the way both my index fingers are skewed slightly and cannot completely straighten. A legacy of ten years of studying martial arts.

Do we make ourselves into what we become or is it built into our genes, into the fate spun for us by whatever shapes events? I was a small child, often alone and often bullied. I was different—raised by old people who babied me, bookish, writing poetry in grade school, talking about animals as if they were people. My grandfather joked when he called me a "mongrel," a mixture of English and Slovak and "French," but others said such things without joking. When I was seven I decided I would grow up to be so big and strong that no one would ever beat me up again. It took me nine years to do it. ("Be careful what you really want," a Tai Chi master told me. "If you really want it, you'll get it.") My junior year in high school I was still the strange kid who dressed in weird clothes, had no social graces, was picked on by the other boys, scored the highest grades in English and biology and almost failed Latin and algebra. That winter of my junior year my grandmother died. My grandfather and I were left alone in the old house. That summer I grew six inches in height. In my senior year, though clothing and social graces showed little evolution, I became a championship wrestler, won a Regents' scholarship, and was accepted by Cornell University to study wildlife conservation.

How can I now, in only a few pages, cover the next twenty-five years? How can I adequately describe five years at Cornell and the

year at Syracuse University, where I held a creative writing fellowship? At Syracuse, told by an expatriate South African writing instructor that my prose was too poetic, I smashed my typewriter in
frustration and burned everything I had written. (Carol, my wife of a
year, looked out the window of our small rented student housing
bungalow and wondered what kind of bear she had married.) What
about the Vietnam protests and the Civil Rights movement, the march
on Washington and that long walk in Mississippi where James
Meredith and Martin Luther King, Stokeley Carmichael and Marlon
Brando took water from canteens I lugged up and down the line
while state troopers with shiny insect eyes took our photographs with
Polaroid cameras, waiting for the night when their eyes would look
out from under white Klan hoods? And what about three years spent
in Ghana, West Africa, where I taught in a school by the Gulf of
Guinea? The Thunder Cult's drum rumbled at night in the next compound and a mad old man asked me to join him in a visit to Mammy
Water under the waves of the man-eating sea. It was in Ghana that
our son James raised his arms to the brightness in the night sky and
spoke his first word, *Moon!* (I fictionalized my Africa experience in a
novel completed in the 1980s. In it a half-breed American teacher dis-
covers himself and his own country through life in a foreign culture—
which he finds less foreign than his white expatriate colleagues. It is
called *No Telephone to Heaven.*) Then came ten years of teaching in
American prisons, and a decade and a half of editing and publishing
multicultural writing: my introduction to *How to Start and Sustain a
Literary Magazine* (Provision House Press, 1980) is a brief autobiography of my life as an editor. And all of that was made richer and more
complicated by twenty years of marriage and sixteen years of learning from two sons—whose accomplishments bring me more pride
than anything I've ever done. There isn't space enough here for more
than the mention of all those things.

• • •

I can only go onward by going back to where my memories
begin. I was not a black belt in pentjak-silat then, not a Ph.D. in Comparative Literature, a Rockefeller Fellow, a published poet, a "well-
known Native American writer," as articles about me usually begin.
(Thoreau might have written his famous "simplify, simplify" for the
average newspaper journalist. How easily a few ill-chosen words can
be used to encapsulate an entire human life!) Then I was only a child,
with few experiences and fewer scars. All that I had in common with
the person I am now is a confused heritage and the house I lived in
then and still live in today. It is an old house with grey shingles, built

by my grandfather on the foundation of a house owned by his wife's parents before it was burned down in a feud. It sits on Splinterville Hill, named for the ashwood baskets once made here. Just to the north of us, the Adirondack Mountains of upstate New York begin. I look out the window of the bedroom where Carol and I sleep and see, below the blue spruce trees my grandfather planted, the yard where I used to play.

How many memories of my childhood are my own and not those someone else had of me and told me about when I was older? I know that the image of a fence taller than my hands can reach is my own. I can still feel the chill, slightly rusted surface of its wire mesh against my face, my tongue almost freezing to its surface as I taste it on a day when the frost has glazed its red weave to the shimmer of a mirror. Is that my first memory or does the litter of puppies in Truman Middlebrooks' barn come before it? A warm milk smell of small animals, the sharpness of their teeth, the gentle insistence of their mother's muzzle nudged between me and them, pushing me away to roll on my back in the straw while someone's adult voice laughs. I know I am not being laughed at, so it is my grandfather's laughter that I hear. I never heard my father or my mother laugh when I was a child, and somehow life seemed too serious to my grandmother for her to indulge in much humor, even though she won her battle to keep me from my parents—that battle which I cannot remember but which has been replayed for me from the reluctant memories of those older than I. My grandfather, though, was often joking, often teasing. When he was serious it was a seriousness that no one laughed at.

The memory of me climbing the ladder, unafraid and right behind the old man, all the way to the roof forty feet up when I was only two, was my grandfather's. But it was recited about me so often that it became inseparably associated with my thoughts of my childhood. I know that I always dreamed of flight. I still do fly in my dreams. Its secret is simple—just lift your legs when you're falling and you'll never touch the ground until you're ready. To this day I don't understand why I can't continue to do it in the seconds after I wake from such dreams. But I have faith that eventually I will solve that problem one way or another and float away, with my body or without it. And though I've had some spectacular falls—at least one of which I should never have survived—I still love high places, cliffs and trees and resounding waterfalls. I inherited that fearlessness about high places and dying from my grandfather, just as I inherited certain stories. Here is one of them which is as much a part of my own fabric as if I had been there when that day was being woven:

I only went to school until I was in 3rd grade.
What happened then, Grampa?
I jumped out the window of the school and never came back.
Why?
I got in a fight with a boy who called me an Indian.

My grandparents raised me. I grew up only a quarter of a mile
away from my mother and father's home on what we always called
"The Farm," a plot of ninety acres with several outbuildings, which
had been the home of my grandparents when they were first married.
My grandfather gave The Farm to them after they'd been married a
few years and were still living with my grandparents. The room where
I type this was my parents' room when I was a baby. They moved to
The Farm with my younger sister, and I stayed "for a while" with my
grandparents. I sat with my grandfather in the wooden chairs he had
made and painted blue and placed in front of his general store: Bowman's Store. I was wearing shorts and my toes couldn't touch the concrete as I dangled them down, using a stick to keep my balance as I
stayed in the chair. There was a shadow in front of me. My parents.
My grandmother took my hand and led me back into the house. "Get
to your room, Sonny."

There my memory is replaced by that of my other grandmother,
the Slovak one who lived three miles away up the South Greenfield
road.

Your fader, he was ready to leave your mother. Dere vere so
many tears, such crying about you. Ah. Den your fader and
mother they come and say they vill take you back, now. Dat is
ven your grandfather Bowman, he goes out of the room. Ven he
come back it is vith the shotgun. And he hold it to his head and
say take him you vill never see me alive again.

Though I did not hear that story until after I was married, I knew
that I was important to my grandfather. I realize now I must have
been, in part, a replacement for my mother's older brother, who died
at birth. I was always close to my grandfather. He delighted in telling
how I was his shadow, how I carried my stick just like a spear and followed him everywhere. But, close as I was, he would never speak of
the Indian blood which showed so strongly in him. I have a tape
recording we made soon after we returned to live with him, back from
three years in West Africa to the old house on Splinterville Hill with
our new son, his great-grandchild, whose life would start the healing
of wounds I had caused by simply being wanted.

Are you Indian, Grampa?
No.
Then why is your skin so dark?
Cause I'm French. Us French is always dark.

Yet I was conscious of the difference, of the way people looked at me when I was with my grandfather. When I was a freshman at Cornell University he came to visit, bringing two of my friends from high school, David Phillips and Tom Furlong. They spent two nights in the dorm, all of them sleeping in my room. My grandfather told everyone that David was my younger brother. They looked at my grandfather and then, more slowly, at me. David was black. When they asked me if it was true, I said, "What do you think?" When the fraternity rushing week came later that semester, I was on more than one "black list."

O my God, Joe, that's Grampa sitting there by the coffin!

I looked at the old man sitting in the front row in Burke's Funeral Home, right next to my grandfather's casket, and my own heart clenched its fist. Then the man looked at us. His face was younger and slightly less dark than that of his last surviving older brother. It was Jack Bowman. Though he lived in Lake George, the home of a more or less underground community of Abenaki Indian people even today, we had never met him before. In the year we had to get to know Jack before his own heart found a weak aorta less strong than his love for the land and his wife of fifty years, we heard more stories about my grandfather and his family. We also heard some of the denials of Indian ancestry, even though Jack offered no more of an explanation than his brother had for my grandfather's cutting himself off from his own side of the family after he married my grandmother, a woman of high education with degrees from Skidmore and Albany Law School, whose marriage to a semi-illiterate and dark-skinned hired man of her father's sparked scandalized comment in Greenfield and Saratoga. In the face of those denials I felt, at times, like one who looks into a mirror and sees a blur over part of his own face. No matter how he shifts, changes the light, cleans the glass, that area which cannot be clearly seen remains. And its very uncertainty becomes more important than that which is clear and defined in his vision.

After Jack's death his wife Katherine fessed up. Yes, she said, Jack and Jesse were Indian. Everyone knew the Bowmans were Indian. She put it into writing and signed her name. It is the closest thing to a tribal registration that I will ever have. But it is enough, for I want to claim no land, no allotments, only part of myself.

There are many people who could claim and learn from their Indian ancestry, but because of the fear their parents and grandparents knew, because of past and present prejudice against Indian people, that part of their heritage is clouded or denied. Had I been raised on other soil or by other people, my Indian ancestry might have been less important, less shaping. But I was not raised in Czechoslovakia or England. I was raised in the foothills of the Adirondack Mountains near a town whose spring waters were regarded as sacred and healing by the Iroquois and Abenaki alike. This is my dreaming place. Only my death will separate it from my flesh.

I've avoided calling myself "Indian" most of my life, even when I have felt that identification most strongly, even when people have called me an "Indian." Unlike my grandfather, I have never seen that name as an insult, but there is another term I like to use. I heard it first in Lakota and it refers to a person of mixed blood, *metis*. In English it becomes "Translator's Son." It is not an insult, like *half-breed*. It means that you are able to understand the language of both sides, to help them understand each other.

In my late teens I began to meet other Indian people and learn from them. It seemed a natural thing to do and I found that there was often something familiar about them. In part it was a physical thing—just as when I opened Frederick John Pratson's book *Land of Four Directions* and saw that the Passamaquoddy man on page 45 was an absolute double of photographs of Jesse Bowman. It was not just looks, though. It was a walk and a way of talking, a way of seeing and an easy relationship to land and the natural world and animals. *Wasn't no man*, Jack Bowman said, *ever better with animals than Jess. Why he could make a horse do most anything.* I saw, too, the way children were treated with great tolerance and gentleness and realized that that, too, was true of my grandfather. He'd learned that from his father, he said.

> Whenever I done something wrong, my father would never hit me. He never would hit a child. He said it jes wasn't right. But he would just talk to me. Sometimes I wisht he'd just of hit me. I hated it when he had to talk to me.

The process of such learning and sharing deserves more space than I can give it now. It involves many hours of sitting around kitchen tables and hearing stories others were too busy to listen to, and even more hours of helping out when help was needed. It comes from travels to places such as the Abenaki community of Swanton, Vermont, and the still-beating heart of the Iroquois League, Onondaga, and from realizing—as Simon Ortiz puts it so simply and so well—that "Indians are everywhere." If you are ready to listen, you'll meet someone who is ready to talk.

This short sketch of my early years, which I shall end here, represents only the beginning of a long apprenticeship I've been serving (*forever*, it seems). I seem to have an unending capacity for making mistakes just as my teachers seem to have an unerring ability to turn my mistakes into lessons. But the patience, the listening that has made it possible for me to learn more than I ever dreamed as a boy, is also the lesson I've begun to learn.

The most widely anthologized of my poems describes one lesson I was taught in the way most good lessons come to you—when you least expect them. Let it represent that part of my life which has come from continual contact with Native American people over more than two decades. Because of that contact my own sons have grown up taking such things as sweat lodges and powwows and pride in Indian ancestry for granted. The small amount that I have learned I've tried, when it is right to do so, to share with others.

BIRDFOOT'S GRAMPA

The old man
must have stopped our car
two dozen times to climb out
and gather into his hands
the small toads blinded
by our lights and leaping,
live drops of rain.

The rain was falling,
a mist about his white hair
and I kept saying
you can't save them all
accept it, get back in
we've got places to go.

But, leathery hands full
of wet brown life
knee deep in the summer
roadside grass,
he just smiled and said
they have places to go to
too

(from *Entering Onondaga*, Cold Mountain Press, 1978)

WRITING ABOUT THE READING

4. Bruchac rejects labels such as "mongrel" and "half-breed." What name does he prefer for himself and why does he choose this label?

5. Explain what you think the following statement means and why you agree and/or disagree with this statement: "If you are ready to listen, you'll meet someone who is ready to talk."

6. Explain what you think the author's statement means and why you agree and/or disagree with this statement: "I can go onward only by going back to where my memories begin."

7. Bruchac's grandfather hid his Native American heritage. Why do you think that he was right or not right to do so?

8. Why do you think that Bruchac concludes this essay with a poem?

WRITING FROM YOUR OWN EXPERIENCE

Note: In these assignments, write about your own experience or use that of someone you know, read about, or saw in a film/TV show.

9. Bruchac reacted violently when his college instructor criticized his writing. Recall a time when someone criticized you, such as a teacher, coach, or someone else in authority. What was your reaction to this criticism and why did you react this way?

10. Bruchac relates how the sport of wrestling was important in his life. Choose a sport, hobby, or other activity and explain why it is important to you.

11. Think of a time when you learned a lesson from a mistake that you made. Why did you make this mistake and what lesson did you learn from it?

WRITING ABOUT RESEARCH

12. Why do you agree (or disagree) that there is a need for Native American studies departments in today's colleges (or in your particular college)?

13. Choose one Native American tribe to study. Explain how and why one (or more) of the following skills or arts was adapted to the land and the tribe's traditional way of life.

    (a) housing

    (b) obtaining food

(c) clothing

(d) sports and/or activities

(e) music

14. Choose a prominent person of Native American heritage and describe his/her achievements. Consider one of the following:

(a) Will Rogers (humorist)

(b) Billy Mills (track and field athlete)

(c) Beverly (Buffy) Sainte-Marie (singer)

(d) Will Sampson, Jr. (actor)

(e) Jay Silverheels (actor)

(f) Maria Tallchief (dancer)

(g) Jim Thorpe (athlete)

15. Research the history of the boarding schools established for Native Americans. Explain the purpose of these schools and whether you think that the government was right to establish boarding schools for Native Americans.

Selection 7

All My Relations

LINDA HOGAN

Linda Hogan *(1947–), a member of the Chickasaw tribe, is noted for writing fiction and poetry that are characterized by a sensitivity to nature and a strong female perspective. Hogan received an M.A. from the University of Colorado, Boulder (1978) and served as associate professor of American/American Indian Studies at the University of Minnesota (1984–1989). Since then, Hogan has been professor of English at the University of Colorado. She received a Pulitzer Prize nomination (1991) for* Mean Spirit, *a novel about the conflict over oil found on Native American lands in Oklahoma in the 1920s. Her 1994 work,* The Book of Medicines, *was a finalist for the National Book Critics Award.*

For many years, Hogan worked as a volunteer in wildlife rehabilitation projects in Minnesota and in Colorado. Both Hogan's poetry and fiction show her deep concern for wild animals and the environment. Hogan views the Earth as a source of life and renewal, as a connection to the spiritual. She often employs images of a sick, barren landscape to represent dislocation, hopelessness, and despair. She believes that as humans learn to reconnect with nature, they become physically well and spiritually regenerated.

The selection "All My Relations" contains many of these themes. This essay first appeared in 1992 in Parabola, *a journal of anthropology published by the Society for the Study of Myth and Tradition. In this reading, Hogan describes the traditional ceremony of the sweat lodge, which heals her and makes her aware again of her connection to all of the universe.*

PREPARING TO READ

1. Explain whether you think that people are more concerned about the environment today than in the past.
2. Why do you think that many people feel a need to get away from the pressures of everyday life to restore themselves?

3. Explain whether you think it is important to understand the different spiritual beliefs of people.
4. Why do you agree (or disagree) that people today are less spiritual than in the past and what are the reasons for your opinion?

ALL MY RELATIONS

It is a sunny, clear day outside, almost hot, and a slight breeze comes through the room from the front door. We sit at the table and talk. As is usual in an Indian household, food preparation began as soon as we arrived and now there is the snap of potatoes frying in the black skillet, the sweet smell of white bread overwhelming even the grease, and the welcome black coffee. A ringer washer stands against the wall of the kitchen, and the counter space is taken up with dishes, pans, and boxes of food.

I am asked if I still read books and I admit that I do. Reading is not "traditional" and education has long been suspect in communities that were broken, in part, by that system, but we laugh at my confession because a television set plays in the next room.

In the living room there are two single beds. People from reservations, travelers needing help, are frequent guests here. The man who will put together the ceremony I have come to request sits on one, dozing. A girl takes him a plate of food. He eats. He is a man I have respected for many years, for his commitment to the people, for his intelligence, for his spiritual and political involvement in concerns vital to Indian people and nations. Next to him sits a girl eating potato chips, and from this room we hear the sounds of the freeway.

After eating and sitting, it is time for me to talk to him, to tell him why we have come here. I have brought him tobacco and he nods and listens as I tell him about the help we need.

I know this telling is the first part of the ceremony, my part in it. It is a story, really, that finds its way into language, and story is at the very crux of healing, at the heart of every ceremony and ritual in the older America.

The ceremony itself includes not just our own prayers and stories of what brought us to it, but includes the unspoken records of history, the mythic past, and all the other lives connected to ours, our family, nations, and all other creatures.

I am sent home to prepare. I tie fifty tobacco ties, green. This I do with Bull Durham tobacco, squares of cotton which are tied with twine and left strung together. These are called prayer ties. I spend the time preparing in silence and alone. Each tie has a prayer in it. I will also need wood for the fire, meat and bread for food.

• • •

On the day of the ceremony, we meet in the next town and leave my car in public parking. My daughters and I climb into the back seat. The man who will help us is drumming and singing in front of us. His wife drives and chats. He doesn't speak. He is moving between the worlds, beginning already to step over the boundaries of what we think, in daily and ordinary terms, is real and present. He is already feeling, hearing, knowing what else is there, that which is around us daily but too often unacknowledged, a larger life than our own small ones. We pass billboards and little towns and gas stations. An eagle flies overhead. It is "a good sign," we all agree. We stop to watch it.

We stop again, later, at a convenience store to fill the gas tank and to buy soda. The leader still drums and is silent. He is going into the drum, going into the center, even here as we drive west on the highway, even with our conversations about other people, family.

It is a hot balmy day, and by the time we reach the site where the ceremony is to take place, we are slow and sleepy with the brightness and warmth of the sun. In some tribes, men and women participate in separate sweat lodge ceremonies, but here, men, women, and children all come together to sweat. The children are cooling off in the creek. A woman stirs the fire that lives inside a circle of black rocks, pots beside her, a jar of oil, a kettle, a can of coffee. The leaves of the trees are thick and green.

In the background, the sweat lodge structure stands. Birds are on it. It is still skeletal. A woman and man are beginning to place old rugs and blankets over the bent cottonwood frame. A great fire is already burning and the lava stones that will be the source of heat for the sweat, are being fired in it.

A few people sit outside on lawn chairs and cast-off couches that have the stuffing coming out. We sip coffee and talk about the food, about recent events. A man tells us that a friend gave him money for a new car. The creek sounds restful. Another man falls asleep. My young daughter splashes in the water. Heat waves rise up behind us from the fire that is preparing the stones. My tobacco ties are placed inside, on the framework of the lodge.

By late afternoon we are ready, one at a time, to enter the enclosure. The hot lava stones are placed inside. They remind us of earth's red and fiery core, and of the spark inside all life. After the flap, which serves as a door, is closed, water is poured over the stones and the hot steam rises around us. In a sweat lodge ceremony, the entire world is brought inside the enclosure. The soft odor of smoking cedar accompanies this arrival of everything. It is all called in. The animals come from the warm and sunny distances. Water from dark lakes is there. Wind. Young, lithe willow branches bent overhead remember their lives rooted in ground, the sun their leaves took in. They remember that minerals and water rose up their trunks, and birds nested in their leaves, and that planets turned above their brief, slender lives. The thunder clouds travel in from far regions of earth. Wind arrives from the four directions. It has moved through caves and breathed through our bodies. It is the same air elk have inhaled, air that passed through the lungs of a grizzly bear. The sky is there, with all the stars whose lights we see long after the stars themselves have gone back to nothing. It is a place grown intense and holy. It is a place of immense community and of humbled solitude; we sit together in our aloneness and speak, one at a time, our deepest language of need, hope, loss, and survival. We remember that all things are connected.

Remembering this is the purpose of the ceremony. It is part of a healing and restoration. It is the mending of a broken connection between us and the rest. The participants in a ceremony say the words, "All my relations," before and after we pray; those words create a relationship with other people, with animals, with the land. To have health it is necessary to keep all these relations in mind.

• • •

The intention of a ceremony is to put a person back together by restructuring the human mind. This reorganization is accomplished by a kind of inner map, a geography of the human spirit and the rest of the world. We make whole our broken off pieces of self and world. Within ourselves, we bring together the fragments of our lives in a sacred act of renewal, and we reestablish our connections with others. The ceremony is a point of return. It takes us toward the place of balance, our place in the community of all things. It is an event that sets us back upright. But it is not a finished thing. The real ceremony begins where the formal one ends, when we take up a new way, our minds and hearts filled with the vision of earth that holds us within it, in compassionate relationship to and with our world.

We speak. We sing. We swallow water and breathe smoke. By the end of the ceremony, it is as if skin contains land and birds. The places within us have become filled. As inside the enclosure of the lodge, the animals and ancestors move into the human body, into skin and blood. The land merges with us. The stones come to dwell inside the person. Gold rolling hills take up residence, their tall grasses blowing. The red light of canyons is there. The black skies of night that wheel above our heads come to live inside the skull. We who easily grow apart from the world are returned to the great store of life all around us and there is the deepest sense of being at home here in this intimate kinship. There is no real aloneness. There is solitude and the nurturing silence that is relationship with ourselves, but even then we are part of something larger.

After a sweat lodge ceremony, the enclosure is abandoned. Quieter now, we prepare to drive home. We pack up the kettles, the coffee pot. The prayer ties are placed in nearby trees. Some of the other people prepare to go to work, go home, or cook a dinner. We drive home. Everything returns to ordinary use. A spider weaves a web from one of the cottonwood poles to another. Crows sit inside the framework. It's evening. The crickets are singing. All my relations.

WRITING ABOUT THE READING

5. Why is it important to the writer that she assist in the preparations for this ceremony?

6. How does Hogan participate actively in the ceremony and why does she do this?

7. How does the opening descriptive paragraph set the tone of the reading?

8. How is the closing paragraph linked to the opening paragraph?

WRITING FROM YOUR OWN EXPERIENCE

Note: In these assignments, write about your own experience or use that of someone you know, read about, or saw in a film/TV show.

9. Although not usually thought of as a "ceremony," many formal events are carried out in an ordered, ceremonious manner. Such "ceremonies" include: the opening of a baseball or football game, a graduation, a play, a formal dinner, a court trial, or a club meeting. Choose one such formal event and explain why you could use the words "ceremony" or "ritual" to describe this event.

10. Have you ever met (or read a book or seen a movie about) someone whose spiritual beliefs were very different from your own. Why did you find this person's beliefs to be interesting and/or different from yours?

11. Recall a time when you had a need for emotional or spiritual "healing." What method did you use for healing and what were some of the reasons for your choice of this method?

12. Hogan has been a volunteer with wildlife rehabilitation projects. Recall an experience that you had with an animal (such as a snake, bear, rabbit, dog, cat, or bird). Why was this experience memorable and what were the consequences of this experience?

WRITING ABOUT RESEARCH

13. Choose one (or more) prominent Native American(s) and explain why this person is significant in American history. Consider one (or more) of the following:

    (a) Black Hawk (warrior)
    (b) Joseph Brant (tribal chief)
    (c) Chief Joseph (Nez Perce)
    (d) Chief Osceola (Seminole)
    (e) Chief Seattle (Suquamish)
    (f) Cochise (warrior)
    (g) Crazy Horse (Oglala Sioux)
    (h) Geronimo (Apache)
    (i) Ishi (tribal survivor)
    (j) Pocahontas (translator)
    (k) Sacajawea (translator)
    (l) Seattle (tribal leader)
    (m) Sequoyah (Cherokee)
    (n) Sitting Bull (Sioux)
    (o) Tecumseh (tribal leader)

14. At the end of the nineteenth century, many Native Americans turned to various spiritual movements. Choose one of the following movements and explain why it was important in the life of these Native Americans:

    (a) the peyote cult and/or the Native American Church
    (b) the Ghost Dance religion
    (c) the Sun Dance religion

15. Choose a current local or national environmental issue. Why is there a concern about this problem and what are some suggested solutions to the problem? Consider issues such as:

    (a) endangered species (or one particular species)
    (b) depletion of nonrenewable resources
    (c) global warming
    (d) nonbiodegradable products
    (e) ozone depletion
    (f) toxic waste

Selection 8

Water Witch

LOUIS OWENS

Louis Owens *(1948–), writer and educator of Choctaw and Cherokee heritage, worked as a farm laborer in California in his early years. He received B.A. (1971) and M.A. (1974) degrees from the University of California, Santa Barbara, and a Ph.D. (1981) from the University of California, Davis. Currently, Owens is professor of English at the University of New Mexico. He has received many awards for his writing, including a National Endowment for the Humanities Fellowship (1987) and a National Endowment for the Arts Fellowship (1989). He received the American Book Award in 1997 for his novel,* Nightland.

Owens often examines the connection of Native Americans to the place where they currently live and the lands from which their ancestors came. In his 1992 novel, The Sharpest Sight, *Owens associates the Salinas River with contemporary life in California and the Yazoo River with traditional life in the ancestral homeland in Mississippi. Owens believes that modern Native Americans of "mixed blood" must integrate traditions of the past with the new world in which they live.*

Owens's sense of place, his use of the contrast between the two river valleys, can be seen in the selection "Water Witch," which was one of a collection of essays, Growing Up Native American: An Anthology *(1993). In this reading, Owens writes about his own "mixed-blood" identity, his youth in the dry Salinas valley, and his family's visit to the humid climate of Mississippi.*

PREPARING TO READ

1. Why do you think some people resort to traditional but "nonscientific" practices (such as water witches, astrologers, psychics, or fortune-tellers)?

2. Why do you think that adolescents and/or adults should (or should not) be allowed to hunt animals or birds for sport?

3. Many environmentalists are concerned about the disappearance of wild areas to accommodate the continuing growth of suburbs. What would be your solution to this problem and why do you think that this is a workable solution?

WATER WITCH

For a while, when I was very young, my father was a water witch. He took us with him sometimes, my older brother and me, and we walked those burned-up central California ranches, wherever there was a low spot that a crop-and-cattle desperate rancher could associate with a dream of wetness. The dusty windmills with their tin blades like pale flowers would be turning tiredly or just creaking windward now and then, and the ranch dogs—always long-haired, brown and black with friendly eyes—would sweep their tails around from a respectful distance. The ranches, scattered near places like Creston, Pozo, San Miguel, and San Ardo, stretched across burnt gold hills, the little ranch houses bent into themselves beneath a few dried up cottonwoods or sycamores, some white oaks if the rancher's grandfather had settled early enough to choose his spot. Usually there would be kids, three or four ranging from diapers to hotrod pickups, and like the friendly ranch dogs they'd keep their distance. The cattle would hang close to the fences, eyeing the house and gray barn. In the sky, red-tailed hawks wheeled against a washed-out sun while ground squirrels whistled warnings from the grain stubble.

He'd walk, steps measured as if the earth demanded measure, the willow fork held in both hands before him pointed at the ground like some kind of offering. We'd follow a few yards behind with measured paces. And nearly always the wand would finally tremble, dip and dance toward the dead wild oats, and he would stop to drive a stick into the ground or pile a few rock-dry clods in a cairn.

A displaced Mississippi Choctaw, half-breed, squat and reddish, blind in one eye, he'd spit tobacco juice at the stick or cairn and turn back toward the house, feeling maybe the stirring of Yazoo mud from the river of his birth as if the water he never merely discovered, but drew all that way from a darker, damper world. Within a few days he'd be back with his boss and they'd drill a well at the spot he'd marked. Not once did the water fail, but always it was hidden and secret, for that was the way of water in our part of California.

When I think now of growing up in that country, the southern end of the Salinas Valley, a single mountain range from the ocean, I remember first the great hidden water, the Salinas River which ran out of the Santa Lucias and disappeared where the coastal mountains bent inland near San Luis Obispo. Dammed at its headwaters into a large reservoir where we caught bluegill and catfish, the river never had a chance. Past the spillway gorge, it sank into itself and became the largest subterranean river on the continent, a half-mile-wide swath of brush and sand and cottonwoods with a current you could feel down there beneath your feet when you hunted the river bottom, as if a water witch yourself, you swayed at every step toward the stream below.

We lived first in withdrawn canyons in the Santa Lucias, miles up dirt roads into the creases of the Coast Range where we kids squirmed through buck brush and plotted long hunts to the ocean. But there were no trails and the manzanita would turn us back with what we thought must be the scent of the sea in our nostrils. Rattlesnakes, bears and mountain lions lived back there. And stories of mythic wild boars drifted down from ranches to the north. In the spring the hills would shine with new grass and the dry creeks would run for a few brief weeks. We'd hike across a ridge to ride wild horses belonging to a man who never knew that the kids rode them. In summer the grasses burned brown and the clumps of live oaks on the hillsides formed dark places in the distance.

Later we lived down in the valley on the caving banks of the river. At six and eight years we had hunted with slingshots in the mountains, but at ten and twelve we owned rifles, .22s, and we stalked the dry river brush for quail and cottontails and the little brush rabbits that, like the pack rats, were everywhere. Now and then a deer would break ahead of us, crashing thickets like the bear himself. Great horned owls lived there and called in drumming voices, vague warnings of death somewhere. From the river bottom we pinged .22 slugs off new farm equipment gliding past on the flatcars of the Southern Pacific.

Once in a while, we'd return to Mississippi, as if my father's mixed blood sought a balance never found. Seven kids, a dog or two, canvas water bags swaying from fender and radiator, we drove into what I remember as the darkness of the Natchez Trace. In our two-room Mississippi cabin, daddy longlegs crawled across the tar papered walls, and cotton fields surged close on three sides. Across the rutted road through a tangle of tree, brush, and vine, fragrant of rot and death, was the Yazoo River, a thick current cutting us off from the swamps that boomed and cracked all night from the other shore.

From the Yazoo we must have learned to feel water as a presence, a constant, a secret source of both dream and nightmare, perhaps as my father's Choctaw ancestors had. I remember it as I remember night. Always we'd return to California after a few months, as much as a year. And it would be an emergence, for the Salinas was a daylight world of hot, white sand and bone-dry brush, where in the fall, red and gold leaves covered the sand, and frost made silver lines from earth to sky. Here, death and decay seemed unrelated things. And here, I imagined the water as a clear, cold stream through white sand beneath my feet.

Only in the winter did the Salinas change. When the rains came pounding down out of the Coast Range, the river would rise from its bed to become a half-mile-wide terror, sweeping away chicken coops and misplaced barns; whatever had crept too near. Tricked each year into death, steelhead trout would dash upstream from the ocean, and almost immediately the flooding river would recede to a thin stream at the heart of the dry bed, then a few pools marked by the tracks of coons, then only sand again and the tails and bones of big fish.

When I think of growing up in California, I think always of the river. It seemed then that all life referred to the one hundred and twenty miles of sand and brush that twisted its way northward, an upside-down, backwards river that emptied into the Pacific near Monterey, a place I didn't see till I was grown. As teenagers, my brother and I bought our own rifles, a .30-.30 and an ought-six, and we followed our father into the Coast Range after deer and wild boar. We acquired shotguns and walked the high coastal ridges for bandtail pigeon. We drove to fish the headwaters of the Nacimiento and San Antonio rivers. And from every ridge top we saw, if not the river itself, then the long, slow course of the valley it had carved, the Salinas. Far across were the rolling Gabilan Mountains, more hawk hills than mountains, and on the valley bottom, ranches made squares of green and gold with flashing windmills and tin roofs.

After school and during summers we worked on the ranches, hoeing sugar beets, building fences, bucking hay, working cattle (dehorning, castrating, branding, ear-clipping, inoculating, all in what must have seemed a single horrific moment for the bawling calf). We'd cross the river to drive at dawn through the dry country watching the clumps of live oak separate from the graying hillsides. Moving shadows would become deer that drifted from dark to dark. Years later, coming home from another state, I would time my drive so that I reached that country at daybreak to watch the oaks rise out of night and to smell the damp dead grasses.

Snaking its way down through our little town was a creek. Dipping out of the Coast Range, sliding past chicken farms and country stores, it pooled in long, shadowed clefts beneath the shoulders of hills and dug its own miniature canyon as it passed by the high school, beneath U.S. 101, around the flanks of the county hospital and on to the river where it gathered in a final welling before sinking into the sand. Enroute it picked up the sweat and stink of a small town, the flotsam and jetsam of stunted aspirations, and along its course in tree shadow and root tangle, under cutbank and log, it hid small, dark trout we caught with hook and handline. From the creek came also steelhead trapped by a vanished river, and great blimp-bellied suckers which hunkered close to the bottom, even a single outraged bull-head which I returned to its solitary pool. At the place where the chicken-processing plant disgorged a yellow stream into the creek, the trout grew fat and sluggish, easily caught. We learned every shading and wrinkle of the creek, not knowing then that it was on the edge already, its years numbered. I more than anyone, fisher of tainted trout, kept what I thought of as a pact with the dying creek: as long as the water flows and the grass grows.

Up on Pine Mountain, not so much looming as leaning over the town of my younger years, a well-kept cemetery casts a wide shadow. From this cemetery, one fine summer evening, a local youth exhumed his grandmother to drive about town with her draped across the hood of his car, an act so shocking no punishment could be brought to bear. Later, when I asked him why, he looked at me in wonder. "Didn't you ever want to do that?" he asked. That fall, after a bitter football loss, members of the high-school letterman's club kidnapped a bus full of rooters from a rival school, holding them briefly at gunpoint with threats of execution. The summer before, an acquaintance of mine had stolen a small plane and dive-bombed the town's hamburger stand with empty beer bottles. The town laughed. Later, he caught a Greyhound bus to Oregon, bought a shotgun in a small town, and killed himself. It was that kind of place also. Stagnant between Coast Range and river, the town, too, had subterranean currents, a hot-in-summer, cold-in-winter kind of submerged violence that rippled the surface again and again. Desires to exhume and punish grew strong. Escape was just around a corner.

Behind the cemetery, deep in a wrinkle of the mountain, was an older burial ground, the town's original graveyard, tumbled and hidden in long grasses and falling oaks. Parting the gray oat stalks to read the ancient stone, I felt back then as astonished as a Japanese soldier must have when he first heard the words of a Navajo code talker. Here was a language that pricked through time, millennia perhaps, with painful familiarity but one that remained inexorably remote.

A year ago, I drove back to the house nine of us had lived in on the banks of the river. The house was gone, and behind the empty lot the river had changed. Where there had been a wilderness of brush and cottonwoods was now only a wide, empty channel gleaming like bone. Alfalfa fields swept coolly up from the opposite bank toward a modern ranch house. "Flood control" someone in the new Denny's restaurant told me later that afternoon. "Cleaned her out clear to San Miguel," he said.

WRITING ABOUT THE READING

4. How is the opening narrative about searching for "subterranean water" related to the end of the essay?
5. Compare the writer's attitude toward the Salinas River valley with that of the Yazoo valley.
6. Why do you think that the writer describes life in the small town as that of "stunted aspirations"?
7. Why does Owens's father's visit to the Yazoo River symbolize his search for his heritage?

WRITING FROM YOUR OWN EXPERIENCE

Note: In these assignments, write about your own experience or use that of someone you know, read about, or saw in a film/TV show.

8. At the end of the essay, Owens returns to his childhood home and finds that the area had changed. Think of a place you know that has changed in the last few years. How has this place changed and what is your feeling about this change?
9. The Salinas River has been an important influence on Owens's life and writing. Choose an important geographical feature (such as a river, lake, ocean, hill, desert, etc.) from an area in which you have lived and explain how and why this feature influences the life of people in that area.
10. Owens relates that some of the actions of young men in his town were designed to shock others. Recall a time when you acted in a way to shock others. Why did you shock people and what was the outcome of this act?

WRITING ABOUT RESEARCH

11. As a boy, Owens learned to use a gun. Research some of the controversy about gun control laws. What is your position on this issue and why do you take this stand?

12. Owens's father was a "water witch." Research this practice and explain why some people still believe in the efficacy of this practice.

13. Choose a Native American tribal organization. Why do you think this organization has been successful (or unsuccessful) in meeting its goals? Some tribal organizations to research include the:
    (a) All-Pueblo Council
    (b) Columbian Powhatan Confederacy
    (c) Iroquois League
    (d) United Sioux Tribes
    (e) United Southeast Tribes

14. Choose a Native American political organization. Why do you think this organization has been successful (or unsuccessful) in meeting its goals? Some organizations to research include the:
    (a) American Indian Civil Rights Council
    (b) American Indian Movement (AIM)
    (c) American Indian Women's League
    (d) Organization of Native American Students
    (e) Young American Indian Council

15. Choose one of the arts and crafts of Native Americans, such as the Cherokee or Iroquois, who lived in the Eastern Woodlands. How were these objects made and what was their purpose? Consider items such as:
    (a) baskets
    (b) beadwork and quillwork
    (c) birchbark utensils
    (d) grave offerings
    (e) masks
    (f) pottery

Language and Literature from a Pueblo Indian Perspective

LESLIE MARMON SILKO

Leslie Marmon Silko *(1948–), poet, writer and educator, grew up on the Laguna Pueblo reservation in New Mexico. After receiving a B.A. from the University of New Mexico in 1969, Silko attended law school until 1971 when she received a National Endowment for the Arts discovery grant. Silko's awards include the Pushcart Prize for poetry (1977), the American Book Award for* Ceremony *(1980), and a John D. and Catherine T. MacArthur Foundation Grant (1983). In 1989, Silko received the University of New Mexico's Distinguished Alumnus award. Since 1978, Silko has been professor of English at the University of Arizona, Tucson.*

Like many other Native American writers, Silko is concerned with the efforts of Native Americans to balance their traditional culture and modern reality. Her celebrated novel, Ceremony, *narrates the struggle of Tayo, a Pueblo war veteran, to adjust to civilian life on the reservation. After learning from a wise old man that a ceremony is a method of achieving harmony with the cosmos, Tayo goes on a journey into the mountains to perform a personal ceremony. Only then can he return to the Pueblo community, rediscover his relationship to the land, and make sense of the disjointed fragments of his life.*

As in Ceremony, *the connection between language, human responsibility, and nature underlies much of Silko's writing. Her essay, "Language and Literature from a Pueblo Indian Perspective," was originally printed in* English Literature: Opening Up the Canon *(1979). In this excerpt, Silko discusses the importance of the oral tradition in bridging the contemporary and traditional cultures.*

PREPARING TO READ

1. Compare listening to a lecture to reading the same material. Which way of learning do you prefer and what are some of the reasons for your choice?

2. Do you think that the media is too intrusive in its desire to get a story about public figures and why do you take this position?

3. Traditional folktales (such as the stories of Cinderella, Sleeping Beauty, or Snow White) have been criticized as teaching girls to be passive and to wait for Prince Charming. What changes would you make in one of these folktales (or another story of your choice) to make it reflect the lives of women today?

LANGUAGE AND LITERATURE FROM A PUEBLO INDIAN PERSPECTIVE

Where I come from, the words most highly valued are those spoken from the heart, unpremeditated and unrehearsed. Among the Pueblo people, a written speech or statement is highly suspect because the true feelings of the speaker remain hidden as she reads words that are detached from the occasion and the audience. I have intentionally not written a formal paper because I want you to *hear* and to experience English in a structure that follows patterns from the oral tradition. For those of you accustomed to being taken from point A to point B to point C, this presentation may be somewhat difficult to follow. Pueblo expression resembles something like a spider's web—with many little threads radiating from the center, crisscrossing each other. As with the web, the structure emerges as it is made and you must simply listen and trust, as the Pueblo people do, that meaning will be made.

My task is a formidable one: I ask you to set aside a number of basic approaches that you have been using, and probably will continue to use, and instead, to approach language from the Pueblo perspective, one that embraces the whole of creation and the whole of history and time.

What changes would Pueblo writers make to English as a language for literature? I have some examples of stories in English that I will use to address this question. At the same time, I would like to explain the importance of storytelling and how it relates to a Pueblo theory of language.

So, I will begin, appropriately enough, with the Pueblo Creation story, an all-inclusive story of how life began. In this story, Tséitsí-nako, Thought Woman, by thinking of her sisters, and together with her sisters, thought of everything that is. In this way, the world was created. Everything in this world was a part of the original creation; the people at home understood that far away there were other human beings, also a part of this world. The Creation story even includes a prophecy, which describes the origin of European and African peoples and also refers to Asians.

This story, I think, suggests something about why the Pueblo people are more concerned with story and communication and less concerned with a particular language. There are at least six, possibly seven, distinct languages among the twenty pueblos of the southwestern United States, for example, Zuñi and Hopi. And from mesa to mesa there are subtle differences in language. But the particular language being spoken isn't as important as what a speaker is trying to say, and this emphasis on the story itself stems, I believe, from a view of narrative particular to the Pueblo and other Native American peoples—that is, that language *is* story.

I will try to clarify this statement. At Laguna Pueblo, for example, many individual words have their own stories. So when one is telling a story, and one is using words to tell the story, each word that one is speaking has a story of its own, too. Often the speakers or tellers will go into these word-stories, creating an elaborate structure of stories-within-stories. This structure, which becomes very apparent in the actual telling of a story, informs contemporary Pueblo writing and storytelling as well as the traditional narratives. This perspective on narrative—of story within story, the idea that one story is only the beginning of many stories, and the sense that stories never truly end—represents an important contribution of Native American cultures to the English language.

Many people think of storytelling as something that is done at bedtime, that it is something done for small children. But when I use the term *storytelling*, I'm talking about something much bigger than that. I'm talking about something that comes out of an experience and an understanding of that original view of creation—that we are all part of a whole; we do not differentiate or fragment stories and experiences. In the beginning, Tséitsínako, Thought Woman, thought of all things, and all of these things are held together as one holds many things together in a single thought.

So in the telling (and you will hear a few of the dimensions of this telling) first of all, as mentioned earlier, the storytelling always includes the audience, the listeners. In fact, a great deal of the story is believed to be inside the listener; the storyteller's role is to draw the story out of the listeners. The storytelling continues from generation to generation.

Basically, the origin story constructs our identity—within this story, we know who we are. We are the Lagunas. This is where we come from. We came this way. We came by this place. And so from the time we are very young, we hear these stories, so that when we go out into the world, when one asks who we are, or where we are from, we immediately know: we are the people who came from the north. We are the people of these stories.

In the Creation story, Antelope says that he will help knock a hole in the earth so that the people can come up, out into the next world. Antelope tries and tries; he uses his hooves, but is unable to break through. It is then that Badger says, "Let me help you." And Badger very patiently uses his claws and digs a way through, bringing the people into the world. When the Badger clan people think of themselves, or when the Antelope people think of themselves, it is as people who are of *this* story, and this is *our* place, and we fit into the very beginning when the people first came, before we began our journey south.

Within the clans there are stories that identify the clan. One moves, then, from the idea of one's identity as a tribal person into clan identity, then to one's identity as a member of an extended family. And it is the notion of "extended family" that has produced a kind of story that some distinguish from other Pueblo stories, though Pueblo people do not. Anthropologists and ethnologists have, for a long time, differentiated the types of stories the Pueblos tell. They tended to elevate the old, sacred, and traditional stories and to brush aside family stories, the family's account of itself. But in Pueblo culture, these family stories are given equal recognition. There is no definite, preset pattern for the way one will hear the stories of one's own family, but it is a very critical part of one's childhood, and the storytelling continues throughout one's life. One will hear stories of importance to the family—sometimes wonderful stories—stories about the time a maternal uncle got the biggest deer that was ever seen and brought it back from the mountains. And so an individual's identity will extend from the identity constructed around the family—"I am from the family of my uncle who brought in this wonderful deer and it was a wonderful hunt."

Family accounts include negative stories, too; perhaps an uncle did something unacceptable. It is very important that one keep track of all these stories—both positive and not so positive—about one's own family and other families. Because even when there is no way around it—old Uncle Pete *did* do a terrible thing—by knowing the stories that originate in other families, one is able to deal with terrible sorts of things that might happen within one's own family. If a member of the family does something that cannot be excused, one always knows stories about similarly inexcusable things done by a member of another family. But this knowledge is not communicated for malicious reasons. It is very important to understand this. Keeping track of all the stories within the community gives us all a certain distance, a useful perspective, that brings incidents down to a level we can deal with. If others have done it before, it cannot be so terrible. If others have endured, so can we.

The stories are always bringing us together, keeping this whole together, keeping this family together, keeping this clan together. "Don't go away, don't isolate yourself, but come here, because we have all had these kinds of experiences." And so there is this constant pulling together to resist the tendency to run or hide or separate oneself during a traumatic emotional experience. This separation not only endangers the group but the individual as well—one does not recover by oneself.

Because storytelling lies at the heart of Pueblo culture, it is absurd to attempt to fix the stories in time. "When did they tell the stories?" or "What time of day does the storytelling take place?"—these questions are nonsensical from a Pueblo perspective, because our storytelling goes on constantly: as some old grandmother puts on the shoes of a child and tells her the story of a little girl who didn't wear her shoes, for instance, or someone comes into the house for coffee to talk with a teenage boy who has just been in a lot of trouble, to reassure him that someone else's son has been in that kind of trouble, too. Storytelling is an ongoing process, working on many different levels.

Here's one story that is often told at a time of individual crisis (and I want to remind you that we make no distinctions between types of story—historical, sacred, plain gossip—because these distinctions are not useful when discussing the Pueblo *experience* of language). There was a young man who, when he came back from the war in Vietnam, had saved up his army pay and bought a beautiful red Volkswagen. He was very proud of it. One night he drove up to a place called the King's Bar right across the reservation line. The bar is notorious for many reasons, particularly for the deep *arroyo* located behind it. The young man ran in to pick up a cold six-pack, but he forgot to put on his emergency brake. And his little red Volkswagen rolled back into the *arroyo* and was all smashed up. He felt very bad about it, but within a few days everybody had come to him with stories about other people who had lost cars and family members to that *arroyo*, for instance, George Day's station wagon, with his mother-in-law and kids inside. So everybody was saying, "Well, at least your mother-in-law and kids weren't in the car when it rolled in," and one can't argue with that kind of story. The story of the young man and his smashed-up Volkswagen was now joined with all the other stories of cars that fell into that *arroyo*.

Now I want to tell you a very beautiful little story. It is a very old story that is sometimes told to people who suffer great family or personal loss. This story was told by my Aunt Susie. She is one of the first generation of people at Laguna who began experimenting with English—who began working to make English speak for us—that is, to speak from the heart. (I come from a family intent on getting the stories told.) As you read the story, I think you will hear that. And here and there, I think, you will also hear the influence of the Indian school at Carlisle, Pennsylvania, where my Aunt Susie was sent (like being sent to prison) for six years.

This scene is set partly in Acoma, partly in Laguna. Waithea was a little girl living in Acoma and one day she said, "Mother, I would like to have some *yashtoah* to eat." *Yashtoah* is the hardened crust of corn mush that curls up. *Yashtoah* literally means "curled up." She said, "I would like to have some *yashtoah*," and her mother said, "My dear little girl, I can't make you any *yashtoah* because we haven't any wood, but if you will go down off the mesa, down below, and pick up some pieces of wood and bring them home, I will make you some *yashtoah*." So Waithea was glad and ran down the precipitous cliff of Acoma mesa. Down below, just as her mother had told her, there were pieces of wood, some curled, some crooked in shape, that she was to pick up and take home. She found just such wood as these.

She brought them home in a little wicker basket. First she called to her mother as she got home, "*Nayah, deeni!* Mother, upstairs!" The Pueblo people always called "upstairs" because long ago their homes were two, three stories, and they entered from the top. She said, "*Deeni!* UPSTAIRS!" and her mother came. The little girl said, "I have brought the wood you wanted me to bring." And she opened her little wicker basket to lay out the pieces of wood but here they were snakes. They were snakes instead of the crooked sticks of wood. And her mother said, "Oh my dear child, you have brought snakes instead!" She said, "Go take them back and put them back just where you got them." And the little girl ran down the mesa again, down below to the flats. And she put those snakes back just where she got them. They were snakes instead and she was very hurt about this and so she said, "I'm not going home. I'm going to *Kawaik*, the beautiful lake place, *Kawaik*, and drown myself in that lake, *byn'yah'nah* [the "west lake"]. I will go there and drown myself."

So she started off, and as she passed by the Enchanted Mesa near Acoma she met an old man, very aged, and he saw her running, and he said, "My dear child, where are you going?" "I'm going to *Kawaik* and jump into the lake there." "Why?" "Well, because," she said, "my mother didn't want to make any *yashtoah* for me." The old man said, "Oh, no! You must not go my child. Come with me and I will take you home." He tried to catch her, but she was very light and skipped along. And every time he would try to grab her she would skip faster away from him.

The old man was coming home with some wood strapped to his back and tied with yucca. He just let that strap go and let the wood drop. He went as fast as he could up the cliff to the little girl's home. When he got to the place where she lived, he called to her mother. "*Deeni!*" "Come on up!" And he said, "I can't. I just came to bring you a message. Your little daughter is running away. She is going to *Kawaik* to drown herself in the lake there." "Oh my dear little girl!" the mother said. So she busied herself with making the *yashtoah* her little girl liked so much. Corn mush curled at the top. (She must have found enough wood to boil the corn meal and make the *yashtoah*.)

While the mush was cooling off, she got the little girl's clothing, her *manta* dress and buckskin moccasins and all her other garments, and put them in a bundle—probably a yucca bag. And she started down as fast as she could on the east side of Acoma. (There used to be a trail there, you know. It's gone now, but it was accessible in those days.) She saw her daughter way at a distance and she kept calling: "Stsamaku! My daughter! Come back! I've got your *yashtoah* for you." But the little girl would not turn. She kept on ahead and she cried: "My mother, my mother, she didn't want me to have any *yashtoah*. So now I'm going to *Kawaik* and drown myself." Her mother heard her cry and said, "My little daughter, come back here!" "No," and she kept a distance away from her. And they came nearer and nearer to the lake. And she could see her daughter now, very plain. "Come back, my daughter! I have your *yashtoah*." But no, she kept on, and finally she reached the lake and she stood on the edge.

She had tied a little feather in her hair, which is traditional (in death they tie this feather on the head). She carried a feather, the little girl did, and she tied it in her hair with a piece of string, right on top of her head she put the feather. Just as her mother was about to reach her, she jumped into the lake. The little feather was whirling around and around in the depths below. Of course the mother was very sad. She went, grieved, back to Acoma and climbed her mesa home. She stood on the edge of the mesa and scattered her daughter's clothing, the little moccasins, the *yashtoah*. She scattered them to the east, to the west, to the north, to the south. And the pieces of clothing and the moccasins and *yashtoah*, all turned into butterflies. And today they say that Acoma has more beautiful butterflies: red ones, white ones, blue ones, yellow ones. They came from this little girl's clothing.

Now this is a story anthropologists would consider very old. The version I have given you is just as Aunt Susie tells it. You can occasionally hear some English she picked up at Carlisle—words like "precipitous." You will also notice that there is a great deal of repetition, and a little reminder about *yashtoah*, and how it is made. There is a remark about the cliff trail at Acoma—that it was once there, but is there no longer. This story may be told at a time of sadness or loss, but within this story many other elements are brought together. Things are not separated out and categorized; all things are brought together, so that the reminder about the *yashtoah* is valuable information that is repeated—a recipe, if you will. The information about the old trail at Acoma reveals that stories are, in a sense, maps, since even to this day there is little information or material about trails that is passed around with writing. In the structure of this story the repetitions are, of course, designed to help you remember. It is repeated again and again, and then it moves on.

• • •

There are a great many parallels between Pueblo experiences and those of African and Caribbean peoples—one is that we have all had the conqueror's language imposed on us. But our experience with English has been somewhat different in that the Bureau of Indian Affairs schools were not interested in teaching us the canon of Western classics. For instance, we never heard of Shakespeare. We were given Dick and Jane, and I can remember reading that the robins were heading south for the winter. It took me a long time to figure out what was going on. I worried for quite a while about our robins in Laguna because they didn't leave in the winter, until I finally realized that all the big textbook companies are up in Boston and *their* robins do go south in the winter. But in a way, this dreadful formal education freed us by encouraging us to maintain our narratives. Whatever literature we were exposed to at school (which was damn little), at home the storytelling, the special regard for telling and bringing together through the telling, was going on constantly.

And as the old people say, "If you can remember the stories, you will be all right. Just remember the stories." When I returned to Laguna Pueblo after attending college, I wondered how the storytelling was continuing (anthropologists say that Laguna Pueblo is one of the more acculturated pueblos), so I visited an English class at Laguna-Acoma High School. I knew the students had cassette tape recorders in their lockers and stereos at home, and that they listened to Kiss and Led Zeppelin and were well informed about popular culture in general. I had with me an anthology of short stories by Native

American writers, *The Man to Send Rain Clouds*. One story in the book is about the killing of a state policeman in New Mexico by three Acoma Pueblo men in the early 1950s. I asked the students how many had heard this story and steeled myself for the possibility that the anthropologists were right, that the old traditions were indeed dying out and the students would be ignorant of the story. But instead, all but one or two raised their hands—they had heard the story, just as I had heard it when I was young, some in English, some in Laguna.

One of the other advantages that we Pueblos have enjoyed is that we have always been able to stay with the land. Our stories cannot be separated from their geographical locations, from actual physical places on the land. We were not relocated like so many Native American groups who were torn away from their ancestral land. And our stories are so much a part of these places that it is almost impossible for future generations to lose them—there is a story connected with every place, every object in the landscape.

Dennis Brutus has talked about the "yet unborn" as well as "those from the past," and how we are still *all* in *this* place, and language—the storytelling—is our way of passing through or being with them, or being together again. When Aunt Susie told her stories, she would tell a younger child to go open the door so that our esteemed predecessors might bring in their gifts to us. "They are out there," Aunt Susie would say. "Let them come in. They're here, they're here with us *within* the stories."

A few years ago, when Aunt Susie was 106, I paid her a visit, and while I was there she said, "Well, I'll be leaving here soon. I think I'll be leaving here next week, and I will be going over to the Cliff House." She said, "It's going to be real good to get back over there." I was listening, and I was thinking that she must be talking about her house at Paguate Village, just north of Laguna. And she went on, "Well, my mother's sister (and she gave her Indian name) will be there. She has been living there. She will be there and we will be over there, and I will get a chance to write down these stories I've been telling you." Now you must understand, of course, that Aunt Susie's mother's sister, a great storyteller herself, has long since passed over into the land of the dead. But then I realized, too, that Aunt Susie wasn't talking about death the way most of us do. She was talking about "going over" as a journey, a journey that perhaps we can only begin to understand through an appreciation for the boundless capacity of language that, through storytelling, brings us together, despite great distances between cultures, despite great distances in time.

WRITING ABOUT THE READING

4. Why does Silko believe that the listener must be included in the telling of a story?

5. Silko uses the image of a web to explain the structure of a Pueblo narrative. How and why does a Pueblo story differ from the usual Western narrative structure?

6. Why does Silko believe that it is important to tell negative stories as well as positive ones?

7. Compare the stories of the smashed-up Volkswagen with that of the girl, Waithea. What are some of the similarities and differences between these two stories?

8. Why does Silko assert that stories serve to connect people despite distances in culture and in time?

9. What advice does she give that you can use to help you in your own writing?

WRITING FROM YOUR OWN EXPERIENCE

Note: In these assignments, write about your own experience or use that of someone you know, read about, or saw in a film/TV show.

10. Recall a time when you were convinced that a person was sincere (or not sincere) about what he/she said. Why did you make this judgment and what were the consequences of this judgment?

11. Have you ever become aware that a poem, reading, or movie had a deeper meaning? How did you become aware of the deeper meaning and what effect did it have on you?

12. Although Silko emphasizes the importance of oral communication, people often use nonverbal ways of communicating (such as hand signals, facial expressions, or body posture). Recall a time when you communicated with someone without using words. What were some of the difficulties you faced using nonverbal communication and what was your reaction to this experience?

13. Silko believes that gossip is just another form of storytelling. Recall a time when you heard or passed on some gossip about someone. Using this experience, explain why you agree (or disagree) that gossip can be useful.

WRITING ABOUT RESEARCH

14. In the Pueblo culture, what was the purpose of the Katcina society into which men were initiated? *(Note: Pronounced "kachina.")*

15. How and why do the features of the houses of the Pueblo people show adaptation to their environment?

16. Many places in the United States have Native American languages preserved in the names of rivers, landmarks, towns, and streets. Unlike European Americans (who often give a place the name of a person), Native Americans usually name a place after a feature of the landscape. Study a map of your state or region. Choose two place names derived from a Native American language and explain their original meanings.

17. Silko says that at the Laguna Pueblo every word has a story of its own. Research the story behind two or three English words. What is the story behind the origin of the word and its present meaning? Consider one or more of the following:

    (a) avant-garde
    (b) boycott
    (c) carnival
    (d) cynosure
    (e) gargantuan
    (f) guillotine
    (g) ketchup
    (h) laser
    (i) maudlin
    (j) mentor
    (k) moccasin
    (l) moose
    (m) mukluk
    (n) narcissism
    (o) nemesis
    (p) procrustean
    (q) pyrrhic
    (r) quixotic
    (s) raccoon
    (t) rigmarole
    (u) robot
    (v) sandwich
    (w) saturnine
    (x) skunk
    (y) tantalize
    (z) tomato

Selection 10

What Part Moon

INEZ PETERSEN

Inez Petersen *(1958–), is a member of the Quinault tribe, from the North-west. Her mother's people are from Taholah, a village at the mouth of the Quinault River; her father is a Dane who worked in the logging industry. Petersen earned her M.A. in creative writing from the University of New Mexico, Albuquerque. She was chosen for residencies in writing at the MacDowell Colony and the Villa Montalvo. Her poetry, fiction, and essays have been widely published in literary journals. Currently Petersen is working on a novel entitled* Missing You.

In "What Part Moon," taken from a collection of works by Native Americans entitled As We Are Now *(1997), Petersen uses the moon as a symbol of her cultural dilemma. Although U.S. culture speaks of the "man in the moon," in many other cultures the moon symbolizes women and the cycle of death and rebirth.*

PREPARING TO READ

1. In greeting others, Americans frequently ask, "How are you?" and are surprised if they get an informative reply. How and why is language used other than to communicate information?
2. Why are some Native Americans offended when nonmembers of this group dress up like and "act like Indians"?
3. How and why do young adults often use body ornaments, dress, and/or gestures to shock members of the older generation?

WHAT PART MOON

"What part Indian are you?" asked a woman whose face told me that she should know better than to ask such an ignorant question. It was a going-away party, summertime in a town which prides itself on the progressive, liberal nature of its political stances, and I was saying goodbye to a gathering of coworkers and their attendant family/significant others. We chatted in groups of twos and threes, milling about a backyard luxuriant with grass, trees, and shrubs. We nibbled at hummus, baby-back ribs, *tzatziki;* drank mineral water, deep Barolos, chilled bottles of long-neck beer; saved ourselves for the indulgent chocolate cake, *la maxine,* this woman's husband had baked for the occasion.

Not long before, at my bother's house, another group had gathered and eaten together: crabs and mussels gathered from the bay, assorted potato salads (some from Safeway), chips, and whatever-was-on-sale sodas. Not exactly your most traditional of Native foods. But then, we ourselves were a mixture of nationalities, of tribes and peoples, some urban, some reservation, others just plain rural. Our tribes included Siletz, Warm Spring, Quinault, and Klamath with sprinklings of French, Irish, Scot, Filipino, and mongrel white. That day we celebrated, not my going away, but our being together. No one in this gathering questions me on blood quantum; here I am always "Auntie Nez," hugged, welcomed, teased for the latest dousing of red to my hair.

"You hear 'bout that big rumor going 'round?"

Bristow, my brother's best friend and next-door neighbor, loves to stir up trouble, and he threw the question out, pure bait. His brown eyes crinkle into ready laughter. He measures the next words, spoken by his wife, as if sighting down the barrel of a rifle.

"You mean about Frank?" Christy asks, innocent enough.

My brother loves the attention, but feigns disbelief.

"I got a rumor?"

"Yeah. Seems that you and this woman . . . " Bristow strings innuendo out better than a fly-fisherman's line.

"Hey! This is great! Me and 'this woman?'" Frank lifts his eyebrows, grabs his chest in mock agony.

I nudge my sister-in-law Bonnie, sitting at the kitchen table beading yet another project for an upcoming powwow. Bonnie smiles down at her beadwork, says "Quit it, Frank," waits for the punch line.

Not until too late do I realize the direction of this elaborate setup. My brother turns to me and says, "I was so happy; here I was about to be the center of some hot gossip."

"Turns out, someone saw him kissing a woman at the last powwow," Bristow turns his broad smile on me. "Some redhead."

"Hot gossip all for nothing—it's my sister," Frank mournfully bows over his bowl of steaming mussels.

We laugh and keep eating.

• • •

Coloring my hair red is one of a series of mini-defiances I have made in my determination to deflate expectations of what a Native American woman should look like. It is hard-won, this minimal acceptance I have of my own appearance. Amidst the variant color tones of my immediate family, I am light-skinned and hazel-eyed. Of the privileges I experience in my life, "passing" ranks high, but for backward reasons: I am invisible to the dominant culture because they do not wish to see "other." It is supremely convenient for some to see me as white, but this "white-only" filter distorts any true picture.

Of course, I am white too; I would just as soon be dead as to think myself the lie of being only of one or the other. My life experience though comes from being a part of a community of Native American peoples. It is here I draw my truest sense of self. Identification is not so simple as the one-letter signifiers on an old application for school: A for Asian, B for Black, C for Caucasian, H for Hispanic, I for Indian. Where is the "M" for mixed-blood?

What would my own brothers and sisters mark on such a questionnaire? We are from multinational bloodlines: Filipino, Dane, African American, and good ole 'Merican white. Perhaps it is from loving my siblings that I can now rest easy amongst a pan-tribal gathering—especially amongst other Native mixed-bloods.

We are told stories live in the blood, yet my blood is not pure. Does that make the story of my life impure? Does that give full-bloods say-so about if I am Indian enough? They would not question my darker mother or elder brother. How can my mama be Quinault, my brother be Quinault, and I not be Indian enough? Who is the arbiter of my existence, telling where I do and do not belong?

I see my silly sallies at defying expectations. I know my fierce determination may be misinterpreted when reddening my brown hair; for me it is the metaphorical hiss between clenched teeth, "I am no Wannabe." Sometimes a person just does not want to play along with the subtle hints of beaded earrings and chiming in with a well-timed, "A-a-a-y."

Who would wish on themselves the curse of not appearing to belong? I rage at colorists and find myself in their midst. Recently, I hear about a well-known Native American author who questioned the blood-quantum of a woman whose book he had been asked to review; knowing this, I find it difficult to praise his very good writing, perhaps out of fear that he would not find me "Indian enough."

What I do know is that if we divide ourselves, we are doing the work of the dominant culture; there is no need for them to keep us down, for we do it to ourselves. What is true too: if I had no need of this generosity of spirit, to include all of us, the mixed-bloods, the traditionals, the urbans, the full-bloods, I might be just as exclusive as my author-colleague.

I do not enjoy the privileged status of only one race, nor can I claim a traditional upbringing. My grandmother died believing it best not to pass on her Salish tongue. My white father abandoned his children and their mother, leaving nothing but his blood in my veins and a twisted belief in the ongoing nature of absented love. I do not know my own traditions.

However, if I do not allow myself the right to dance intertribals, or sit in on non-Quinault sweat house ceremonies, or participate in rituals not specific to the Northwest, is not this the expected acquiescence of assimilation? Because my untaught mother taught me no tradition whatsoever, am I to refuse when a loving older Kiowa woman wants to teach me about fringing shawls? If I should exclude myself from belonging on the basis of my nontraditional upbringing and on the color of my skin, it would bring about unbearable loneliness.

• • •

At the same time, I find myself careful when about to meet other Native Americans, especially when addressing a crowd. Asked to read a poem for the opening of Joy Harjo's band one year at a "Columbus Day" celebration (the organizers determined to put the day on its head and celebrate ethnicity at the University of New Mexico), I nervously prepared at home for the event. I chose carefully: black dhoti pants, a sweater, black beads on black cotton would give just the right signifiers; classy, urban, nothing to prove (yeah, right). I hated the discomfort of my light skin once again and decided to address the crowd from that ambivalence.

Walking the few blocks from my cramped apartment to campus, I looked skyward, beyond the city lights of Albuquerque, and saw the tiniest crescent of moon in a bruised purple sky. Cupped within the sliver of bright light rested the dimmed round fullness of the moon, and I wondered if people questioned what part moon they could see or doubted the moon's wholeness when it was not full.

"What part Indian are you?" I intoned into the mike, my voice pleasingly amplified, rounder than real life. And I went on to tell the reactions of different mixed-blood Indian men, friends of mine. When asked this question, these men have, at one time or another, stood up and pretended to unzip their pants. A defiant gesture that delights me, even if somewhat vulgar and rude. At the mike, in front of 200 or so, I mimic my male friends' response, "unzipping," and get the laugh that puts me at ease. It is the laughter of Native people that makes me belong again.

As if speaking to Frank and Bonnie and Bristow and Christy, I tell them of the woman at that going-away party; I tell them of her dark skin, brown eyes, round face—maybe Chicana, maybe Asian. I say what I saw: a woman who did not recognize her own self anymore, who maybe thought herself white. I said how I wanted to slap her, shake her up; but more important I wanted her to know the ridiculousness of her question. And so when she asked me, "What part Indian are you?"

I said, "I think it is my heart."

WRITING ABOUT THE READING

4. What is Petersen's initial reaction to the woman's question and why does the writer react in this way?

5. How does the closing statement by Petersen serve to respond to the question and to summarize the essence of what she discusses in the body of the essay?

6. How and why does the writer use the image of the moon as expressive of her identity dilemma?

7. Why is it so difficult for Petersen to be recognized as a Native American?

8. Why does the writer find it important to proclaim her status as a Native American?

WRITING FROM YOUR OWN EXPERIENCE

Note: In these assignments, write about your own experience or use that of someone you know, read about, or saw in a film/TV show.

9. Petersen is upset that she is often asked what part of her is Native American. Recall a situation when you were asked a similar disconcerting question. How was this situation handled and what happened as a result?

10. Petersen dyes her hair to defy expectations of what a Native American woman should look like. Have you ever changed your appearance to meet or defy expectations of others? Why did you do this and what was the outcome of this defiance?

11. One friend teases Petersen's brother by telling a story about the brother kissing a girl. Have you ever been teased or teased someone else? What do you think was the reason for this "kidding around" and what was the result of this behavior?

WRITING ABOUT RESEARCH

12. Why do many Native Americans (such as those in prison) feel that their right to freedom of religion (under the First Amendment) is being impinged upon or denied?

13. Why has there been a controversy between scientists and Native Americans over the rights to the human remains of the 9,300-year-old Kennewick Man?

14. What is the current scientific explanation of when and how the indigenous peoples came to North and South America?

15. How and why has discrimination and/or reservation life resulted in major social problems, such as alcoholism and/or drug use, for Native Americans?

COMPARING SELECTIONS: NATIVE AMERICAN WRITERS

1. Compare attitudes toward the natural environment in the readings by **Louis Owens** and **Linda Hogan**. How and why do both writers show a respect for nature?

2. Compare the importance of storytelling in the readings by **N. Scott Momaday** and **Leslie Marmon Silko**. Why are stories so important to each writer?

3. Compare the search for identity of **Gerald Vizenor** and **N. Scott Momaday**. How does each writer create a representation of his father or grandfather?

4. Compare the discussion of socioeconomic problems faced by Native Americans in readings by **Elizabeth Cook-Lynn** and **Vine Deloria**. How does Cook-Lynn's account of the destruction of Native Americans result in the reservation conditions discussed by Deloria?

5. Compare the attitudes toward assimilation to the dominant culture in readings by **Simon J. Ortiz** and **Joseph Bruchac**. What are some of the ways they show that they are divided between the two cultures?

6. Compare the importance of Native American traditions in readings by **Linda Hogan** and **Simon J. Ortiz**. Why are these traditions important to each writer?

7. Compare the importance of special places in the essays by **N. Scott Momaday** and **Louis Owens**. Why are these places important in keeping memories alive?

8. Compare the attitudes toward the traditional language discussed in readings by **Simon J. Ortiz** and **Leslie Marmon Silko**. How and why is it important to retain the traditional language and stories?

9. Compare the role of the storyteller in the essays by **N. Scott Momaday** and **Joseph Bruchac**. How and why is the storyteller important in Native American culture?

10. Compare the ways in which **Joseph Bruchac** and **Inez Petersen** deal with their "mixed blood." How and why does each identify as Native American?

11. Compare the criticisms of the assimilation process in the selections by **Elizabeth Cook-Lynn** and **Simon J. Ortiz**. Why is each writer critical of the way Native Americans have been coerced into adopting the dominant culture?

SELECTED BIBLIOGRAPHY—NATIVE AMERICAN WRITERS

Allen, Paula Gunn, ed. *Voice of the Turtle: America Native American Literature 1900–1970*. New York: Ballantine Books, 1994.

Bataille, Gretchen M., and Kathleen M. Sands. *American Indian Women: A Guide to Research*. New York: Garland, 1991.

Bruchac, Joseph. *Roots of Survival: Native American Storytelling and the Sacred*. Golden, CO: Fulcrum Pub., 1996.

———. *Survival This Way: Interviews with Native American Poets*. Tucson: Univ. of Arizona Press, 1990.

Bruchac, Joseph, ed. *Aniyunwiya/Real Human Beings: An Anthology of Contemporary Cherokee Prose*. New York: Greenfield Review Press, 1995.

———. *Smoke Rising: The Native North American Literary Companion*. Detroit: Visible Ink Press, 1995.

Cook-Lynn, Elizabeth. *From the River's Edge*. New York: Arcade-Little, Brown, 1991.

———. *The Power of Horses and Other Stories*. New York: Arcade-Little, Brown, 1990.

———. *Why I Can't Read Wallace Stegner and Other Essays: A Tribal Voice*. Madison: The Univ. of Wisconsin Press, 1996.

Cook-Lynn, Elizabeth, and Mario Gonzalez. *The Politics of Hallowed Ground: Wounded Knee and the Struggle for Indian Sovereignty*. Urbana: Univ. of Illinois Press, 1998.

Dearborn, Mary. *Pocahontas's Daughters: Gender and Ethnicity in American Culture*. New York: Oxford Univ. Press, 1986.

Deloria, Vine, Jr. *American Indian Policy in the Twentieth Century*. Norman: Univ. of Oklahoma Press, 1985.

———. *Behind the Trail of Broken Treaties*. New York: Delacorte, 1974.

———. *Custer Died for Your Sins: A Native American Manifesto*. New York: Macmillan, 1969.

———. *God Is Red: A Native View of Religion*. New York: Grosset, 1973; 2nd ed., North American Press, 1992.

———. *We Talk, You Listen: New Tribes, New Turf*. New York: Macmillan, 1970.

Deloria, Vine, Jr., and Clifford Lytle. *American Indians, American Justice*. Austin: Univ. of Texas Press, 1983.

———. *The Nations Within: The Past and Future of American Indian Sovereignty*. New York: Pantheon, 1984.

Frazier, Ian. *On the Rez*. New York: Farrar, Straus, Giroux, 2000.

Gish, Robert Franklin. *Beyond Bounds: Cross-Cultural Essays on Anglo, American Native American, and Chicano Literature.* Albuquerque: Univ. of New Mexico Press, 1996.

Hobson, Geary, ed. *The Remembered Earth. An Anthology of Contemporary Native American Literature.* Albuquerque: Univ. of New Mexico Press, 1981.

Hogan, Linda. *The Book of Medicines.* Minneapolis: Coffee House Press, 1993.

———. *Dwellings: A Spiritual History of the Living World.* New York: Norton, 1995.

———. *Mean Spirit.* New York: Atheneum, 1990.

———. *Power.* New York: Norton, 1998.

———. *Seeing through the Sun.* Amherst: Univ. of Massachusetts Press, 1985.

Klein, Barry T., ed. *Reference Encyclopedia of the American Indian.* West Nyack, NY: Todd Publications, 1993.

Kornblum, William. *Sociology in a Changing World.* 4th ed. Fort Worth: Harcourt Brace, 1997.

Krupat, Arnold, ed. *Native American Autobiography: An Anthology.* The Univ. of Wisconsin Press, 1994.

Lincoln, Kenneth. *Native American Renaissance.* Berkeley: Univ. of California Press 1983.

Littlefield, Daniel F., Jr., , and James W. Parins. *Native American Writing in the Southeast: An Anthology, 1875–1935.* Jackson: Univ. Press of Mississippi, 1995.

Marger, Martin N. *Race and Ethnic Relations: American and Global Perspectives.* Belmont, CA: Wadsworth Pub. Co., 1997.

Momaday, N. Scott. *The Ancient Child.* New York: Doubleday, 1989.

———. *House Made of Dawn.* New York: Harper, 1968; reprinted, 1989.

———. *In the Presence of the Sun: Stories and Poems, 1961–1991.* New York: St. Martin's Press, 1992.

———. *The Names: A Memoir.* New York: Harper, 1976; reprinted, Univ. of Arizona Press, 1996.

———. *The Way to Rainy Mountain.* Albuquerque: Univ. of New Mexico Press, 1969; reprinted, New York: Ballantine, 1973.

Neihardt, John G. *Black Elk Speaks: Being the Life Story of a Holy Man of the Oglala Sioux.* Lincoln: Univ. of Nebraska Press, 1961.

Olson, James S. *The Ethnic Dimension in American History.* 2nd ed. New York: St. Martin's Press, 1994.

Ortiz, Simon J. *After and Before the Lightening*. Tucson: Univ. of Arizona Press, 1994.

———. *Fight Back: For the Sake of the People, For the Sake of the Land*. Albuquerque: Univ. of New Mexico, 1980.

———. *Woven Stone*. Tucson: Univ. of Arizona Press, 1992.

Owens, Louis. *Bone Game*. Norman: Univ. of Oklahoma Press, 1994.

———. *Dark River*. Norman: Univ. of Oklahoma Press, 1999.

———. *Mixedblood Messages: Literature, Film, Family, Place*. Norman: Univ. of Oklahoma Press, 1998.

———. *Nightland*. New York: Dutton, 1996.

———. *Other Destinies: Understanding the American Indian Novel*. Norman: Univ. of Oklahoma Press, 1992.

Penn, William S., ed. *As We Are Now: Mixblood Essays on Race and Identity*. Berkeley: Univ. of California Press, 1997.

Riley, Patricia, ed. *Growing Up Native American: An Anthology*. New York: William Morrow and Co., Inc., 1993.

Rosen, Kenneth, ed. *The Man to Send Rain Clouds: Contemporary Stories by American Indians*. New York: Viking, 1974.

Rothenberg, Paula S. *Race, Class, and Gender in the United States*. New York: St. Martin's Press, 1998.

Ruoff, A. LaVonne. *Literatures of the American Indian*. New York: Chelsea, 1991.

Silko, Leslie Marmon. *Almanac of the Dead*. New York: Simon & Schuster, 1991.

———. *Ceremony*. New York: Viking Press, 1977.

———. *Laguna Woman: Poems*. New York: Greenfield Press, 1974.

———. *Storyteller*. New York: Seaver Books, 1981.

Swann, Brian, and Arnold Krupat, eds. *I Tell You Now: Autobiographical Essays by Native American Writers*. Lincoln: Univ. of Nebraska Press, 1987.

Vizenor, Gerald. *Dead Voices: Natural Agonies in the New World*. Norman: Univ. of Oklahoma Press, 1992.

———. *Griever: An American Monkey King in China*. Minneapolis: Univ. of Minnesota Press, 1990.

———. *The Heirs of Columbus*. Hanover, NH: Univ. Press of New England, 1991.

———. *Interior Landscapes: Autobiographic Myths and Metaphors*. Minneapolis: Univ. of Minnesota Press, 1990.

———. *Manifest Manners: Postindian Warriors of Survivance*. Hanover, NH: Univ. Press of New England, 1994.

———. *The People Named the Chippewa: Narrative Histories*. Minneapolis: Univ. of Minneapolis Press, 1984.

———, ed. *Native American Literature: A Brief Introduction and Anthology*. New York: HarperCollins College Publishers, 1995.

Welch, James. *Fools Crow*. New York: Viking, 1986.

Wiget, Andrew, ed. *Handbook of Native American Literature*. New York: Garland Publishing, Inc., 1996.

SELECTED INTERNET RESOURCES—NATIVE AMERICAN WRITERS

Note: Unless otherwise noted, all URL addresses listed begin with http://www.

Bureau of Indian Affairs/Department of the Interior. <doi.gov/bureau-indian-affairs.html<

The Cherokee National Historical Society. <powersource.com/powersource/heritage>

Ethnic Studies at the University of Southern California. <usc.edu/isd/archives/ethnicstudies/ index.html>

First Nations/First Peoples. <dickshovel.com/www.html>

Index of Native American Cultural Resources on the Internet. <hanksville.org/ NAresources/>

Native American Resources. <kstrom.net/isk/mainmenu.html>

Native American Resource Guide. <usc.edu/isk/archives/ethnicstudies/Native American_main.html>

Native Nations (Guide to Tribal Sites). <kstrom.net/isk/tribes/tribes.htm>

NativeNet. <http://niikaan.fdl.cc.mn.us/natnet/>

Native Web. <http://www.nativeweb.org>

Office of Indian Education Programs. <oiep.bia.edu>

Pueblo Cultural Center.

Wordcraft Circle of Native Writers and Storytellers. <wordcraftcircle.org>

U.S. Census Bureau. <census.gov>

Connecting Writers Across Ethnic/Racial Groups

1. What similarities do you see in the way **Frank Chin** and **Inez Petersen** challenge the usual stereotypes of their ethnic group and why do you think that they do this?

2. Compare the feelings of nostalgia that **Gustavo Perez Firmat** and **Louis Owens** have for their lost homelands.

3. **Elizabeth Cook-Lynn** and **Ralph Ellison** discuss the desire of the white majority to rid the country of Native Americans and African Americans. What similarities can you see in the treatment of the two groups?

4. As immigrants, both **Fae Myenne Ng** and **Pablo Medina** faced discrimination upon their arrival in the United States. Compare their experience of discrimination. Which was more overt and why was this so?

5. Compare the roles of the fathers in the essays by **Helen Zia** and **Sandra Cisneros**. Why was each father so influential in the life of his daughter?

6. Compare the roles of the mothers and/or grandmothers in the essays by **Chang-rae Lee** and **Gary Soto**. Why were these women so significant in the lives of these writers?

7. Evaluate **Pablo Medina's** or **Simon Ortiz's** educational experience in view of the criteria for a good teacher discussed by **Claude Steele**.

8. Discuss the consequences of poverty in the essay by **Luis Rodriguez** in light of **Cornel West's** discussion of the importance of income.

9. Consider how **Amy Tan** was affected by her teacher's remarks in light of **Claude Steele's** discussion of the importance of self-esteem.

10. Compare the emphasis on the emotions and spirit in the writings of **Frederick Douglass** and **Sandra Cisneros**.

11. Both **Gary Soto** and **Bharati Mukherjee** married outside their ethnic group. What are some of the similarities or differences in the ways their families regarded such intermarriages?

12. Compare the type of jobs held by **Jesus Colon** and **Louis Owens**. How and why did their work influence their lives and/or writing?

13. Compare the selections by **Frederick Douglass** and **Jesus Colon.** How and why do these readings illustrate the psychology of those who are excluded from the dominant culture?

14. How and why do the essays by **David Mura** and **Henry Louis Gates** illustrate the concept of "social mobility," the movement into a higher socioeconomic class?

15. To what extent are both **Pablo Medina** and **Le Thi Diem Thuy** victims of political circumstances?

16. How and why does the essay by **Fae Myenne Ng** illustrate **Richard Rodriguez's** belief that illegal immigration has occurred in the past?

17. How and why do the selections by **Harriet Jacobs** and **Judith Ortiz Cofer** show the prevalence of sexual harassment from past to modern times?

18. In what ways do both the essays by **Gerald Vizenor** and **Luis Rodriguez** illustrate the violence of life in the United States?

19. How and why do the essays by **Eric Liu** and **Gustavo Perez Firmat** both illustrate the assimilation process?

20. How does the selection by **Maya Angelou** illustrate what **Christine Granados** says about the importance of strong mothers or grandmothers?

21. What insight into the cultural significance of food do you get from the selections by **Sandra Cisneros** and **Chang-rae Lee?**

22. What differing perspectives on assimilation are found in the essays by **Bharati Mukherjee** and **Vine Deloria, Jr.?**

23. Contrast the way **Shawn Wong** deals with discrimination to the way that **Joseph Bruchac's** grandfather handles the issue. Why do you think these men reacted so differently to the attitudes of society toward their group?

24. Compare the discussions by **Nikki Giovanni** and **Judith Ortiz Cofer** of the influence of the media. Why is one writer more positive than the other about the effects of the media?

25. Why do **Marcus Mabry** and **Joseph Bruchac** have different attitudes toward the relationship of sports and academics?

26. Compare the discussion of language in the essays by **Simon Ortiz** and **Joseph Torres.** How and why can these essays be used to support the assertion that the movement to forbid the use of native languages is discriminatory?

27. Compare the importance of ritual and tradition in the essays by **Linda Hogan** and **Sandra Cisneros**. How do these familiar routines help to give meaning to their lives?

28. Compare the ways **Frank Chin's** Ben Fee and **Frederick Douglass** defy cultural expectations.

29. Compare the memories of childhood of **Helen Zia** and **N. Scott Momaday**. How and why did the experiences of these early years shape their later lives?

30. What similar concern for equality do you see in the writings of **Frederick Douglass** and **Elizabeth Lynn-Cook**?

31. Evaluate **Eric Liu's** stories about his father in view of **Leslie Marmon Silko's** belief about the importance of stories.

32. Compare the essays by **Barbara Reynolds** and **Le Thi Diem Thuy**. How and why do these selections show the effects of discrimination on individual lives?

33. Evaluate the effectiveness of the persuasive essays of **Ralph Ellison** and **Joseph Torres**. Which essay do you think is more effective and why do you think so?

34. **Cornel West's** essay stresses the importance of self-esteem. In light of this essay, why did their internment during World War II have such an influence on **David Mura's** parents?

35. Compare the importance of music in the selections by **Ralph Ellison** and **Gustavo Perez Firmat**.

36. Compare the importance of childhood friends in the selections by **Gary Soto** and **Pablo Medina**. How and why did these friends help the writers to better understand themselves and/or others?

Glossary

---

abolitionists   Those who attacked the institution of slavery.

acculturation   Transference of the rules and behaviors of one cultural group to another cultural group; the way a person incorporates values and behaviors of a new culture.

affirmative action   Government programs to advance the economic and educational achievement of minorities, particularly in admission to educational programs, hiring, and promotion on the job.

African American (black)   Persons whose primary identity is black or African American. In the United States, persons of mixed race with any identifiable black ancestry are usually considered African American.

Anglos   Americans (usually white) who are not Hispanic.

assimilation   The "melting pot" theory; the belief that the minority group should be blended into the larger society.

barrio   A neighborhood in which a mixture of Spanish and English is spoken.

bilingual education   The teaching of non-English speaking immigrant children in their home language (often Spanish) until they can understand English.

blues   A musical tradition, rooted in the African American experience of the post–Civil War period, that blends European and African traditions. Often autobiographical, the lyrics to these songs deal with unhappy situations, such as betrayal or unrequited love.

Bracero Program   A government program to bring temporary farm-workers from Mexico to the United States. The program began in 1942 and ended in 1965.

Chicanos   See "Mexican Americans."

class   The ranking of people in a society from high to low according to attributes such as income, occupation, and wealth.

Cuban Americans   Hispanics originally from Cuba; these people often are political refugees from the regime of Fidel Castro.

423

cultural assimilation   The degree to which individuals associate with their own cultural group or the majority culture or both.

cultural pluralism   The belief that different groups should maintain their own distinctive cultures even as they gain equality in society.

culture   The system of shared meanings that people learn from their society and use to make sense of their world.

discrimination   Unfair treatment of members of a group.

dominant group   That group with control of wealth and political power. In the United States, white Anglo Saxon males are regarded as the dominant group.

essay   A moderately brief composition dealing with a topic from a limited or personal point of view.

ethnic emergence   A period of identity exploration, usually occurring in adolescence or early adulthood.

ethnic group   People who feel a sense of group identity based on a common ancestry or shared culture.

ethnic identity incorporation   A time when a member of an ethnic minority comes to terms with his/her minority status.

ethnicity   A person's affiliation with an ethnic group.

ethnic stratification   The valuing of differing groups based on how closely they resemble the dominant standards of appearance and culture.

ethnocentrism   The judging of other cultures as inferior to one's own culture.

Hispanics   Those persons of any race with a heritage that is a mixture of Spanish with Native American (and some African American) populations. The term includes those of Hispanic descent born in the United States and those who were foreign-born but immigrated to this country. According to the results of the Year 2000 Census, of the total (native-born and foreign-born) Hispanic population, 66 percent were of Mexican origin. About 14 percent were from Central or South America, 9 percent from Puerto Rico, and 6 percent from Cuba and other Hispanic countries.

in-group   See "other."

jazz   A musical form, often improvisational, developed by African Americans; it is often characterized by its use of blues and speech intonations.

Jim Crow   "Jim Crow" laws were passed in the 1880s (primarily in the South) and ratified by the Supreme Court decision in *Plessy* v. *Ferguson* (1896). Jim Crow laws segregated African Americans in theaters, buses, trains, waiting rooms, schools, hospitals, parks, prisons, and at drinking fountains.

La Raza   A term ("the race") denoting a common heritage of Hispanic peoples.

Latinos   See "Hispanics."

Mexican Americans   Hispanics originally of Mexican origin.

minority group   A group that is singled out for discriminatory treatment. In the United States, Native Americans, African Americans, Hispanic Americans, and Asian Americans often are spoken as being members of a "minority group," even when they are numerically the majority in a community.

other / out-group   A person's differentiation between acceptable people (the "in-group") and unacceptable people or the "out-group" (the "other"). This discrimination is often based on class, income, race, or religion.

passing (as white)   The practice of some light-skinned African Americans as identifying themselves as white.

people of color   A term often used for members of minority groups.

pluralistic society   A society in which different racial/ethnic groups are able to maintain their own cultures while they gain equality.

prejudice   An attitude that prejudges a person based on the stereotypes of a group to which the person belongs.

Puerto Ricans   Hispanic Americans originally from the territory of Puerto Rico. Puerto Ricans are not immigrants but American citizens.

race   A sociopolitical term (not a biological term) for the classification of people; the assignment of people to a group in which membership is determined by perceived physical differences, such as skin color.

racial identity   The extent to which a person identifies with a racial group; the person perceives that he/she shares a common racial heritage with other members of that group.

racial profiling   The law enforcement practice of questioning persons based on their physical similarities to others who have committed crimes.

racism   The belief that a minority group should receive discriminatory treatment because of a trait such as skin color.

resiliency   The ability to overcome negative environmental circumstances (such as poverty or substandard housing) and to become well-adjusted persons.

segregation   A separation of groups either by law (*de jure*) or by social custom (*de facto*).

slavery   The system of ownership of an enslaved population; the owner has complete control over the enslaved person, including the right to buy and sell the enslaved person.

Spanish Americans (Latin Americans)   A term sometimes used by early Hispanic settlers to distinguish themselves from later-arriving people of Mexican origin.

stereotype   Fixed image of a racial or cultural group. This term often has a negative connotation.

voice   Voice emerges from the writer's style, including choice of words, ways of constructing sentences, and attitude toward the subject.

worldview   The way a person organizes information about the self, other individuals, the environment, and institutions.

Acknowledgments and Permissions

PART 1: AFRICAN AMERICAN WRITERS

1. Jacobs, Harriet Ann. "Incidents in the Life of a Slave Girl." Public domain (published 1861).

2. Douglass, Frederick. "Narrative of the Life of Frederick Douglass, an American Slave, Written by Himself." Public domain (published 1845).

3. Ellison, Ralph. "What Would America Be Like Without Blacks." Originally published in *Time*, 6 April 1970. From *Going to the Territory* by Ralph Ellison. Copyright (c) 1986 by Ralph Ellison. New York: Random House, 1986. Reprinted with permission from Random House, Inc.

4. Angelou, Maya. "My Brother Bailey and Kay Francis." From *I Know Why the Caged Bird Sings*. New York: Random House, 1969. Copyright (c) 1969 and renewed 1997 by Maya Angelou. Reprinted with permission from Random House, Inc.

5. Reynolds, Barbara. "Our Sons Under Siege." Originally published in *Essence* Magazine, Nov. 1999. Reprinted with permission of the author.

6. Giovanni, Nikki. "Black Is the Noun." From *Racism 101*. New York: William Morrow and Co., 1994. Reprinted with permission of the author.

7. Steele, Claude M. "Race and the Schooling of Black Americans." Originally published in *The Atlantic Monthly*, April 1992. Reprinted with permission of the author.

8. Gates, Henry Louis, Jr. "The Two Nations of Black America." *The Brookings Review*, 16 (Spring 98).

9. West, Cornel. "Beyond Affirmative Action: Equality and Identity." From *Race Matters*. Boston: Beacon Press, 1993. Reprinted with permission from Beacon Press.

10. Mabry, Marcus. "When the Game Is Over." Originally printed in *Black Collegiate Magazine*, Mar./Apr. 1993. Reprinted with permission of the author.

PART 2: HISPANIC AMERICAN WRITERS

1. Colon, Jesus. Sketches from *A Puerto Rican in New York* (1982). Reprinted in: Faythe Turner. *Puerto Rican Writers at Home in the USA*. Open Hand Publishing Co., 1991. Reprinted with permission from International Pub. Co.
2. Torres, Joseph. "The Language Crusade." *Hispanic* Magazine. June 1996. Copyright (c) October 1999 by Hispanic Publishing Corporation.
3. Rodriguez, Richard. "Illegal Immigrants: Prophets of a Borderless World." Originally published *NPQ: New Perspectives Quarterly* 12 (Winter 1995) : 61. Reprinted with permission from *NPQ*.
4. Medina, Pablo. "Arrival: 1960." From *Exiled Memories: A Cuban Childhood*. Austin: Univ. of Texas Press, 1990. Reprinted with permission from the Univ. of Texas Press.
5. Perez Firmat, Gustavo. "Earth to Papi, Earth to Papi." From *Next Year in Cuba*. New York: Anchor/Doubleday, 1995. Reprinted with permission of the author.
6. Cofer, Judith Ortiz. "The Myth of the Latin Woman." From *The Latin Deli: Prose and Poetry*. Athens: Univ. of Georgia Press, 1993. Reprinted with permission from the Univ. of Georgia Press.
7. Soto, Gary. "Like Mexicans." From *Small Faces*, 1986. Reprinted in *Visions of America*. New York: Persea Books, 1993. Reprinted with permission from Persea Books.
8. Cisneros, Sandra. "Un Poquito de Tu Amor." From Santiago, Esmeralda and Joie Davidow, eds. *Las Christmas: Favorite Latino Authors Share Their Holiday Memories*. New York: Random House, 1998. Reprinted with permission from Frederick T. Courtright, The Permissions Company.
9. Rodriguez, Luis J. "Turning Youth Gangs Around." Originally printed in *The Nation Journal* 21 (Nov. 1994): 605. Reprinted with permission from *The Nation*.
10. Granados, Christine. "Young, Single ... and a Mom." *Hispanic* (June 1997): 24–27. Reprinted with permission of the author.

PART 3: ASIAN AMERICAN WRITERS

1. Chin, Frank. "Confessions of a Chinatown Cowboy." From *Bulletproof Buddhists and Other Essays*. Honolulu: Univ. of Hawaii Press, 1998. Reprinted with permission of the author.

2. Mukherjee, Bharati. "American Dreamer." From *Race: An Anthology in the First Person*. New York: Clarkson Potter, 1997. Reprinted with permission of the author.

3. Wong, Shawn. "The Chinese Man Has My Ticket." From Susan Shreve, and Porter Shreve, eds. *How We Want to Live*. Boston: Beacon Press, 1998. Reprinted with permission of the author.

4. Mura, David. "Where the Body Meets Memory." From *Where the Body Meets Memory* by David Mura, copyright (c) 1996 by David Mura. Used by permission of Doubleday, a division of Random House, Inc.

5. Tan, Amy. "Mother Tongue." Copyright (c) 1990 by Amy Tan. First appeared in *The Threepenny Review*. Reprinted by permission of the author and the Sandra Dijkstra Literary Agency.

6. Zia, Helen. "Beyond Our Shadows: From Nothing a Consciousness." From *Asian American Dreams*. New York: Farrar, Straus and Giroux, 2000. Reprinted with permission from Farrar, Straus and Giroux.

7. Ng, Fae Myenne. "False Gold." Originally published in *The New Republic*, 19 and 26 July 1993. Reprinted by permission of *The New Republic,* (c) 1993, The New Republic, Inc.

8. Lee, Chang-rae. "Coming Home Again." Originally published in *The New Yorker Magazine*. Reprinted in Atwan, Robert, ed. *The Best American Essays*. Boston: Houghton Mifflin Co., 1996. Reprinted with permission of the author.

9. Liu, Eric. "Song for My Father." From: *The Accidental Asian: Notes of a Native Speaker*. New York: Random House, 1998. Reprinted with permission from Random House.

10. Thuy, Le Thi Diem. "The Gangster We Are All Looking For." Reprinted from *The Massachusetts Review,* (c) 1996, The Massachusetts Review, Inc.

PART 4: NATIVE AMERICAN WRITERS

1. Cook-Lynn, Elizabeth. "America's Oldest Racism: The Roots of Inequality." From *Why I Can't Read Wallace Stegner and Other Essays:*

A Tribal Voice. Madison: Univ. of Wisconsin Press, 1996. Reprinted with permission from the Univ. of Wisconsin Press.

2. Deloria, Vine, Jr. "The Reservation Conditions." *National Forum*, 71 (Spring 1991) : 10. Reprinted with permission of the author.

3. Momaday, N. Scott. From *The Names: A Memoir*. New York: Harper, 1976; reprinted Univ. of Arizona Press, 1996. Reprinted with permission of the author.

4. Vizenor, Gerald. "Measuring My Blood." From: *Interior Landscapes: Autobiographical Myths and Metaphors*. Univ. of Minnesota Press, 1990. Reprinted with permission from the Univ. of Minnesota Press.

5. Ortiz, Simon J. "The Language We Know." From: *I Tell You Now: Autobiographical Essays by Native American Writers*, edited by Brian Swann and Arnold Krupat (1987) University of Nebraska Press, 1987. Permission from the Univ. of Nebraska Press.

6. Bruchac, Joseph. "Notes of a Translator's Son." From Brian Swann and Arnold Krupat, eds. *I Tell You Now: Autobiographical Essays by Native American Writers*. Lincoln: Univ. of Nebraska Press, 1987. Reprinted with permission from the Univ. of Nebraska Press.

7. Hogan, Linda. "All My Relations." Originally published in *Parabola* 17 (Spring 1992) : 33. Reprinted with permission of the author.

8. Owens, Louis. "Water Witch." From *Growing Up Native American: An Anthology*. New York: William Morrow and Co., Inc., 1993. Reprinted with permission of the author.

9. Silko, Leslie Marmon. "Language and Literature from a Pueblo Indian Perspective." Copyright (c) 1979 by Leslie Marmon Silko. Reprinted with the permission of The Wylie Agency, Inc.

10. Petersen, Inez. "What Part Moon." From *As We Are Now*, William S. Penn, ed. Univ. of California Press, 1997. Reprinted with permission from the Univ. of California Press.

Index of Authors
and Titles